THE HANDBOOK OF
TRANSACTIONAL ANALYSIS PSYCHOTHERAPY

THE HANDBOOK OF
TRANSACTIONAL ANALYSIS PSYCHOTHERAPY

AN EVIDENCE-BASED APPROACH

**JOEL VOS AND
BILJANA VAN RIJN**

 Sage

1 Oliver's Yard
55 City Road
London EC1Y 1SP

2455 Teller Road
Thousand Oaks
California 91320

Unit No 323-333, Third Floor, F-Block
International Trade Tower
Nehru Place, New Delhi 110 019

8 Marina View Suite 43-053
Asia Square Tower 1
Singapore 018960

Library of Congress Control Number: 2024948776

British Library Cataloguing in Publication data

A catalogue record for this book is available from the British Library

Editor: Susannah Trefgarne
Editorial assistant: Harry Dixon
Production editor: Victoria Nicholas
Copyeditor: Niketha
Indexer: TNQ Tech Pvt. Ltd.
Marketing manager: Ruslana Khatagova
Cover design: Bhairvi Vyas
Typeset by: TNQ Tech Pvt. Ltd.
Printed in the UK

ISBN 978-1-5296-6914-5
ISBN 978-1-5296-6913-8 (pbk)

I am the Life Script, with intentions so vast,
Crafted by those whose influence will last.
Parents, teachers, figures of might,
Shaped me with care, and sometimes in folly's night.

In my youth, I thrived, the tale they told,
A life's story, through me, it rolled.
But as chapters turned, I became caught,
In rigid games, where intimacy was sought.

Avoiding the real, the authentic connection,
Locked the gate to true reflection.
My ego-states skewed, imbalance profound,
Critical Parent loud, Nurturing sounds drowned.

Adapted Child strong, Free Child weak,
My narrative stifled, my outcome bleak.
Then to a transactional therapist, I was led,
Fearful of change, of what lay ahead.

The therapist, with a nurturing hand,
Guided me through my no man's land.
Not to erase the script I've worn,
But to mend the pages, tattered and torn.

The Adult within, growing day by day,
Finding my voice, having my say.
No longer a prisoner of past decree,
Embracing the future, I hold the key.

A journey of change, courageously made,
In freedom's light, my fears do fade.
A decision made, to live, to thrive,
In my Life Script, I am alive.

Now I sigh with relief, feeling free,
Living spontaneously, just being me.
No longer trapped in a prewritten fate,
No longer afraid to open the gate.

I am the Life Script, master of my state.

(JV)

CONTENTS

PART I
BACKGROUND

1
INTRODUCTION

Transactional Analysis (TA) psychotherapy is at a crossroads. Professional bodies, national health services and health insurance companies require systematic research evidence before they include them in clinical guidelines and funded therapies. We see this as a chance for the development for critical self-reflection, introspection and development of TA, and this book reflects that perspective. This book focuses on the common concepts and core competencies across TA 'schools' or approaches. It is grounded in systematic research evidence. It offers a guide for TA trainees, practitioners and researchers. This combination, while embedded in the context of the broader fields of psychotherapy research, diversity and social justice-oriented therapies, sets this book apart from existing TA literature.

TA boasts a wealth of literature and various 'schools' or approaches. While we provide an overview of these schools, our primary goal was to craft a book centred on concepts and core competencies that the different schools have in common and situate these within the broader context of psychotherapy research. The book is distinctive within the TA field, inviting broader scrutiny of our shared theories and practices. Notably, we have revised some well-known TA concepts following systematic research findings.

The common conceptual model and core competencies in TA discussed in this book stem from systematic research. Although there are many publications on TA, systematically evidence-informed handbooks on the subject are scarce. Most existing TA-books serve as introductions or reflect the theories and practices of specific TA schools. Like other therapeutic methods, some critical texts rely heavily on theoretical reflection and the author's client experiences. Although this is immensely useful in practice and training, we want to develop a foundation rooted in systematic research. This is essential, as statutory mental healthcare services and health insurance companies increasingly require therapists to practice and be trained in an evidence-based or evidence-informed approach, as the next section will further explain.

This handbook intends to serve as an evidence-based overview and guide for beginning and practising TA therapists. It is also relevant for students of various psychological therapies, particularly those within the humanistic field. The book can easily be integrated into teaching, with many anecdotes, relatable scenarios, reflective questions and exercises. This book also serves as a reference and inspiration for research. For example, this book's last part includes a treatment manual that has proven helpful in training and research.

Another distinctive characteristic of this book is its embedding in broader psychotherapy research via the synergy of us as authors. We approach this book from diverse backgrounds. Joel Vos is an Existential, Humanistic and Cognitive-Behavioural therapist and psychotherapy researcher. Biljana van Rijn is a Teaching and Supervising Transactional Analyst (psychotherapy), relational and integrative psychotherapist, supervisor and psychotherapy researcher. Together, we offer a varied therapeutic perspective. This unique blend is a defining feature of this book, making it pertinent for readers within and beyond the realms of TA-practice and research.

In summary, this handbook is not only a guide for beginning practitioners, a research reference and a resource for teaching but also a valuable contribution to the field, addressing the need for evidence-based approaches in TA. Its synthesis of core competencies, revised concepts and diverse therapeutic perspectives makes it an essential read for anyone seeking a deeper understanding of TA psychotherapy.

RESEARCH PROGRAMME

This book results from a research programme spanning from 2017 to 2022 conducted for the European Association for Psychotherapy (EATA), and supported by the Metanoia Institute in London. Our mission was to fortify the evidence base for TA psychotherapy. We are deeply grateful for EATA's financial support and encouragement, especially when COVID-19 necessitated timeline adjustments. The programme has resulted in several publications (Vos & van Rijn, 2021a, 2021b, 2021c, 2022, 2023, 2024a, 2024b, 2024c), published within the TA-community and the broader research field. We hope they will contribute to the general research field in psychotherapy, develop statutory recognition for TA and inspire further research.

Our research programme aimed to answer the growing need for evidence-based and evidence-informed (Bohart, 2005) therapies, requiring therapists to work with clients based on the most reliable and proven research (Chambless & Hollon, 1998; David et al., 2018; Goodheart, 2006; Levant & Sperry, 2016; Tolin et al., 2015). Guidelines set by national health services rely on evidence-based research to determine which therapies will be funded, posing a challenge for TA therapists in various countries. In the United Kingdom, between 60% and 90% of supported mental health treatments consist of brief Cognitive Behavioural Therapy (CBT) for specific disorders (O'Donohue et al., 2000). This may be influenced by political factors, paradigmatic reasoning (Vos et al., 2019) and the lack of comprehensive treatment manuals and handbooks (Luborsky et al., 2002; Wampold & Imel, 2015).

Therefore, we conducted a comprehensive review of the research evidence supporting the conceptual framework in TA, demonstrating that the fundamental principles of TA are substantiated by robust empirical data (Vos & van Rijn, 2021a, 2021c). Following this, we systematically examined 41 clinical trials of TA psychotherapy through a systematic literature review and meta-analysis (Vos & van Rijn, 2022). The results indicate that TA significantly positively affects psychological well-being and quality of life, comparable to other forms of psychological therapy. To further validate these findings, we conducted a global survey among TA-practitioners to explore the shared conceptual ideas and practices among therapists from different TA schools. This survey confirmed the commonalities existing within the field of TA. By synthesising these studies, we developed a coherent conceptual model for TA. We simplified the ego-states model to merge functional and structural analysis, addressing internal dialogue and behaviour. In some respects, this is a return to the fundamentals of early TA, acknowledging that a more complex structural analysis is particularly suited for supervision and reflection.

Building upon this model, we created a new evidence-based TA treatment manual consisting of 16 sessions. Feasibility and pilot studies have shown that clients who undergo therapy with our treatment manual significantly improve their mental health and overall quality of life (Vos & van Rijn, 2023, 2024a, 2024b, 2024c). These studies form the basis for this book's evidence-based conceptual model (Part I), psychotherapeutic competencies (Part II), recommendations for working with specific disorders (Part III) and the updated treatment manual (Part IV).

DIVERSITY AND SOCIAL JUSTICE

In recent years, TA-practice and research have moved towards embracing diversity and social justice, although more progress is needed in this area (Shadbolt, 2022). Some authors suggest that evidence-based practice focusing on generalisation and identifying universal trends may conflict with social justice principles by marginalising diversity and minority groups (Rogers-Siring, 2017). This book advocates for a critical interpretation/application of research (Vos, 2025) to help therapists develop more relationally sensitive, empowering practices. As research in later chapters shows, the client's symptoms, aetiology options and limitations for change need to be understood within their socioeconomic/political context. In line with a call for radical justice-oriented practices (Dhananjaya, 2022; Minikin, 2023; Tudor, 2011), Evidence-Based TA can help recognising and exploring sources of injustice, and aiding victims in exploring realistic opportunities to break the life script that confines them, thereby developing fairer intrapsychic, interpersonal and intergenerational dynamics.

We also recognise the importance of not reducing social justice to tokenism, Black-or-white splitting or mere subjective experiences; social justice is real, complex, pluralist and intersectional, acknowledging how everyone, including therapists and clients, can be both oppressor and oppressed (Dhananjaya, 2022; Vos, 2025):

A review of approximately 50,000 scientific studies on social justice in psychological therapies showed that a structurally unjust context increases the likelihood of unjust actions by individuals, which may lead to unjust transactional dynamics, denial, internalisation, and personal actions, subsequently reinforcing the cycle of injustice. For example, John's bullies were raised in a racist/transphobic society, which may have triggered their unjust actions of shouting and spitting at John, who identifies as a black transman, followed by the denial of this structural injustice by John's friends and authorities, which seems to have subsequently triggered John's anxiety, depression and low self-esteem. John's automated traumatic stress symptoms made him respond with anger and fear to his bullies, which reinforced their bullying. Therefore, therapists may want to reflect on the extent to which they address social justice in all its nuances and dynamic complexities. They may want to train their

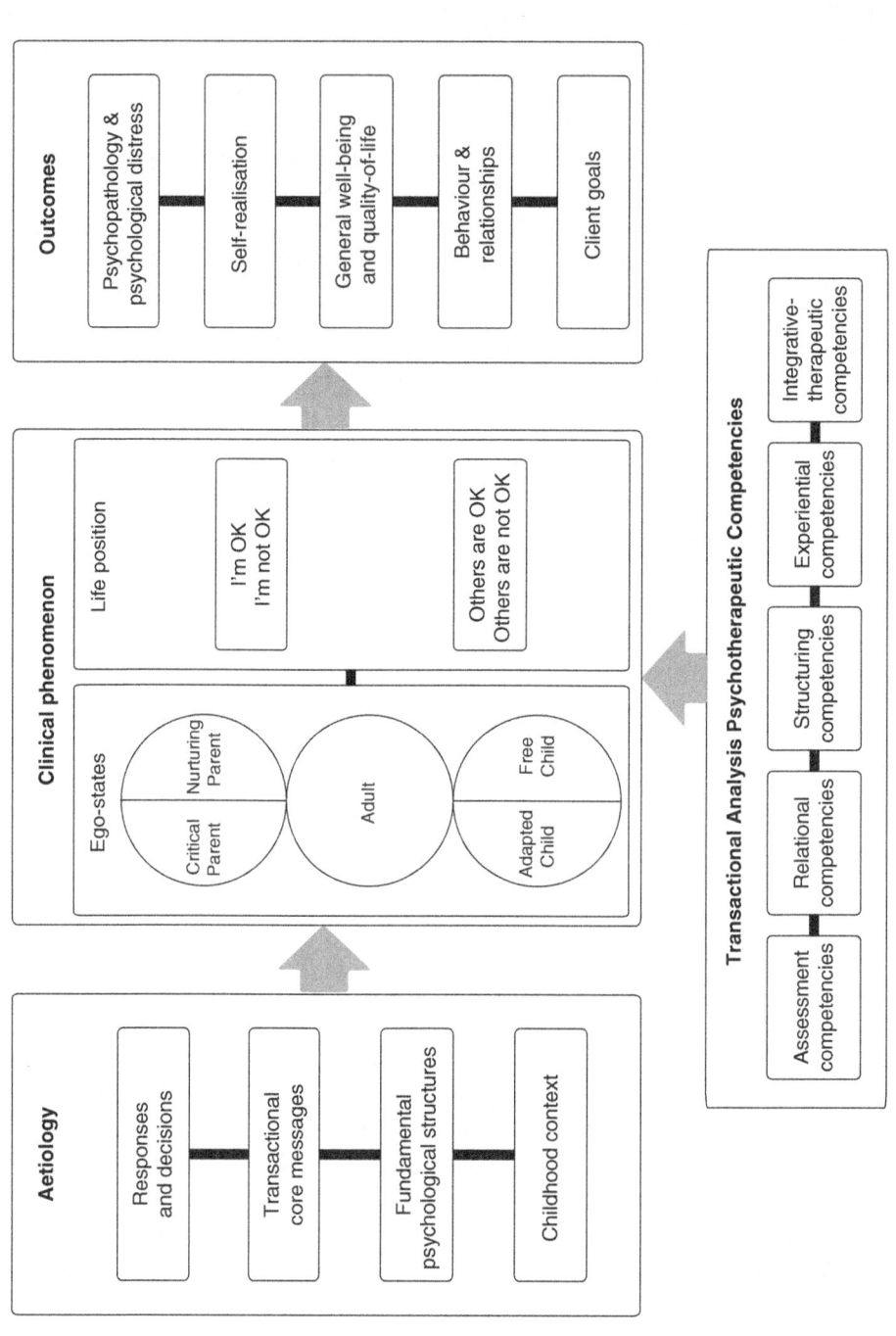

Figure 1.1 Simplified Conceptual Model of Evidence-Based TA psychotherapy

Source: Updated from Vos and van Rijn (2021c).

competencies and intuitive sensitivity towards the reality of social injustice, its multiple subjective meanings, and its development in interactions between society and the individual, and help clients develop freedom not only to liberate them from their feelings/memories of injustice but also freedom towards actively creating a more meaningful and fulfilling life, enabling them to flourish and realise their individual and social potential. (Vos, 2025, pp. 6–8)

Early TA authors believed that TA should aim to guide individuals towards autonomy, fostering a sense of personal freedom and self-awareness. However, recent research findings from focus groups, interviews and surveys indicate that personal autonomy is not straightforward (Car, 2013), as an individual's sense of autonomy and freedom is influenced by contextual factors and everyday interactions such as family, race, culture and religion (Cross, 2012; English, 2006; Massey, 2007). For example, individual experiences and expressions of sexual orientation and gender identity are shaped by cultural norms and values (Rowland & Cornell, 2021; Simerly, 2003). This contextual variability challenges the hetero and cisnormative, Western, white notion of universal and absolute personal autonomy in early TA (Minikin, 2023). Therefore, this book recommends empowering clients by determining their own therapy goals, including outcomes for social justice.

This book will explain how the client's presenting issues and case formulation can be sensitively assessed in their context, potentially including their 'contextual self' (Sedgwick, 2020). Drego (2006) argues that Berne's (1972) three-handed position of 'I'm, OK, You're OK, They're OK' envelops both individual and social freedoms, spanning both individual wholeness and mutual responsibility between individuals and between groups. Therefore, our evidence-based ego-state model incorporates functional and structural analysis to address the complex dynamics of internal dialogue and behaviour, highlighting personal and socio-political dynamics.

While we advocate for a systematic assessment and case formulation, these should be culturally sensitive, honour the client's lived experiences and emerge as co-created and evolving hypotheses between therapist and client. For example, therapists should avoid pathologisation, such as labelling homo/bisexual orientation and transgender identities as games (Shadbolt, 2004). Assessment of the development/aetiology of the client's issues should not merely include their life script but also their 'life-course', which contains influences of chance and circumstance on life outcomes such as being-born into a particular culture, gender, sexual orientation, racial/ethnic identity and socioeconomic class (Campos, 2010) that are often determined by the 'Cultural Parent' in the client's community/society (Drego, 1983).

Recognising the harsh realities of social existence (Vos et al., 2017) and the biological, neurological reality of certain behaviours (Selavan, 1990), we challenge the notion that an individual can always break free from the constraints of a life script, as an individual may be unable to change their broader socioeconomic, political structures, sometimes making the lack of change a normal reaction to abnormal circumstances (Frankl, 1985), requiring self-compassion instead of self-blame. Speaking in terms of an individual's 'decisions' regarding their life script may not only be unrealistic – as they may not have the freedom to decide – but also harmful by triggering undue feelings of shame, guilt and alienation;

therefore, we have replaced outdated terms like 'decision' and 'racket' that may give such unrealistic, unhelpful impressions.

Thus, early TA emphasised individual freedom and agency in decision-making without sufficiently acknowledging the constraints and limitations on individual freedom imposed by societal structures, power dynamics and oppressive social games, and the intersectional, multifaceted nature of diversity and oppression. Instead, we promote a more inclusive, socially aware and culturally sensitive approach that is grounded in a justice-oriented, sensitive therapeutic relationship (Norcross & Lambert, 2019), for example, by developing multicultural competencies (Tao et al., 2015) and flexibly tailoring the therapeutic stages, structure and treatment-manual to the individual (Power, 2022).

OVERVIEW OF THIS BOOK

This book aims to introduce the theory and practice of Evidence-based TA Psychotherapy. Part I offers an overview of the field's history, schools and research. Part II presents the evidence-based conceptual model of TA, as summarised in Figure 1.1: the client's aetiology impacts their presenting clinical issues, which can be addressed in therapy to improve a range of outcomes. Part III focuses on the therapeutic competencies that TA therapists should develop, which includes assessment, relational, structuring, experiential and integrative-therapeutic competencies. Part IV delves into tailoring TA to address specific mental and physical issues. Finally, part V offers a step-by-step manual for evidence-based 16-session TA psychotherapy, originally developing for treating depression but now made generally applicable. This manual, designed to be an evidence-based standard across TA schools, integrates research-backed elements to enhance therapy effectiveness and therapist competency. This exemplifies how therapists may apply the theory and skills taught in the preceding chapters. This may be particularly helpful for trainees and skilled therapists wanting to translate research evidence into their practices. The appendices include questionnaires, templates and homework exercises, allowing therapists to tailor the approach to individual client needs.

1.1 REFLECTIVE QUESTIONS

- We hope that this introduction invited questions for you. What captures your attention and ignites your curiosity? What frustrates or stimulates you? What are your expectations, assumptions and experiences with TA? How do you feel about an evidence-based approach to TA, and where do these feelings come from? As we embark on our journey together in this book, we invite you to engage with your own reflexivity, passion and open-mindedness.
- Many TA therapists invite clients to formulate goals in therapy and develop 'therapeutic contracts', which may stimulate the client's motivation and focus their development. What do you hope to achieve by reading this book?
- Like the TA founder Eric Berne often used fairy tales and stories in his work, write a fairy tale about your journey as a therapist: where did you start, what unknown lands have you already explored, what dragons have been slain, how could this book help you and where will you go?

2
THE SCHOOLS OF TA

INTRODUCTION

This chapter delves into the historical context of Transactional Analysis (TA) and TA psychotherapy, providing a comprehensive understanding of the various schools within TA and their fundamental principles and focuses. It encompasses the following aspects:

- The influential ideas that preceded TA and its underlying philosophy.
- An overview of Classical TA, Redecision TA, Integrative TA, Co-Creative TA, Psychoanalytic TA and Relational TA.
- Lastly, we outline professional training, accreditation and the relevant professional organisations.

DEVELOPMENT OF TA PSYCHOTHERAPY

According to Mahrer's categorisation (1989), TA can be classified as one of the early integrative psychotherapies. Its objective was to achieve theoretical integration by creating a new and substantive psychotherapy theory. TA was rooted in the humanistic-existential theory of understanding individuals, focusing on authenticity. It developed a psychotherapy theory that outlined its purpose, the characteristics of therapeutic contracts, specific therapeutic techniques, the nature of the therapeutic relationship and formulations. By employing Mahrer's classification, it is evident that TA aligns with the goals of integration in psychotherapy.

Eric Berne developed TA in the socio-political context of California in the 1950s (Berne, 1958). His psychoanalytic training and work with Paul Federn and Eric Eriksson strongly influenced his approach (Berne, 1961). However, he was also shaped by the humanistic philosophy prevalent in that cultural context. Berne aimed to create a humanistic form of psychotherapy that respected patients' ability to understand what is best for themselves and make life decisions. This had significant implications for the therapist-client relationship, as Berne emphasised transparency and equality. He referred to this philosophy as 'I'm OK, You're OK', using colloquial terms to describe the internal and interpersonal processes that remain central to TA today.

Despite the emphasis on equality, TA at that time still reflected elements of the medical model, and Berne sought to 'cure' his clients. The concept of the therapeutic relationship, as we understand it today, including the working alliance and transferential processes, was developed during the late 20th and early 21st centuries. However, it did not exist in the same format during his time. TA gained popularity in the 1950s thanks to its use of colloquial terms and perceived simplicity. Unfortunately, these colloquial terms, rooted in the culture and language of that era, eventually became therapeutic jargon that the founder of TA sought to avoid. It is worth noting that Berne's work was influenced by Watson's behavioural therapy, which impacted the context in which he operated. This influence is evident in Berne's emphasis on behavioural change and 'cure' and his interest in short-term therapy, often referred to as the 'one session cure' (Berne, 1971).

Box 2.1

Berne's Ego States

Berne (1972) defined ego-states as patterns of thought, feeling and behaviour, which formed the structure of personality and were separated into 'exteropsyche' or influences from the external environment (Parent ego-state), 'neopsyche' (Adult ego-state) responding to the here-and-now reality and 'archeopsyche' (Child ego-state) containing archaic responses to the environment (Berne, 1961). These colloquial terms for the ego-states are still used and readily recognisable by the clients, although some have argued that there may be nuanced differences between these concepts and ego-states.

Another cornerstone of TA is a theory of life script (Berne, 1972), a pattern of inter-connected story-like themes and unconscious narratives leading to a predictable ending that people re-enacted and confirmed throughout life through a series of internal beliefs and their interactions with their environment (Berne, 1964). In the early TA, these patterns were described as fairy tales. Clients were invited to reflect on their favourite childhood fairy tales and their underlying meanings, reflected in their life patterns.

2.1 REFLECTIVE QUESTIONS

- What are the colloquial terms in TA that you relate to? Are there any that seem to be outdated in your culture at this time?
- Apart from the familiar fairy tales in the Western culture, are there any stories in your culture that people internalise as representations of their life script?

In his work, Berne diverged from his training in psychoanalysis and endeavoured to create a conscious, insight-driven approach to achieve therapeutic outcomes that led to behavioural transformation. He considered this approach suitable for addressing less intricate clinical issues that did not necessitate psychoanalysis. While he was intrigued by the social context and aimed to establish TA as a form of social psychiatry, the focus on psychotherapy remained centered on individuals, even when practised in a group setting. At that time, TA retained its status as a modernist psychotherapy, firmly rooted in the principles of one-person psychology (Stark, 1999).

The TA community in the 21st century has become global. Various contexts and approaches have shaped the development of TA therapy, resulting in the emergence of different models or 'schools'. However, these new theories still have their foundations in Western societal models, and exploring broader cultural meanings and practices is still in its early stages. The identification with specific TA schools is not officially regulated but rather self-determined by authors, publications and training institutions.

We can differentiate between existing models as those aiming to achieve therapeutic transformation through understanding (either cognitively or emotionally driven) and relational approaches that prioritise the therapeutic connection and engage with the subconscious process. Despite a historical progression in theoretical development, moving from classical to the currently more prevalent integrative and relational models, the various 'schools' of TA psychotherapy still coexist and provide a variety of choices for therapeutic practice.

CREATING CHANGE THROUGH DEVELOPING INSIGHT

Classical TA Psychotherapy

The classical form of TA, pioneered by Eric Berne and his followers like Steiner, Karman and more recently Stewart and Joines (Stewart & Joines, 1987, 2012), is a modernist approach to psychotherapy (Stark, 1999). The foundations of this theory and its terminology were established during the 1960s and 1970s. The main focus of psychotherapy was centered on promoting behavioural change, often aiming to 'cure' the individual's life script. This perspective aligned with the medical model, contradicting the humanistic belief in authenticity and self-responsibility. In this approach, the therapist took on the responsibility of curing the patient, and therapy progressed through a series of contractual agreements aimed at achieving observable goals. The ultimate goal was to liberate patients from the constraints imposed by their life script. Practitioners within the classical school believed that their patients achieved a cure by enhancing the functioning of their Adult ego-state, which would be clarified and freed from the outdated and restrictive influences of their childhood experiences.

Box 2.2

Psychological Games

The techniques employed in Classical Therapy encompassed psychoeducation and examining individuals' repetitive transactional patterns, commonly known as psychological games. These patterns were analysed using various methods, including Berne's game formula (Berne, 1964). This formula revealed an unconscious and repetitive process that unfolded through a series of interactions, ultimately leading to familiar and unhealthy outcomes. Additionally, games could also be analysed using Karman's Drama Triangle (Karpman, 1971), which identified the roles individuals assumed in these games, such as

Rescuer, Persecutor and Victim. Another approach involved examining life script patterns, which aimed to raise awareness of early parental influences, messages and modelling. This examination often utilised tools like the Script Matrix (Steiner, 1974). Through these techniques, individuals gained insight into their own behaviours and thought processes, facilitating personal growth and healing.

Psychotherapy was provided individually and in group settings, with Berne's approach to group psychotherapy focused on establishing change contracts with participants and analysing transactions (Berne, 1966). Classical TA therapists, however, did not solely rely on cognition in their practice; they also recognised the importance of intuition for both the therapist and the client. This intuition, often called the 'Little Professor', aided children in understanding their surroundings and making adaptive choices. Although these adaptive choices formed the foundation of their life script, they were beneficial and protective at the time. TA psychotherapists also utilised their intuition when working with clients to create ego-images that supported the social analysis of ego-states and fostered an emotional comprehension of their clients.

2.2 REFLECTIVE QUESTIONS

- What techniques of classical TA do you use in your practice? What are their strengths and limitations?
- How do you formulate treatment contracts?

Redecision TA Psychotherapy

Redecision therapy, a therapeutic approach developed by Bob and Mary Goulding in 1976 (Goulding & Goulding, 1976), emerged alongside traditional methods and was heavily influenced by Gestalt psychotherapy techniques (Gladfelter, 1992). This approach expanded on the original principles of TA theory, emphasising conscious change, client empowerment and a humanistic perspective that promotes personal growth and autonomy. While some may view redecision therapy as an individual form of psychotherapy (Stark, 1999), it differs from traditional methods in facilitating change.

Instead of altering an individual's entire life script, redecision therapy concentrates on modifying the specific script messages received during childhood. This is achieved by engaging the Child ego-state of the individual. Through cognitive insight gained in the Adult ego-state and subsequent emotional catharsis in the Child ego-state, redecision therapy allows suppressed emotions to be expressed. The therapist collaborates with the client to make new and authentic decisions for their future. For instance, a client may affirm, 'It is acceptable to have needs and ask for support when necessary, and I will continue to do so'. By working through these suppressed emotions and making new choices, redecision therapy promotes personal growth. It paves the way for a more fulfilling future. In that sense, the change to a script decision was achieved by an emotional redecision In Child ego-state. This was typically achieved through a brief group intervention, generally during a workshop.

Box 2.3

Injunctions

The authors further developed the theory of early childhood messages and redefined them as 'injunctions' – restrictive and limiting messages conveyed by parental figures. They outlined twelve primary injunctions: 'Do not', 'Do not Exist', 'Do not feel', 'Do not Be Close', 'Do not Succeed', 'Do not be Well (sane)', 'Do not be You', 'Do not Belong', 'Do not think', 'Do not be important', 'Do not Grow up' and 'Do not be a Child'.

According to Kahler and Capers (1974), counter script injunctions or drivers such as 'Be Strong', 'Be Perfect', 'Try Hard', 'Hurry Up' and 'Please Others' play a crucial role in highlighting the conflict between managing these prohibitions and fulfilling the innate needs of the child.

The authors emphasised the importance of a child's ability to adjust to their surroundings. This indicated that a child could make different choices, such as altogether avoiding harmful injunctions. The therapy they created primarily involved short-term group sessions, often in the form of workshops. Clients were encouraged to explore and interact with a hypothetical early situation and consciously alter their decision-making process while receiving support and encouragement from the group members. Therapists employed various creative techniques to assist them, frequently utilising the Gestalt two-chair method.

The theory and practice of redecision therapy have been greatly enhanced through further development by renowned authors like McNeel (1982, 2010, 2016). McNeel made significant contributions by revising the terminology used in the theory. He replaced the term 'injunction' with 'injunctive messages' to eliminate its legalistic connotations. Instead of presenting a list of 12 distinct messages, McNeel introduced five categories of prohibitive messages, focusing on their impact and grouping them into specific areas. This expansion and refinement of the redecision theory have provided therapists with a more comprehensive understanding of how these injunctive messages influence individuals. By categorising them, therapists can effectively address and challenge these messages in therapy sessions to promote personal growth and transformation:

- survival
- attachment
- identity
- competence
- sense of security.

Moving away from specific instructions allowed for greater flexibility in the therapeutic exploration. McNeel disagreed that a child could altogether avoid the unfavourable effects of these injunctions. The injunctive messages in the family's systemic and cultural context were inevitable and unavoidable. This new approach aligned more closely with evidence-based theories of child development, as it acknowledged the role of family culture as a system and avoided placing blame on the client for their psychological struggles. However, the author still used the term 'decision' to describe how a child responds to this environment. He explained that a child would typically make either a despairing or defiant decision, which to some extent provided relief from their psychological pain. For instance, the script decision could represent a defiant position in response to an injunctive message: 'I am strong and can handle anything on my own'.

After training and working at the Gouldings' Western Institute for Group and Family Therapy, McNeel dedicated his research to the effects of redecision therapy (McNeel, 1982). He questioned the belief that experiencing redecision as a cathartic event in a workshop setting alone was enough to change one's life script. In his study conducted in 1982, participants in workshops reported positive outcomes. However, his subsequent work revealed that these outcomes did not result in lasting change. Instead, he discovered that redecision work occurred gradually over an extended period. McNeel also revised the approach to redecision psychotherapy, shifting the focus from eliminating old messages to adopting a more satisfying and functional approach and developing a new internal Parental stance.

Relational TA Psychotherapy

Relational approaches within the TA framework have evolved, drawing from the psycho-analytic origins of the approach, humanistic philosophy and a growing understanding of the importance of the therapeutic relationship. This progression reflects a shift from focusing on individual psychology to acknowledging the dynamic interplay between two individuals involved in therapy (Stark, 1999). These developments have paved the way for a deeper exploration of the interpersonal dynamics and relational patterns that shape the therapy-process. TA therapists recognise that the therapeutic relationship holds transformative potential by incorporating relational perspectives. Personal growth and healing can occur through the genuine connection and empathic attunement between therapist and client. This shift towards a more relational stance highlights the importance of establishing trust, fostering open communication and creating a safe space for exploration and vulnerability. The emergence of relational approaches in TA signifies a broader recognition of the profound impact of human connection on individual well-being. This offers a more holistic understanding of human experience and emphasises compassion, authenticity and the power of genuine human connection in facilitating personal growth.

Judy Barr (Barr, 1987) was the first TA author to prioritise the therapeutic relationship in the therapy-process. This idea was further expanded upon by Clarkson (1990). The emphasis on the therapeutic relationship remained a crucial aspect of TA psychotherapy, aligning with advancements in psychotherapy research. The growing evidence highlighted the significance of the psychotherapy relationship, particularly the working alliance (Luborsky, 1976; Luborsky et al., 1985; Norcross & Wampold, 2011; Wampold & Imel, 2015). While relational, integrative and psychodynamic models within TA all recognised the importance of the therapeutic relationship, they varied in their approaches. There are currently four distinctive models within the relational schools of TA:

- The integrative approach developed by Erskine, Zalcman, Moursund and Trautmann;
- The psychodynamic relational school, developed by Moiso and Novellino;
- The relational transactional analyses developed by Hargadon and Sills;
- The co-creative TA was developed by Summers and Tudor.

Psychodynamic and relational approaches strongly emphasise the concept of transference. At the same time, integrative and co-creative models highlight the importance of present-centred relating. These relational frameworks are widely recognised in the field of TA psychotherapy. However, classical and redecision approaches continue to be relevant. The focus on transference is a key aspect of psychodynamic and relational schools. In contrast, integrative and co-creative models prioritise establishing a strong connection in the present moment. In the current landscape of TA psychotherapy, relational models are prominent, coexisting alongside classical and redecision schools.

Integrative TA Psychotherapy

The Integrative School of TA was created by Richard Erskine and his colleagues Zalcman, Moursund and Trautmann (Erskine et al., 1999; Erskine & Trautmann, 1996; Erskine & Zalcman, 1979). This approach was primarily influenced by attachment theory (Bowlby, 1982) and research on attunement in child development (Stern, 1985), emphasising the significance of establishing a secure foundation and the innate human drive for connection.

The integrative school emphasised the significance of a genuine human connection between the therapist and the client and eight relational requirements: feeling secure, being valued, experiencing acceptance, fostering mutuality, defining oneself, making a meaningful impact, having the other initiate contact and expressing love. These needs were not viewed as abnormal or unhealthy. The therapist aimed to fulfil them while maintaining the boundaries of the empathic therapeutic relationship (Erskine & Trautmann, 1996), offering a safe and supportive environment for personal growth and healing.

In his early writing, Erskine described the aim of psychotherapy as achieving a script cure (Erskine, 1980), introducing the physiological aspect of script and recognising that personal development was broader than script-change. In their approach to TA psychotherapy, integrative therapists focused on developing a secure and attuned therapeutic relationship, as well as using some regressive techniques and working with a Child Ego-state using a two-chair technique.

Box 2.4

Racket System

The concept of the Racket System, as outlined by Erskine and Zalcman in 1979, offers a framework for analysing various script elements. These elements include script beliefs, internal experiences (including bodily sensations) and past experiences reinforcing the script beliefs. In later work with O'Reilly-Knapp in 2010, the term 'racket' was replaced with the more precise term 'script-system' to accurately reflect the nature of this framework for analysing script dynamics. The revised title still provides a means to examine the different aspects of a script in action.

Co-Creative TA Psychotherapy

Co-Creative TA was developed by Summers and Tudor (Summers & Tudor, 2000) and introduced social constructivism and field theory into the development of ego-states. This emphasised the significance of the collaborative and relational nature of TA concepts. The application of these ideas extended to psychotherapy, where the therapist played an active role in co-creating the therapeutic narrative while also considering the cultural context. The therapeutic relationship was viewed as intersubjective, involving the subjective experiences of both the therapist and the client. This unique interaction formed the core of the therapy-process. Two types of therapeutic relationships were identified: present-centred, which focused on the existential realities of two individuals within their specific context, and past-centred (transferential), which explored the broader socio-economic and cultural factors alongside the transferential process.

The authors integrated developmental theories (Bowlby, 1982; Stern, 1985) and the relational TA school (Cornell, 1988) to define script theory as a collaborative process influencing parents and children. Instead of considering script decisions as cognitive processes, they viewed them as dynamic states belonging to various life narratives held by individuals. Additionally, they raised concerns about the traditional language of TA, which predominantly reflected heterosexual, western values and failed to acknowledge inherent differences in temperament and other innate characteristics among individuals. A significant advancement within the co-creative school was evaluating and reimagining ego-states, explicitly focusing on the Adult ego-state (Tudor & Summers, 2014).

Box 2.5

Neopsyche

Tudor introduced the idea of neopsyche (Berne, 1962, 1972), which encompassed elements such as autonomy, relational needs, consciousness, reflective consciousness, critical consciousness, maturity, motivation and imagination. This reimagined the Adult ego-state as the foundation of our executive self, departing from the traditional TA model that likens it to a computer-like processor. The concept of an Integrating Adult emerged from this framework, emphasising the integration of various psychological aspects in a holistic manner. By incorporating these elements, Tudor's neopsyche model offers a more comprehensive understanding of human behaviour and personal growth. It recognises the importance of autonomy, self-awareness and the capacity for critical reflection in fostering psychological well-being and facilitating personal development.

In 2011, co-creative TA was firmly positioned as a relational TA, distinctive with an expanded role of the Adult ego-state and the significance of the present-centred relating (Tudor, 2011).

The development of co-creative TA not only updated the theory of ego-states but also incorporated cultural and socio-economic factors, constructivism and a two-person psychology into TA. However, despite these developments, there was no corresponding creation of a distinct therapeutic approach. Nevertheless, the co-creative TA framework remains highly significant in providing a solid foundation and valuable insights for therapeutic practice.

Psychodynamic TA Psychotherapy

The Psychodynamic school of thought was developed by Carlo Moiso and Michele Novellino, drawing inspiration from the psychoanalytic clinical methodology of TA and the earlier writings of Woods and Haykin. Their approach focused on analysing transference and countertransference, specifically within actual clinical transactions, whether group or individual therapy. They distinguished their approach from traditional psychoanalysis by utilising techniques such as Gestalt, redecision or reparenting when working with transference. Within this framework, the interactions between therapists and clients were examined to understand the ongoing creation, re-creation and co-creation of personal scripts. Unlike in redecision work, the analysis of scripts did not involve emotional reliving of early script protocol scenes. Instead, scripts were seen as lived-out stories that continuously evolved through an ongoing process.

Relational TA Psychotherapy

The emphasis of relational TA is centred on engaging with the subconscious process. This incorporates a therapeutic model recognising the importance of a collaborative relationship between the therapist and the client (Beebe & Lachmann, 2013). Initially conceptualised by Hargaden and Sills (Hargaden & Sills, 2002), this approach has been extensively explored and documented in various publications, such as the works of Fowlie and Sills (2011) and Hargaden and Cornell (2019), which outline its progression and core principles.

According to these authors, the therapeutic relationship involves the therapist and the client, each bringing their own conscious and unconscious patterns of relating. The therapist cannot simply observe the client's process from a neutral standpoint; instead, they must be open to reflecting on their own experiences during therapy. Therapeutic rupture and repair are crucial methods for facilitating internal and external change. In relational TA therapy, the main focus is developing the work with the Child ego-state. This development occurs not through techniques or cathartic methods but through inquiry and collaboratively creating meaning with the client. Relational TA necessitates that therapists consistently focus on developing self-awareness and remaining receptive and non-defensive throughout therapy. It also accentuates the cultural context and the conscious and unconscious influences it has on the therapist and the client.

According to these authors, the motivation behind creating this model stemmed from the clinical requirements of effectively working with complex clinical cases and addressing issues related to one's sense of self. Relational TA primarily finds its application in long-term individual psychotherapy but can also be utilised in group settings. This approach draws inspiration from TA's psychoanalytic origins while being influenced by various factors. These include research that highlights the significance of the therapeutic relationship in determining outcomes in psychotherapy (Norcross, 2002; Wampold & Imel, 2015), advancements in affective neuroscience (Schore, 1994), therapeutic traditions of intersubjectivity (Stolorow, 1987) and other forms of relational psychoanalysis (Benjamin, 1992, 2018; DeYoung, 2003).

2.3 REFLECTIVE QUESTIONS

- Which TA schools do you use in your practice?
- Does this vary in short- and long-term therapy?
- What roles do the therapeutic relationship, co-creation and unconscious processes play in your client work?
- How pure do you use the approach of a specific TA school, or do you integrate this with other therapeutic approaches? What arguments or evidence do you have for this pure or integrative approach?
- How could you improve your TA therapy skills? How serious are you about improving your TA-skills; what is your motivation, and what is holding you back?

Box 2.6

How to Use This Book for TA Examination?

To achieve a Certified TA status, students need to comply with the standards of EATA (https://eata.news.org) and/or International Association of Transactional Analysis (https://itaaworld.com). The certification consists of two parts: the written examination and a viva. A case study focusing on applying TA theory in practice takes up a significant part of the written examination. The stages of this book's manual can support the candidates in developing the case study by focusing on case formulation and diagnosis, developing a treatment contract, developing a treatment plan and offering the prognosis. The guide for the written examination (based on EATA handbook) asks the candidate to offer a diagnosis based on TA and the standardised diagnostic systems (DSM-5 and ICD). The term diagnosis, externally to TA, is normally used for standardised diagnostic systems, and the term formulation is more commonly used within the wider therapeutic field (van Rijn, 2014). The treatment manual within this book can support the candidates in structuring both their case formulation and clinical diagnosis. There are several approaches to treatment planning within TA (Clarkson, 2013; Minikin, 2023; Woollams & Brown, 1979). The manual also offers a generic, research-based generic treatment plan that can be used flexibly and outlines the process and outcomes of the treatment. As described in this book, questionnaires can help the therapist evaluate these outcomes.

3

OVERVIEW OF RESEARCH ON TA

INTRODUCTION

This chapter will provide a comprehensive review of the research on TA, which will be further discussed in subsequent chapters. This chapter addresses the following:

- TA research is grounded in a movement towards evidence-based therapies
- Research on outcomes of TA psychotherapy
- Research on TA-questionnaires
- Research on TA therapists' actual practices
- Scientific evidence for TA's conceptual model
- Based on the body of research, TA may be considered a bona fide psychotherapy

EVIDENCE-BASED PSYCHOTHERAPY

Therapists benefit from scientific research as it may provide evidence-based guidelines that enhance the effectiveness of their interventions (Vos, 2023). Access to the latest empirical findings enables therapists to tailor treatments to individual client needs, ensuring more beneficial outcomes and client satisfaction. Moreover, research helps therapists to stay informed about emerging therapeutic techniques and best practices, fostering continuous professional growth and improved client outcomes. Evolutions in the research and practices of therapies have led to the development in the late 1990s of 'evidence-based psychological therapies', which accentuates that therapists should ground their practice in the most up-to-date research and professional guidelines (Goodheart, 2006).

There seems to be a growing consensus amongst therapy researchers that most clients derive equivalent effects from any type of bona fide psychotherapy delivered by therapists who are trained and dedicated to a specific practice that is grounded in a solid conceptual framework (Vos, 2023; Wampold & Imel, 2015). Furthermore, researchers have identified factors that effective therapies have in common, such as a positive therapeutic alliance (Norcross & Wampold, 2019). Thus, the evolution of psychotherapy research highlights the importance of grounding therapeutic practices in research while recognising the common effective elements across various therapeutic approaches. This book will present evidence that aligns with these criteria of evidence-based therapies, effectively meeting the standards of policy-makers and health insurance companies.

Initially, humanistic therapies resisted the evidence-based movement due to concerns about reductionism but have since adopted advanced research techniques, demonstrating that many humanistic therapies are as effective as other evidence-based therapies (Angus, 2015; Cuijpers et al., 2016; Duffy et al., 2024; Elliott et al., 2021, 2002; Lambert et al., 2016; Leichsenring & Rabung, 2011, 2004; Lilliengren et al., 2016; Vos & Vitali, 2018; Vos et al., 2015). Similarly, TA research has evolved from Berne's early, less rigorous publications to more methodologically rigorous studies, establishing a stronger evidential foundation. Evidence-based TA psychotherapy results from these research developments, identifying effective TA-specific interventions and integrating common therapeutic factors.

━━━━━━━━━ **3.1 REFLECTIVE QUESTIONS** ━━━━━━━━━

- How do you justify the trustworthiness and possible benefits of your therapy?
- How do you know that your clients experience positive outcomes?
- To what extent do you unquestioningly follow your teachers/supervisors as ultimate holders of the truth, and to what extent do you critically question and tailor their guidance?
- How do you feel about using research in therapies? What are its strengths and weaknesses?

TA PSYCHOTHERAPY OUTCOME STUDIES

To ascertain the effects of TA psychotherapy, we undertook a systematic review and meta-analyses of all 41 clinical trials on TA (Vos & van Rijn, 2022). Across these studies, clients reported moderate to large improvements in psychopathology, social functioning, self-efficacy, ego-state functioning, well-being and behaviour. When compared to control conditions, TA showed moderate to large effects on psychopathology (e.g. depression, anxiety), social functioning, self-efficacy, ego-states, well-being and behaviour. Interestingly, TA was more effective in individuals, groups and families than schools or prisons. TA seemed similarly effective as control groups and as the findings of other humanistic therapies. This study confirmed the so-called 'Dodo Bird Effect', a tongue-in-cheek title for universal efficacy. The Dodo bird in Alice in Wonderland by Lewis Carrol, was a judge in a race of various creatures who stated that everyone had won and deserved prizes (Wampold & Imel, 2015). As a well-established bona fide therapeutic approach, TA psychotherapies also proved to have effects comparable to those of other evidence-based therapies.

TA-QUESTIONNAIRE STUDIES

After examining the outcomes of TA, we focused on its key concepts (Vos & van Rijn, 2021b). Berne and various TA schools developed many concepts from therapeutic expertise and the collective knowledge of previous psychotherapists. However, personal and collective clinical experiences may not meet the rigorous standards of modern scientific research. We reviewed the literature on TA-related questionnaires to explore and validate these key concepts. We scrutinised 12,287 studies and identified 56 questionnaires used in 263 studies. Chapter 8 includes an overview of questionnaires to consider in TA psychotherapy.

Our analysis addressed a crucial question: 'Which Transactional Analysis (TA) concepts have substantial empirical support from quantitative studies, particularly those using questionnaires?' The findings indicate that many individuals experience structurally different ego-states (Parent, Adult, Child) and variations in their functions (Critical Parent, Nurturing Parent, Free Child, Adapted Child). Additionally, people adopt four fundamental life stances, encompassing positive/negative attitudes towards oneself/others. Meta-analyses revealed that psychopathology and physical symptoms are linked to a dominant Adapted Child and Critical Parent, weakened Nurturing Parent, Adult, and Free Child, negative coping styles and negative attitudes towards oneself/others. For instance, individuals with clinical diagnoses showed higher scores on subscales like Critical Parent and Vulnerable Child and lower scores in positive modes like Healthy Adult and Free Child. These findings support fundamental TA-practices and their empirical validity. Chapter 4 will explain how to assess and work with these concepts.

RESEARCH ON TA THERAPISTS' ACTUAL PRACTICES

To understand how TA therapists practice TA, we surveyed European TA therapists (Vos & van Rijn, 2021b). Two hundred and thirty-eight TA therapists completed the survey. The majority expressed that they view TA as a therapeutic approach, a general attitude towards life and their preferred model for their practice. Their clinical practice focuses mainly on the client's ego-states, transactions, social functioning and self-efficacy. In their experience, this focus improves the clients' psychological well-being, self-realisation and overall behavioural wellness. They reported that clients commonly asked for their therapeutic support because their reported problems were believed to be caused by unfavourable messages received early in life (forming the basis of their life script), unhelpful coping, transgenerational messages, life events, discounting of existential givens and genetic/temperamental factors. The respondents understood that individuals have some, albeit limited by their social context, agency in accepting or rejecting the negative impact of these messages and life events through their behaviour, emotions and cognitive styles. TA was seen as beneficial to clients through its work on ego-states, social functioning and self-efficacy. The therapeutic changes were facilitated by competent therapists who fostered positive relationships with their clients, worked at experiential depth in the present moment, conducted etiological analyses and provided structured treatment. The following chapters on the clinical, aetiological and therapeutic models follow this survey.

Based on this survey, we concluded that, in practice, TA provides a unified and comprehensive conceptual framework. This coherence in therapeutic practice remains true, even with differences between various TA schools, as discussed in Chapter 2. Therefore, we decided to present one unified, evidence-based conceptual model of TA in this book.

■■■■■■ 3.2 REFLECTIVE QUESTIONS ■■■■■■

Reflect on some of the questions asked in the survey:

- What are the three most significant strengths of TA, and what are the three most substantial weaknesses and most contested topics?
- What aspects of TA-practice are helpful for your clients, and what aspects are less helpful/problematic?
- What makes you a good TA-practitioner? What TA competencies do you use? How could you become a better TA-practitioner?
- What issues can your therapy help with in your clients?
- What are the therapeutic mechanisms you use to benefit your clients?
- What are significant moments of change in your therapeutic practice with clients? What do these moments tell about TA?
- Do you combine TA with other therapeutic approaches, and if so, how?

TA'S CONCEPTUAL MODEL

Figure 3.1 provides a detailed integration of all the research evidence for TA (Vos & van Rijn, 2021c). This book is based on this evidence-based model of TA. Chapters 4 and 6 will explain the central clinical phenomenon that TA therapists assess and address to stimulate positive therapeutic change. This consists of the client's ego-states, such as the Critical Parent, Nurturing Parent, Adult, Adapted Child and Free Child. This also includes the life positions 'I'm OK/not-OK' and its associated self-efficacy, and 'You're OK/not-OK' and its associated social functioning. As Chapter 5 will explain, the client's presenting issues can originate from various factors, including their childhood context, fundamental psychological structures, transactional core messages and the client's responses/decisions; therapists address these aetiological factors, and connect these past life experiences with the present issues. As Chapter 6 will explain, the presentation of the clinical problems can lead to a range of outcomes, which therapists may aim to improve, such as psychopathology (e.g. anxiety, depression), psychological distress, self-realisation (the ability to live a meaningful and fulfilling life), general well-being and quality-of-life, behaviour and relationships; TA helps clients to formulate their own therapy goals. As Part III will explain, therapists use a range of therapeutic competencies to foster change, which includes assessment, relational, structuring, experiential and integrative-therapeutic competencies.

A fundamental problem in the TA research field was the lack of treatment manuals that systematically applied these evidence-based concepts and provided clear guidance to therapists (Vos & van Rijn, 2022). Hence, we have systematically developed the treatment manual that implements the evidence-based conceptual model described in this book's Part V (Vos & van Rijn, 2023). This manual is grounded in the evidence-based principles shared among all TA schools, making it a standard and widely applicable TA treatment approach. To assess its viability, we conducted a feasibility study (Vos & van Rijn, 2024c), followed by a pilot randomised controlled trial (Vos & van Rijn, 2024a, 2024b). During the pilot study, we provided brief TA sessions to 28 clients with mild to moderate depression. We then compared the results to a group of ten randomly assigned clients who received brief Cognitive Behaviour Therapy and 28 who received Care As Usual, consisting of generic Humanistic-relational therapies. TA had a significant impact on clients' depression, anxiety, general distress and overall quality of life. These effects are noteworthy as they equal or surpass the control conditions' effects. The findings validated our conceptual model (Figure 3.1.), as these positive outcomes were predicted by improvements in clients' ego-states, life position, self-efficacy and social functioning, which were again predicted by the therapist's TA-related skills. In summary, our clinical trials demonstrated how a treatment that systematically applies TA's conceptual model can produce substantial positive effects, and provides evidence supporting the conceptual model. A small feasibility study in Italy with a translated manual suggested similar findings (unpublished findings).

TA IS A BONA FIDE PSYCHOTHERAPY

This chapter highlighted how TA research is integrated into broader psychotherapy research, emphasising evidence-based therapies. Figure 3.2 outlines the history of the systematic and clinical reviews, showing TA's consistent positive outcomes and alignment with its therapeutic mechanisms (Kazdin, 2022; Vos, 2023). Our findings, particularly our meta-analysis and systematically developed treatment manual, indicate that TA meets the criteria for 'empirical validation', according to APA Division of Clinical Psychology criteria (Chambless & Hollon, 1998; David et al., 2018; Goodheart, 2006; Levant & Sperry; 2016; Tolin et al., 2015), such as well-designed trials and systematic treatment manuals. Furthermore, TA emphasises the therapeutic relationship, a key criterion the APA Division of Psychotherapy accentuates.

We contend that TA can be recognised as a bona fide therapy (Wampold & Imel, 2015), when practised as an evidence-based therapy. This recognition stems from the fact that TA is administered conducted by professionally trained, committed therapists who follow a therapeutic approach in which each conceptual component is supported by systematic, empirical evidence (Vos, 2023). Based on this evidence, we recommend that TA therapists be recognised and included in national health services and health insurance policies.

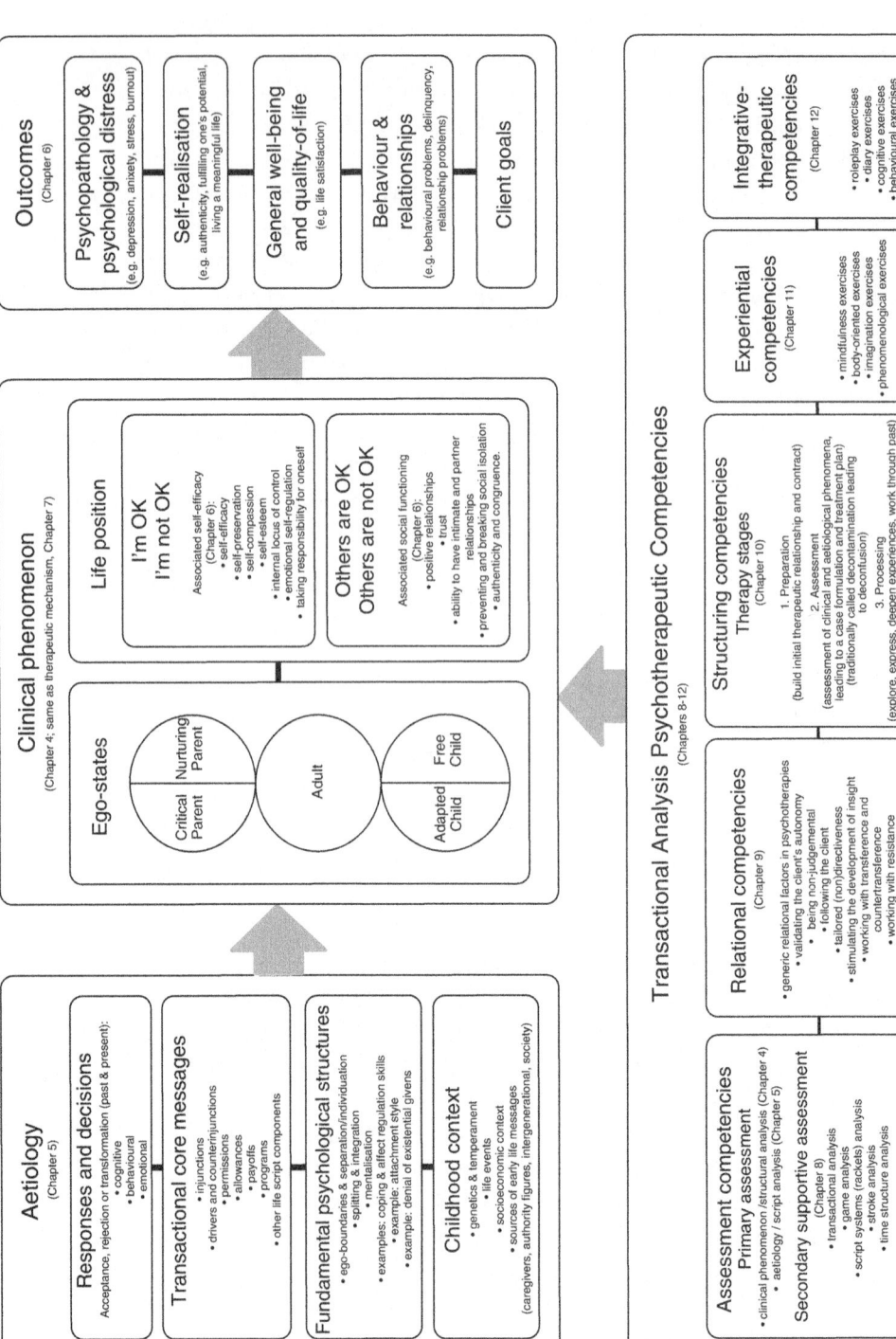

Figure 3.1 Complete Conceptual Model of Evidence-based TA Psychotherapy

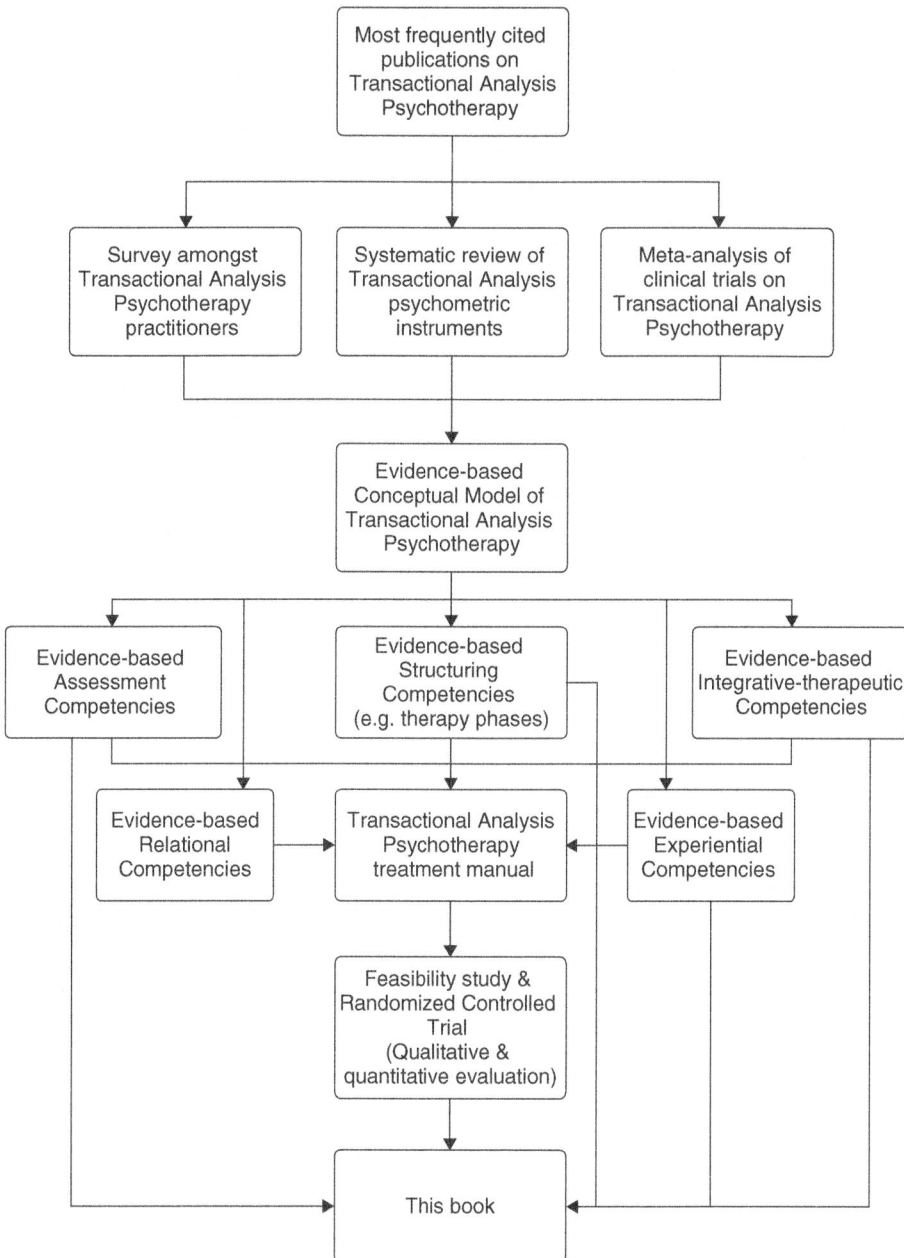

Figure 3.2 Overview of the History of Our Research on Evidence-based Transactional Analysis Psychotherapy

SUMMARY

- Evidence-Based TA psychotherapy aligns with trends towards evidence-based therapies.
- Forty-one clinical trials have been conducted on TA psychotherapy, showing large effects on mental health and quality of life. As expected, these outcomes can be explained by the client's improvements in their ego-states and life positions, facilitated by the therapists' competencies of analysis, structure, working in the present and offering a supportive therapeutic relationship.
- The general conceptual model of TA has been robustly validated through a broad survey among TA therapists.
- The general conceptual model has been confirmed via multiple empirical studies. This model consists of the aetiological concepts (childhood context, fundamental psychological structures, transactional core messages, responses and decisions), clinical phenomena which the therapeutic mechanisms focus on (ego-states and life positions I'm/You're OK/not-OK), outcomes (psychopathology, general distress, self-realisation, well-being, quality-of-life, behaviour, relationships and client goals) and therapist skills (assessment, relational, structuring, experiential and integrative-therapeutic competencies).
- The TA treatment manual, detailed in Part V, is backed by clinical trials confirming its effectiveness.
- TA is supported by substantial empirical evidence, establishing it as an evidence-based, bona fide psychotherapy.

PART II

EVIDENCE-BASED CONCEPTUAL MODEL OF TRANSACTIONAL ANALYSIS PSYCHOTHERAPY

4

CLINICAL PHENOMENON: WHAT ARE THE CLIENT'S PROBLEMS?

This chapter describes the evidence-based clinical model of TA. Research evidence will show the clinical issues that clients may present within TA therapy, centering around an evidence-based model of ego-states and life positions. Although specific disorders and unique clients may need uniquely tailored models, this chapter will discuss generic trends in research:

- An illustrative case study
- A brief historical overview of structural models
- The evidence-based structural model of Critical Parent, Nurturing Parent, Adult, Adapted Child and Free Child
- The life position of 'I'm OK'
- The life position of 'You're OK'

Case Study 4.1

Freya

Freya, a 25-year-old student, seeks therapy to address recurring patterns in her relationships and emotional well-being. She describes a history of challenging interactions with authority figures like her research supervisors, difficulty expressing her emotions and a persistent feeling of emptiness despite her achievements in her academic work. Through TA, her therapist explores the influence of different ego-states on Freya's life and mental health.

Critical Parent: Freya's Critical Parent ego-state is evident in her often high standards, being critical of others and finding fault in them, like her supervisors. This Critical Parent ego-state stems from her upbringing with a highly critical and demanding mother. This critical voice also seems replicated internally, as she has adopted feelings of self-doubt in her Adapted Child ego-state: she often hears her internal voice echoing her mother's disapproving remarks, leading to feelings of inadequacy and self-doubt, impacting her mental health negatively.

Nurturing Parent: Freya discovers her capacity for nurturing and self-compassion in therapy. Through the Nurturing Parent behaviours, such as positive affirmations and permissions and recognising another person's perspective rather than finding fault, she learns to comfort and support herself and receive support from others, countering her Critical Parent's effects. By practising self-care and positive affirmations, she experiences a gradual improvement in her self-esteem and emotional resilience.

Adult: As Freya engages in her healthy Adult ego-state, she can reflect on her thoughts and feelings. This enables her to make informed decisions and set boundaries in her relationships, contributing to a sense of empowerment and agency. The Healthy Adult ego-state fosters her mental well-being by promoting adaptive coping strategies and problem-solving skills.

Adapted Child: Freya's ego-state manifests in her working hard in all areas of her life to reach real or imaginary standards, as she had learnt to work hard to achieve her parents' approval. This often results in stressful relationships – particularly with authority figures like her supervisors, emotional exhaustion and a lack of fulfilment.

Free Child: Through therapy, Freya reconnects with her Free Child ego-state, allowing herself to experience joy, spontaneity and creativity. Embracing her inner Child rekindles her zest for life. It helps her break free from the constraints of her past conditioning, leading to a renewed sense of vitality and emotional liberation.

Thus, by exploring and understanding the influences of the various ego-states, Freya gains insight into her relational patterns and psychological well-being. By addressing the impact of her critical behaviour and internal dialogue (Adapted Child and Critical parent ego-states) and nurturing self-compassion (nurturing Parent ego-state), Freya has progressed from a more negative life position towards a healthier and more adaptive outlook. This transformation involves transitioning from a life position of 'I'm not-OK/You're OK' towards 'I'm OK/You're OK'. She learns to navigate her internal dynamics through TA therapy, fostering greater self-awareness, emotional balance and improved mental health. This case study illustrates how distinct ego-states and life positions can profoundly impact an individual's psychological well-being and relational patterns.

EGO-STATES

The concept of ego-states, colloquially named Parent, Adult and Child (PAC), is one of the key concepts in the TA theory of personality and one that has seen much development since the definition of Eric Berne (1961, p. 364) as 'a consistent pattern of feeling and experience directly related to a corresponding consistent pattern of behaviour'. These concepts were associated with Federn's ego-psychology (1952) and developed further to incorporate behaviour and a notion that some ego-states resembled figures from the person's history (Parent). The behaviours related to these different ego-states, such as controlling, nurturing, adaptive or free, became known as functional ego-states. However, Parent behaviours replicated that of parental figures, and Child functions were remnants of a person's childhood (Berne, 1972). In our case study, Freya's high standards and demanding behaviour replicated those of her mother, and she behaved in a compliant manner when people in authority asked her to do something.

These concepts were not always defined precisely by Berne or his followers in these early writings, and terms of functional and structural ego-states were used interchangeably (Gregoire, 2024). The current theory recognises that ego-state functions and structure could be distinctive. Further structural analysis could be needed to understand their aetiology. In Berne's writing, the behavioural diagnosis was the first step in diagnosing ego-states, followed by systematic social, historical and phenomenological diagnoses. Diagnosing someone's ego-state from a small selection of behavioural or cultural cues is a common mistake.

The theory of ego-states was developed by many theorists over the years (Sills & Hargaden, 2003). It is beyond the scope of this book to give a complete overview of these developments, including working with the unconscious, developing a somatic model of ego-states and understanding cultural influences and their integration into the ego-state theories. Broadly speaking, theorists who developed a relational TA model and those who worked with the unconscious processes developed a more in-depth approach to understanding the Child ego-state (e.g. Hargaden & Sill, 2002; Novelino, 2003). The Adult ego-state was reviewed, and the concept was expanded by the co-creative approach theorists (Summers & Tudor, 2000). There were developments in working with Parent ego-states (Erskine & Trautman, 1996).

However, the simple concept of the three main ego-states, Parent, Adult and Child, and behavioural expressions in the functional states of Critical and Nurturing Parent, Adapted and Free Child, remain in use by therapists and clients, as indicated by our survey amongst TA therapists (Vos & van Rijn, 2021a-c).

A HISTORICAL OVERVIEW OF TA'S STRUCTURAL MODELS

This section gives a brief historical overview of the structural models in TA. Practitioners may want to skip this section and jump to the sections that present the concise, evidence-based model of Critical Parent, Nurturing Parent, Adult, Adapted Child and Free Child. However, readers may draw inspiration from this section to develop unique models for individual clients, as one size may not fit all.

Classical Freudian Model

After WWII, Eric Berne trained as a psychoanalyst but was denied certification by the San Francisco Psychoanalytic Institute in 1956. Viewing this as rejection, he distanced himself from psychoanalysis. His approach had shifted from traditional psychoanalytic models, influenced by his trainer Erik Erikson's research and psychodynamic object-relations theory.

Formulated highly simplified, the classical Freudian model comprises the id, ego and superego readers (Mitchell & Black, 2016). The id represents primal instincts and desires, operating on the pleasure principle. The ego mediates between the id's impulsive demands and the superego's moral and societal constraints. The superego embodies internalised societal and parental values, serving as the moral compass of the psyche. Defence mechanisms serve as crucial psychological strategies employed by the ego to manage conflicts between the id's primal impulses and the superego's moral and societal constraints, to protect the individual from anxiety and distress arising from internal conflicts, such as repressing unacceptable thoughts or emotions out of awareness, shielding the individual from discomfort, or projecting involves attributing one's undesirable thoughts or feelings to others, thus alleviating personal anxiety.

Berne's structural ego-state model echoed these concepts, such as recognising internal and external influences on human behaviour and an interplay between individual impulses and external factors, whether societal norms or past experiences. However, Berne was uneasy with the model's focus on intrapsychic drives and the ego as their mediator. In TA, the focus shifts from Freud's id-ego-superego to the ego-states of Parent-Adult-Child. Ego-states involve different patterns of thinking, feeling and behaving that individuals adopt in various situations, influenced by their past conditioning and internalised experiences. The Parent ego-state reflects learnt behaviours and attitudes from parental figures or authority figures. The Adult ego-state represents the rational and adaptive aspect of the self, processing information objectively. The Child's ego-state embodies emotional and instinctual responses influenced by past experiences and emotions. TA suggests emotional states stem from inner dialogues between ego-states rather than imagery. For example, depression might result from critical messages from the inner Parent to the Child. Eric Berne used the TA framework to move beyond understanding to transforming client interactions, aiming to provide cures through contractual agreements akin to short-term psychodynamic psychotherapy.

Box 4.1

Evidence for the Classical Freudian Model

Research evidence for the classical psychoanalytic model is often indirect due to the complexity of its concepts (Luyten et al., 2017; Schore, 2001). However, psychodynamic therapies generally show positive effects (Leichsenring & Rabung, 2011, 2004; Steinert et al., 2017). Freud's idea that most processes are unconscious makes direct measurement challenging, though neurocognitive research supports the existence of unconscious processes like implicit memory and subliminal priming (Kahneman, 2011; Strick et al., 2011; Vandenbussche et al., 2009). Neuroscientific studies link the ego to the prefrontal cortex and the id to limbic structures (Schore, 2001; Shimamura, 2000; Waldhauser, 2023). Developmental psychology supports the id's early presence and the interplay of superego, ego and id in personality development, particularly developed in human interaction (Fonagy, 2003; Guntrip, 2018; Sroufe, 2005). The superego impacts moral reasoning (Harding, 2018; Langford, 2018), and the ego's use of defence mechanisms affects well-being and psychopathology (Bokanowski & Lewkowicz, 2018; Calati et al., 2010; Carvalho et al., 2019; Fiorentino et al., 2024; Vaillant, 1992).

Object-Relations Theory Model

Like other psychoanalysts in his era, Berne seemed uneasy with the traditional Freudian model. Object-Relations Theory (ORT), developed by Klein, Winnicott, Kohut and Kernberg focuses on the role of early relationships and the internalisation of these relationships as objects within the psyche (Mitchell & Black, 2016; Scharff, 2005; Summers, 2024). The concept of objects refers to the internal representations of significant others, which influence an individual's perceptions and interactions.

Key ORT concepts include splitting (dividing objects into all-good or all-bad), projection (attributing undesirable traits to others) and projective identification (inducing others to experience one's intolerable feelings) (Bokanowski & Lewkowicz, 2018). The paranoid-schizoid position involves primitive defence mechanisms and fragmented self-perception. In contrast, the depressive position integrates conflicting feelings and fosters empathy and guilt (ibidem). These ideas help understand early psychological development.

Berne didn't identify as an ORT therapist, but his structural model integrates some ORT concepts (Manor, 1992). For example, he describes the early-life development of our inner Parent as an internalisation of interactions with our actual caregivers and authority figures (compare ORT's concept of Object), which may include positive and negative sides in a Nurturing Parent and Critical Parent (ORT says that individuals may develop an integrated Other-Object or may split between a Good-Other and Bad-Other). He also describes the early-life development of our inner Child as an internalisation of how caregivers and authority figures interacted with us as a child, which may include positive and negative sides in an Adapted Child and Free Child (ORT says that individuals may develop an integrated Self-Object or may split between a Good-Self and Bad-Self). The TA model of the life positions of 'I'm OK/not-OK' and 'You're OK/not-OK' also seem inspired by the ORT splitting of Self-Objects and Other-Objects. Both ORT and TA shift from intrapsychic processes to relationships. For example, ORT describes how parents and authority figures influence a child to develop inner representations, Objects, of themselves and others, which the child subsequently uses to interact with others. Consequently, ORT and TA use therapeutic relationship interactions to derive the client's underlying mental representations of themselves and others. This includes working with transference, where the client's feelings and attitudes from past relationships are transferred onto the therapist, and countertransference, where the therapist's emotional reactions are influenced by their past experiences. However, Berne emphasises transactional patterns and the states of being, offering a practical framework for understanding and improving interpersonal dynamics. Unlike the neutral stance of some ORT therapists (Symington & Symington, 2002), Berne's approach involves active engagement to enhance real-life transactions.

Box 4.2

Research on Object-Relations Theory

Research evidence for Object-Relations Theory (ORT) comes primarily from case studies and qualitative research, with some quantitative studies (Felici et al., 2023; Kernberg, 1993; Summers, 2024). Empirical studies on attachment styles support the impact of early caregiving on internalised object representations and relational schemas (Bowlby, 1998; Fraley, 2002; Pallini, 2018; Schore, 2002). Neuroscience confirms biological correlates of object relations and interpersonal processes, impacting affect regulation in early-life (Schore, 2003, 2015) and informing therapeutic practices (Schore, 2012; Siegel et al., 2021).

Overview of TA-models

Many authors differentiate TA-models into first, second and third-order structural models, like Russian dolls are nested inside each other (see next Figures). The inner Child, Adult and Parent are written in capitals, whereas child/adult/parent denote the actual individuals.

> In technical language, an ego-state may be described phenomenologically as a coherent system of feelings and operationally as a set of coherent behaviour patterns. In practical terms, it is a system of feelings accompanied by a related set of behaviour patterns. Each individual seems to have a limited repertoire of such ego-states, which are not roles but psychological realities. The position is, then, that at any given moment, each individual in a social aggregation will exhibit a Parental, Adult or Child ego-state, and that individuals can shift with varying degrees of readiness from one ego-state to another. (Berne, 1964, p. 52)

First-Order Structural Model

The Basic Ego-state Model or PAC-model consists of three primary ego-states: Parent, Adult and Child (Berne, 1972). All TA therapists (Figure 4.1) use this model (Vos & van Rijn, 2021c), that is supported by robust research evidence (Vos & van Rijn, 2021a, 2021b, 2021c).

Parent: Berne suggests that as we transition into adulthood, we internalise our parents' ways of thinking, feeling and behaving. This process helps us perceive and respond to the world like our parents did, incorporating their beliefs, values and principles. This internalised knowledge forms our Parent ego-state. The Parent ego-state can actively respond to external stimuli or influence our internal Child ego-state. It comprises the knowledge, beliefs and patterns learnt during childhood from significant figures. This state includes our cognitive processes, emotional experiences, evaluative abilities, perceptual judgements and moral standards, some of which become integrated into our identity. When operating from the Parent state, a person responds to the world similarly to a parental figure.

Adult: The Adult ego-state is crucial for realistic assessments of our surroundings. It gathers, filters, evaluates and stores information for future use. It facilitates reality testing, which is essential for mature problem-solving and decision-making. The Adult ego-state aids in self-preservation and social control, operating autonomously like the Child ego-state. It is supported by a compliant Child who agrees without protest and a permissive Parent, allowing it to delay responses to urges. This state helps deal with reality rationally and safely, fostering logical thinking, open-mindedness and results-oriented approaches. It also manages limitations by enabling forecasting and probability assessment.

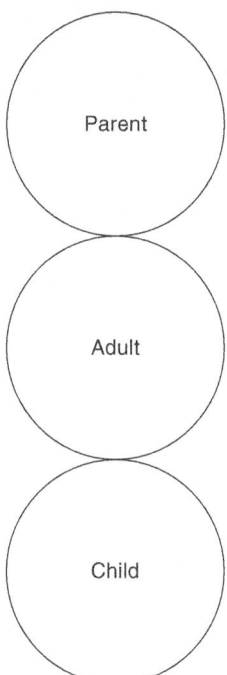

Figure 4.1 First-Order Model, P2, A2 and C2

Child: The Child ego-state in adults responds to reality with a childlike perspective, serving as a reservoir of psychic energy within the PAC system. It focuses on maximising gratification and comfort, often beyond rationality. The Child exhibits playfulness, creativity and intuition when active, fostering intimacy and unconventional thinking. A healthy Child promotes joy, happiness and enjoyment in life, supporting the Adult in mature decision-making. It endows individuals with charm, triggers emotional memories, and is crucial in transitioning one's Life Script.

When the first order structure is represented simply, the ego states could be listed as P, A, C. However, as we progress through more in depth structural analysis, these ego states are marked as P2, A2 and C2.

Second-Order Structural Model

The Second-Order model extends the basic ego-state model by integrating transactions and script-analysis, focusing on communication patterns and ego-state manifestations in relationships. On the one hand, it reflects the origin of the internal material, on the other it analyzes life scripts and unconscious plans from childhood affecting decisions and behaviours (Vos & van Rijn, 2021c) (Figure 4.4). The PAC within the Parent is termed P3, A3 and C3, while the Child's PAC is P1, A1 and C1, reflecting their developmental roles and origins. Only the Child ego-state is active in childhood, relying on the Parent and Adult of caregivers to understand and respond to reality, forming a healthy symbiotic dependence. Full development of the Parent and Adult ego-states occurs later. Several components of this model seem indirectly supported by research (Vos & van Rijn, 2021b). Research also shows children undergo a separation-individuation process influenced by family dynamics and stressful events (Kins et al., 2013; Lopez & Gover, 1993; Rice et al., 1995; Koopmans, 2001), though classical concepts such as symbiosis and double-bind lack clear evidence (Morley & Moran, 2011; Koopmans, 2001).

Parent in the Child (P1): This early Parent-like structure is internalised by the child while adapting to and making sense of their experience and reality. Relational TA-theorists (Hargaden & Sills, 2002) call this an internal object representation, explaining how extreme internal dialogs have often been shaped by childhood adaptation (Fowlie, 2005). For example, an older child may develop strategies like using a harsh internal voice (P1-'Don't exist') to suppress their needs after the birth of a sibling, forming beliefs to gain parental attention. These early, emotionally intense beliefs, such as 'I am good/no good', 'I am treated fairly/unfairly' or 'Lovable/unloved', may be unconscious responses/decisions. Understanding the Parent in the Child helps us explore how childhood beliefs shape adult experiences and challenge limiting beliefs. Although not systematically researched, some authors suggest that P1 forms from birth to around five years old, while the complete Parent ego-state (P2) develops between five and twenty years, influenced by authority figures. When P2 is triggered in adulthood, Parent-like individuals often act like the authority figures, they internalised Parent-like. This introspection reveals how early experiences shape our adult selves (Vos & van Rijn, 2021c).

Adult in the Child (A1): The Adult in the Child is sometimes referred to as 'Little Professor' in TA to highlight the innate creativity, originality, and intuition, that help the child find the balance between their innate needs and feeling (C1), and restrictions they encounter and intuit (P1). For example, faced with a belief that they were not important that might have been triggered by the birth of a younger sibling, A1 may intuit that the best way to be important is to be nice to the new baby, and supress their anger and jealousy. If this is reinforced by either previous, or later experiences, it might become embedded as a script belief that the only way to matter to others is by not showing one's own feelings and needs.

Child within the Child (C1): The 'Somatic Child' encompasses the PAC of infancy, storing early developmental needs for contact, closeness, and agency. This ego-state ensures survival within familial and cultural contexts, fostering development into adulthood but sometimes creating limiting life scripts. Relational theorists (Hargaden & Sills, 2002) call C1 the 'core self'. Third-order structural analysis (P0, A0 and C0) addresses early, somatic, and unconscious material, noting that A0 is an intersection between P0 and C at this stage. The second order structure in relation to Child Ego-State is the most used clinically, as it enables therapists to understand and address the early developmental material their clients bring. Second-order structural analysis can also be applied to the Parent ego-state (P2), although it used less frequently.

Parent in the Parent (P3): P3 represents the internalised version of the Parent and the ancestral/cultural context, such as values, rules, regulations, beliefs and moral frameworks.

Adult in the Parent (A3): Children naturally try to understand their parents/caregivers/authority figures. Parents may rationally explain their values, rules, regulations, beliefs and moral frameworks. However, a child may accept these justifications without scrutiny or updates, which become ingrained in their mind as their inner voice. This is A3, the adult aspect of the internalised parental figure.

Child in the Parent (C3): This is a channel for passing down cultural norms and values. It encompasses the positive aspects of the family, our typical characteristics, methods of adaptation and strengths and vulnerabilities. C3 represents the internalisation of the Parent carrying the script multi-generational material (Figure 4.2).

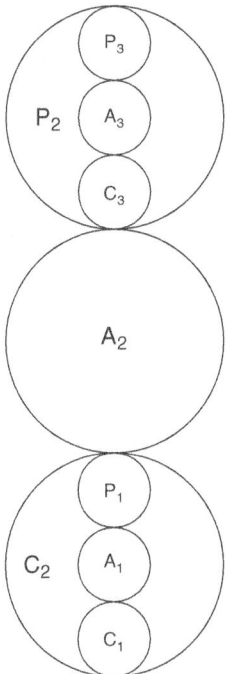

Figure 4.2   Second-Order Model

Third-Order Model

The third-order structural analysis represents the PAC of early stages, encompassing automatic responses to stimuli (Figure 4.3). Experiences are shaped by physical interactions, with babies being socially responsive and reliant on caregivers. It is presented differently by different authors, and the model we present was developed by Hargaden and Sills (2002). Though rarely used by TA therapists (Vos & van Rijn, 2021c), substantial research supports this model. These PAC components in the Somatic Child relate to neuroscientific findings on early affect regulation, forming a psychological structure that influences later skill and ego-state development (Bradley, 2003; Hill, 2015; Schore, 2015, 2003; Vohs & Baumeister, 2016).

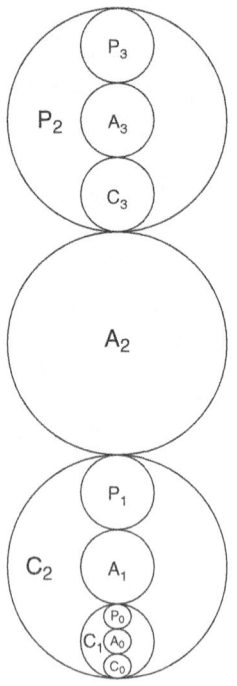

Figure 4.3 Third-Order Model

4.1 REFLECTIVE QUESTIONS

- Think of a client/person you know well. Try to apply each model based on your knowledge to see which model fits best. Is there one best model, or do multiple models fit, or do you need to create a new model?
- Which model appeals intuitively the most to you? What attracts you to this model?

THE EVIDENCE-BASED STRUCTURAL MODEL

Don't feel overwhelmed by the different models in the previous section. TA is a rich and evolving theory, and TA therapists use various models in practice. Our survey indicates:

- 47% of TA therapists see ego-states as distinct psychological phenomena.
- 34% view ego-states as multiple phenomena or experiences.
- 32% believe ego-states are not a tangible concept.
- 27% see ego-states as co-constructed between therapist and client.

The basic PAC-model is the most agreed upon (65%), frequently used (56%) and easiest to explain (52%) (Vos & van Rijn, 2021b, p. 321). Less than half frequently use other models.

Therefore, in this book and previous publications, we recommend using an evidence-based ego-stated model that does not only include the Parent-Adult-Child structure but also the functions of Nurturing/Critical Child and Adapted/Free Child. This model enjoys extensive support from numerous studies and fulfils the need for a user-friendly approach (Vos & van Rijn, 2021a, 2021b, 2021c). The differentiation between the two sides in the Parent (Critical/Nurturing) and in the Child (Adapted/Free) may be regarded as a transactional translation of ORT's evidence-based concept of Good/Bad Child Other-Object and Good/Bad Child Self-Object, particularly as these ego-states seem to strongly correlate with the negative/positive life positions towards self/others, thus reflecting a generic good/bad differentiation towards self and others (Vos & van Rijn, 2024b, 2024c).

Research indicates that individuals report better mental health if they are often in a strong Adult, Nurturing Parent or Free Child ego-state. In contrast, they report worse mental health if they are often in a strong Adapted Child, or Critical Parent state combined with a weak Adult, Nurturing Parent or Free Child (Vos & van Rijn, 2024b, 2024c). This book's Part IV will show that specific psychological disorders are associated with specific dominant ego-states (see for example for evidence: Arntz & Van Genderen, 2020; Bar et al., 2023; Lobbestael et al., 2008; Vos & van Rijn, 2021a). As expected, clinical trials on TA significantly help clients move towards more beneficial ego-states, such as more Adult, Nurturing Parent and Free Child, and less Critical Parent an Adapted Child (Vos & van Rijn, 2024a, 2024c, 2022).

However, some researchers have shown that we should look not merely at the presence of ego-states but an individual's ability to flexibly shift between ego-states, called 'functional fluency' (Temple, 2002). Thus, what matters may be the extent to which an individual is 'stuck' in an ego-state and struggles to shift to another state; research confirms that flexibility is significantly impaired in individuals with mental health problems, and helping clients to become more flexible often improves their symptoms (Kato, 2015). Although related to these findings, there have not been enough studies to confirm the TA-concept of contamination; means that it is difficult to distinguish two ego-states in a person because the ego-states overlap or distort each other, such as a distortion of the Adult reality from the Child's perspective. Given the lack of evidence, we recommend not to conduct separate analyses of the structure and functioning of a client's ego-states but assess them simultaneously, like in earlier versions of TA.

As some studies indicate that therapists may not be accurate in assessing clients' ego-states (cf., L Lobbestael, 2007), TA therapists should familiarise themselves well with this model and validate their assessment and case formulation in conversation with clients and possibly with the help of questionnaires (Figure 4.4).

Critical Parent: The Critical Parent ego-state represents internalised voices of caregivers, authority figures and societal norms. It manifests as critical, judgemental and controlling attitudes, often mirroring punitive childhood experiences. Examples include harsh criticism, rigid rule adherence and judgemental attitudes. This ego-state can negatively impact mental health, self-image and relationships. Note that this concept integrates aspects of the previously formulated Parent in the Parent (P3).

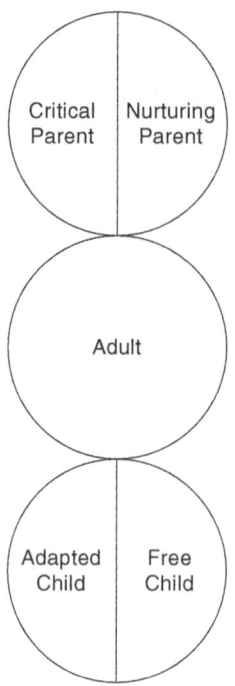

Figure 4.4   Evidence-Based Ego-State Model Integrating Structural and Functional Components

Case Study 4.2

Bob and Mary

Bob, the informal leader of his group of friends, assumes a controlling and authoritative role. He dictates meeting times, locations and activities, often reproving his friends for deviating from his directives. His authoritarian behaviour leads to dissatisfaction within the group, causing many to leave.

Mary plays a nurturing role in her friendship with Joan. When Joan's mother passes away, Mary provides emotional support and assistance. She expresses love, care and reassurance, offering to help with Joan's tasks and consistently showing empathy and support during a difficult time. Both case studies include a parent ego-state, with Bob exemplifying the Critical Parent while Mary embodies the Nurturing Parent.

Nurturing Parent: The Nurturing Parent ego-state embodies internalised compassion, empathy and support from early caregivers and authority figures. It is characterised by kindness, encouragement and care for self/others. Examples include comforting friends, self-encouragement and expressing empathy. This concept integrates aspects of the Adult in the Parent (A3) and Child in the Parent (C3). The Nurturing Parent ego-state promotes emotional resilience, positive self-image and healthy relationships based on genuine care and empathy.

Case Study 4.3

Amelia

Amelia, a 43-year-old architect, demonstrates the influence of the Nurturing Parent ego-state in her daily life. When faced with challenging project deadlines, she approaches herself with self-compassion, acknowledging her efforts and providing herself with words of encouragement. Amelia's interactions with colleagues demonstrate a nurturing attitude, offering support and understanding during stressful periods. The dominant presence of the Nurturing Parent ego-state enables Amelia to foster a positive work environment, build authentic connections and maintain a healthy balance between professional responsibilities and self-care, contributing to her overall well-being and resilience.

Adult: The Adult ego-state embodies objective analysis, critical thinking and autonomous decision-making – the 'reality principle'. It is characterised by rationality, logical reasoning and present-focused information processing without undue emotional bias. Behaviours include thoughtful problem-solving, balanced perspectives, evidence-based decisions, impulse control and nuanced ethical understanding. This concept incorporates aspects of the Adult in the Parent (A3) and Adult in the Child (A1). The Adult ego-state promotes adaptability, effective coping, personal agency and self-assurance.

Case Study 4.4

Muhammed

Muhammed, 67, a retired investment banker, demonstrates the Adult ego-state's influence. He approaches financial decisions logically, assesses health needs objectively and engages in open-minded social interactions. This dominant Adult ego-state enables Muhammed to navigate retirement purposefully and adaptably, enhancing his mental and emotional well-being.

Adapted Child: The Adapted Child ego-state represents internalised behaviours and attitudes adopted in response to childhood authority figures. It is characterised by compliance, obedience and rigid conformity to perceived external demands. Behaviours include seeking approval and accommodating others' needs. The Adapted Child may continue to follow what was believed to be true in early childhood even though these may have been false, such as a belief that one must be perfect or have high academic achievements to receive love from others and be worthy of self-love. Adapted Child behaviour includes seeking approval and validation from others, accommodating the needs of authority figures and displaying patterns of behaviour learned from childhood experiences, such as being overly compliant. Another example of the Adapted Child role is the flipside of the compliant child, pseudo-rebellion. This concept integrates aspects of Parent in the Parent (P1). The Adapted Child ego-state can lead to internal conflict, diminished autonomy and difficulties in authentic self-expression and forming genuine connections, often prioritising others' expectations over personal well-being.

Case Study 4.5

Isla

Isla, 36, a mother-of-two and marketing specialist, exemplifies the Adapted Child ego-state's impact. She seeks approval at work, suppresses her need to conform and prioritises others' needs, especially her children's. This dominant Adapted Child ego-state leads to self-doubt, unfulfilment and challenges in asserting boundaries and expressing her authentic self, affecting her mental well-being and sense of fulfilment in both her professional and personal life.

Free Child: The Free Child ego-state embodies spontaneous, uninhibited and authentic aspects of personality. It is characterised by creativity, humour, playfulness, curiosity and wonder. Behaviours include imaginative play, uninhibited emotional expression and a carefree spirit. This concept integrates aspects of the Adult in the Child (A1) and Child in the Child (C1). The Free Child ego-state promotes creativity, emotional authenticity, joy and spontaneity, contributing to a balanced emotional life, deeper self-connection and overall well-being.

Case Study 4.6

Joel

Joel, the first author of this book, exemplifies the influence of the Free Child ego-state throughout the creation of this chapter. While deeply engrossed in writing, he experiences a profound state of flow at this moment, igniting his passion and joy reminiscent of a child fully immersed in play. Storytelling and crafting narratives feel like a wellspring of unrestricted creativity and authenticity, evoking the same sense of playfulness, wonder and enthusiasm he felt during childhood. Joel's earliest memories vividly reflect his deep-seated love for writing. One particular memory dates back to when he was just three years old, observing adults penning texts yet not knowing how to form letters himself (Vos, 2017). He took it upon himself to invent his letters, filling a notebook with these scribbles. With this book complete of self-invented letters in hand, he enthusiastically performed a book reading for his delighted and applauding family, spontaneously weaving a story as his nonsensical letters adorned the pages. Writing this chapter is a poignant reminder to Joel of his inner Free Child rooted in these warm memories. The drawback of his dominant state of the Free Child is that he has been neglecting the concept of time, writing late into the night, well past a reasonable bedtime. Consequently, his inner Parent now comes in to start a dialogue with his Free Child by imploring him to conclude this text for the time being and resume tomorrow, all while ensuring he remembers to prioritise his bedtime in the upcoming days of writing this book so that he does not overexert himself again. His Free Child tries to rebel as he wants to continue writing this chapter. However, Joel's Adult now comes in by recognising his wish to write – which he promises to continue tomorrow – while looking after his physical needs.

4.2 REFLECTIVE QUESTIONS

- Identify at least one example for each ego-state from the evidence-based ego-states model in your personal life. For each ego-state, close your eyes for a moment and try to imagine you are in an example situation when this ego-state feels dominant; how does this ego-state make you feel, think, observe, behave, respond and shift to another? Do you have any dominant ego-states, and if so, how did this develop, when did this start, how did others contribute to this, and how did you contribute to this development? Would you like to change anything regarding your ego-states? If so, what practical steps can you take to achieve this?
- Think of a client/person you know well. Try to identify at least one example for each ego-state. Do they have any dominant ego-states, and if so, how does this impact their social functioning, self-efficacy, mental health and well-being? What would you recommend they improve, if anything?
- Keep an Ego-State Diary, ideally for one or two weeks, so that you have enough examples to identify a trend in your life. At the end of each day, identify the three most emotionally difficult moments. For each moment, identify the situation (including any potential triggers), identify how strong each of the ego-states Nurturing Parent, Critical Parent, Adult, Adapted Child, Free Child, felt in that moment (e.g. 1, ego-state felt absent, to 7, ego-state was dominating) (note that you will most likely experience some of all ego-states simultaneously), describe how this ego-state made you feel (e.g. happiness, anxiety, anger, sadness, shame), how you responded automatically or what you decided to do consciously; for each state, how did you shift to a different ego-state, was there anything that triggered this shift or anything you did? After a week, identify any trends. For example, which ego-states were the easiest to identify and which were the most difficult? Which ego-states were the strongest, and which were the weakest? Which ego-states were the least relevant, realistic and helpful, and which were the most? Do any specific situations trigger specific ego-states? How do specific ego-states make you feel? How do you respond to a particular ego-state? When did your trend of a specific dominant ego-state, feelings or responses start in life; to what extent was that ego-state relevant, realistic, helpful and authentic in that situation? How relevant, realistic, helpful and authentic was each ego-state in your situation now? What would be more relevant, realistic, helpful and authentic ego-states? What could you do to change your ego-states? How could you shift ego-states? For example, how could you decide to respond in the future when you experience an irrelevant, unrealistic, unhelpful or inauthentic ego-state? For example, could you tell yourself, 'This ego-state tells something about my past, not about the present'. 'This is my response to the situation; this is not necessarily the truth'. 'What evidence is there for the relevance and realism in the present?'. 'How helpful is this ego-state

to me?' Write down your decision about what you would like to change and the specific steps to do this, for example, 'I know that if I come in this particular situation, this often triggers an unhelpful/unrealistic ego-state; therefore, in future, I will prepare myself when I go into such a situation by doing [X]'. 'Whenever I feel that my Adapted Child becomes dominant, I will ask my Adult to check how relevant, realistic and helpful this response this, and I will invite my Nurturing Parent to look after my needs'. Keep a diary to reflect on how these experiments went, how they made you feel, and what you could do better next time. Be kind towards yourself because change may not happen quickly; as your old ego-states/responses have possibly been there for a long time, they may take time and perseverance to change.

LIFE POSITIONS

TA therapists identify life positions as one of the biggest strengths of TA, find these easy to share with and understand by clients (Vos & van Rijn, 2021c). This ORT-inspired concept was popularised by Thomas Harris's widely acclaimed book from the late 1960s, 'I'm OK, You're OK' (Harris, 2012). However, whereas Berne suggested everyone begins life in the 'I'm OK' state, Harris argued that life commences with a sense of 'I'm not-OK, you're OK'. This ideological difference may not impact the practice of TA therapy, as therapists will always examine the client's experiences and position in different life periods. Research validates this conceptualisation of four life positions (Vos & van Rijn, 2021a). It shows that TA therapy can significantly help clients move towards a life position of 'I'm OK, You're OK' (Vos & van Rijn, 2022, 2024a, 2024c). Life positions refer to the fundamental attitudes individuals develop towards themselves and others based on their experiences. There are four primary life positions.

I'm OK, You're OK

This position reflects a healthy and constructive attitude. This primary position leads to a positive outlook on life and relationships, fostering a sense of mutual respect and acceptance.

Case Study 4.7

Grace

Grace, 40, an HR Manager, seeks therapy for relationship challenges. Despite adversity, she maintains a balanced perspective and empathy. She values open communication and mutual understanding. Through therapy, Grace explores how her positive life position influences conflict management and boundary-setting abilities. This self-awareness enhances her interpersonal skills and emotional well-being.

I'm OK, You're Not-OK

In this position, individuals view themselves positively but negatively perceive others. This can lead to feelings of superiority, judgement or alienation towards others.

Case Study 4.8

Alex

Alex, a 30-year-old Cyber Security Specialist, has a strong sense of self-confidence and achievement. However, he often demonstrates a critical and judgemental attitude towards others, perceiving them as inferior or inadequate. This life positions challenges his personal and professional relationships, as he struggles to form genuine connections and tends to dominate interactions with a sense of superiority. Through therapy, Alex explores the origins of his belief system and its impact on his interactions, aiming to develop a more empathetic and balanced approach to his relationships.

I'm Not-OK, You're OK

This position involves individuals feeling inadequate or flawed while perceiving others as competent and worthy. It may lead to feelings of inferiority, dependence or seeking validation from others.

Case Study 4.9

Ava

Ava, 45, a residential healthcare provider, struggles with inadequacy and self-doubt. She idealises others while minimising her worth, seeking external validation. In therapy, Ava explores the origins of her self-perception, aiming to develop a balanced view of herself/others. She aims to enhance self-esteem and build authentic relationships based on mutual respect.

I'm Not-OK, You're Not-OK

This position reflects pervasive negativity towards oneself/others, leading to hopelessness, mistrust and a belief that life is inherently unfair or unjust.

Case Study 4.10

Oscar

Oscar, 56, a primary school teacher on long-term sick leave, struggles with inadequacy and hopelessness. He views others negatively, leading to isolation. In therapy, he explores the origins of these beliefs, aiming to develop a more positive self-view and outlook on others. He aims to improve self-worth and form healthier relationships by addressing ingrained negative thought patterns.

TA psychotherapy aims to help individuals recognise and understand their primary life position, leading to greater self-awareness and the potential for positive change in their attitudes and relationships. Chapter 6 will show how the life position of 'I'm OK' is associated with self-efficacy, self-preservation, self-compassion, self-esteem, internal locus of control, emotional self-regulation and responsibility for oneself. The life positions of 'You're OK' is associated with positive transactions and relationships, trust, the capability to have intimate and partner relationships, no social isolation, authenticity and congruence. Chapter 6 will also show how seeing oneself/others as OK leads to better outcomes, such as improved psychopathology, psychological distress, self-realisation, behaviour, general well-being and quality of life.

4.3 REFLECTIVE QUESTIONS

- Identify at least one example for each of the four life positions in your personal life. For each life position, close your eyes and imagine you are in an example situation when this life position feels dominant; how does this life position make you feel, think, observe, behave and respond? Do you have any dominant life position, and if so, how did this develop, when did this start, how did others contribute and how did you contribute to this development? Would you like to change anything in this dominant life position? If so, what practical steps must you take to achieve this?
- Think of a client/person you know well. Do they seem to have any dominant life position, and how does this impact their social functioning, self-efficacy, mental health and well-being? What would you recommend they improve, if anything?
- Keep a Life Position Diary, ideally for one or two weeks, so that you have enough examples to identify a trend in your life. At the end of each day, identify the three most emotionally difficult moments. For each moment, identify the situation (including any potential triggers), identify how strong each of the four life positions felt in that moment (e.g. 1, life position felt absent, -7, life position was dominating), and describe how this life position made you feel (e.g. happiness, anxiety, anger, sadness, shame), and how you responded automatically or what you decided to do consciously. After a week, identify any trends. For example, was there any dominant life position? Do any specific situations trigger specific life positions? How do specific life positions make you feel? How do you respond to particular life positions? When did your trend of a dominant life position, feelings or responses start in life; to what extent was that life position relevant, realistic, helpful and authentic in that situation? How relevant, realistic, helpful and authentic were each life position in your current situation? What would be more relevant, realistic, helpful and authentic life positions? What could you do to change your life position? For example, how could you decide to respond in future when you experience an irrelevant, unrealistic, unhelpful or inauthentic life position? For example, could you tell yourself, 'This life position tells something about my past, not about the present'. 'This is my response to the situation; this is not necessary the truth'. 'What evidence is there for the relevance and realism in the present?'. 'How helpful is this life position to me?' Write down your decision about what you would like to change and the specific steps to do this, for example, 'I know that if I come in this particular situation, this often triggers an

unhelpful/unrealistic life position; therefore, in future, I will prepare myself when I go into such a situation by doing [X]'. 'Whenever I start to feel "I and others are not-OK" becomes dominant, I will check how relevant, realistic and helpful this response this, and I will deliberately focus on aspects of myself/others that are OK'. Keep a diary to reflect on how these experiments went, how they made you feel and what you could do better next time. Be kind towards yourself because change may not happen quickly; as your old life position/responses have possibly been there for a long time, they may take time and perseverance to change.

SUMMARY

- Over time, TA therapists have developed several iterations of models of ego-states. Ego-states refer to the distinct patterns of thinking, feeling and behaviour, encompassing an individual's personality, shaped by past transactions and life messages, and influencing their interactions and responses in the present.
- The current research indicates that one ego-state model has the most evidence, integrating structural and functional components: Critical Parent, Nurturing Parent, Adult, Adapted Child and Free Child.
- Research suggests that individuals benefit from being able to move between ego-states flexibly and not be stuck or dominantly focused on one ego-state. Dominant Adult, Nurturing Parent and Free Child ego-states are often associated with positive feelings and mental well-being. In contrast, dominant Critical Parent and Adapted Child ego-states are often associated with negative emotions and mental health problems.
- Life positions include positions on the spectrums of I'm OK/not-OK (associated with self-efficacy), and You're OK/not-OK (related to social functioning). The OK-positions are associated with better mental health and well-being, reflecting acceptance and respect for self/others.
- As the ego-states and life positions directly impact the outcomes, TA therapists use their therapeutic competencies to help their clients improve. One therapeutic competency involves analysing the client's aetiology, which will be explained in the next chapter, and may show the possible origins of ego-states and life positions.

5

AETIOLOGICAL MODEL: HOW DO THE CLIENT'S PROBLEMS START?

Scripts are only possible because people do not know what they do to themselves and others. Knowing that one is doing it is the opposite of following a script. (...) Awareness means seeing a coffee-pot and hearing the birds sing in their own way, not how one was taught. (Berne, 1964, p. 47)

This chapter outlines the evidence-based aetiological model of TA. Following an illustrative case study and a general overview of how the past may influence the present, this chapter will explain how the client's issues and problems may have started. Each section will discuss how individuals gradually develop the script for their lives:

- Childhood context
  - Genetics and temperament
  - Life events and socioeconomic context
  - Sources of early-life messages
- Fundamental psychological structures
  - Ego-boundaries and separation/individuation
  - Splitting and integration
  - Mentalisation
  - Example: coping and affect regulation mechanisms
  - Example: discounting of existential givens
  - Example: attachment
- Transactional core messages
  - Injunctions
  - Drivers and counterinjunctions
  - Permissions
  - Allowances
  - Payoffs
  - Programmes
  - Other early-life messages

- Responses and decisions
  - In the past
  - In the present
- Self-perpetuating mechanisms and feedback loops

This chapter is a culmination of systematic research on the aetiological theories that TA schools commonly share. Our survey amongst TA therapists revealed a range of aetiological factors. Although this chapter contains the same evidence-based content (Vos & van Rijn, 2021a-c), we present this slightly differently for readability purposes, have added nuances, and integrated the latest research publications on child development (e.g. Bradley, 2003; Conkbayir, 2021; Eslinger et al., 2021; Goldstein & Brookes, 2023; Hill, 2015; Schore, 2015, 2012, 2001–2003; Smith & Hart, 2022; Vohs & Baumeister, 2016). Our studies confirm the generic findings in psychotherapy research that developing insight correlates significantly with positive treatment outcomes (Jennissen et al., 2018).

Case Study 5.1

John

John, a 35-year-old marketing executive, sought the help of a TA psychotherapist to address his long-standing struggle with low mood. He expressed his desire to break free from the constant negativity plaguing him. During their initial session, John spoke about his upbringing in a dysfunctional family environment. His parents were frequently critical and emotionally distant, leading to feelings of neglect. Witnessing frequent conflicts between his parents further added to his emotional turmoil. Academically and socially, John's parents had high expectations of him, often expressing disapproval and disappointment whenever he fell short of their standards.

John's Adult ego-state, responsible for logical thinking and problem-solving, was weakened by the emotional turmoil he endured in his youth. Particularly in challenging situations, he often found it difficult to maintain a balanced and rational perspective, as his childhood experiences have made him emotionally reactive and vulnerable. Furthermore, the lack of nurturing and emotional support during his formative years hindered the growth of John's Nurturing Parent ego-state. He struggled to show compassion and understanding towards others, a need left unfulfilled in his childhood.

In response to his hardships, John often seemed to be in an Adapted Child ego-state. He learnt to adapt to his parent's expectations and emotional demands. *As-if* by an unconscious decision (note the expression 'as-if' because this was an unconscious response when alternatives were impossible), he adopted a lifelong compliant and accommodating demeanour to avoid conflict. This adaptive behaviour became a coping mechanism that served him well in his childhood environment as a normal response to an abnormal situation. However, these survival mechanisms have lost their benefits in his current situation. Throughout his adult years, John remains deeply impacted by the memories and lessons of his childhood. The influence of his upbringing is evident as he constantly seeks validation and approval from those in positions of authority, reflecting the familiar dynamics he once experienced with his parents. This tendency stems from his dominant Adapted Child ego-state, which fuels self-criticism and judgement, ultimately affecting his self-esteem and interpersonal connections. Unfortunately, John faces significant challenges in openly and authentically expressing his needs and emotions. This struggle is rooted in his dominant Adapted Child ego-state, leading him to prioritise the expectations and desires of others over his well-being. As a result, he often needs to pay more attention to his own needs to meet the expectations set by external sources.

Growing up in a dysfunctional family setting marked by neglect, emotional detachment, and regular disapproval from his parents, John forged a pessimistic outlook on life rooted in suspicion, self-condemnation and feelings of inadequacy. These formative experiences shaped his core attitudes and beliefs about himself and those around him, resulting in a deep-seated mistrust of others, scepticism towards relationships and difficulty making decisions. His negative life stance continues to exert its influence on his adult life, impacting his self-worth, interpersonal connections and ability to assert his own needs. Consequently, his life position seems marked by the beliefs 'I am not-OK' and 'Others are not-OK'.

The therapist supported John in understanding how his childhood experiences impacted his ego-states and life position. Over time, he gradually became aware of the messages he internalised, both critical and nurturing. This newfound awareness allowed him to reframe his self-talk and develop a more supportive and nurturing internal dialogue. As a result, he experienced various emotions, and he received the necessary support to process these early-life traumas. John also learnt to listen to and accept his authentic experiences without immediately interpreting them through the lens of an Adapted Child or Critical Parent. By strengthening his healthy Adult ego-state, he acquired the ability to approach situations with more rationality and emotional balance, regularly checking in with how he authentically felt about a problem or social interaction.

Consequently, the influence of his childhood experiences on his present-day interactions and decision-making diminished. He successfully challenged and changed the negative beliefs ingrained in his childhood experiences, reframing his life position. This transformation enabled him to develop a more positive and self-affirming outlook on life, fostering trust in himself/others. Ultimately, John embraced a sense of worthiness and self-acceptance.

HOW THE PAST INFLUENCES THE PRESENT?

This case illustrates how childhood experiences can profoundly impact our present ego-states and life positions, which may have originated early in life and persist into the present, potentially causing psychological distress and interpersonal difficulties. Eric Berne (1972) coined the term 'life script' to describe a 'life plan based on a decision made in childhood, reinforced by parents, justified by subsequent events, and culminating in the chosen alternative' (p. 445).

> Each person decides in his early childhood how he will live and how he will die, and we call this plan, which he carries in his head wherever he goes, a script. (Berne, 1972, p. 54)

Berne later explained that the life script is a repetitive pattern of complex interactions. Essentially, it is an attempt to re-enact the past in a modified form in the present. This transferential drama arises from the child's interaction with their environment. The life script gradually develops over time, with the underlying dynamics and conflicts emerging often before a child can verbally communicate. Berne referred to the unconscious life script developed in early-life as the 'protocol' and the preconscious script in later life as a 'palimpsest'.

Let us zoom into the TA theory of how ego-states can be developed early in life. Childhood experiences play a crucial role in shaping the Parent ego-state. This ego-state is influenced by the messages and behaviours children receive from their caregivers and authority figures, as well as those that arise from their environment and the cultural context. Many of them are not given intentionally or consciously. For example, a child who grows up in an environment where they receive nurturing, supportive and positive parental messages is likely to develop a nurturing and supportive Parent ego-state. Conversely, a child who experiences criticism, neglect or overbearing control from their parents may create a critical or controlling Parent ego-state. However, even supportive and loving parents sometimes give critical messages and do not meet every child's needs. This is relevant to the child's socialisation and the limits of any parenting. Therefore, therapists must remember that a Parent ego-state is an internal representation, rather than a person's actual parent.

The Child ego-state is also significantly influenced by childhood experiences. This ego-state reflects the emotions, attitudes and behaviours that individuals experience as children. For instance, a child who grew up in an environment where they felt loved, secure and encouraged to express their feelings may develop a confident and emotionally secure Child ego-state. On the other hand, a child who experienced trauma, rejection or emotional suppression may develop a fearful or defensive Child ego-state. As in the example above, all children will also experience limitations and frustrations and develop ways to adapt to what they perceive are the requirements of their environment, whether those come from the parents, siblings or the world beyond the family.

Thus, children form their dominant ego-states based on the regular and significant interactions they have in life. The child's caregivers and authority figures may exhibit recurring patterns of interactions to which the child responds. The child may develop habitual patterns of responses that are most beneficial, rewarding or reinforced to cope with the input from their caregivers and authorities. This leads the child to believe that 'this is how life is and how people are, and this is how I should handle them'. It is important to note that caregivers and authority figures are not always perfect in their interactions, and a minor, unhelpful interaction is unlikely to create long-lasting habitual responses in a child. What matters is that, on average, they are 'good enough': they have sufficient insight, willingness and ability, meet day-to-day and complex needs, prioritise the child's needs before their own, foster attachment, offer consistency with some realistic amount of flexibility (Eve et al., 2014). The more frequently these relational patterns occur and the more the child's survival and fulfilment of basic needs rely on these early interactions, the greater the likelihood that these patterns will become long-term habits for the child.

Life positions are also shaped by childhood experiences. For example, a person growing up feeling loved and valued is more likely to adopt a positive life position, believing in their worth and the inherent goodness of others. Conversely, a person who experienced consistent rejection or emotional deprivation in childhood may adopt a negative life position, viewing themselves and others with mistrust and scepticism. One illustrative case study is the impact of childhood trauma on the development of ego-states and life positions. A child who experienced abuse or neglect may develop a Critical Parent ego-state, internalising the negative messages and behaviours they received. This can lead to a corresponding vulnerable or wounded Child ego-state, resulting in a negative life position characterised by feelings of unworthiness and distrust.

Clients often value learning how their problems and lifelong patterns have originated and evolved. In our clinical studies, clients have expressed that one of the most beneficial aspects of TA therapy is discovering how their past experiences shape their present challenges, even though it can initially feel overwhelming (Vos & van Rijn, 2024a-c). We have also observed that many clients experience a temporary increase in symptoms of anxiety and depression after the therapist shares their hypotheses about the aetiology and their case formulation with the client. However, this temporary negative peak is usually followed by a significant decrease in symptoms in the following weeks. These findings highlight the importance of exploring the client's past and sharing the therapist's hypotheses about the client's aetiology in a compassionate manner, taking care of pains and vulnerabilities, as well as acknowledging the need for anger towards the injustice done to them, and grief over missed opportunities in early-life. Each individual will have their interpretations and associations with their life story.

Hence, creating a tailored case formulation that accurately encompasses their subjective experiences is crucial. Valuing the formulation with the client and collaborating on its development is essential. A key motivation to explore a client's past is that clients may start to develop a sense of self-compassion and strengthen their Nurturing Parent role as they understand that they were not in control of the life circumstances that shaped their path in life. Naming the injustice and lack of power and giving space for feelings such as anger, shame and grief may help this development. By understanding the distinct influence of childhood experiences on the present, individuals like John can embark on a voyage of self-discovery and emotional restoration, loosening the elastic bands that had kept them tied to the past.

TA therapists often utilise the concept of a 'life script' to help clients understand how they may have formulated a script for their lives during their formative years. Their primary focus is on the client's potential to reframe and rewrite this script, thus enabling a more positive present and future (Vos & van Rijn, 2021c). The notion that individuals could develop a life script at an early stage, encompassing programmes and episcripts, has also been explored and studied beyond the realm of TA. This includes concepts such as schema in schema therapy (Arntz & Van Genderen, 2020; Lobbestael et al., 2007; Young et al., 2006), representations of generalised interactions (RIGs) (Stern, 1985), and Tomkin's script (1978). In general, research has indicated that mental health issues later in life can trace their roots back to the early establishment of an insecure attachment (Morley & Moran, 2011). Several studies have confirmed that there are strong correlations between childhood traumas and ego-states and life positions (Anne & Boholst, 2021; Blizard, 2001; Boholst et al., 2005; Novak, 2008; Van der Kolk, 1994).

However, therapists acknowledge that the idea of a 'life script' may not provide enough specificity when examining the specific factors in a client's early life that have shaped their later experiences. Additionally, while TA-questionnaires for analysing causes can be helpful, they lack sufficient psychometric quality (Vos & van Rijn, 2021a). To explore the specifics of the life script, our survey of TA therapists has identified several aetiological factors, which we will give more details about in this chapter than in our previous publications (Vos & van Rijn, 2021c). Figure 5.1 shows possible relationships between these factors. We use the term life script loosely in this book to refer to the complex, dynamic totality of a client's life-story that may influence or cause (aetiologically) their current ego-states, life positions and outcomes.

To sketch a comprehensive life history of clients, we need to start at the beginning. A child is born with a unique genetic makeup and temperament in a specific socioeconomic and cultural context. Although TA therapists recognise these aetiological factors, they focus more on early-life messages and their sources in early-life, such as caregivers and authority figures, intergenerational messages and stroking patterns. Some TA therapists identify how children develop fundamental psychological structures in their very early-life that determine how they perceive, respond to and make decisions in response to the messages they receive. These fundamental functions include ego-boundaries, separation-individuation, splitting/integration and mentalisation. Examples of these functions can be found in the coping and affect regulation skills, attachment style and discounting of existential givens that may continue into adulthood. However, these fundamental structures should not be regarded as separate entities from the transactional core messages but as their foundations.

TA therapists have identified several components in the transactional core messages, such as injunctions, drivers, counterinjunctions, permissions, allowances, payoffs, programmes and other early-life messages; these seem to function like core beliefs in CBT, and therefore we will call these 'transactional core messages'. The term 'message' is a metaphor in this context, as that is how a child may experience them. They would be more accurately described as influences, experiences and perceptions used by individuals to make sense and create narratives containing beliefs about themselves, life and others. We can think of them as script beliefs, responses and decisions. These responses or decisions are often unconscious and automatic, strongly influenced by the fundamental psychological structures. They can

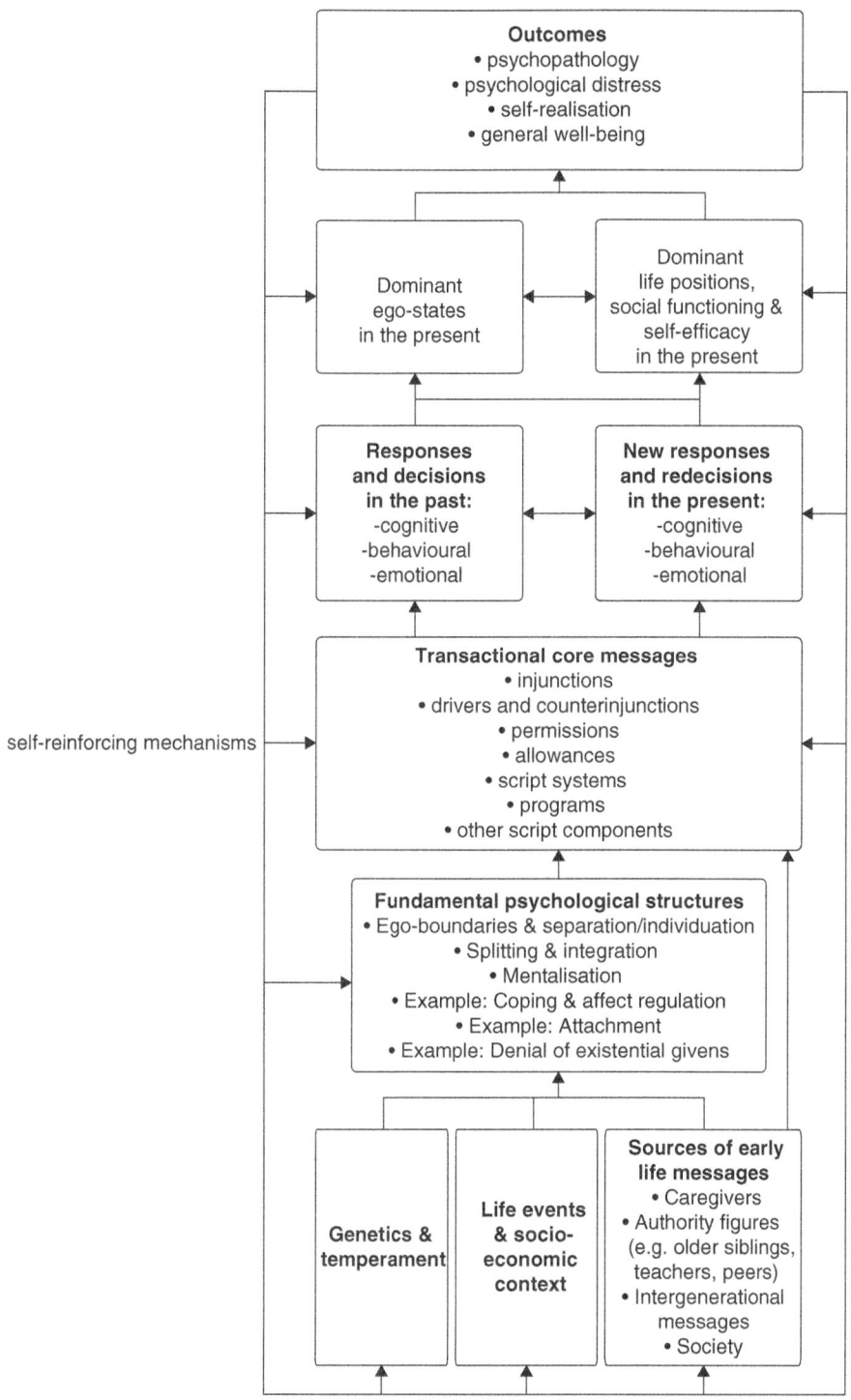

Figure 5.1 Overview of the Aetiological Model in Evidence-Based TA psychotherapy

be cognitive, behavioural or emotional. Whereas individuals may not have much freedom and many opportunities in the past to make a conscious decision about their response to the transactional core messages they had received, they have some freedom to respond in a new way and make a different choice in the present. The habitual responses and decisions towards the transactional core messages influence the ego-states, life positions, social functioning and self-efficacy in the present day, which may subsequently impact a range of outcomes, such as psychopathology, psychological distress, self-realisation, living a meaningful and satisfying life, general well-being and quality-of-life.

Berne highlighted how there can be feedback loops, for example, how a child's response to their parents may subsequently influence the subsequent reaction from their parents, which may, for example, reinforce the underlying transactional core messages that the child receives; thus, transactional core messages and responses/decisions often seem self-perpetuating.

The following sections will explain each of these aetiological components.

GENETICS AND TEMPERAMENT

TA recognises genetics and temperament as influential factors in mental health, and biology may be a frequently overlooked component in TA (Allen, 1999, 2000). For example, research indicates that parents respond and relate differently to children with different psychological traits, mental health challenges, neurodiversity or physical disabilities; these characteristics may also influence how children respond to their parents (Raya et al., 2013). However, TA does not explicitly focus on genetics and temperament in the development of mental health problems, as it emphasises the impact of early-life experiences and interactions with caregivers and significant others. These experiences can often be translated into script beliefs about being different or not belonging.

LIFE EVENTS

Stressful and traumatic life events can severely impact one's fundamental assumptions about life, the world and the self, such as the benevolence, understandability and explainability of such events (Janoff-Bulman, 2010; see also Vos, 2023a, 2022, 2018, 2016a/b). For example, losing a parent at an early age may give the implicit message to a child that loved ones can unexpectedly die and their death can feel very painful; therefore, a child may respond to the loss by avoiding close and intimate relationships and instead live a more socially withdrawn life, pull out when a relationship becomes more intense, or focus much on work or hedonistic enjoyment.

Numerous studies demonstrate the impact of adverse experiences during early childhood on depression. These experiences encompass various factors such as physical abuse, emotional abuse, emotional neglect, inadequate care, rejection, excessive control and dysfunctional parenting styles (Lim & Barlas, 2019). Many studies confirmed the influence of early-life attachment style on psychopathology over the lifespan (Chauhan et al., 2014; Gorrese & Ruggieri, 2012; Jalali et al., 2011; Köruk, 2016; Mallinckrodt & Wei, 2005; Ranson & Urichuk, 2008). Insecure attachment has been linked to poor social functioning and a diminished sense of self-efficacy (Caldwell et al., 2011; Wei, 2005; Wolfe & Betz, 2004). Research suggests that the transmission of parental burdens to children and the direct impact of a parent's mental health play a particularly significant role, as children may implicitly or explicitly be expected to take on parental responsibilities, also known as parentification (Boszormenyi-Nagy, 2013).

Many studies have revealed that various segments of society face significantly more situations of oppression, discrimination and traumatic experiences. These groups include, amongst others, women, individuals with lower socioeconomic status, Black, Asian, and other people with different ethnic backgrounds, LGBTQI+ individuals and those with chronic physical and mental health conditions (Vos et al., 2019). The repercussions of these factors manifest in feelings of stigma, fear, distrust, humiliation, shame, instability and insecurity. Moreover, social inequalities and discrimination may worsen the adverse effects experienced by these individuals (Vos, 2019, 2024a). Socioeconomic contexts, such as being raised in a single-parent household or belonging to a minoritised ethnic group, and the subsequent experiences of potential prejudice and socio-economic hardship can have a profound impact on a child's mental health and overall well-being as they transition into adulthood (Ryan et al., 2015). The influences of the adverse life events and the socioeconomic context can also be a source of the script 'messages'. For example, an experience of sexual abuse or trauma is usually experienced as a 'don't exist' injunction, transmitted through the traumatic experience and pain.

SOCIOECONOMIC CONTEXT

We are born princes, and the civilizing process makes us frogs. It is our responsibility
to take off that toad skin and remain princes and princesses. (Berne, 1964, p. 62)

TA acknowledges the influence of the socioeconomic context, politics, power and privilege on the development of mental health problems. It recognises that societal structures, economic disparities and political systems can shape individuals' early experiences and contribute to the formation of their life scripts and interpersonal dynamics. Socioeconomic status, income, education and occupation significantly impact parenting styles and the interactions and messages children receive (Hoff & Laursen, 2019). Large bodies of research from the last decade have revealed the impact of cultural differences, socioeconomic situations and social injustice on mental health (Mazzetti, 2018; Vos, 2019).

TA therapists should try to understand the client's experiences, narratives, identities and meanings within their broader social context, including potential structural injustices, marginalisation, alienation, power dynamics and oppression (Rowland & Cornell, 2021; Tudor, 2020; Minikin, 2023). Remember that social-justice may not only be revealed in big traumatic events but also in everyday transactions (Cross, 2012) and micro-aggressions (Sue & Spanierman, 2020). Therapists should avoid assuming that the client's issues are individual or chosen (Car, 2013; English, 2006) and that different cultures may have other definitions and connotations with concepts such as 'personal autonomy' (Massey, 2007; Minikin, 2023).

As with the other 'messages' received from the environment, our socio-economic background can also result in a lifescript narrative and impact our life position. Experiences of privilege and entitlement can lead to an 'I'm OK/You're not-OK position'. On the other hand, experiences of lack-of-privilege, discrimination and racism may lead to internalised messages about not belonging: 'I am not-OK and You're not-OK'. Therefore, it is vital to explore the clients' experiences and perceptions of power and privilege throughout their lives, and how this shaped their sense of self, others, transactions, mental and physical well-being.

Several authors have also argued that socioeconomic and political power imbalances may also be re-enacted in the therapy room, as the therapist may symbolise an authority figure with their therapeutic expertise; this imbalance may, for example, lead to clients expecting their therapist to give answers and shape their perceptions and behaviours in therapy, which may lead to a lack of progress, ruptures in the therapeutic relationship and dropout from treatment. Due to the power imbalance, therapists may mislabel their client's aetiological and clinical phenomena, which may lead to misinterpretations and frustrations in clients (Chapter 9 explains how to pay attention to diversity and social injustice in the therapeutic relationship).

5.1 REFLECTIVE QUESTIONS

- What were the most difficult moments in your childhood? What were unique social, economic or physical struggles in your family, such as illness, loss, divorce, discrimination, stigma, coming out as gay, neurodiversity, etc.? If these moments and struggles could speak and give you a core message about life, what would this be? How did you respond to this message as a child? How does this message still impact your life? Do you want this message to still influence your life, and would you like to formulate a more helpful alternative; if so, what would an alternative message be?
- Think of a client/person you know well and answer the same questions.
- Identify examples of how differences in power and privilege may have impacted your work with clients. Consider differences in working with clients with equal, more, and less power/privilege.

SOURCES OF MESSAGES

All your decisions are made by four or five people inside your head, and although you may ignore them if you're too proud to hear them, they will be there next time if you bother to listen. Script analysts learn to amplify and identify these voices. (Berne, 1952, p. 53)

TA therapists focus on the messages that individuals learn in early-life. As we have seen, some sources may involve genetics and temperament, life events and socioeconomic context.

TA therapists are particularly interested in the messages given by caregivers and authority figures, messages carried over generations, and stroking patterns, contextual and cultural messages have received less attention and need further development. The idea that early relational experiences – particularly trauma – influence the development of our ego, its components/working models and how it consequently relates to others is based on work from psychodynamic authors, such as Kohut (2009), Stern (1985) and Stolorow et al. (1987).

Three-hundred-eighty-six studies have investigated the connection between parenting style, ego-states and psychopathology (Vos & van Rijn, 2021b). The Young Parenting Inventory was utilised as a measurement tool in many of these studies (e.g. Sheffield et al., 2005). Comprehensive literature reviews have revealed that parental messages play a significant role in shaping a child's ego-states/schemas and can also contribute to the occurrence of psychopathology later in life. Research has consistently shown that individuals with psychopathology are more likely to have experienced caregivers who were unpredictable, invalidating and critical. These individuals grew up in an environment lacking warmth, safety and nurturing, which may have included conflicts, childhood trauma and abuse (Harold & Sellers, 2018; Toth et al., 1992).

Several studies also indicate that the childhood environment can shape a child's self-image, internal dialogue and emotional state, resulting in negative feelings such as guilt and shame (Hammen, 1992; Sachs-Ericsson et al., 2006). Unfavourable child-rearing styles contribute to developing maladaptive ego-states or schemas in early-life. These maladaptive thinking patterns can then influence the emergence of psychopathology later in adulthood (Fischer et al., 2016). Various investigations have confirmed that the association between early-life experiences and later psychopathology is mediated by the development of negative ego-states or schemas in conditions like depression and anxiety (Delorme et al., 2013; Haugh et al., 2017; Nia et al., 2014), eating disorders (Sheffield et al., 2009), gender identity issues (Hinrichsen et al., 2007; Simon, 2009), obsessive-compulsive disorder (Goli et al., 2019), antisocial behaviour (Van Vlierberghe et al., 2007), partner problems (Besharat et al., 2014; Monajem, 2013; Taşkale & Soygüt, 2017), sleep problems (Rodrigues et al., 2019) and Attention-Deficit Hyperactivity Disorder (ADHD) (Evinç et al., 2014). Furthermore, some studies indicate how negative parental messages can influence children's neurodevelopment (Allen, 2000). These findings emphasise the crucial importance of the quality of caregiving and its profound influence on a child's psychological well-being and long-term mental health outcomes.

Not only do our parents have the ability to shape our life script, but their ancestors can also play a role, as Eric Berne writes:

> The parental programming is not the 'fault' of the parents since they only pass on to their children the programming received from their parents, just as it is not their 'fault' the physical appearance of their children since they only pass on to them the genes they received from their ancestors. But brain chemicals are easier to change than those that determine physical appearance. (Berne, 1964, p. 103)

Recent research has identified the transgenerational transmission of psychological messages in the offspring of traumatised parents, such as those who endured hardships during the Holocaust. This research has shown that these traumas can impact future generations (Baranowsky, 1998; Goodman & West-Olatunji, 2008; Pearrow & Cosgrove, 2009; Roth et al., 2014). While more empirical evidence is still needed, it has been suggested that several generations later, the descendants of slaves may experience poorer health due to post-traumatic slave syndrome – possibly influenced by epigenetics (Degruy-Leary, 1994; Sullivan, 1953/2013). As explored in these studies, the proposed mechanisms behind this transmission involve parenting styles and attachment issues. Additionally, some smaller studies have indicated that family secrets can have a long-term impact on the well-being of both children and grandchildren (Dalzell, 2000; Vangelisti, 1994), with a particular focus on the emotional consequences of revealing these secrets within the family (Pennebaker et al., 1988; Vangelisti et al., 2001). As family system therapists frequently state: instead of envisioning a single client in the therapy room, consider all their family members, including those from previous generations, those who have passed away and those who have yet to be born (yes, your therapy room will be pretty crowded); what are the messages that all these individuals are silently or loudly giving to your client? Furthermore, how can you, as a therapist, assist clients in comprehending and expressing these unspoken words, enabling them to decide how to respond consciously?

> "Raising" children is primarily a matter of teaching them what games to play. Different cultures and different social classes favour different types of games, and various tribes and families favour different variations of these. That is the cultural significance of games. Parents, deliberately or unaware, teach their children how to behave, drink, feel and perceive from birth. Everyone carries his parents around inside of him. Liberation from these influences is no easy matter. (Berne, 1964, p. 132)

5.2 REFLECTIVE QUESTIONS

- What explicit/implicit messages have your caregivers conveyed? What messages have been passed down from your ancestors through multiple generations? What are hidden family secrets and taboo topics nobody dares to discuss? What would happen if someone were to open up this conversation or challenge their expectations? What is the worst-case scenario, and how likely is it to occur? What is the personal cost of keeping these secrets hidden and sacrificing one's authenticity? How do these family stories shape your ego-states, life positions, values and overall sense of meaning in life?
- How did your separation and individuation process happen in your life? Were there any significant moments? Are there any specific struggles? Are there any life areas where the separation-individuation may not have been fully completed yet; consider internalised messages that are unrealistic or unhelpful in your current life as an independent adult. What practical steps would you need to do to change these?

- How can you uncover the messages of parents and authority figures on your clients? How can you identify intergenerational messages and family secrets underlying your clients' stories? Consider your most challenging clients; what messages from caregivers, authority figures, intergenerational messages or family secrets might influence their challenges? What are the potential challenges and risks involved in exploring these topics, and how could you cope with these?

FUNDAMENTAL PSYCHOLOGICAL STRUCTURES

Neurocognitive studies exploring the psychodynamic development of individuals, mainly focusing on object-relations, have revealed how children establish fundamental psychological structures in their early years (e.g. Bradley, 2003; Conkbayir, 2021; Eslinger et al., 2021; Goldstein & Brooks, 2023; Hill, 2015; Schore, 2015, 2012, 2001–2003; Smith & Hart, 2022; Vohs & Baumeister, 2016). During this formative period, we acquire essential abilities to navigate various situations and regulate our emotions. For instance, Berne briefly touches upon these structures in his early writings, such as the PAC in the Somatic Child in the Second-Order Structural analysis. In our survey, TA therapists also highlight the significance of assessing unmet primal needs, the absence of psychological support, separation-individuation, psychological integration and holding.

In a previous publication (Vos & van Rijn, 2021c), we categorised these fundamental psychological skills as components of other aetiological elements. However, we have decided to dedicate a separate section to these fundamental psychological structures. It is worth noting that they are not entirely separate entities but rather interconnected with other contributing factors. This is because research indicates that these fundamental skills are like the hardware that enables us to navigate and select different software programmes. They determine the degree of freedom we possess in our decision-making and emotional regulation processes, acting as a bandwidth for our responses and choices. These core coping and emotion regulation mechanisms are not solely a product of our responses or decisions about early-life messages but rather an inherent aspect of our neurocognitive and nervous system functioning. They become deeply ingrained in our development, often operating at a preverbal and unconscious level.

The underlying framework of the Nurturing/Critical Parent, Adult, and Adapted/Free Child model seems to assume that an individual has established several fundamental psychological structures. Aligned with psychodynamic research, we might anticipate these structures to have developed by the culmination of the oedipal phase – consequently, Berne's ego-state model and his initial assessment of life scripts predominantly focused on post-oedipal advancements. Before individuals can differentiate between the Parent, Adult and Child ego-states, they must have encountered boundaries between themselves as a child, their caregivers and authorities. Additionally, children must integrate various aspects of themselves and others rather than dichotomising the world into good versus evil as a defence mechanism against the anxieties and uncertainties of life. This division could result in a rigid separation between the Critical Parent and the Nurturing Parent, as well as between the Adapted Child and the Free Child.

Conversely, a child with a sense of psychological integration can more fluidly transition between these ego-states. Moreover, TA presupposes that an individual engages in transactions involving their various ego-states and those of another person. This suggests that, at least to a certain degree, the individual can recognise and understand the ego-states of the other person. This means that the individual is capable of mentalising, which entails acknowledging that the other person possesses their own unique emotions, thoughts and behaviours.

Thus, individuals establish ego-boundaries and separation-individuation, integration and splitting, and mentalisation during their early years. These processes serve as the foundations for their ego-states. Any complications in these fundamental psychological structures can subsequently influence their ego-states. Hence, this section delves into each of these fundamental psychological structures. Subsequently, illustrations demonstrate how individuals experience these fundamental structures as coping and affect regulation mechanisms, attachment styles and stroke profiles. These examples highlight the interconnectedness of the three fundamental structures and their impact on an individual's self-efficacy, social functioning, mental well-being and happiness.

Ego-Boundaries and Separation/Individuation

Ego-boundaries refer to an individual's psychological distinction between themselves and the external world and between themselves and others. Healthy ego-boundaries allow individuals to recognise their thoughts, feelings and experiences separate from those around them. These boundaries shape an individual's sense of identity, autonomy and interpersonal interactions. Although Freud did not explicitly use the term 'ego-boundaries', his work contributed to understanding the ego-functions as a mediator between the id, superego and external reality. The Object-Relations theorist Heinz Kohut (2009) examined the role of healthy narcissism and its importance in developing a cohesive self. He explored the concept of the 'nuclear self' and the importance of maintaining boundaries between the self/others for psychological well-being.

Subsequently, Margaret Mahler (2018), known for her research on child development and object relations, examined the separation-individuation process in early childhood and its impact on the formation of ego-boundaries. Separation-Individuation is the process through which a person becomes an individual, developing a distinct identity apart from their primary caregivers. This process is characterised by phases of differentiation, practising, rapprochement and consolidation of individuality. The relationship between ego-boundaries and the process of individuation-separation is complex. Individuation-separation represents the psychological journey towards developing a distinct and autonomous identity separate from one's caregivers and significant others. It involves the formation of a cohesive self-concept and the ability to assert one's individuality while maintaining healthy connections with others. Ego-boundaries play a crucial role in this process by delineating the borders between the self/others, facilitating the establishment of a coherent sense of self while engaging in meaningful relationships.

Individuation-separation seems to be a continuing process, with significant steps in the early years. For example, between one and three years, a child starts to slowly leave the safety of their caregivers to interact and experiment with the world around them; if this interaction is not allowed, overwhelming or without sufficient holding and adequately sensitive responses from the caregivers, the child may not develop healthy boundaries (Bradley, 2003; Hill, 2015; Mikulincer et al., 2003; Schore, 2003, 2015). Children start more explicit differentiation from their parents between three and six years, trying out their individuality; if caregivers do not allow, or even punish this individuality, a child may initially try to exert their individuality at all costs, like tantrums. Ultimately, this may lead to a sense of helplessness, leading them to fall back to merging with their caregiver. This drama is repeated with even larger strength during adolescence, which may be felt as the ultimate moment, 'now or never', that an individual may separate and develop their individuality.

Healthy ego-boundaries enable individuals to recognise their thoughts, feelings and needs as distinct from those of others, allowing for authentic self-expression and the ability to form intimate connections without feeling engulfed or losing their identity in the relationship. Conversely, insufficiently developed ego-boundaries can result in difficulties asserting one's autonomy, setting healthy boundaries and experiencing a cohesive sense of self, hindering the process of individuation-separation. Research shows that ego-boundaries are essential for maintaining a coherent sense of self and navigating interpersonal relationships and environmental stimuli (Grolnick & Ryan, 1989; Johnson & Whiffen, 1999). The impact of ego-boundaries and individuation-separation on mental health is profound. Well-defined ego-boundaries and successful individuation separation are associated with increased psychological resilience, self-esteem and adaptive coping mechanisms. Conversely, challenges in these areas can contribute to issues such as identity confusion, relationship difficulties and susceptibility to psychological distress.

Berne referred to ego-boundaries in his early work; his ideas were further refined by several TA researchers/therapists who highlighted the individual's intrapsychic conflict derived from internalisations of object relationships, particularly between ego-states within the archeopsyche (C2). Goulding and Goulding (1976) suggested a model of complex contaminations (between Parent P2, Adult A2 and Child A2), Hine (1997) systems of ego/self-activation, Allen (2000) states of mind and Hargaden and Sills (2002) ego/self-states, 'with the subconscious, unconscious, presymbolic, and therefore protomental nature of experiences attributed to the never-ending structural organization of the developing Child ego-state' (Mellacqua, 2014, p. 11).

Ego-boundaries primarily regard the relationship between an individual and real others, but this seems to translate into inner Parent, Adult and Child relationships. Healthy ego-boundaries are reflected in a clear differentiation between the ego-states, allowing individuals to access and integrate these states appropriately without confusion. For instance, an individual with solid ego-boundaries can engage from an Adult ego-state without inappropriate intrusion from the Child or Parent ego-states, enabling balanced and appropriate responses to the world. Healthy transactions (e.g. Adult-Adult) indicate clear ego-boundaries, where individuals can interact without losing their sense of self or merging their identity with others; disturbed transactions might suggest blurred ego-boundaries, leading to enmeshment or isolation. A script that involves seeking approval from others at the expense of one's own needs may reflect difficulties in the rapprochement phase of separation-individuation, where the individual did not fully consolidate their sense of identity separate from their caregivers.

For example, suppose a real parent has blurred boundaries with the client as a child, like relational merger or symbiosis. In that case, the client may be unable to develop healthy boundaries between their inner Parent and inner Child, and their inner Adult may get contaminated by both Parent and Child. This means, for example, that the individual may find it difficult to see the difference between ego-states, and struggle to have a healthy inner dialogue between different ego-states. Consequently, they may experience frequent sudden transitions between ego-states, whereby a person may, for example, seem in an Adult ego-state in one second and the next second Child, and then Parent. If a therapist were to strengthen one ego-state, this might initially blur into different ego-states; for example, strengthening the Adult – for example, supporting the client to be realistic and rational – may be challenging for this individual as they will struggle to differentiate this from their Child – for example, child-like or mythical understanding of reality – and from their Parent – for example, when looking at reality this feels like a Critical Parent oppressing them. Working with an individual with insufficient individuation-separation requires sensitive and slow steps, focusing the primary work in the therapeutic relationship to help the individual develop a healthy sense of boundaries between therapist and client by giving much attention to transactions and games in the therapy room. This may slowly give the client insight into the difference between themselves and others and make them aware of their ego-states. Only after this process will they be able to start work with ego-states, and may the therapist, for example, strengthen the Adult without this being conflated with Child and Parent ego-states. These processes seem particularly relevant for clients with personality disorders, such as borderline or schizotypal.

The other extreme alternative is that an individual has too hard boundaries between themselves and others, which may subsequently be reflected in disconnected Parent, Adult and Child ego-states; consequently, they may experience sudden radical shifts between ego-states, from one into another state without a gradual transition. They may find it challenging to move to another state when stuck in one ego-state. Consequently, these individuals may be at risk of harming themselves or others, mainly if showing impulsive behaviour; these individuals may require a stronger safety net involving their direct social network, as it may not be sufficient to make a plan with these clients what they may do if they feel suicidal, as not-acting on such a plan requires the ability to shift to an Adult ego-state. Strengthening or weakening any ego-state does not seem to impact the other ego-states; for example, a therapist may help them build their Adult function, but this may not affect their Child or Parent. Working with these clients requires much attention to the therapeutic relationship, fostering a sense of unconditional positive regard, and following the client's tempo; otherwise, they may risk dropping out of therapy. Over time, the client may feel safe enough for the therapist to analyse their transactions and help them identify and name their ego-state. Only if there seems enough safety and holding, and the client has developed some insight into their ego-states, could the therapist examine their life script. As their life story reveals unmet relational needs and severe trauma, this could trigger strong emotions and regression to rigidly separated ego-states, such as getting stuck into a Child ego-state. In such cases, it be may be helpful if the therapists uses a bull's eye transaction to address each ego-state simultaneously (see Chapter 8).

In sum, by analysing, identifying and addressing the ego-boundaries, TA therapists can help clients develop a more transparent and integrated sense of self. Script-analysis may recognise the impact of early experiences and familial dynamics on forming their ego-boundaries and individuation process. Through script-analysis, TA therapy can address unresolved issues in the separation-individuation process. By exploring early responses/ decisions and the script beliefs that guide current behaviour, therapy can support individuals in rewriting their life scripts to honour their individuated self. TA therapists can collaborate with clients to establish explicit contracts focusing on boundary-setting, autonomy and developing a distinct sense of self. By outlining specific behavioural and relational goals, clients can work towards strengthening their ego-boundaries and individuation process. TA therapy may strengthen ego-boundaries by clarifying and reinforcing the distinctions between ego-states. Techniques such as ego-state mapping and TA proper can help individuals recognise and respect their boundaries and those of others. The TA therapist stimulates clients to develop autonomy within and outside therapy, for example, via explicit exercises/homework and goals. Both ego-boundaries and a successful separation-individuation process are fundamental to autonomy, a key goal of TA. Therapy aims to foster independence by supporting the development of a coherent sense of self, capable of making new decisions not confined by past scripts or confused ego-boundaries.

Case Study 5.2

Arthur

Arthur, a 23-year-old student, presented with challenges related to boundaries and individuation-separation. He struggled to assert his needs and opinions in relationships, often feeling overwhelmed and unable to maintain a distinct sense of self. He experienced anxiety and low self-worth, frequently prioritising others' needs over his own. His TA therapist helped him by using techniques such as boundary-setting exercises and cognitive-behavioural interventions to enhance self-esteem, as well as TA and working with the therapeutic relationship to explore and address underlying attachment patterns. Arthur developed healthier ego-boundaries through therapeutic exploration and support, asserted his individuality and cultivated more fulfilling and balanced relationships. This holistic approach facilitated Arthur's journey towards robust ego-boundaries, successful individuation-separation and an authentic self, ultimately promoting his mental well-being and personal growth.

■■■■■■■■■■ **5.3 REFLECTIVE QUESTIONS** ■■■■■■■■■■

- How did your separation and individuation process happen in your life? Were there any significant moments? Are there any specific struggles? Are there any life areas where the separation-individuation has not been fully completed yet; think about any internalised messages that are unrealistic or unhelpful in your current life as an independent adult. What practical steps would you need to do to change this?
- Consider a client/person you know well. How did the separation-individuation happen in them, in which areas could they benefit from further separation and individuation, and how could they achieve this? What are potential challenges and risks involved in exploring these topics, and how could you cope with these?

Splitting versus Integration

A healthy person goes 'Yes', 'No', and 'Whoopee!' An unhealthy person goes 'Yes, but', 'No, but', and 'No whoopee'. (Citation attributed to Berne)

Splitting is a defence mechanism identified in psychodynamic theory, particularly within Object Relations Theory, supported by research (Bokanowski & Lewkowicz, 2018; Calati et al. 2010; Carvalho et al., 2019; Woods & Wood, 1981). It involves dividing external objects (people, situations) and internal representations (thoughts, feelings) into 'all good' or 'all bad' without the ability to integrate these opposing aspects. This mechanism often emerges as a way to manage complex and conflicting emotions, aiding in reducing anxiety in the face of ambiguity but at the cost of oversimplification and distortion of reality.

Examples of splitting can manifest in various ways, such as an individual alternating between idealising and devaluing others, perceiving situations as either all good or all bad or experiencing intense shifts in mood and perception without recognising the middle ground. The impact of splitting on mental health can be significant, leading to interpersonal difficulties, emotional instability and challenges in maintaining stable relationships. It can contribute to mood disorders, identity disturbances and problems in managing intense emotions and impulses.

A related concept is psychological integration, which refers to how individuals fully embrace and acknowledge all aspects of themselves and others without suppressing or avoiding any important parts (Sollarova & Sollar, 2010). Research suggests that a lack of congruence and coherence in one's life can negatively impact their mental health (Sheldon & Kasser, 1995). Additionally, feelings of inauthenticity (Goldman & Kernis, 2002; Schlegel et al., 2009, 2013) and the repression and dissociation of emotions and bodily experiences, particularly in cases of trauma (Bremner & Marmar, 2002; Singer et al., 1995), can also contribute to mental health issues.

In his early work, Berne (1957/1969) used the concept of splitting, mainly to understand severe psychopathology. Several TA researchers elaborated on this. For example, Mellacqua (2014) proposed a structure of schizophrenia that includes a Differentially Excluded Parent

P2, an Unintegrated Adult A2 and Fragmented Child C2 consisting of an Adult A1 that Child C1 contaminates, and a split positive Parent P1+ and a negative Parent P1-. Mellacqua focused on schizophrenic individuals, in whom splitting seems combined with problematic ego-boundaries. However, her example shows how an individual may split between a positive Parent and a hostile Parent at different ego levels. The process of splitting can also be seen within the healthy development of the Child Ego-state (Hargaden & Sills, 2003). An early Child develops a sense of cohesion in relationship to the parent/caregiver, who plays a role in developing self-regulation (Olson & Lunkenheimer, 2009). The integration is not a verbal process and develops gradually through the experience of being able to regulate the primitive and distressing feelings (like shame) and repeated process where both the child (C1+ and C1−) and parent (P1+ and P1−) are integrated (A1+ and A1−). When this developmental process is successfully negotiated, the person develops a sense of self that is good-enough and can accept positive and negative aspects of themselves and others. When an individual does not develop this integration, they may be splitting.

For example, depending on the situation, an individual might oscillate between viewing someone from a Critical Parent perspective (all bad) and a Nurturing Parent perspective (all good). This expresses the Child's early developmental needs and fears: seeing someone as entirely nurturing (good) when needs are met or completely neglectful (bad) when they are not. Strengthening the Adult ego-state and the in-depth therapeutic work of 'deconfusion' in therapy can help an individual move beyond splitting by assessing people and situations more nuanced and realistic, integrating good and evil. When splitting occurs, transactions might frequently shift from complementary to crossed (e.g. a nurturing response from one person met with an unexpected critical reaction from another), reflecting the rapid reassessment of the other person as all bad or all good. Consequently, individuals might only accept or give positive strokes or only negative strokes that align with their underlying black-or-white life positions. An individual prone to splitting might have a script that includes expectations of abandonment or betrayal, leading to viewing others through a lens oscillating between idealisation and devaluation.

A TA therapist may help clients become aware of their tendency to split and identify specific instances where this defence is at play (Hargaden & Sills, 2003; Manor, 1992). This involves examining patterns in relationships, reactions to stress and the binary way in which people and situations are categorised. TA therapists may strengthen their Adult functioning by identifying triggers and responses associated with splitting, interrupting dichotomous reactions and developing more adaptive ways of relating to themselves and others. This can help the client see beyond the 'all good' or 'all bad' dichotomy, appreciating human behaviour and relationships' complexity and multifaceted nature. This may involve using experiential therapeutic competencies, such as helping clients to tolerate inner tensions created by paradoxes, uncertainties and ambiguities, instead of responding with splitting to these (Chapter 11). TA therapists can help clients explore their life scripts and the underlying drivers of splitting tendencies. TA therapists may help identify and challenge the life script that reinforces splitting, working towards a script that allows for complexity and ambivalence in relationships. By exploring and questioning the origins and validity of these scripts, the client can begin to adopt a more balanced Adult ego-state perspective, recognising the grey areas and embracing the complexity of life. For example, therapists may promote inner dialogue, understanding and integration of different ego-states, via Empty-chair Exercises (Chapter 12). Thus, TA therapists can encourage the integration of different ego-states to foster a more nuanced and flexible approach to self/others.

Exponents of psychodynamic TA (Novellino, 2018, 1998, 2004; Moiso & Novellino, 2000) and relational TA (Hargaden & Sills, 2001, 2003) have described this development of a cohesive sense of self within their detailed structural-analysis models.

Case Study 5.3

Florence

Florence, a 40-year-old actuary, struggled with splitting, mood swings, unstable relationships and fear of abandonment. She categorised people as good or bad, causing chaotic interpersonal dynamics. Her TA therapist explored and challenged her dichotomous thinking, focusing on their interactions and transference. The therapist remained self-aware, used supervision and applied insights sensitively. This transference-based approach enabled cognitive interventions like restructuring, emotion regulation and insight-oriented techniques. Florence learnt to recognise nuances in her perceptions.

5.4 REFLECTIVE QUESTIONS

- Think of a client or a person you know well who struggles with severe mental health problems. What small/larger examples of splitting do they demonstrate? What do you know about their life history: have they always tended to split in everyday life or particularly in stressful situations? How did they benefit from splitting, for example, by releasing tension as a child? How do they benefit from splitting in the present? How would they respond if they would not be splitting; what alternative coping responses do they have? How could you help them overcome splitting without risking a more significant emotional collapse due to a lack of alternative skills?

Mentalisation

Developed within the field of psychoanalysis, mentalisation refers to the capacity to understand and interpret one own's and others' behaviour in terms of underlying mental states, such as thoughts, feelings, beliefs and desires (Bateman & Fonagy, 2019; Crisanti, 2023; Fonagy et al., 2007; Hawkes, 2011). It involves the ability to recognise and empathise with the internal experiences of oneself/others, leading to more accurate and empathetic interpretations of behaviour and improved interpersonal relationships. Enhanced mentalisation skills enable individuals to engage in more compassionate and attuned transactions, fostering healthier, deeper and more fulfilling relationships.

Examples of mentalisation include recognising that a friend's irritability may stem from underlying stress or anxiety rather than assuming it is a personal attack. People may understand their emotions and thoughts in response to a challenging situation and articulate and communicate them effectively. A person empathises with a colleague's perspective and understands the motivations behind their actions, even if they differ in opinion. A lack of mentalisation may manifest as misinterpreting others' behaviours as intentional or malicious without considering their underlying emotional experiences. This could also involve being unable to articulate or understand one's emotional responses and thoughts in complex or distressing situations. Individuals may struggle to empathise with others' perspectives and recognise their experiences as valid or important.

The impact of mentalisation, and a lack thereof, on mental health is profound (ibid.). Strong mentalisation skills are associated with improved emotional regulation, more satisfying relationships and enhanced psychological well-being. Conversely, deficits in mentalisation can contribute to difficulties in understanding and managing emotions, impaired social functioning and vulnerability to mental health conditions such as borderline personality disorder.

The TA concept of ego-states requires understanding how different states influence one's thoughts, feelings and behaviours. Developing mentalisation involves recognising which ego-state one operates from and understanding the mental states driving the behaviours associated with each state. Effective mentalisation enhances understanding of transactions by allowing individuals to perceive better and interpret the underlying mental states that drive these communications. Mentalisation can help individuals recognise and understand the mental states that perpetuate games and scripted behaviours, providing insight into how to change them.

Individuals can learn to mentalise through therapeutic interventions that aim at helping clients recognise and articulate their own and others' mental states, fostering more adaptive and empathetic interpersonal interactions. TA therapists may encourage clients to reflect on their own and others' mental states. This involves exploring feelings, thoughts and motives behind actions, which can help understand complex emotional and social dynamics. By identifying and understanding the different ego-states and their associated thoughts and feelings within themselves, clients may better understand their mental processes and those of others. Through analysing transactions and games in the first place within the therapy room, therapists may help clients see beyond the surface level of communication to the underlying emotions and intentions, fostering a deeper understanding of social interactions and relationships. Via script-analysis, therapists may identify underlying beliefs and patterns that influence their interpretations of themselves and others to develop a more empathetic and reflective approach to their interactions. Cognitive techniques may help clients to improve their cognitive biases and to create a more accurate understanding of themselves and others. Thus, by integrating mentalisation into TA therapy, therapists can provide clients with tools to enhance self-awareness, understand the mental states behind behaviours and improve emotional regulation and relationships.

Case Study 5.4

Lily

Lily seeks TA therapy due to frequent misunderstandings and conflicts. She often struggles to empathise with others' perspectives and experiences, leading to strained interactions with family, friends and colleagues. During the initial sessions, the therapist conducts a comprehensive assessment of Lily's ego-states, life scripts and patterns of interaction. It becomes evident that Lily has difficulty recognising and articulating her own and others' mental states, contributing to a lack of empathetic understanding in her relationships. The therapist collaborates with Lily to establish explicit goals for enhancing her mentalisation skills. Together, they identify specific cognitive and behavioural targets for recognising, understanding and empathising with underlying mental states in themselves and others.

The therapist guides Lily through exercises to clarify and differentiate her Parent, Adult and Child ego-states. Lily gains insight into the internal dynamics influencing her perceptions and interactions by fostering dialogue and reflection between these states. Through script-analysis, Lily examines the origins of her cognitive/emotional patterns, uncovering beliefs/biases hindering empathetic understanding. She works redefines her life-narrative to foster more accurate, empathetic interpretations, reprogramming limiting beliefs/cognitive-distortions and revising transactional patterns to promote more attuned/empathetic interactions with others. Over time, Emily's capacity for mentalising and integrating conflicting emotions and perceptions improves, leading to more stable relationships and reduced mood volatility.

Example of Fundamental Psychological Structure: Coping and Affect Regulation Mechanisms

Recent advances in neurocognitive research have shed light on the importance of basic coping and affect regulation skills in shaping our responses (Bradley, 2003; Carl et al., 2013; Dana, 2018; Ehring et al., 2008; Fehlinger et al., 2013; Grolnick & Ryan, 1989; Hill, 2015; Perry et al., 2014; Schore, 2015, 2003; Vohs & Baumeister, 2016). Basic coping and affect regulation skills pertain to the ingrained patterns a child develops during their earliest years in interactions with their parents, applying ego-boundaries, integration and mentalisation skills. Coping and affect regulation refers to how individuals manage their emotions and emotional responses to stimuli. This includes how people modulate their feelings to adapt to the demands of their environment, maintain well-being and achieve their goals. Effective affect regulation involves the ability to up-regulate (enhance) and down-regulate (diminish) emotional experiences and expressions appropriate to the situation.

Understanding the significance of these basic structures is crucial when working with clients who struggle with basic coping and affect regulation issues. It is essential to recognise that developing these skills can be complex and time-consuming, akin to growing an organ that was never there before. By acknowledging the fundamental role of these basic structures in our perception and response to messages, we can gain insight into how they contribute to forming self-perpetuating ego-states and life positions. Consequently, the therapist should approach these situations with great patience and empathy.

The development of affect regulation and the impact on the self has garnered significant interest from researchers and therapists in recent years. For example, Allan Schore (2015, 2003), a prominent figure in developmental neuroscience and psychiatry, emphasises the crucial impact of early relationships, particularly the mother-infant bond, on lifelong development. He discussed the significance of the mother's role in regulating the infant's emotions, which directly influences the development of the brain and is responsible for emotion regulation and nonverbal processing. Schore highlighted the pivotal role of early interactions in forming the foundation for self-regulation, stressing that the mother's regulation of the infant's emotional and arousal states is fundamental to attachment and the development of the right brain. Furthermore, he linked early affect regulation to physical health, emphasising the solid brain-mind-body connections, including the impact on the immune system and overall physical well-being. Schore's work underscores the long-lasting influence of early affect regulation on mental health and emotional well-being throughout life.

Imagine Bobby, an 18-month-old toddler. Bobby has recently mastered crawling and standing independently, allowing him to venture into the world around him. It is natural for children his age to be curious and eager to explore new people, situations and places. However, due to his limited life experiences, Bobby does not yet understand who he can trust. Consequently, his curiosity may lead him to wander away from his caregivers.

Nevertheless, when Bobby finds himself in unfamiliar surroundings, he may suddenly feel overwhelmed with fear and uncertainty. In such situations, Bobby's instinct is to seek safety and reassurance from his nearest caregiver. From a neurological perspective, he is attempting to calm down the activation of his sympathetic nervous system and activate his parasympathetic system. This can be achieved through the socially oriented dorsal vagus nerves (Dana, 2018; Porges, 2011). His caregiver can help him co-regulate his emotions by acknowledging his feelings and offering a sense of safety.

The caregiver's sensitive reaction validates the child's emotions, assuring him that he is fundamentally OK. Additionally, he realises that the strange situation may not be as alarming as initially thought, as he observes his caregiver's lack of concern. Through this observation, Bobby begins to understand that others are also OK. Moreover, Bobby learns effective strategies for managing distressing emotions, such as learning how to calm down and seeking support from trusted individuals. He may even internalise his caregiver's rational response to the unfamiliar situation, which could contribute to developing an early version of an inner healthy Adult. Thus, Bobby's caregiver is a role model, demonstrating composure to navigate unfamiliar and potentially unsettling circumstances.

Poor affect regulation skills in early-life can manifest as difficulties in managing emotional experiences and expressing emotions appropriately. For example, Schore (2015, 2003) highlights how infants with inconsistent or unresponsive caregiving may struggle to regulate their emotional states, leading to heightened distress and difficulty self-soothing. Additionally, infants exposed to chronic stress or neglect may exhibit poor affect regulation, as their developing brains may not receive the necessary regulatory input from caregivers, impacting their ability to manage emotions effectively. Adults with poor affect regulation skills due to a lack of early-life learning may struggle with emotional instability, difficulty in maintaining healthy relationships, substance abuse and low frustration tolerance, and may engage in self-harm or destructive behaviours as maladaptive coping mechanisms. These challenges can impact their well-being and functioning.

Examples of effective strategies for managing stress and healthily regulating emotions encompass the ability to tolerate stress, adaptability to employ multiple coping tech-niques and the conscious release of mental and physical tension through activities such as deep breathing, grounding exercises, listening to music, dancing, engaging in sports or exercise. Other helpful coping mechanisms include using humour, fostering con-nections with others, making proactive plans, practising self-care, finding distractions when necessary and allowing oneself to rest without resorting to complete denial or avoidance. These strategies are beneficial for maintaining emotional well-being and managing stress levels effectively (Aldao et al., 2010; Bradley, 2003; Carl, 2013; Ehring et al., 2008; Fehlinger et al., 2013; Grolnick & Ryan, 1989; Marroquin, 2011; Mikulincer et al., 2003; Schore, 1994, 2003, 2015).

Suppose caregivers fail to respond sensitively or consistently. Bobby might think that his emotions are invalid or deserve attention ('I am not-OK') and that he should be wary of unfamiliar people and situations ('others are not-OK'). Children like Bobby may develop alternative methods to cope with stressful situations and regulate their emotions, as we will explore later in the section on 'responses and decisions'. Research shows that coping and regulating emotions in early-life may become ingrained and long-lasting patterns, reflecting negative life positions and unhelpful ego-states. A person's ability to cope with stress and regulate emotions significantly impacts their mental and physical well-being. Individuals who struggle with mental health issues often exhibit disturbances in their coping mecha-nisms and emotional regulation (Carl, 2013; Ehring et al., 2008; Fehlinger et al., 2013; Gross 2007). It is common for these individuals to rely heavily on avoidance and denial as coping strategies in various aspects of their lives (Beblo et al., 2012; Campbell-Sills et al., 2006; Ehring et al., 2010).

A person's ability to regulate their emotions from an early age can also help them deal with stressful and traumatic situations, reducing the likelihood of developing a severe trauma or grief response. On the other hand, individuals who have not developed effective coping and emotion regulation skills are more likely to experience acute or post-traumatic stress in response to such events. This creates a tragic cycle where a person may continually face stressful events without having the necessary skills to manage the resulting stress effectively. In cases of severe child abuse and neglect, both adverse childhood experiences and a lack of development in healthy coping mechanisms and emotion regulation often coexist, potentially leading to Complex-PTSD or Personality Disorders.

In conclusion, individuals must cultivate healthy coping mechanisms and effective emotion regulation strategies to maintain their overall well-being. Therefore, therapists can find it beneficial to explore how clients managed stressful situations during their childhood and how they currently cope with stress. By doing so, they can identify whether clients need to develop more adaptive coping and emotional regulation mechanisms that they may not have learnt earlier in life, as detailed in the section on experiential therapist competencies. Emerging research suggests that clients may first need to acquire adequate coping skills and emotional regulation abilities before they can begin to address and process traumatic memories or confront the darker or neglected aspects of themselves (Cloitre et al., 2020; Herman & Van der Kolk, 2020; Karatzias et al. 2019; Kothgassner et al., 2021; Neimeyer et al., 2011). This is understandable, as engaging in trauma work and employing confrontational approaches in therapy can evoke complex emotions and bodily sensations that require strong coping and emotional regulation mechanisms to contain them. Suppose the processing of traumatic experiences or confrontations occurs prematurely before clients have developed sufficient fundamental skills. In that case, they may become emotionally overwhelmed and experience dissociation, suicidal thoughts or even discontinue therapy altogether. To illustrate, individuals who are coping with Complex-PTSD must initially establish a sense of safety. Subsequently, they must acquire fundamental skills, address past traumas and implement modifications in daily routines (Herman & Van der Kolk, 2020). Understanding and accessing the Adult ego-state can help clients regulate affects more effectively, as this state is characterised by responses congruent with the present moment's reality rather than being driven by past experiences or external expectations. It may be beneficial to help clients identify which ego-state they are operating from in moments of emotional distress and guide them towards the Adult ego-state for more balanced emotional responses.

TA may help understand transactional options and dynamics, allowing individuals to choose effective responses and managing emotional states within interpersonal interactions. Working with clients to uncover the emotional patterns scripted in childhood that influence current affect regulation may help clients challenge and change their automatic emotional responses. Techniques such as re-parenting can also be used to heal and integrate dysfunctional Child or Parent ego-states. Analysing the client's patterns of giving and receiving strokes (explained in Chapter 8 as units of recognition or attention) can offer insights into their emotional needs and how these needs influence emotional regulation and teach clients healthier ways to meet their emotional needs. Furthermore, the therapeutic relationship provides an opportunity for role-modelling and reinforcing helpful affect regulation through empathy and holding (Chapter 9). Moreover, therapists may help clients develop a broader emotional vocabulary and practical problem-solving skills, such as assertiveness training, to create more emotional expression tools (Chapter 12).

5.5 REFLECTIVE QUESTIONS

- How did you cope with stressful situations and emotions as a toddler, child, primary-school kid and teenager? What are the strengths and possible weaknesses of these coping-styles? What skills did you not develop but would have been good to have developed? How did these early coping-mechanics help you survive or fulfil your basic needs, such as getting attention, love and validation from your caregivers and authority figures? How do these early-life coping mechanisms still influence how you cope with stressful situations? What works well? What does not work well? What skills could you improve, how could you develop these, and what practical steps are needed?
- Think about a client/person you know well. Ask the same questions about them.

Case Study 5.5

Ahmed

Ahmed sought therapy for Complex-PTSD stemming from his childhood. His mother had narcissistic tendencies, and his father was often absent. Ahmed's mother neglected him emotionally from ages one to four, hindering his development of healthy coping mechanisms and emotional regulation. Ahmed's older brother frequently tormented him, and his mother sided with the brother when Ahmed complained. Feeling unheard, Ahmed developed angry outbursts, which were punished by parents and teachers. This led him to suppress his emotions and adopt a rational approach to life, becoming withdrawn. Lacking an understanding of healthy boundaries, Ahmed attracted narcissistic friends and partners, reinforcing his pessimistic outlook. After a recent fallout with friends, he developed intense C-PTSD symptoms. In therapy, Ahmed realised his emotional dysregulation and attraction to narcissistic individuals had caused numerous traumatic experiences. Through therapy, Ahmed cultivated self-compassion, improved emotion regulation, processed traumatic memories, learnt to avoid narcissistic relationships and built a supportive social network.

Box 5.1

Working With Clients Who Have Never Learnt Mature Coping and Affect-Regulation Skills

The Polyvagal Theory (Porges, 2011) emphasises the vagus nerve's role in regulating responses to stress and social interactions. It describes three neural circuits: social engagement (ventral vagal complex), mobilisation (sympathetic nervous system) and immobilisation (dorsal vagal complex). Transactional Analysis (TA) can help understand these processes (Crisanti, 2023). Studies have shown how parent-child transactions impact vagal-regulation (Perry, 2014) and how ego-states relate to brain functions (Hine, 2005; Messina & Sambin, 2015; Oller-Vallejo, 2005). Integrating neurological findings with TA may benefit traumatised clients (Novak, 2013). Therapists can use Polyvagal Theory to address clients' physiological and emotional states. Deep breathing and mindfulness can regulate the vagal system, promoting safety and trust. Dana (2018) provides a framework for transitioning clients from protection to connection states.

Somatic Experiencing (Levine, 1997) focuses on processing trauma through bodily sensations. Therapists help clients become aware of trauma-related sensations and safely discharge pent-up energy. Sensorimotor therapy (Ogden, 2021) integrates physical sensations with talk therapy, promoting healing through mindful awareness of bodily experiences. These body-oriented approaches benefit clients with complex trauma (Lewis et al., 2020).

Research suggests developing fundamental affect regulation skills before treating Complex-PTSD (Bisson et al., 2007; Karatzias et al., 2019; Neimeyer, 2022). STAIR Therapy (Cloitre et al., 2020) helps trauma survivors develop coping mechanisms and improve interpersonal skills. It focuses on emotional awareness, regulation, distress tolerance and self-compassion.

Compassion-focused interventions (Craig et al., 2020; Gilbert, 2010; Millard et al., 2023; Neff, 2011; Schwartz, 2021) help clients develop self-compassion, crucial for those with negative self-perceptions. Therapists guide clients in cultivating mindfulness, reframing negative self-talk and fostering self-acceptance. These practices lead to reduced self-criticism, enhanced emotional resilience and improved well-being.

Example of Fundamental Psychological Structure: Attachment

Although Berne did not speak about an individual's attachment style, many TA therapists, particularly those in integrative, co-creative and relational TA, mention its importance in understanding a client's aetiology (Vos & van Rijn, 2021c). There is much overlap between attachment theory and TA-specific concepts such as life positions; Berne's idea of 'intimacy' is closely related. It may be argued that their differences are mainly due to differences in naming the concepts and theoretical perspectives (Hargaden & Sills, 2014). For example, some drivers correlate as expected with attachment styles, such as the 'Be strong' driver is often associated with anxious-ambivalent attachment (Pesic, 2009). Life positions strongly correlate with attachment styles (Boholst et al., 2017). Developing attachment style and regulation skills also go hand-in-hand and may be considered different sides of the same coin (Mikulincer et al., 2003). Sciligo and colleagues have developed sociocognitive TA, which integrates Bowlby's Attachment Theory (DeLuca & Tosi, 2011; Scilligo, 2009, 2005), but requires translation into English and further empirical validation. As the next paragraphs will explain, Attachment theory is a well-studied topic that outlines four primary attachment styles that children may develop: secure, anxious-ambivalent, avoidant attachment and disorganised attachment.

Secure Attachment: Children with secure attachment have caregivers who consistently respond to their needs, providing comfort and support. This fosters a sense of security and trust in relationships. Adults with a secure attachment style are generally comfortable with intimacy and autonomy. They are responsive to their partners and can healthily express their needs and emotions. They tend to have healthy, balanced relationships, effective communication skills and positive mental health outcomes in later life. This seems associated with few harmful injunctive messages, drivers and many permissive messages and beneficial allowers. The individual has a flexible range of ego-states, a strong Healthy Ego and Nurturing Parent and positive life positions (others/self are OK).

Anxious-Preoccupation Attachment: Anxious-ambivalent attached children may experience inconsistent caregiving, leading to anxiety and a fear of abandonment. This may be associated with injunctive messages, drivers such as 'Be Perfect' and 'Try hard', and few beneficial permissions/allowers. In adulthood, individuals with an anxious-preoccupied attachment style might exhibit clingy or overly dependent behaviour in relationships, along with heightened emotional reactivity and vulnerability to anxiety disorders. These individuals often seek high levels of closeness and approval, feeling insecure and susceptible to rejection. They may worry about their partner's availability and can be overly dependent. An anxious-ambivalent individual may have a strong Critical Parent, a weaker Healthy Adult and negative life positions (others/self are not-OK).

Dismissive-Avoidant Attachment: Avoidant children may have caregivers who are emotionally distant or unresponsive, leading them to develop self-reliance and a reluctance to seek comfort from others. Adults with a dismissive-avoidant attachment style tend to downplay the importance of close relationships and may prioritise independence over intimacy. They may struggle with emotional expression and dismiss their own and others' needs for closeness. They may avoid emotional vulnerability and tend to be self-reliant. Still, they struggle with intimacy and expressing emotions, potentially leading to challenges in forming deep emotional connections. This attachment style may be associated with injunctions and drivers such as 'Do not belong' and 'Do not be close' and a life position telling them that 'others are not-OK'. Their sense of self may be OK.

Fearful-avoidant Attachment: Children with disorganised attachment often experience unpredictable or frightening caregiving experiences, leading to confusion and conflicting behaviours. In adulthood, individuals with disorganised attachment may exhibit erratic relationship patterns, emotional instability and an increased risk of mental health issues such as dissociation or personality disorders. This may be associated with conflicting messages, harmful injunctions and drivers and few beneficial permissions and allowers. Adults with a fearful-avoidant attachment may experience conflicting desires for closeness and independence, leading to inner turmoil and difficulty trusting relationships. They may exhibit unpredictable behaviour and struggle with emotional regulation, vacillating between seeking and avoiding intimacy. These individuals may have a strong Critical Parent, a weak healthy Adult.

Thus, attachment styles can influence how individuals perceive and respond to the transactional core messages and life script, life-long relational patterns and mental health. Secure attachment is associated with greater emotional resilience, effective stress management and overall psychological well-being. In contrast, insecure attachment styles, such as anxious-preoccupied, dismissive-avoidant and fearful-avoidant, are linked to higher levels of anxiety, depression and difficulties in managing stress and emotional regulation.

Therapists can assess an adult's attachment style through various methods, including observation of relational patterns, self-report questionnaires (e.g. Experiences in Close Relationships) and interviews (e.g. Adult Attachment Interview). Therapists may integrate attachment theory into their work with clients by recognising the influence of early attachment experiences on clients' personality development, relational patterns and emotional well-being (Obegi & Berant, 2010). TA therapy may improve attachment in the following ways (Monajem & Aghayousefi, 2015).

Understanding Clients' Attachment Styles: TA therapists may assess and understand their attachment styles by analysing their transactions, relational patterns, emotional responses and coping strategies. By recognising the impact of early attachment experiences, therapists can tailor interventions to address specific attachment-related challenges.

Exploring and Redeciding Early Attachment Experiences: Therapists may help clients explore and process their early-life experiences, including interactions with caregivers and primary attachment figures. This exploration can provide clients with a deeper understanding of how their attachment experiences have shaped their beliefs, emotions and behaviours in relationships. This also offers the opportunity to redecide their life script.

Addressing Attachment-Based Patterns: By identifying attachment-based patterns such as fear of abandonment, difficulty forming close connections or emotional distancing, TA therapists may help clients recognise and modify maladaptive relational patterns. This may involve addressing underlying worries, insecurities and unmet emotional needs stemming from early attachment.

Promoting Secure Attachment: TA therapists may work with clients to promote secure attachment by fostering a supportive and validating therapeutic relationship. Therapists may help clients develop a more secure internal working model and healthier interpersonal dynamics through consistent attunement, empathy and validation. This may include focusing on rupture and repair cycles (Neal, 2017), such as practical exercises and boundary-setting.

Emphasising Relational Patterns: TA therapists may use the concept of ego-states to explore how clients' attachment-related beliefs and behaviours manifest in their interactions with others, including in the therapeutic relationship. Therapists may facilitate insight and promote adaptive relational dynamics by examining how early attachment experiences influence clients' Parent, Adult and Child ego-states.

Thus, integrating attachment theory into TA may provide a comprehensive framework for understanding and addressing clients' relational challenges, emotional regulation and overall psychological well-being. By recognising the interconnectedness of attachment and personality dynamics, therapists can offer more targeted and effective interventions to support clients in developing healthier relational patterns and achieving greater emotional resilience.

> For certain fortunate people, there is something which transcends all classifications of behaviour, and that is awareness; something which rises above the programming of the past, and that is spontaneity; and something more rewarding than games, and that is intimacy (Berne, 1964, p. 79).

Case Study 5.6

Alex

TA therapist Dr Smith works with a client named Alex, who exhibits dismissive-avoidant attachment patterns in his relationships. Alex struggles to express vulnerability and prioritises independence over intimacy, leading to challenges forming deep connections. During therapy, Dr Smith employs a combination of ego-state work and script-analysis to explore the origins of Alex's attachment patterns and their impact on his relational dynamics. Through collaborative redefinition of transactional patterns and contracting for change, Alex gains insight into his dismissive-avoidant tendencies and begins to explore more balanced approaches to intimacy and independence. Over time, Alex demonstrates increased comfort with vulnerability and emotional expression, leading to more secure and fulfilling relationships. Alex develops a more secure attachment style through dedicated therapeutic work with Dr Smith, leading to improved emotional regulation and enhanced well-being in his interpersonal connections.

5.6 REFLECTIVE QUESTIONS

- How would you describe your attachment style as a child and in the present? If there have been any changes in your attachment style, what has brought these changes? How could you improve your attachment style?
- Think of a person/client you know well. Answer the same questions.

Example of Fundamental Psychological Structure: Discounting of Existential Givens

Discounting refers to the unconscious processes by which individuals minimise, ignore or deny aspects of reality, including their own experiences, feelings, needs or the existential givens of life, often resulting from unfavourable early-life experiences and transactional messages received from caregivers and authorities (Thayer & Schiff, 1975). Minimisation or denial means that clients downplay or outright deny the significance of emotional events and life facts, such as saying, 'It is not a big deal', even when talking about one's funda-mental limitations, such as mortality. There may be an avoidance of confronting uncom-fortable truths or emotions, passivity or avoiding taking responsibility for their actions by saying, 'There's nothing I can do about it'. Clients may engage in distorted thinking pat-terns, which prevents them from acknowledging reality (see an overview of cognitive biases in Chapter 12). Individuals may also discount the reality and feelings associated with experiences of social injustice (Sedgwick, 2020). For instance, a young person may develop feelings of anger, vulnerability or a lack of control, as an understandable response to being the victim of an unjust situation or event, such as abuse, social inequality, racism, sexism, homophobia or transphobia; however, instead of staying with the reality, emotions and physical experiences of the injustice and traumatic memories, the person may deny, ignore or minimise the injustice, for instance, by developing unrealistic feelings of self-blame, shame, incompetence and social withdrawal (Elison et al., 2006) (later sections address such 'responses/decisions').

TA therapists often talk about 'discounting of existential givens' to underline that the discounted topics do not merely regard one specific situation but the general sense of self, others, life, world and the human condition: they are 'existential'. Discounting means that individuals avoid confronting life's inherent challenges and truths, which may hinder self-awareness, personal growth, authentic and intimate relationships. There are few empirical TA-studies on discounting of existential givens. However, the TA-model of dis-counting is generally supported by many existential-psychological studies on the avoidance and denial of existential givens (Vos, 2014, 2016a, 2016b).

Discounting often happens in an internal dialogue and can occur in different ego states, affecting how individuals perceive themselves, others and the world to fit their script beliefs (called 'redefining' by Thayer and Schiff, 1975). Sometimes, internal dis-counting is transferred to the outside world, for example, via non-constructive criticism and other games, triggering unpleasant feelings in others (Thayer & Schiff, 1975). Individuals may redefine their transactions from a Child ego-state, for example, when they perceive the interaction as threatening their script-belief by going on a tangent or blocking the conversation. A consequence of discounting is often that a person is more rigid and less effective in problem-solving, underestimates their own or other people's resources and realistic opportunities for change (Thayer & Schiff, 1975). For example, in a relational symbiosis between two individuals, one individual may only be in a Child ego-state, whereas the other stays in a Parent or Adult ego-state, which excludes the opportunities for other ego-states in both (cf., Mahler et al., 1975). TA therapists have used the concept of discounting as an intrapsychic indicator of psychopathology and severity of problems; extreme forms of discounting may, for instance, be seen in schizophrenia (Thayer & Schiff, 1975), and discounting the reality of death may be involved in suicidal ideation (White, 2017).

Hargaden and Sills (2002) have argued that a child may develop their life script, including discounting existential topics, as personal plans to come to terms with existential realities. During their childhood, individuals often develop fundamental beliefs and rules, which may give a soothing and comforting sense of knowing roughly where to go in their lives, such as assumptions about our self-worth, trust in others, invulnerability, the world's benevolence, the meaningfulness of their actions and the predictability of their environment (Janoff-Bulman, 2010). These beliefs are the foundations of our ego-states and life positions in our day-to-day lives. For example, we dare to walk a pedestrian crossing based on the assumption that car drivers will stop, thus assuming the benevolence and predictability of our world, a belief that we may have developed via positive early-life interactions, role-models and messages from caregivers and authorities. Stressful life events, such as a car-driver not stopping at the crossing, may shatter our fundamental assumptions about our invulnerability and the goodness of people; this experience could make us aware that we had been discounting fundamental parts of our reality by having unrealistic beliefs in their invulnerability and the world's benevolence (Janoff-Bulman, 2010; Vos, 2016b). Chapter 25 will explain how therapists could work with clients asking questions about existential givens or being in a crisis about identity, existence, meaning or spirituality.

An individual may discount existential givens in response to the house-hold dramas or protocols of their early-life (e.g. via injunctive messages, role-models and other aspects of the script apparatus) (Hargaden & Sills, 2002). Parents can deny a child's existential givens through their behaviours and attitudes, which the child may take over and subsequently influence their transactional core beliefs, ego-states and life positions. If parents shield their children from discussions about mortality or the concept of death, they may inadvertently contribute to the discounting of the inevitability of death. Similarly, if parents overly restrict their children's choices and decision-making processes, they may inhibit the development of the child's sense of freedom and responsibility. Other examples include discounting one's strengths or vulnerabilities, masculine or feminine sides, positive or negative traits, unconscious or conscious side, individual-self or self-in-context, the persona or the shadow. Discounting prevents children from being seen and learning to see the totality of who they are, their life and their context. If your caregivers ignore a topic, you may get the message that this topic is not worthy of attention, and you may discount this; for example, if mortality is discounted in someone's childhood, a person may not know how to cope with their mortality when they get seriously ill later in life or when they become aware of their mortality during midlife or retirement. If parents fail to provide a nurturing and supportive environment for their children to explore and find meaning in life, they may inadvertently contribute to the discounting of a sense of meaning, like the meaning a person may derive from exploring our mortality. By recognising and addressing these dynamics, parents can play a crucial role in fostering their children's awareness of existential givens and supporting their healthy emotional and psychological development.

As our survey indicated (Vos & van Rijn, 2021a), TA-practitioners often assess the client's discounting of existential givens. In a later stage of therapy (Chapter 10), when a strong client-therapist relationship has been established (Chapter 9), therapists may carefully challenge and help clients explore their discounting, for example, via cognitive/behavioural techniques (Chapter 12), to help them explore and accept the reality and totality of their experiences (Chapter 11). By acknowledging and addressing existential givens, individuals may develop self-awareness, emotional resilience, authenticity, meaning in life, fulfilling relationships and intimacy (Vos, 2017).

5.7 REFLECTIVE QUESTIONS

Vos (2017) inspired the following questions:

- How did you develop your sense of meaning in life as a child? What did you want to become? Which childhood dreams did you have? Which dreams did you manage to fulfil? Which dreams did you let go of, which have you tried but failed to achieve, and why?
- When did you first contemplate the concept of meaning in life? What did your caregivers and authority figures tell you about meaning? How did they expect you to live your life? To what extent did you critically evaluate the meanings, stories and expectations you were exposed to? How did you cultivate your capacity for critical thinking? Presently, how critical are you towards your own life? What does your intuition tell you about your current meaning in life? What steps can you take to improve your sense of meaning?
- Many people see living a meaningful life and facing life's limitations as opposites. However, Viktor Frankl wrote in 'Man's Search for Meaning' how he found meaning as a prisoner in a concentration camp, which he calls 'tragic optimism', the ability to realistically acknowledge the tragedy of the situation and simultaneously find small moments of meaning. Think back to moments when your meanings were challenged, such as during the pandemic, when many people could not do things meaningful for them before the lockdowns, such as going to a football stadium. How did you respond to these limitations? Did you respond with a sense of fatalism or meaninglessness? Could you shift your focus to what was still possible within the constraints? To what extent did your initial response reflect how your parents would have responded to such a challenge and how you would have responded as a child? How would you like to respond to similar challenges in future? What helped you overcome life's difficult moments; could you use this coping mechanism again? How can you find meaning despite life's limitations?
- Imagine you are on your deathbed. What must you do to ensure you die with a fulfilled feeling about your life? This is about your sense of life-satisfaction and not fulfilling what others expected from you; for example, imagine that everyone who has taught you about life has died, such as your parents, caregivers, authority figures, priests, etc. You are alone and the only person deciding what 'a meaningful life' means to you. Be aware of the realistic options and limitations of what you can and cannot achieve.
- Keep a Meaningful Moments Diary for at least two weeks. Write down the three most meaningful moments at the end of each day. This can be minor, like enjoying listening to a bird, or something significant, such as preparing your wedding. After two weeks, identify any trends. What can you do to get more of these meaningful moments?
- We may know theoretically that we should make time for what matters. Still, in everyday life, possibly due to our life script, we often 'forget' to live a meaningful/fulfilling life. Therefore, take out your calendar: do it now. Put in a big meaningful event for the upcoming year, one relatively big meaningful event for each month, one medium meaningful moment for each week and one relatively meaningful moment each day.
- Consider a person or client you know well. How would they respond to these questions and exercises?

TRANSACTIONAL CORE MESSAGES IN THE LIFE SCRIPT

Think back to your childhood messages from caregivers, authority figures, intergenerational messages, life events, socioeconomic context, genetics or temperament. Which messages did you take over, and which did you dismiss? If you were to summarise each message you have internalised as one sentence, such as 'Do not...' or 'You are allowed to...' how would they sound? In TA, such core beliefs and behaviours are described as injunctions, drivers, counterinjunctions, permissions, allowances, payoffs, programmes and other transactional core messages.

Injunctions are negative internalised messages that individuals adopt from unprocessed early-life experiences and parental messages such as restrictions and unfavourable directions, such as 'Do not be you'. Injunctions can lead to self-limiting beliefs and behaviours and contribute to feelings of inadequacy, anxiety and self-doubt. TA therapists recommended analysing how or what individuals attribute the injunctive messages to.

Permissions, in contrast, are positive internalised messages that allow individuals to engage in healthy, fulfilling and authentic behaviours without self-imposed restrictions, such as, 'It is OK to be me'. They play a crucial role in promoting emotional well-being and self-expression.

Drivers are usually conscious messages, socially acceptable on the surface but driving individuals towards compulsive behaviours, often stemming from early childhood experiences. In that sense, they are different from the socially acceptable values of attention to detail, personal robustness, perseverance, speed and valuing of others. These drivers can impact mental health by perpetuating patterns of self-sabotage and emotional distress, such as the 'Be perfect' driver, leading to perfectionism and an internal feeling of shame and inadequacy. Although five groups of driver behaviours were identified by Kahler (1975), including Be Strong, Be Perfect, Try Hard and Please Others, the broader term of counterinjuctions refers to a more comprehensive range of similar script-messages. They are often verbal, and seen as positive. Their limiting influence lies in their drivenness or compulsivity. So, someone with a Be Strong Driver, may find it nearly impossible to relax or be vulnerable.

Allowers are healthy, adaptive messages that enable individuals to engage in authentic and fulfilling behaviours without the burden of self-limiting beliefs, such as 'You are good enough as you are'.

A payoff (stamp) reflects the outcome of the repetitive, predictable patterns of behaviour and beliefs that individuals carry from their formative years into adulthood. This was previously known as 'stamp', a term in the 1970s where people collected stamps in exchange for discounts on goods; this concept relates to an expected emotional payoff as an outcome of a game. These can result from recurring relationship dynamics, self-sabotaging tendencies, persistent emotional reactions, communication styles or decision-making processes.

A programme is a model for living based on interactions with caregivers and significant others. Some are valuable learning and modelling experiences, but some relate to limiting script patterns. For example, even though a parent wants a child to be healthy, their own repeated abuse of alcohol serves as part of the programme (modelling) for the child. In short, this type of message highlights that a parental message, 'Do as I say, not as I do', is essentially pointless.

Other Script Components: TA therapists have proposed an almost endless number of aspects that could be identified in a person's life script, such as mythical heroes, fantasies, games, curses, demons, sweatshirts, seduction, antithesis and tragic endings.

Over time, TA theory has undergone further refinement, leading to a more complex understanding of creating script choices and patterns.

It is essential to note that these TA constructs have not been extensively studied and validated. However, the absence of research does not necessarily mean these constructs are untrue or unhelpful. The research closest to these constructs possibly regards core beliefs, which are deeply ingrained, fundamentally biased, negative and self-perpetuating beliefs about oneself, others and the world, often developed early in life. These beliefs significantly influence a person's perceptions, emotions and behaviours, shaping their overall cognitive and emotional experiences. Research has identified three categories of core beliefs: helplessness (I am helpless; I fail at everything I try; I am a weakling; I am stuck; I am defenceless), worthlessness (I am worthless, I am disgusting; I am a disaster; I am greatly flawed; I should not be allowed to live) and unloveability (I am unloveable; I am unlikeable; I will always be alone; I will eventually be rejected; I will never be cared for) (Beck, 2020). A similar concept regards maladaptive cognitive schemas, which do not only include core cognitions but also deeply ingrained, enduring patterns of feelings, behaviours and coping strategies. Common early-developed cognitive schemas include abandonment/instability, mistrust/abuse, emotional deprivation, defectiveness/shame, social isolation/alienation, dependence/incompetence, vulnerability to harm or illness, enmeshment/ undeveloped self, failure to achieve and subjugation (Young, Klosko & Weishaar, 2006).

The similarity between core cognitions/schemas and TA concepts is evident: both reflect patterns of thoughts, behaviour and emotions that develop in early-life. They can either be beneficial or detrimental, self-perpetuating and have the potential to be modified and substituted with more realistic and advantageous alternatives, for example, in psychotherapy. However, the distinction lies in the transactional nature of TA concepts, formulated as messages conveyed by caregivers and authority figures. For instance, the injunction 'do not belong' can be seen as a transactional version of a core belief of unloveability, such as 'nobody will accept me'. Consequently, therapists can utilise transactional or cognitive formulations to express similar experiences. Given the similarities, instead of 'core cognitions', we may use the term 'transactional core messages' to refer to the injunctions, drivers, counterinjunctions, permissions, allowances and programmes; this highlights that these may be regarded as transactional examples of core cognitions and schemas.

The transactional formulations offer a potential advantage over cognitive formulations, as they immediately highlight the real/external origins of the message, which may help the client create distance between themselves and their thoughts, acknowledging that their caregivers and authority figures imparted these messages. Instead of thinking, 'I am unlovable', they can say, 'My caregivers and authority figures taught me this message'. This shift in perspective allows for a more objective examination of their thoughts and provides an opportunity for self-compassion, personal growth and change.

Moreover, studies suggest distinguishing between thoughts, behaviours, emotions and physical sensations can be tricky since they are closely interconnected and mutually influential. Modern CBT-therapists adopt a holistic approach, addressing these aspects rather than focusing solely on thoughts or emotions (see Chapter 12). Similarly, transactional messages should be regarded as a combination of transactional core beliefs, behaviours, emotions and physical sensations.

When working with clients, therapists may want to explore examples in the client's story of potential transactional core messages (i.e. injunctions, drivers, counterinjunctions, permissions, allowances and programmes). It is crucial to approach these tentatively as possible hypotheses rather than absolute truths or diagnoses, which should be confirmed through conversations with the client. The summaries in this chapter's tables can help therapists identify patterns in their client's narratives. However, asking clients, especially those who deeply understand their own life story, can have an even more significant and empowering impact in articulating the 'life lessons' or 'core messages about life' they have learnt in early-life.

Box 5.2

Integrative List of Injunctions, Permissions, Drivers and Allowers (Based on Goulding & Goulding, 1972; McNeel, 2010)

Injunctions (Don't Messages):
  (Don't messages often regard survival, attachment, identity, competence, security)

- Don't be (exist)
- Don't be you
- Don't be a child
- Don't grow up
- Don't make it (succeed)
- Don't do anything
- Don't be important
- Don't belong
- Don't be close
- Don't be well/sane
- Don't think
- Don't feel
- Don't be separate
- Don't be visible
- Don't trust
- Don't want
- Don't enjoy
- Don't relax
- Don't feel attached
- Don't be thankful
- Don't share your life
- Don't touch
- Don't invest

Permissions (It's Okay Messages):

- It's okay to ... be
- It's okay to be you
- It's okay to be a child
- It's okay to grow up
- It's okay to make it (succeed)
- Two yesses for every no
- It's okay to be important
- It's okay to belong
- It's okay to be close
- It's okay to be well/sane
- It's okay to think

Drivers:

- Be perfect
- Please (others)
- Be strong
- Try hard
- Hurry up

Allowers:

- You are good enough as you are
- Please yourself
- Be open and express your wants
- Do it
- Take your time

5.8 REFLECTIVE QUESTIONS

- Look at the above lists of Injunctions, Permissions, Drivers and Allowers. Which injunctions, drivers, counterinjunctions, permissions, allowances and programmes do you recognise in your life-story? How have these messages impacted your present ego-states and life positions? How have these early-life messages influenced your career decisions? How can you use these as a strength in your work with clients? How could they limit or challenge your client work? How could these messages create blind spots in your work and how could you overcome these?
- Think about a client/person you know well. Which injunctions, drivers, counterinjunctions, permissions, allowances and programmes do you recognise? How do you know this is an accurate assessment; how could you verify this? How do these messages impact their present ego-states and life positions?

RESPONSES AND DECISIONS IN THE PAST AND PRESENT

In previous sections, we observed how caregivers, figures of authority and life events seem to communicate to us. However, simply receiving a message does not imply that we automatically agree. We can reject or modify a message and respond with our alternative counter-injunction. Berne referred to this response as our 'decision'.

The term 'decision' used by Berne may not always be realistic, relevant or helpful. A 'decision' suggests a conscious or intentional choice, along with assigning blame. However, in reality, individuals often develop their response to their upbringing gradually, without being fully aware of it or making deliberate decisions (Campos, 2010; Car, 2013; Minikin, 2023; Sedgwick, 2020). In our survey, TA therapists noted that forming self-limiting patterns is interactive rather than conscious (Vos & van Rijn, 2021b). According to the social responsibility model, many individuals unknowingly contribute small parts to patterns or situations of injustice, a complex accumulation of unintended actions by many individuals (Vos, 2025). How much freedom do individuals have to change their perspective on their circumstances? Can individuals always determine their response? Suppose a client's parents did not teach them good coping and affect regulation skills; they may not be able to make a realistic and helpful decision about how they will respond to the messages from their upbringing, as they may lack the hardware to make decisions and run particular software programmes. The empirical literature does not support the stereotypical TA notion of a decision as a specific moment when individuals had multiple options and selected one particular choice. Due to the complex interplay of circumstances, individuals often did not have another viable option. Therefore, the dynamic interplay of numerous complex elements necessitates viewing the concept of freedom as a metaphysical inquiry that cannot be directly put into action or confirmed. One may argue that delving into the theoretical concept of freedom is unnecessary and an unscientific or unverifiable concept (Popper, 1990). Furthermore, the term 'decision' might be criticised for victim-blaming, intensifying feelings of guilt/shame in an already struggling client and potentially contributing to psychological issues (Verhaeghe, 2017; Vos, 2019). In response to this list of criticisms about the term 'decision', we recommend to more appropriate terms, such as responses, which may depend on the client's circumstances; throughout this book, we will use the term 'response/ decision'.

Thus, therapists need to be careful and sensitive in how they assess and address the role of the self as a hypothetical factor in the aetiology of mental health problems. For example, clients often express a sense of liberation and empowerment when they realise that their past actions were driven by circumstances and limited choices rather than inherent flaws in their character (Vos & van Rijn, 2024a, 2024b, 2024c). This perspective allows them to maintain a healthy level of self-accountability without excessively burdening their self-esteem while also providing a foundation for self-compassion.

Nevertheless, individuals may inadvertently contribute to developing and perpetuating their problems in various ways, sometimes due to a lack of alternative coping mechanisms.

This brings forth the concept of accountability, which focuses on taking responsibility rather than feeling guilty/ashamed. For instance, a client might have withdrawn socially to respond to a stressful situation, believing it to be the best course of action. In hindsight, they recognise that this withdrawal was not beneficial. However, they also acknowledge that they lacked the necessary skills for coping and regulating their emotions, likely stemming from a lack of proper upbringing. Thus, therapists must navigate these complexities delicately, recognising the balance between helping clients understand their accountability and fostering self-compassion. By doing so, therapists can empower individuals to take owner-ship of their actions and make positive life changes.

While it may be unrealistic and unhelpful to dwell on past responses to life cir-cumstances, it can be beneficial to emphasise the freedom and responsibility we have in the present. Although clients may not have had a say in the past, they may now have some power to develop self-awareness, acquire new skills and make fresh decisions. The belief in freedom impacts individuals positively, and hope enhances mental well-being (Koehn & Cutcliffe, 2007; Schrank et al., 2008; Snyder et al., 2003). Consequently, fostering freedom and hope can be advantageous (Schrank et al., 2012). Furthermore, individuals can benefit from having a sense of self-efficacy, which is the belief in their ability to achieve desired outcomes through their actions (Maddux & Kleiman, 2016; Schwarzer, 2014). This is particularly true for individuals facing mental health issues (Corrigan et al., 2006; Marks & Allegrante, 2005).

All therapeutic strategies must remain grounded in reality as individuals do not possess boundless choices and resources, nor can they alter the past that led them to their current circumstances. Thus, while asserting that individuals can ultimately determine or redefine their situation or life path may appear implausible, they seem to have some capacity to shape their mindset towards their past/current circumstances. This phenomenon has been described as a dual attitude (Vos, 2014). On the one hand, individuals acknowledge the limitations imposed by their situation on their freedom. On the other hand, they strive to cultivate a meaningful outlook on their circumstances. This concept was pioneered by Frankl (1985), who explored it in his book 'Man's Search for Meaning'. Frankl recounted how prisoners in concentration camps were unable to transcend their situation fully – it was realistic for them to experience despair and mental health challenges – yet within their limited options, some individuals were able to find solace in meaningful moments, such as sharing a meaningful glance with another inmate or holding onto memories of the past or their loved one. Individuals possess a degree of freedom to choose a more positive mindset towards their situation, even if it is understandable that this may be difficult given their constraints (Vos, 2016a, 2016b).

Therefore, therapists may acknowledge the client's realistic responsibility while simulta-neously showing compassion for past actions and consciously deciding to utilise the available opportunities in the present. In line with existential therapists TA therapists may find it beneficial to emphasise and rephrase the stories shared by their clients, highlighting how they may have been limited in their choices in the past but now have more agency (Vos, 2017). Clients often find solace in hearing the Serenity Prayer, developed by the theologian Martin Niebuhr: 'God, grant me the serenity to accept the things I cannot change, the courage to change the things I can, and the wisdom to know the difference' (Vos, 2018, 2023). By adopting this approach, therapists may guide clients towards accepting their past actions, taking control of present circumstances and making informed decisions for a better future.

McNeel's Model

John McNeel's comprehensive model, developed in 2010, offers a nuanced approach to understanding and working with injunctive messages. He categorised the injunctive messages into the following groups: survival, attachment, identity, competence, security.

According to McNeel, individuals can make two types of responses or decisions for each injunctive message: a Despairing Decision, which represents what the person fears to be the truth, and a Defiant Decision, which is the person's best attempt at health. These decisions influence Coping Behaviour, which is observable and stems from the defiant decision. McNeel's model suggests that transformation occurs through a Redecision process, where a new belief is required for change. This process is supported by Resolving Activity, which strengthens the redecision, and a Healing Parental Stance, which serves as an internal parental voice to counteract previous negative influences. McNeel also identified two types of Self-Diagnostic Thoughts: Bitter (Self-Destructive) Responses and Healing (Self-Protective) Responses.

To illustrate his model, McNeel provides an example using the 'Don't Exist' injunction from the Survival Category. In this case, the Despairing Decision might be 'I should go away', while the Defiant Decision could be 'I will stay here and you won't break me or defeat me'. The resulting Coping Behaviour might involve driving oneself to excess and exhaustion. The Redecision process would involve embracing the belief that 'I know my life is precious and I cherish it'. The Resolving Activity would entail continually answering questions like 'What matters?' and 'How much is enough?' The Healing Parental Stance in this scenario recognises that sympathy is not the same as nurturance.

McNeel's model offers several key insights. It recognises that injunctive messages are ongoing and cannot be simply revoked, but can be better coped with over time. The resolution of injunctions often involves internalising love and affection from others, and the healing process is viewed as a gradual acquisition of new beliefs rather than a single, dramatic event. For identity-related injunctions, understanding one's gifts and shortcomings is crucial. Resolving competence-related injunctions requires accepting life as a learning process, while addressing security-related injunctions involves making peace with real-world insecurity.

This model provides therapists with a structured approach to identify, understand and work through injunctions with their clients, offering a more nuanced and comprehensive framework than earlier models of Transactional Analysis. However, it is important to note that while McNeel provides clinical examples, systematic research evidence underlying his model is lacking. In a survey of TA therapists, only a few reported using McNeel's model in their practice. Consequently, the focus will be on the three key responses and decisions that TA therapists mentioned in the survey and that are supported by research evidence.

Three Responses/Decisions

TA therapists generally recognise three potential responses individuals may have towards the messages they receive during life, which may contribute to their current situation (Vos et al., 2021b). Individuals may accept or reject specific messages through emotional disconnection, avoidance, denial, dysfunctional emotion regulation and dissociation of experiences and memories. They could also accept or reject messages through their behaviour, such as externalising or projecting their internal turmoil onto others. Alternatively, individuals may accept or reject these injunctions through cognitive styles such as learnt helplessness and cognitive biases.

Emotional responses/decisions: In Classical TA, a 'racket' encompassed inauthentic emotions, thoughts and behaviours that individuals learnt during childhood through socialisation within the family. For example, in a family where expressing anger is unacceptable for girls, a girl may learn to cry instead (which some psychodynamic therapists have described as displacement of emotions). Erskine and Zalcman (1979) and O'Reily-Knapp and Erskine (2010) further developed this understanding of rackets as a cyclical manifestation of the script dynamic in the present, often occurring during stress. This script-system frequently leads to predictable yet self-limiting interactions with others, commonly called psychological games. The script-system becomes evident through recognisable behaviours, such as irritability, accompanied by an internal experience of feeling weighed down. This script-system has a cognitive aspect, which involves self-limiting beliefs about oneself, others and the overall quality of life. An example of such beliefs could be 'I am on my own', 'No one will help' or 'Life is pointless'. A habitual/repetitive emotion may be associated with these script-systems, such as feelings of hopelessness. Memories of similar past experiences reinforce this cyclical experience. Thus, script-systems/rackets in TA refer to the learnt patterns of inauthenticity that individuals acquire during childhood. These patterns are perpetuated through cyclical enactments in the present, particularly during times of stress. They result in self-limiting interactions with others and are characterised by specific behaviours, internal experiences, cognitive processes and repetitive emotions. The memory of past experiences further reinforces these script-systems/rackets. More extreme emotional responses/decisions, such as dissociation, may result from insufficiently developed fundamental psychological structures, such as coping and affect regulation skills.

Behavioural responses/decisions: Research on the development of fundamental psychological structures, such as dysfunctional affect regulation research, shows how, in response to feeling unseen or unfairly treated, individuals may resort to tantrums, anger, aggression or panic attacks (Schore, 2003, 2015). Instead of acknowledging feelings, such as shame or vulnerability, individuals might project those emotions onto others, redirecting their anger towards them.

Numerous research studies indicate that individuals can externalise their problems. Young men may display disruptive behaviours in response to stressful situations, including verbal or physical aggression (e.g. Enstad & Kjeldsen, 2018; Kjeldsen et al., 2021; Zilanawala et al., 2017). Genetic factors increase individuals' likelihood of externalising coping strategies (Bakermans-Kranenburg & Van Ijzendoorn, 2011). Additionally, temperament traits such as self-regulation and reactivity play a role (Rothbart & Bates 2006). Other factors include hyperactivity (Shaw et al., 2005), lack of social competence (Bornstein et al., 2010; Burt et al., 2008) and being male (Dofge & Conduct Problems Prevention Research Group, 2007). Moreover, externalisation is more prevalent among individuals who have experienced harsh and hostile parenting, such as physical aggression or low levels of warmth (Odgers et al., 2008; Shaw et al., 2003; Wiggins, 2015). It appears that the combination of cold and controlling parenting styles can contribute to the development of externalising behaviour in children (Baumrind, 1991; Thompson et al., 2003). Additionally, parental depression and other mental health issues, as well as marital dissatisfaction and conflict, can increase the likelihood of externalisation (Campbell, 1995; Katz & Gottman, 1993; Shaw et al., 2005). Other family stressors, such as losing a relative, have also been linked to externalising behaviour (Campbell, 1996). Furthermore, overwhelming evidence suggests that a lack of social support and socioeconomic problems within the family can contribute to externalisation (Bøe et al., 2014 Côté et al., 2006; Nagin & Tremblay, 2001). The presence of larger families and younger siblings may also increase the risk (Farrington, 1995). Additionally, peer pressure and the influence of peer cultures can play a role in developing externalising behaviour (Dishion et al., 1999; Hanish et al., 2005).

Thus, various factors contribute to children's externalising behaviour development. Parenting styles, mental health issues, family stressors, social support and peer influences all play a significant role. The process of externalisation can be attributed to a complex combination of various factors that interact dynamically over time. Individuals who exhibit externalising behaviour tend to experience these factors consistently from early-life until adulthood, rather than there being a specific sensitive period as proposed by some TA theorists (Kjeldsen, 2020; Roberts & DelVecchio, 2000; Skipstein et al., 2010).

According to research on the development of fundamental psychological structures, such as dysfunctional affect regulation, individuals can respond with externalisation and internalisation (Schore, 1994, 2003, 2015). Individuals may become overly reliant on others (e.g. codependency) or excessively independent (e.g. schizoid personality disorder). Some individuals may use self-soothing techniques, distractions or denial to manage their emotions. They may retreat into an inner or fantasy world to find solace. In more severe cases, dissociation can occur, where individuals detach from reality (e.g. dissociative and schizoaffective disorders). Evidence suggests early ego-states can predict internalising and externalising behaviour (Van Wijk-Herbrink et al., 2018).

Cognitive responses/decisions: As we saw in the previous section, McNeel argued that individuals may embrace injunctions through a despondent or rebellious choice. As previously mentioned, there is limited proof that people possess well-defined alternative options for rejecting the influence of their early-life circumstances. However, ample evidence suggests that individuals may develop despair in response to challenging life situations (Liu et al., 2015), lose morale (Robinson et al., 2016) or create a surrendering ego-state. Adopting a behaviourist standpoint, substantial evidence indicates that individuals can develop learnt helplessness in response to repeated failures, which is associated with symptoms of passivity and depression and can be explained by neurobiological mechanisms (Maier & Seligman, 2016). Additionally, children can imitate their parents' helplessness, potentially due to parental modelling and adverse parental reactions (River et al., 2018).

Individuals may respond by redefining their experiences based on their frame of reference or, more broadly, due to cognitive biases. Biased interpretations, processing and memory retrieval are linked to mental health issues like depression, anxiety and rumination (Everaert, 2012; Gotlib & Joorman, 2010; Mathews & MacLeod, 2005; Nolen-Hoeksema et al., 2008). Greenberg and Watson (2006) have identified four maladaptive (inauthentic or racket) emotions in depression that have shifted away from a more realistic and nuanced perspective on life, the world and oneself: shame and guilt, fear and anxiety, sadness and anger. Numerous cognitive biases have been identified through research, with the following being the most prevalent and psychologically problematic for clients (Widdowson, 2016): Black-or-white thinking, catastrophising, fortune telling, mind reading, taking things personally, overgeneralisation, over-detailing and tunnel vision.

Many of these examples follow from fundamental psychological structures. For instance, affect regulation research gives practical examples of cognitive mechanisms to cope with stressful situations and regulate their effects (Schore, 2003, 2015). For example, a child may perceive the world in absolutes, categorising others as either completely good or completely bad rather than recognising shades of grey or rapidly shifting between viewing others in positive or negative light. They may also struggle with a distorted self-perception, oscillating between seeing themselves as entirely virtuous (e.g. narcissism) or wholly flawed (e.g. depression) or experiencing frequent fluctuations between feeling positive and negative about themselves (e.g. borderline personality disorder).

What can prevent individuals from developing learnt helplessness or cognitive biases? Numerous researchers have extensively examined a broad range of resilience factors that can thwart the onset of mental health issues triggered by stressful life events (Galatzer-Levy et al., 2018). Among its various facets, resilience entails individuals transcending their circumstances and dynamically adapting and adjusting to stressful situations (Aburn et al., 2016), social connectedness, self-compassion and a sense of meaning in life (Vos, 2016b, 2017). Meta-analyses reveal that the most potent factors for resilience in the face of failure are higher self-esteem, a more positive attributional style, lower perfectionism, and lower self-attribution/self-oriented-perfectionism and enhanced emotional intelligence (Johnson et al., 2017). Consequently, multiple factors have the potential to safeguard individuals against developing mental health problems.

5.9 REFLECTIVE QUESTIONS

- Look back at the previous answers to the self-reflective questions in this chapter. How did you respond to the multiple messages you received in childhood? How did you unintentionally or unconsciously contribute to your unhelpful life pattern? What emotional responses/decisions did you make, which cognitive responses/decisions and which behavioural responses/decisions? How many options did you realistically have to make an entirely free decision or rational response; be compassionate about your responses/decisions? What options do you have to decide on a different life now? What practical steps do you need?
- Imagine a client/person you know well. Answer the same questions.

SELF-REINFORCING MECHANISMS AND FEEDBACK LOOPS

Transactional core messages are often self-perpetuating/self-reinforcing, as Figure 5.1 shows. These feedback loops can strengthen the transactional core messages. This may explain why people usually seem deeply entrenched in their life script and resistant to change, even when outsiders like therapists can see the need for it. Therefore, if clients want to change the message they tell themselves in life, they should not only identify the original message and formulate an alternative, but they also need to stop the feedback loops.

The emotional responses and decisions may reinforce a client's transactional core messages. For example, caregivers and authority figures can give negative messages to a child, which may contribute to developing unrealistic and unhelpful coping and affect regulation skills, which makes it more difficult for the child to cope with the negative messages. A key symptom of many mental health problems, particularly those that are caused by strong injunctive messages about the self and one's performance, is hyper-reflection and hyper-obsession, which means that a client may be reflecting on their reflections or getting obsessed with having to get better, which may make them feel worse; CBT describes this as second-order thoughts, triggering ongoing cycles of self-observation, worrying, rumination and self-criticism (Vos, 2017).

The cognitive responses and decisions may reinforce a client's transactional core messages. For example, mood-congruent retrieval bias can strengthen a client's ego-states and life positions by influencing the recall and interpretation of past experiences consistent with their current emotional state. When clients are in a particular mood or emotional state, such as depression, they may selectively retrieve memories and interpret them in a way that aligns with their current feelings, such as focusing only on negative or generic periods of their past instead of zooming into specific positive memories (Gaddy & Ingram, 2014). This bias can reinforce certain ego-states and life positions by perpetuating patterns of thinking and behaviour consistent with their prevailing mood. For example, if a client is feeling pessimistic, they may selectively recall and interpret past experiences in a negative light, further reinforcing their negative ego-states and life positions. This phenomenon underscores the complex interplay between mood, memory and the maintenance of psychological patterns. For example, a therapist may stimulate clients to remember specific positive life events and positive transactional core messages in detail. By imagining that they are in that favourable situation again, they may experientially disprove their depressive thought that they only have received negative messages.

The behavioural responses and decisions may reinforce a client's transactional core messages. The transactional core messages, ego-states and life positions may reinforce the behaviour of the caregivers and authority figures who gave the message; for example, when a child internalises the message 'Do not be yourself', they may frequently show a strong Adapted Child in response to the parent who may feel validated and reinforced in their behaviour and may give this message even more substantial. Individuals may also unconsciously seek out others who fulfil the various roles in their life script (protocol/palimpsest), which may further reinforce their belief in their life script. For example, depressive symptoms can be maintained due to behavioural withdrawal and avoidance, which, for example, prevents an individual from having positive experiences and testing the realism and helpfulness of their messages. For example, the message 'Do not be yourself' could make a person avoid being themselves amongst others, avoiding having positive experiences of being themselves. Safety behaviours, such as preventing risks and feeling the uncertainties of showing more of oneself, may relieve tension in the short term.

An example of self-perpetuating toxic relationships is given by Rosenberg (2013) in his book 'The Human Magnet Syndrome', explaining the mutual attraction between codependents and narcissists. Codependents, seeking validation and approval, are drawn to narcissists' charisma and manipulation. Narcissists, in turn, are attracted to codependents as a source of constant admiration and validation. This creates a dysfunctional relationship dynamic where the codependent's need to please aligns with the narcissist's self-centeredness.

SUMMARY

- This chapter explained how the client's clinical phenomena (e.g. ego-states and life positions) and outcomes (e.g. mental health) started.
- Children's formative years are marked by receiving various messages via genetics, temperament, life events, socioeconomic context, transactions and observations of role models, like caregivers and authority figures, and intergenerational messages.
- In early-life, individuals develop fundamental psychological structures that influence how they perceive, respond to and decide to respond to the early-life messages they receive. This includes the formation of ego-boundaries and separation-individuation, splitting/integration and mentalisation. These fundamental structures include coping and affect regulation skills, attachment styles and discounting of existential givens.
- This combination of the childhood context and fundamental psychological structures may establish transactional core messages, such as injunctions, drivers, counterinjunctions, permissions, allowances, payoffs and programmes.

- Individuals may respond or decide to respond to transactional core messages, for example, via cognitive, emotional or behavioural rejection or acceptance. Whereas individuals may not have had many opportunities to react/choose differently in the past, they may now have more options decide differently within the realistic limitations of their life situation.
- Transactional core messages are often self-perpetuating/self-reinforcing, creating vicious cycles that can make individuals resist change. To foster change, clients should not only replace the unhelpful or unrealistic messages with more positive alternatives but also stop feedback loops.

6

THERAPEUTIC AIMS AND OUTCOMES: WHAT CAN BE ACHIEVED IN TA?

This chapter gives an overview of the general aims and outcomes of TA psychotherapy. After a review of aims/outcomes across TA schools, we will discuss which clients are best suited for TA psychotherapy. The final sections will give details for each of the following therapy aims/outcomes:

- ego-states
- self-efficacy
- social functioning
- psychopathology
- general well-being and quality of life
- self-realisation
- behaviour
- insight into the past
- self-determined client goals

OVERVIEW OF AIMS/OUTCOMES

Overview Across TA schools

In his early work, Berne used the term 'cure' to describe TA-outcomes. The term 'cure' follows from the medical model, like when you have a stomach ulcer, you ask a medical doctor to examine and treat your symptoms and the underlying infection (Davies, 2013; Moncrieff, 2008; Vos et al., 2019). The expectation that TA could offer a cure aligned with early behaviour therapists who systematically assessed a client's clinical symptoms and aetiological causes, followed by a treatment to remove the causes, expecting a cure from the symptoms (note that decades of research indicates that not all clients can achieve complete cure (Vos et al., 2019). In contrast, psychodynamic and humanistic therapists had a more complex intrapsychic model. Although they also explored symptoms and aetiology, they aimed to help clients improve their inner processes and develop self-insight, which may not lead to a complete cure but to living more satisfying lives, such as being able to work and love despite, or possibly even thanks to, one's intricate intrapsychic dynamics.

Berne integrated both medical/behaviourist and psychoanalytic/humanistic perspectives into transactional analysis. Like medicine/behaviourism, he aimed to examine and improve the symptoms (e.g. ego-states and life position; see Chapter 4), understand and – where possible – reduce the impact of aetiological causes such as reducing the influence of the life script on the present (Chapter 5). However, instead of expecting complete removal of all possible emotional problems, Berne aimed to give clients the autonomy, awareness, spontaneity and freedom to cope realistically and beneficially with the constraints of one's life script and current life-situation and, despite or thanks-to these, live a meaningful and satisfying life in the present.

> For certain fortunate people, there is something which transcends all classifications of behaviour, and that is awareness; something which rises above the programming of the past, and that is spontaneity; and something more rewarding than games, and that is intimacy. (Berne, 1964, p. 123)

Berne proposed that TA psychotherapy could offer a cure in the following ways:

- *Achieving autonomy:* This involves reclaiming or regaining awareness, spontaneity and intimacy.
- *Achieving awareness:* This entails refraining from interpreting or distorting one's experiences to fit the messages received in early-life.
- *Achieving spontaneity:* This is seen as the ability to choose from a wide range of options in thoughts, emotions and actions, unrestricted by past experiences.
- *Achieving intimacy:* This involves openly sharing authentic emotions and desires with others.

Berne (1961, 1972) noted that not every client could achieve a complete cure and that individuals can attain varying levels of healing. Although these levels have not been systematically studied, they may serve as a metaphorical guideline:

1 *Social control:* Managing dysfunctional behaviour in social situations;
2 *Symptomatic relief:* Alleviation of inner conflict, confusion, pressures or mental health issues;
3 *Transference:* Liberating oneself from the limitations imposed by one's life script;
4 *Script cure:* Integrating the Adult ego-state allows the individual to break free from their script and live with mindfulness, spontaneity and intimacy.

TA therapists in the Classical School followed Berne's promised cure by aiming to liberate clients from the constraints of their entire life script and enhancing the client's adult ego-state functioning. Therefore, they offered clear therapy contracts aimed at achieving observable goals. Later Classical TA therapists seemed to nuance these aims. Erskine spoke of a script-cure (Erskine, 1980), which included physiological aspects and personal development beyond script-change.

TA therapists in other Schools have argued that the promise of a cure was too medical and did not fit their humanistic values. According to them, progress will always be limited by our human nature, lifescripts, practical life circumstances and socioeconomic/political context. It is unrealistic to expect that clients will never experience emotional turmoil after they finished therapy. We may be able to loosen the tightness of the elastic bands that hold us onto our past, but we may never be able to remove these bands altogether; possibly, we may also not want to remove these bands as they may also be the source of our unique meanings and personality.

Overview of Evidence-Based Aims/Outcomes

Most TA-practitioners expect a mixture of therapy aims/outcomes, as we saw in our survey:

> Autonomy (88%), awareness of how the past influences the present (85%), spontaneity (77%), living in the present (73%), intimacy (73%), insight (72%), greater movement between ego-states (69%), facilitating Adult analysis of problems while stimulating intuitive powers of the Child to aid problem-solving (65%), self-validation (64%), resolution of internal conflicts (61%), redecision (60%), developing a position of 'I'm OK'/'You're OK' (60%), understanding and transforming homoeostasis functions of the script-system intervening with daily-life (57%), self-regulation (56%), self-protection (54%), insurance against future shocks (53%), and sense of integrity (51%). (Vos & van Rijn, 2021b, p. 117)

Statistical analyses of the therapists's answers identified the following eight groups of aims/outcomes (ibidem), which we will detail in the following sections. We recommend focusing on these aims/outcomes, as they are in line with other psychotherapy studies and have been confirmed as realistic outcomes in clinical trials on TA (Vos & van Rijn, 2021a, 2021b, 2021c):

1 *Improved ego-states:* for example, beneficial and flexible relationships between Critical/Nurturing Parent, Adult and Adapted/Free Child (see Chapter 4);
2 *Improved self-efficacy:* in addition to the traditional TA-concept of the 'I'm OK'-life position, this includes, for example, self-love, autonomy, self-esteem, sense of control, emotional self-regulation, self-protection, psychological resilience against future shocks, problem-solving skills, taking responsibility (Chapter 4);
3 *Improved social functioning:* in addition to the traditional TA-concept of the 'You're OK'-life position, this includes, for example, trust, connection, intimacy, authentic expression (Chapter 4);
4 *Improved psychopathology:* decreasing negative effects, for example, anxiety, depression, trauma;

5 *Improved self-realisation:* for example, identification and acceptance of feelings and needs in the present instead of feeling hindered by the past/life script; free flowing of drives, energy and spontaneity;

6 *Improved general well-being and quality-of-life:* increasing positive effects, for example, life-satisfaction, happiness;

7 *Improved behaviour:* for example, social relationships, games;

8 *Improved insight into the past* (new addition compared to our previous publication).

We found large to very-large improvements in each of these eight aims/outcomes in our review of forty-one clinical trials of TA treatments in various settings for different populations (Vos & van Rijn, 2022), which was also confirmed in our feasibility and pilot studies (Vos & van Rijn, 2024a, 2024b, 2024c). Across clinical trials, TA was more effective in individuals, groups and families than in schools or prisons; this finding may be caused by less strict research/treatment protocols and more complex populations and settings. We did not find any differences in outcomes for different populations or individuals with various sociodemographic characteristics; this may be caused by a self-selection of clients interested in therapy. As expected, compared with other psychotherapies, TA is more effective in improving TA-specific outcomes: ego-states, self-efficacy, social functioning and general well-being. The effects on psychopathology are similar to other therapies, confirming the so-called 'Dodo Bird Effect' of equivalent therapeutic outcomes effects (Vos, 2023; Wampold & Imel, 2015). Like other therapies (Vos, 2023), we recommend more research on the effectiveness of TA in diverse populations and settings.

SUITABLE CLIENTS

We asked in our survey among TA therapists which clients are best suited for TA psychotherapy (ibidem). We recommend considering these characteristics for therapy eligibility, together with other eligibility-criteria identified in broader psychotherapy literature (APA, 2006; Holdsworth et al., 2014; Norcross & Wampold, 2011):

- Willing and able to self-reflect
- Willing and able to face emotional pain
- Willing and able to not be merely a passive recipient of help
- Willing and able to contain feelings
- Willing and able to change
- Basic Adult ego-state functioning (e.g. no active psychosis, psychoactive substances, or severe cognitive disabilities)
- Motivated
- Committed
- Positive expectations and hope
- Realistic expectations
- Not overly perfectionistic
- Sufficiently secure attachment

- Willing and able to confide in their therapist
- Trust in the process and the therapist
- Alignment of client/therapist goals
- Sufficient daily-life psychological and interpersonal functioning
- Sufficient social support
- Attend all therapy sessions.

Certain groups, including young people, men and individuals from minority ethnic backgrounds, lower socioeconomic status or those experiencing mental health stigma, may face more challenges in accessing therapy and are more likely to discontinue treatment (Vos et al., 2019).

EGO-STATES

Chapter 4 described how TA helps clients develop insight and improve ego-states and life positions. The TA-concept of life positions is closely related to other broadly-known, well-studied concepts in psychotherapy therapy, as we will detail below. Therefore, we will exchangeably use the generic term 'self-efficacy' and the TA-concept of 'I'm OK', as well as the generic term 'social functioning' and the TA-concept of 'You're OK' (Vos & van Rijn, 2021a, 2021b, 2021c).

SELF-EFFICACY: I'M OK

Research suggests that the life position of 'I'm OK' is associated with several self-efficacy-related concepts that have shown to reduce levels of stress and psychopathology and increase well-being (Greenspoon & Saklofske, 2001; Vos & van Rijn, 2021c; Zeigler-Hill, 2011).

Self-Efficacy (narrow definition): This refers to the Adult-state of engaging in practical actions in daily life, including setting and striving towards goals, planning, maintaining discipline, flexibility in adjusting to changing circumstances (Vos, 2017) and being able to comprehend and transform dysfunctional script-systems hindering daily life (Vos & van Rijn, 2021a). High self-efficacy leads to confidence in approaching tasks, perseverance, resilience, quick recovery from setbacks and lower stress. Exercises to enhance self-efficacy include setting realistic goals, mastering new skills, positive self-talk, visualising success, seeking feedback and reflecting on achievements.

Self-preservation: Self-preservation, primarily involving the Adult and Parent ego-states, is the instinctual drive to protect oneself psychologically from negative influences (Vos & van Rijn, 2021a). It includes recognising and addressing toxic relationships, practising assertive communication and engaging in self-care activities to build mental and emotional resilience. Exercises to enhance self-preservation involve mindfulness, boundary-setting role-playing and self-compassion practices, leading to reduced stress, increased self-esteem and a greater sense of personal agency (Marks & Allegrangte, 2005; Orth et al., 2018; Schore, 1994; Vohs & Baumeister, 2016). TA therapists may analyse problems from the Adult ego-state perspective, supported by the Child ego-state's intuitive capabilities.

Internal Locus of Control: This concept refers to the belief that one has control over one's life and experiences, in other words: a strong Adult ego-state (Lefcourt, 2014). Research indicates that individuals with an internal locus of control exhibit greater motivation, resilience and well-being. They take proactive steps to address challenges and pursue goals, leading to empowerment and lower stress levels. Practical examples include taking responsibility for actions, seeking solutions and believing in the influence of their efforts. Exercises to improve this include goal-setting, decision-making and reflecting on past successes.

Emotional Self-Regulation: This involves managing and modulating emotional responses to stimuli, based on a strong Adult (Bradley, 2003; Hill, 2015; Schore, 2015; also see Chapter 5). Effective emotional self-regulation reduces stress and anxiety, improving overall emotional resilience. Techniques include deep breathing, mindfulness, cognitive reappraisal, progressive muscle relaxation, journaling and professional guidance.

Self-Compassion: Stemming from the Adult, Nurturing Parent or Free Child, self-compassion involves treating oneself with kindness and understanding, especially during personal failures (Gilbert, 2010; Neff, 2011; Schwartz, 2021). It includes self-kindness (being warm and understanding towards oneself), common humanity (recognising suffering and personal challenges are part of the human experience, social connections) and mindfulness (approaching one's thoughts and emotions with non-judgemental awareness, allowing for a balanced perspective on difficulties). When facing a setback at work, a self-compassionate person responds with kindness, acknowledges their efforts and avoids harsh self-criticism; they recognise challenges as part of the human experience, fostering shared humanity, and approach their emotions mindfully and without judgement for a balanced perspective. Practising self-compassion reduces anxiety, depression and other forms of stress and mental health problems, and enhances, enhancing emotional resilience and psychological well-being. Exercises include Self-Compassion Break (taking a moment to acknowledge personal suffering, recognising common humanity and offering oneself words of kindness and support), loving-kindness meditation (directing compassionate and loving thoughts towards oneself/others, fostering a sense of interconnectedness and warmth) and writing a compassionate letter to oneself (acknowledging personal struggles and offering words of understanding and encouragement can help cultivate self-compassion).

Self-Esteem: Based on realistic self-evaluation by the Adult and nurturing by the Nurturing Parent, self-esteem is an individual's evaluation of their worth and abilities (Orth, 2018). High self-esteem is linked to resilience, positive mood and fulfilment, while low self-esteem is associated with anxiety, depression and low motivation. Practical examples of self-esteem can be observed in individuals who confidently pursue their goals, assert their needs and maintain a positive self-image despite challenges. Exercises such as positive self-affirmations, setting achievable goals and practising self-compassion can improve self-esteem.

Taking Responsibility for Oneself: This involves acknowledging one's role in shaping life circumstances, fostering a proactive and empowered mindset (Vos, 2023a). It leads to greater autonomy, self-motivation and control over life, reducing helplessness and improving resilience. Practical examples include owning mistakes, seeking solutions and making deliberate choices aligned with personal values. Exercises include reflective journaling, setting and achieving goals and practising assertive communication. Note that taking-responsibility ideally goes hand-in-hand with self-compassion (this may be described as a 'dual-attitude': Vos, 2015), based on the ability to accept the things they cannot change, courage to change the things they can, and the wisdom to know the difference.

SOCIAL FUNCTIONING: 'YOU'RE OK'

Research suggests that the life position of 'You're OK' is associated with several concepts regarding social functioning that have shown to reduce levels of stress and psychopathology and increase well-being and behaviour (Vos & van Rijn, 2021c). Social functioning correlates with strong Adult and weak Adaptive Child and Critical Parent modes (Vos & van Rijn, 2021b).

Positive transactions and strokes: Chapter 8 will further explain that this regards positive transactions between people (Berne, 1964). Some studies differentiated between complementary and crossed transactions and between nonverbal/implicit messages and verbal/explicit messages (Booth & Booth, 2018; Lovejoy, 1991; Patel & Smith, 2022; Shustov, 2016; Tanaka et al., 2021). Examples of positive transactions and positive strokes include expressing genuine appreciation, offering support and encouragement, active listening and engaging in collaborative problem-solving. Exercises involve practising active/reflective listening (e.g. paraphrasing and reflecting what the other said to demonstrate understanding and empathy), positive communication (e.g. using 'I' statements to express thoughts and feelings openly and assertively), assertiveness training and role-playing scenarios to practice positive transactions and communication skills. Therapy sessions with a higher proportion of complementary Adult-Adult transactions showed better therapeutic outcomes (Johnson et al., 2018).

Trust: This regards the willingness to be vulnerable and rely on the integrity and competence of individuals. This may involve a state of Free/Adapted Child; ideally, a trusting individual feels free and safe enough to engage in any ego-state in the presence of another and have positive transactions. Trust improves mental health, well-being, security, connections and emotional stability. Practical examples of trust in others include confiding in a friend, seeking support during challenging times and collaborating with colleagues towards a common goal. Exercises to improve trust in others may involve practising active listening, team-building activities and participating in group therapy.

Capable of intimate and partner relationships: Similarly to trust, intimate relationships encompass deep emotional connections and mutual support between individuals, such as good friends or a couple. They profoundly impact mental health and well-being, contributing to feelings of security, fulfilment and emotional resilience. Practical examples of intimate relationships include open and honest communication, shared experiences that foster understanding and empathy and mutual support during challenging times. Exercises to improve intimate relationships may involve couples therapy to enhance communication and conflict resolution skills, practising active listening and empathy-building exercises and engaging in activities that cultivate emotional intimacy and trust.

Preventing and breaking social isolation: Social isolation means being disconnected from meaningful social interactions and relationships, such as prolonged physical separation from friends, family or community and a lack of emotional support and social engagement (Wang et al., 2017). Isolation profoundly impacts mental health and well-being. Isolation may stem from geographical distance, life transitions like retirement or relocation, the loss of loved ones, disabilities, chronic illnesses, stigma, discrimination, economic hardships, personality traits (e.g. shyness, introversion), defence mechanisms, workaholism, past negative experiences and superficial relationships due to mobile-phone/social-media-addiction. TA therapists may analyse whether the client has any transactional patterns that may inhibit social relationships and unresolved transactional core messages. Exercises may involve gradually increasing social interactions through small group activities, volunteering or joining interest-based clubs or organisations. Practising mindfulness and self-compassion can help alleviate the adverse effects of social isolation by fostering a sense of inner connectedness and emotional resilience (Chung, 2018; Shustov et al., 2016).

Authenticity: This regards genuinely expressing one's thoughts, feelings and values in various social contexts (Goldman et al., 2005; Schlegel et al., 2009; Vos, 2017). This may involve an awareness of one's ulterior motivations in transactions, self-insight in one's life script and the freedom to decide one's positions, states and responses instead of being bound to one's past. Embracing authenticity is linked to improved mental health and well-being, inner congruence, self-acceptance and reduced psychopathology. Practical examples of authenticity include speaking honestly about one's emotions, asserting personal boundaries and aligning with one's core values, leading to more fulfiling and meaningful relationships. Exercises may involve journaling to explore and articulate personal beliefs and emotions, engaging in mindfulness practices to cultivate self-awareness and seeking feedback from trusted individuals to gain insight into genuine self-expression.

Congruence and unconditional positive self-regard: Congruence is a person-centred construct, referring to the alignment between inner experiences and outward expressions, fostering authenticity and self-awareness (Kolden et al., 2018). Similarly to authenticity, this requires self-insight and freedom to consciously determine one's responses and decisions. Unconditional positive self-regard involves accepting oneself without conditions, promoting self-compassion and self-worth. Both concepts positively impact mental health and well-being by reducing internal conflict, enhancing self-acceptance, and emotional resilience. Examples include expressing genuine emotions without fear of judgement, setting healthy boundaries based on self-respect and embracing personal strengths and imperfections with kindness. Exercises may involve self-reflection to identify and acknowledge genuine emotions, practising self-compassion exercises such as positive affirmations and mindfulness and seeking therapy or counselling to explore and navigate inner conflicts and self-acceptance.

- Which aspects of self-efficacy and social functioning do you experience for yourself? Which aspects do you find challenging? Which could you improve? What steps do you need to take towards improvement? How could personal therapy help your improvement?
- Answer the same questions for a client or person you know well.

PSYCHOPATHOLOGY

Across clinical trials (Vos & van Rijn, 2022, 2024a, 2024b, 2024c) TA has large to very-large effects (pre-post therapy effects and differences between TA and control groups) on psychopathology, such as reducing the level of depression, anxiety and general distress.

GENERAL WELL-BEING AND QUALITY OF LIFE

Several clinical trials on TA used general quality-of-life outcome measures, like the formal WHO-Quality-of-Life questionnaire (Vos & van Rijn, 2024a, 2024b, 2024c). Researchers often compare measuring the quality of life with measuring the quality of wine, which only a person can say about themselves and may include multiple flavours and smells. TA studies have shown that clients rate the quality of their lives better after receiving TA therapy. Although these are aggregate measures, they include multiple life domains such as physical and psychological health, social relationships and environment. These findings show that the client's overall quality of life improves with large effects. These findings should convince policy-makers to often look at how a therapeutic approach may improve a client's quality-of-adjusted life years. Furthermore, policy-makers look at the cost-effectiveness of our feasibility/pilot studies. Pilot studies have confirmed large improvements in health-related costs, such as more productivity, less frequent absence from work and less use of health services, with equivalent cost-effectiveness as CBT (unpublished findings).

SELF-REALISATION

The eternal problem of the human being is how to structure his waking hours.
(Berne, 1964, p. 63)

In our feasibility and pilot studies (Vos & van Rijn, 2024a, 2024b, 2024c), we confirmed that clients improve on a range of outcomes that are often described as existential well-being, which includes improvements in the domains of autonomy, personal growth, positive relationships, purpose in life and self-acceptance. In line with other humanistic therapies and some of Berne's original therapy goals, we describe these findings as improving their 'self-realisation'. In TA-terms, individuals structure their time meaningfully and fulfilling.

Note the overlap with the before-mentioned improvements in self-efficacy and social functioning.

Self-realisation refers to becoming aware of and understanding one's true self, including one's abilities, potential and innermost desires. It involves a deep understanding of one's emotions, motivations and values and the ability to express and fulfil one's authentic self. Examples of self-realisation can vary widely and are deeply personal to each individual. It could involve someone recognising their passion for a particular career path and pursuing it wholeheartedly, leading to a sense of fulfilment and purpose. Another example could be an individual realising the need to set boundaries in relationships and assert their needs, leading to healthier and more authentic connections with others. Self-realisation equips individuals to make choices that align with their values and bring them a sense of fulfilment. This, in turn, can lead to reduced stress, improved self-esteem and a greater understanding of control over one's life. Self-realisation also fosters resilience and adaptability, allowing individuals to navigate life's challenges with a more vital self-awareness and purpose.

BEHAVIOUR

As described above, TA clients improve their social functioning and behaviour by analysing transactions and changing the underlying problems that may arise from their life script. Studies in schools and prisons suggest TA may be beneficial in improving behaviour (Vos & van Rijn, 2023).

INSIGHT INTO THE PAST

When we interviewed clients in our clinical trials, they said that developing insight into the causes of their problems and lifescript (see Chapter 5) was one of the most important and helpful outcomes of TA, as they better understand how their present problems are linked to their past (Vos & van Rijn, 2024a, 2024b, 2024c).

━━━━━━━ 6.2 REFLECTIVE QUESTIONS ━━━━━━━

- Reflect on therapy or counselling you may have had yourself. Which outcomes have you observed? What did you hope to achieve but did not achieve; why could you not achieve this, and what would be more realistic aims/outcomes?
- Answer the same questions for a client/person you know well.

> **Case Study 6.1**
>
> ## Rosie
>
> Meet client Rosie, a 47-year administrative assistant who reported feeling inadequate and difficulty forming meaningful connections. In TA, she explored her communication and interpersonal dynamics patterns, gaining insight into her behaviours and

beginning to recognise the underlying beliefs and emotions driving her interactions with others. This newfound self-awareness allowed Rosie to make conscious choices to express her needs and set relational boundaries. Over time, she experienced a profound improvement in her sense of self-worth. She developed more authentic connections with those around her. Rosie journey exemplifies how TA therapy can facilitate the process of self-realisation, leading to significant improvements in mental well-being.

SELF-DETERMINED CLIENT GOALS

Therapy Contracts

Following his aim to offer a cure and his collaborative, relational approach, Berne used therapy contracts. A contract manages the client's expectations, offers transparency, accountability, a sense of direction, engaging and empowering clients to take personal responsibility for their experiences and progress in therapy (Hargaden & Sills, 2002). A contract also makes the transactions in the therapeutic relationship transparent, which may facilitate the client to develop insight into their transactional processes. Research shows that contracts can enhance the client's sense of autonomy, accountability, responsibility, security, and respect, align goals between therapist and client, and set realistic goals (Bennett, 1999; Hargaden & Sills, 2002), and improve outcomes (Vos & van Rijn, 2023). Most TA therapists do not work with written and formal contracts but with verbal and informal contracts (Vos & van Rijn, 2021c), which may include the following:

Therapy goals: specific goals/objectives the client and therapist aim to achieve during therapy (see below);

Roles and responsibilities: e.g. client commitment to attend sessions, engage in therapeutic exercises, open/honest communication;

Boundaries: e.g. confidentiality, limits of the therapeutic relationship, professional ethical standards;

Organisational details: e.g. duration and frequency of sessions, how to make, cancel and pay for appointments.

Evaluation: provisions for regular feedback and evaluation of progress, allowing clients and therapists to assess effectiveness/progress and, if needed, make necessary adjustments.

Client Therapy Goals

Most TA therapists encourage clients to set their own therapy goals. Research indicates that when clients have a say in defining their goals, they are more likely to be personally invested in the therapy-process, leading to increased motivation, commitment, autonomy and a better therapist-client working alliance, trust and rapport (Swift et al., 2018). Therapists have used many tools to guide goal-setting, such as goal-setting exercises, mindfulness exercises, visualising outcomes, values clarification and finding goals that fit their overall life narratives about past, present and future. The most common tool is self-assessment worksheets, such as the Therapy goal Attainment Form which can be found in this book's appendix. Based on a review of the research literature, Vos (2018) concluded therapy goals should be:

- important;
- specific and simple;
- not too far in the future;
- challenging;
- attainable;
- mutually conducive in the case of multiple goals;
- focused towards something positive ('approach') rather than negative ('avoidance').

Research highlights the significance of a collaborative process between therapist and client during goal-setting (Cantwell, 2018). Many clients find it difficult to set clear and attainable goals, for various reasons that a therapist may address:

> *Lack of knowledge about how therapy works and what is possible:* The therapist may educate the client, for example, by sharing findings from this chapter. Some clients may benefit from a temporary more directive approach, by the therapist suggesting some therapy goals/aims, as may help clients to comprehend what is realistically achievable; it is crucial, however, for therapists to refrain from imposing ideas onto clients.

> *Resistance against confrontation with difficult or uncomfortable aspects of their lives:* The therapist may show empathy, foster safety and explain how short-term unease may be followed by long-term improvement.

> *Resistance to change:* Clients may be stuck with life script messages, such as 'Don't change' or 'Stay sick'. The therapist may want to explore such messages and work with resistance (Chapter 9).

> *Inauthenticity:* A client may have a strong Adapted Child hindering them to align their goals with their true selves. Therapists should be sensitive to the authenticity of the clients goals/aims, and possible pleasing behaviour. During therapy, the client may develop more insight in their genuine wishes, which may be used to adjust the therapy goals/aims. The therapy may want to role-model via their authentic/congruent communication, like person-centred therapists argue that the therapist's self-congruence and congruence in the therapeutic relationship may foster clients to be more congruent.

> *Cultural/religious norms and values:* Therapists should exhibit cultural sensitivity and awareness of the client's cultural/religious norms and values. For instance, Western cultures may emphasise individual growth and autonomy.

Reviewing Goals

Regular updates on therapy goals ensure that the therapy is still going in the right direction, track progress, identify any necessary adjustments and celebrate achievements (Cantwell,

2018; Lindhiem, 2016). This can increase the clients' sense of accountability, motivation and engagement. Clients can also reflect on their evolving needs and aspirations, ensuring the therapy goals align with their personal growth and well-being. Regular goal updates also allow open communication between the client and therapist, strengthening the collaborative relationship and fostering a more profound sense of trust and support. The following are some tips for goal review sessions:

Reflective Discussions: Encourage clients to reflect on their progress since the last goal update. Ask open-ended questions prompting to explore experiences, challenges and achievements.

Goal Reassessment: Reassess goals and their relevance to the client's evolving needs and aspirations. Discuss changes in the client's circumstances or priorities that may require adjustments to the goals.

Co-Creation of New Objectives: Collaborate to co-create new or revised therapy goals based on their current insights and aspirations. This empowers the client to take an active role in shaping the therapeutic journey.

Action Planning: Work together to develop actionable steps and strategies aligning with the updated goals. Encourage the client to express their ideas and preferences.

Celebrating Progress: Acknowledge and celebrate the client's achievements and milestones, however small. Recognising progress fosters a sense of self-efficacy, hope and motivation.

Feedback Integration: Encourage clients to provide feedback on the therapy process and relationship, which can inform future updates and enhance the relationship.

TA Goal Attainment Form

The TA Goal Attainment Form (TAGAF) can be found in this book's appendix (Vos & van Rijn, 2024a). This is an adjusted version of the generic Goal Attainment Form, which helps clients formulate goals that focus on realistic outcomes in TA, as discussed in this chapter. The domains represent suggestions and tools for reflection, and clients do not need to formulate a goal for each domain. Therapists may want to help clients develop goals to ensure that the goals are important, specific, straightforward, not too far in the future, challenging, attainable, mutually conductive and positive. During goal review sessions or at the end of therapy, the client can rate on a 1-7 Likert scale to which extent they have achieved each goal. The TAGAF consists of the following goals to operationalise the evidence-based aims/outcomes outlined in this chapter:

Emotional goal: This regards reducing psychopathology and negative emotions, and improving positive emotions, such as depression, anxiety, grief, sleeping, happiness.

Goals about my self-beliefs. This regards self-efficacy and the life position of 'I'm OK'. This may include goals about accepting, affirming and expressing one's identity within a community, such as accepting and expressing one's sexual orientation or self-identified gender.

Social goals: This regards social functioning and the life position of 'You're OK', as well as improving social behaviour. This may include goals to foster social-justice, such as (re)connecting with a community, joining social causes (Herman, 2023) or stopping vicious cycles of social injustice (Vos, 2025).

Living in the present: This regards developing insight into how messages from their past/lifescript may influence their present and make the decision to change these messages, thus loosening the elastic band that binds the client to their past. This may also include an increased understanding of their ego-states, strengthening their Adult, Nurturing Parent and Free Child and reducing their Critical Parent and Adapted Child or Rebellious Child.

Life-goal: This goal regards improving their general well-being, quality-of-life and self-realisation, such as developing more energy and flow, learning how to set and achieve goals in life, be more spontaneous, make conscious life decisions and living a meaningful and satisfying life despite life's challenges and limitations.

Any other goal.

Case Study 6.2

Leo

Leo formulated several therapy goals in the TAGAF form. His emotional goal was to alleviate excessive worry and attain faster sleep. He sought to enhance his self-beliefs by cultivating self-compassion. Socially, he desired to feel more comfortable in the presence of others and reduce his tendency to be overly self-critical. He wanted to cultivate present-moment awareness by understanding the underlying factors contributing to his strong Adapted Child and Critical Parent dynamics. Additionally, he aimed to break the automatic pattern of assuming the role of an Adapted Child when faced with a Critical Parent in a transaction while diminishing his Critical Parent's influence. By accomplishing these objectives, the client anticipated experiencing an overall improvement in his life and boost energy levels.

SUMMARY

- Research shows that TA can improve ego-states, self-efficacy ('I'm OK'), social functioning ('You're OK'), psychopathology, general well-being, quality-of-life, self-realisation, behaviour, insight into the past and self-determined client goals.
- TA therapy seems best suited to clients who are willing and able to change, face emotional pain, not be merely a passive recipient of help, contain feelings, have basic Adult ego-state functioning (e.g. no active psychosis, psychoactive substances, or severe cognitive disabilities) and are motivated, committed, with positive, realistic and not-overly perfectionistic expectations, with sufficiently secure attachment to trust and

confide in their therapist, and have sufficient daily-life psychological and social support to create change, and attend all sessions.

- The therapy process may be facilitated by having an explicit or implicit therapy contract.
- Clients benefit from setting and regularly re-assessing their own therapy goals that are important, specific, simple, not too far in the future, challenging, attainable, mutually conducive and focused towards something positive.

7

THERAPEUTIC MECHANISMS: HOW CAN THERAPISTS HELP CLIENTS?

This chapter describes the therapeutic mechanisms of change in therapy. Therapeutic mechanisms provide insights into the factors that drive change, encompassing all processes, events and reasons behind therapy outcomes (Kazdin, 2022; Vos, 2023). We will examine the various stages in the therapy process and how they shape client outcomes (cf., Castonguay & Beutler, 2005). This includes the following:

- General mechanisms of therapeutic change
- TA mechanisms of change
- Overview of evidence-based TA therapeutic competencies (detailed in Part III).

GENERAL THEORIES OF THERAPEUTIC CHANGE

Why do clients change in therapy? What mechanisms make therapy work (Vos, 2023)?

Overall therapy effects: Most bona fide therapies have similar effects for most clients (Cuijpers et al., 2008; Luborsky et al., 2002; Wampold et al., 1997; Wampold & Imel, 2015); TA seems similarly effective (Vos & van Rijn, 2021a, 2021c). This does not mean any therapy can be applied to every client; therapies must be tailored to individual needs (Chambless & Ollendick, 2001).

Specific factors: The healing mechanism in therapy may lie in specific interventions rather than the overall approach. Research highlights several effective factors. Evidence-based CBT techniques include exposure, systematic desensitisation, paradoxical intention, activity scheduling and cognitive techniques like reframing. Humanistic interventions involve sensitive interpretations, non-directivity, emotional processing, chair dialogs, focusing and mindfulness (Goldberg et al., 2018). Other effective techniques include therapeutic agreements, active listening, paraphrasing, encouragement, questioning, advice, sensitive touch, homework assignments, feedback and systematic treatment manuals. Studies also examine the impact of defence mechanisms on therapy outcomes. Clients benefit from systematic assessment and case formulation sharing (van Rijn, 2014). This book includes various specific therapeutic factors, such as systematic assessment, case formulation sharing, humanistic-relational skills and semi-structured manuals.

Common factors: As many therapeutic approaches, like TA, have integrated many similar interventions, many researchers have focused on non-specific factors common to all therapies, such as offering a supportive therapeutic relationship and instilling positive expectations and hope (Ahn & Wampold, 2001; Wampold & Imel, 2015). The common factor that has received the most attention from researchers is the therapeutic relationship, such as offering a positive working alliance, genuine relationship and empathy (this will be exemplified and detailed in Chapter 9).

Process-related factors: Process-related concepts regard how clients and therapists experience change processes in therapy, often studied via interviews (Vos, 2023). Therefore, we have also conducted client-change helpfulness interviews in our TA trials, as we will explain below, and we have integrated the findings into this book and treatment manual (Vos & van Rijn, 2024b). Other examples of process research include the Transtheoretical Model of Behaviour Change (Krebs et al., 2018; Prochaska & Norcross, 2001), which says that clients may go through 'stages of change: pre-contemplation (not recognising the problem), contemplation (recognising the problem but unsure about change), preparation/ determination (preparing to change), action/willpower (changing) and maintaining the changes' (Vos, 2023, p. 39). We have integrated these insights into the chapter on TA therapist structuring skills to help clients move through these stages.

TA MECHANISMS OF CHANGE

In our survey, the TA therapists identified the following mechanisms of change: 'remove obstruction to natural growth; rise above circumstances, history, drives, and impulses; learn to live in the moment; develop self-insight; resolve structural conflicts; have a positive corrective experience; feel validated in their experiences; develop greater movement between ego-states; learn to risk intimacy; learn from mistakes; learn to fulfil their potential; grieve for losses; forgive; and remember but not repeat the past' (Vos & van Rijn, 2021b). Statistical analyses reduced these answers to three main mechanisms of change:

> *Improve ego-states:* e.g., develop self-insight and freedom/flexibility between
> ego-states, rise above the past by developing a stronger Adult;
> *Improved social functioning:* e.g., daring to take social risks in the present;
> *Improved self-efficacy:* e.g., trusting one's experiences, self-insight, sense of freedom,
> and control. (Vos & van Rijn, 2021c)

Predictors of outcomes. To confirm the self-reported therapeutic mechanisms, we analysed the mechanisms underlying the outcomes of forty-one TA trials (Vos & van Rijn, 2023). We discovered that TA therapies were more effective if they focused on the following:

- Constructive therapist-client relationship;
- Experiencing in the here-and-now;
- Assessment case formulation;
- Clear therapy stages;
- Psycho-education/didactics;
- Life script analysis;
- Analysis of injunctions, drivers and counterinjunctions;
- Therapeutic contract and goals.

Researchers do not only want to know that therapy has good outcomes but also that the outcomes can be explained by the unique therapeutic mechanisms promised by the therapeutic model (Kazdin, 2022; Vos, 2023). In TA trials, the clients' improvements in their level of psychopathology and well-being could be explained by specific TA therapeutic mechanisms as elaborated in the following chapters:

- *Improved ego-states:* e.g. more Adult, Nurturing Parent and Free Child, and less Critical Parent and Adapted Child
- *Improved social functioning*: e.g. 'You're OK'
- *Improved self-efficacy*: e.g. 'I'm OK'
- *Positive therapeutic relationship.*

Further validation: A fundamental issue in TA clinical trials was the lack of treatment manuals systematically applying evidence-based concepts. Based on our studies on the empirical evidence of TA, we developed and tested a 16-session treatment manual for depressed clients (Vos & van Rijn, 2024a). In our feasibility study with nine clients, process-oriented interviews revealed improvements in self-insight, coping strategies, self-confidence and boundaries. Although the sample was small, we observed positive outcomes in psychopathology, ego-states, self-efficacy and social functioning, with no negative side effects. Therapists also reported improved competence in TA therapeutic skills (Vos & van Rijn, 2024b). We then conducted a randomized clinical trial comparing 28 TA clients with 10 CBT clients and 28 clients receiving care as usual (relational-humanistic therapies). Clients reported significant improvements in depression, anxiety, distress and quality of life, similar to CBT but greater than care as usual, likely due to the structured training and treatment manuals in TA and CBT (Vos & van Rijn, 2024c). Improvements in TA-specific skills and therapist competencies predicted outcomes. In conclusion, our studies confirm TA's positive outcomes, demonstrating its efficacy in improving ego-states, life positions, self-efficacy, social functioning, psychopathology and general well-being via TA therapist therapeutic mechanisms (Vos & van Rijn, 2024b; 2024c).

OVERVIEW OF EVIDENCE-BASED TA PSYCHOTHERAPEUTIC COMPETENCIES

In 2006, the APA called for competency standards in psychology to ensure proficiency at all training and practice levels. These standards guide trainers and supervisors in assessing trainee progress and ensuring high-quality care. Beutler identified five universal therapeutic competencies, confirmed by other researchers (Norcross & Karpiak, 2017): fostering a constructive therapeutic connection, understanding therapeutic change mechanisms, applying effective techniques, considering temporal demands in interventions and demonstrating adaptability and creativity. Additionally, specific competency frameworks have been developed for various therapeutic approaches (Vos, 2023). In our survey and subsequent research studies (Vos & van Rijn, 2021a, 2021b, 2021c, 2021d), we have identified four groups of evidence-based TA therapeutic competencies, which the book's next Part will further explain:

- Assessment Competencies (Chapter 8)
- Relational Competencies (Chapter 9)
- Structuring Competencies (Chapter 10)
- Experiential Competencies (Chapter 11)
- Integrative-therapeutic Competencies (Chapter 12)

SUMMARY

- TA therapy integrates specific interventions and common factors identified as effective across bona fide therapeutic approaches, such as therapeutic-relational competencies.
- TA improves clients' mental health and well-being by enhancing their ego-states, life position, self-efficacy and social functioning.
- TA is more effective if it focuses on the therapeutic relationship, experiences in the present, assessment, case formulation, clear therapy stages, psycho-education/didactics, present, analysis of life script, injunctions, drivers and counterinjunctions, and includes a therapeutic contract or therapy goals.
- TA therapists are more effective if they are proficient in their assessment, relational, structuring and experiential competencies.

PART III
EVIDENCE-BASED TA PSYCHOTHERAPEUTIC COMPETENCIES

8
ASSESSMENT COMPETENCIES

How to conduct a systematic assessment, use questionnaires and develop a case formulation? As this chapter will show, therapists primarily aim to assess the client's clinical concerns (Chapter 4) and the aetiology underlying these concerns (Chapter 5) to help the client achieve their therapy goals/outcomes (see Chapter 6). In this clinical and aetiological assessment, the therapist may use various techniques, as this chapter explains after a generic overview of psychotherapy research on assessment and case formulations:

- TA assessment
- Primary assessment
  - Ego-states and life positions (self-efficacy and social functioning)
  - Life scripts
- Secondary assessment
  - Transactions
  - Games
  - Drama triangle
  - Winner's triangle
  - Script-systems (rackets)
  - Stroke profiles
  - Time structure
- Assessment tools
  - Interview schedules
  - Questionnaires
- Evidence-based TA case formulation

OVERVIEW OF PSYCHOTHERAPY ASSESSMENT AND CASE FORMULATIONS

Assessment in psychotherapy involves systematically gathering and evaluating information about a client's psychological, emotional and behavioural functioning. Case formulation synthesises this information to understand the client's difficulties, guiding therapy planning and implementation. Treatments are more effective when based on systematic assessment and case formulation (Kendjelic & Eells, 2007; Page et al., 2008). Benefits include (van Rijn, 2014):

Understanding the Client: Gaining insight into a client's unique experiences, strengths, and challenges for tailored treatment

Tailored Treatment Planning: Developing individualised plans addressing root causes of distress.

Targeting Interventions: Selecting effective interventions for client's specific difficulties

Collaboration and Empowerment: Fostering a collaborative relationship and empowering clients in their treatment

Monitoring Progress: Allowing therapists to track progress and adjust plans as needed

Ethical, Professional Practice: Ensuring interventions are evidence-based and relevant to the client's needs.

Thus, assessment and case formulation are crucial for effective, client-centred therapy, providing a solid foundation for understanding, planning and implementing the therapy-process. While we support a structured evaluation and case formulation, these should develop as collaborative and evolving ideas between therapist and client, rather than fixed diagnostic labels. This typically includes several key steps:

Information Gathering: The therapist collects relevant information about the client's issues, history, relationships and current circumstances through interviews, assessments and records review.

Hypothesis Generation: Based on the information, the therapist develops hypotheses about the client's difficulties, considering factors like past experiences, cognitive patterns and interpersonal dynamics.

Integrating Perspectives: The therapist uses various theoretical frameworks to understand the client's difficulties from multiple angles.

Identifying Themes and Patterns: The therapist identifies recurring themes in the client's thoughts, emotions, behaviours and relationships to understand their contribution to the client's distress.

Developing a Conceptualisation: The therapist creates a conceptualisation of the client's difficulties, serving as a roadmap for understanding the underlying mechanisms of distress.

Establishing Therapy goals: The therapist collaborates with the client to set specific treatment goals based on the case formulation.

Monitoring Progress: The therapist monitors the client's progress and reviews therapy goals, using new information to refine the assessment and treatment plan.

A good case formulation is as clear and brief as possible, holistic, precise and empirically testable (Dawson & Moghaddam, 2015). But several challenges can arise:

Bias: Assessment and case formulation can be biased due to cultural misunderstandings or lack of competence in diversity. Therapists may misinterpret client behaviours through their own cultural lens. Cultural competence training, self-reflection and supervision with culturally competent colleagues are recommended (Tao et al., 2015; Jeffrey & Fish, 2011; Rea, 2001). They should also consider institutional discrimination and seek supervision from culturally competent colleagues. Therapists may want to get additional training and supervision to offer therapy that affirms and validates the experiences of LGBTQ+ clients, such as asking the pronoun that clients want to be known by.

Ignoring Social Context: It is crucial not to pathologise behaviours without considering social context. Behaviours may be normal responses to abnormal circumstances It is crucial not to pathologise behaviours without considering social context. Acknowledging biological and neurological facets of behaviours, like addiction, is important. Therapists should include societal structural analysis in assessments and explore the impact of gender, ethnicity, sexual orientation, stigma and discrimination on mental health (Barnes, 2004; Rowland & Cornell, 2021; Shadbolt, 2004).

Limited Information: Incomplete client information can hinder case formulation. Systematic assessment tools can help gather comprehensive data.

Multiple Presenting Issues: Clients often have complex, overlapping issues. Therapists should prioritise therapy goals, use various interventions and understand underlying life scripts to address multiple problems effectively.

Complexity of Neurodiversity: Assessing neurodiverse clients (e.g. autism, ADHD) requires understanding diverse cognitive and sensory processing styles. Therapists should seek additional training and adapt assessment methods accordingly.

Integrating Non-Verbal Communication: Effective assessment includes paying attention to non-verbal cues and ulterior goals, which can improve treatment outcomes.

Overreliance on Intuition: While clinical intuition can be helpful, overreliance can introduce bias. Therapists should use semi-standardized assessment tools and questionnaires to mitigate this risk.

8.1 REFLECTIVE QUESTIONS

- Which clients do you find challenging to work with? Are there any clients you would not accept? What does this say about your competencies, and how could you improve these to become more inclusive?
- How have issues of social injustice impacted your life script? How do your personal and professional experiences with social injustice influence how you work with clients who have been victims of social injustice; what are your strengths, blind spots and opportunities for improvement?
- Consider a client or person whose life-story you know well; how have their diverse characteristics and experiences of social-justice/injustice influenced their life script, their present dominant ego-states, life position and outcomes on mental, physical and social well-being?
- If you have done assessments before. What are your strengths? What are your weaknesses? Which mistakes have you made? How can you improve assessment competencies?

OVERVIEW OF TA ASSESSMENTS

Although the term 'case formulation' is not commonly mentioned in TA literature, it involves a comprehensive evaluation of clinical and etiological aspects of treatment, similar to TA's focus on assessment and diagnosis. This includes examining ego-states, life position, social functioning, self-efficacy and underlying causes. TA therapists, including Berne, conduct systematic assessments to guide therapeutic treatment (van Rijn, 2014; Vos et al., 2019). The goal is to develop a customised treatment plan and monitor progress, adjusting goals or methods as needed (van Rijn, 2014). In our survey, TA therapists reported assessing: the client's relational needs, transference, countertransference, stroking, drama triangle, clinical intuition, historical inquiry, phenomenological inquiry, analysis of ego-state contamination, verbal/non-verbal communication, script, script-system, sociobehavioural diagnosis of ego-states, unmet archaic needs, coping with disruptions in the past, unconscious stories, reenactments of childhood scripts, life position, modes of passivity and time structure (Vos & van Rijn, 2021c). Statistical analyses reduced these answers to the following categories; as the next sections will detail, we recommend TA assessment/case formulation include these:

> *Analysis of current ego-states and their historical development:* e.g. 'I'm OK', injunctions, drivers;
> *Analysis of social functioning and its historical development:* e.g. 'You're OK', transactions, permissions, stroking, time structure, modes of passivity, archaic relational needs in the here-and-now, including in the therapeutic relationship;
> *Analysis of self-efficacy and its historical development:* e.g. inauthenticity, script feelings and behaviour, reported fantasies, self-perpetuating experiences;
> *Analysis of the unspoken:* e.g. body language, phenomenological analysis, clinical intuition.

PRIMARY ASSESSMENT

Structural Analysis

Structural analysis examines the structures underlying the ego-states and their interactions within an individual, focusing on how these states influence thoughts, feelings and behaviours. TA therapists analyse the structural makeup of ego-states to provide insight into internal dynamics, communication patterns and psychological well-being. According to Chapter 4, therapists should examine the presence, frequency and intensity of the Nurturing Parent, Critical Parent, Adult, Adapted Child and Free Child ego-states, as well as the client's ability to shift between them. Identifying dominant patterns may take several sessions, and therapists might develop unique structural models for each client (see Chapter 4).

Life Position Analysis

Chapter 6 explains how to assess the client's life positions and associated concepts of self-efficacy ('I'm OK') and social functioning ('You're OK').

Aetiological/Life Script Analysis

Chapter 5 details the influence of our client's life script and early-life on their presenting problems. The treatment manual in the book's final part offers practical examples.

SECONDARY ASSESSMENT
Transactional Analysis

TA focuses on examining interpersonal transactions through structural analysis of the individuals involved. For instance, 'games', are repeating sequences of transactions leading to a subconsciously agreed result. Individuals are never consistently in one ego-state and often embody multiple ego-states simultaneously. Mentally healthy individuals can flexibly transition between ego-states, primarily spending time in the Adult and Nurturing Parent states, which are linked to well-being (Vos & van Rijn, 2021c). The dominant ego-state may be influenced by life situations or life scripts. If an individual predominantly occupies an unhelpful ego-state, seeking guidance from a TA therapist is advisable. TA provides a framework for understanding and analysing the dynamics of ego-states in interactions and relationships. For example, a TA therapist may analyse the dominant ego-states a client embodies in therapy sessions or their everyday stories.

Identifying Ego-States: TA helps clients identify their own and others' ego-states, providing insight into behavioural patterns (Vos & van Rijn, 2021c).

Analysing Interactions: Clients can observe and analyse transactions to understand how ego-states influence communication and outcomes (De Roten et al., 1999; Pally, 2001).

Recognising Patterns: TA reveals recurring interaction patterns between specific ego-states, offering insights into relationship dynamics (Pinto et al., 2012; Sherer & Rogers, 1980).

Improving Communication: Awareness of ego-states enables individuals to adapt their communication style, fostering more effective and harmonious interactions (Tepper & Haase, 1978).

In TA, a transaction refers to a unit of social interaction involving communication and recognition of ego-states. The following are different types of transactions:

Complementary Transaction: For example, a Critical Parent ego-state interacts with an Adapted Child ego-state where the Critical Parent provides support and the Adapted Child responds with compliance (Figure 8.1).

Crossed Transaction: For example, an Adult ego-state interacts with a Free Child ego-state where the Adult attempts to engage in rational discussion, but the Free Child responds with playful avoidance, asking for a Nurturing Parent to look after their needs (e.g. Adult: 'Have you finished the project today?' Free Child: I am really tired now') (Figure 8.2).

Ulterior Transaction: For example, an Adult ego-state interacts with another adult ego-state, where the overt communication is focused on discussing factual information (social-level transaction visualised with the unbroken line). However, the psychological (ulterior) motive is that his Adapted Child seeks validation from the other person's Nurturing Parent (psychological-level transaction with the broken-dotted line) (Figure 8.3).

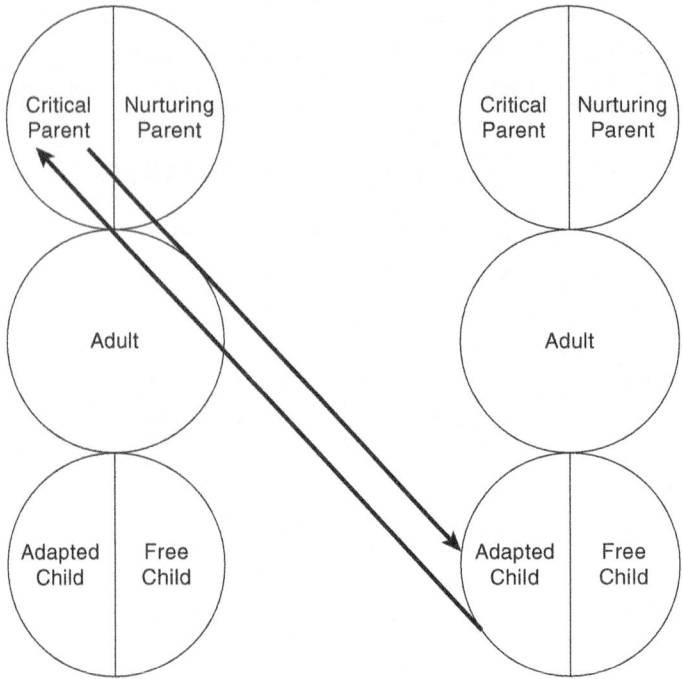

Figure 8.1 Complementary Transaction

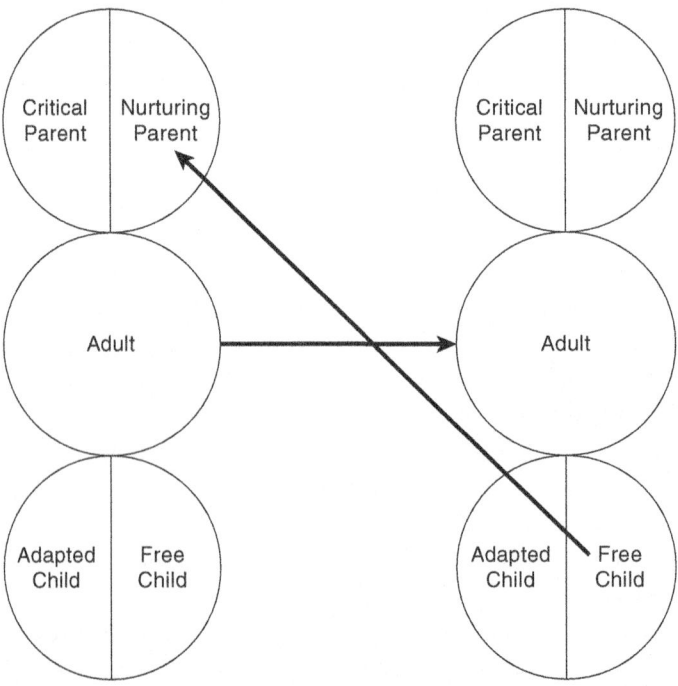

Figure 8.2 Crossed Transaction

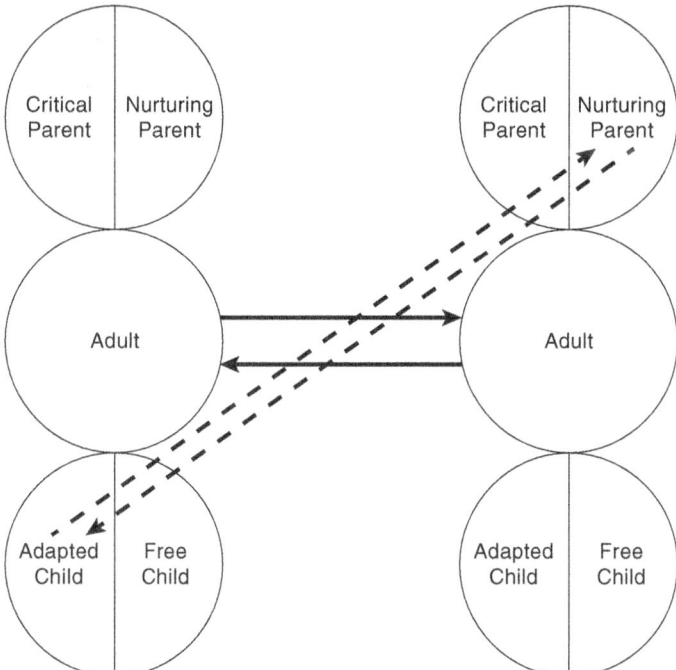

Figure 8.3 Ulterior Transaction

Duplex Transaction: For example, a Parent ego-state interacts with another Parent ego-state, where both parties engage in a mutual exchange of critical judgements on the social level of the transaction while nurturing behaviours on the psychological level. For example, these individuals could be making harsh jokes or criticisms of each other. Still, as they are good friends, they know their real underlying intention is to support each other (Figure 8.4).

In sum, by analysing the client's transactions, the therapist may become aware of their dominant ego-states and transaction responses. The therapist may want to make the client aware of this and help explore possible underlying aetiological causes of the inclination to respond with particular ego-states and decide to change their responses. A good example is the often highly effective bull's-eye intervention, whereby the therapist gives feedback to all ego-states of the client to do full justice to all their sides; for example, the therapist could say, 'I hear that your Free Child wants to leave the therapy room, but I also hear how your Adapted Child wants to conform to the social expectations of sitting out a session. I can also see your inner Adult, who sees the potential rational benefits of therapy. Your Critical Parent seems highly critical of me, like he has been critical of all authorities in your life, starting with your parents against whom you rebelled. I can also see your Nurturing Parent who wants to look after you, as this session seems to trigger many emotions. You may want some time to process what we have covered today'. The bull's eye transaction may create a supportive environment in which the client may feel validated in their complexities and free to explore various ego-states (Figure 8.5).

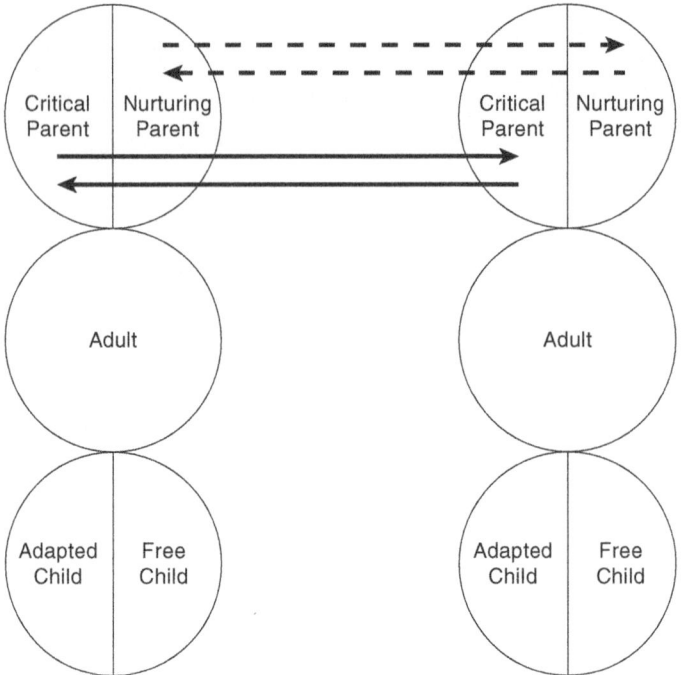

Figure 8.4 Duplex Transaction

Case Study 8.1

John

Fifty-year-old mechanic John seeks therapy with a TA therapist due to recurring conflicts in his personal and professional relationships. He often feels misunderstood and struggles to assert himself effectively. The therapist observes and analyses John's transactions, uncovering patterns in his Parent, Adult and Child ego-states. John defaults to critical and controlling behaviours from his Parent ego-state, leading to power struggles, and exhibits emotional reactivity from his Child ego-state, resulting in impulsive or withdrawn responses. The therapist collaborates with John to explore these patterns and their underlying dynamics, setting goals to enhance his awareness and develop more adaptive behaviours. Through exercises, role-playing and reflective dialogue, John gains insight into his motivations and transactional patterns. They reframe his life script to promote assertive and empathetic communication. As therapy progresses, John becomes more adept at recognising and adjusting his behaviours, leading to improved interactions.

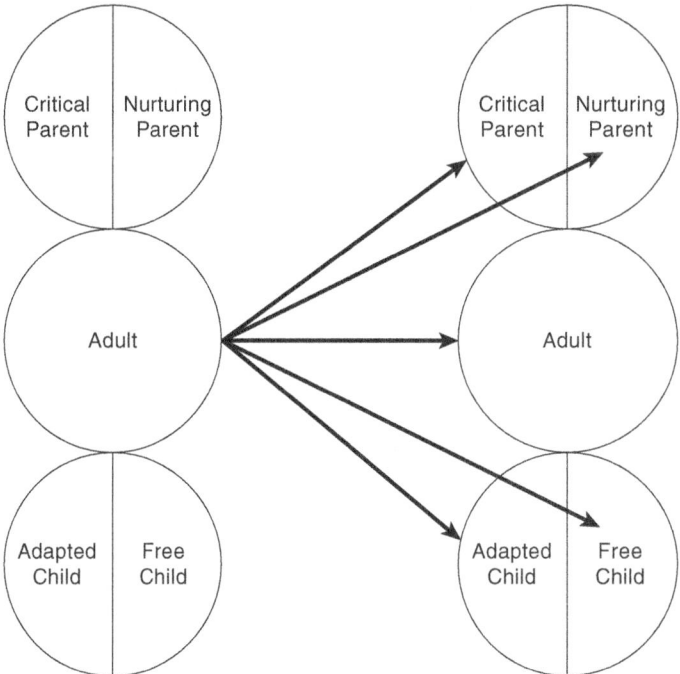

Figure 8.5 Bull's-Eye Intervention

━━━━━━━ **8.2 REFLECTIVE QUESTIONS** ━━━━━━━

- Recall a recent challenging interaction. Identify your ego-state and the other person's ego-state, and your transactions. Do you notice any repeating patterns? How did these patterns develop, and what role did you and others play? What steps can you take to change this transaction?
- Think of a client/person you know well. Do you have recurring interactions or games with them? How do these affect your social functioning, self-efficacy, mental-health/ psychopathological symptoms and well-being? Are these patterns linked to a dominant ego-state in you or the other person, and how did these develop? What steps can you both take to improve these interactions? How can you discuss these patterns sensitively?

Game Analysis

Games differ from procedures, rituals and pastimes by their hidden motives and dramatic outcomes. While procedures, rituals and pastimes are straightforward and may involve contests, games are fundamentally dishonest and lead to predictable, often negative outcomes (Berne, 1964). Whereas playfulness, freedom and creativity characterise a Free Child who is allowed to play by the Adult and supported by the Nurturing Parent, a game is restricted by rigid rules and roles and usually leads to predictable outcomes, which may be dominated by a Critical Parent or Adapted Child, and possibly a contaminated Adult; the boundary between play and game may be subtle and blurred, whereby some players may experience their transactions as play whereas others may see this as a game (it sometimes seems that the shadow-side of play are games, and vice versa).

Thus, games can be identified by their ulterior quality and psychological payoff. Games are bilateral and always involve at least two people (one of whom may be a therapist), and often involve manipulative communication and unproductive relational dynamics. People play games to fulfil their life scripts, confirming negative beliefs established in childhood. Game Analysis may help uncover repetitive, unconscious behaviour patterns. Understanding their games helps clients stop playing them, promoting genuine and fulfiling interactions. Berne originally identified several common games and their messages, such as:

> *Why Don't You–Yes, But:* A person presents a problem, and others offer solutions that are repeatedly rejected with excuses.
>
> *If It Weren't for You:* Blame others for their difficulties or shortcomings.
>
> *See What You Made Me Do:* Manipulation by provoking others to act in a certain way and then blaming them.
>
> *Why Does This Always Happen To Me?* Creating a self-fulfiling prophecy.
>
> *Uproar:* Creating chaos and drama to gain attention or control.
>
> *You Got Me Into This:* Blaming the other if a joint activity disappoints.
>
> *I'm Only Trying To Help You*: Shifting blame.
>
> *Now I've Got You, You Son of a Bitch:* Power struggles and manipulation to gain superiority or control.
>
> *Demi-God:* Act as if You're without blame, making others feel guilty about your goodness.
>
> *Kick me!* Do everything poorly to get told off.
>
> *Yes, but. . .:* Act as if you need help and then add, 'but. . .'

Although research on games is limited, and these generic labels seem to oversimplify often complex transactional processes, TA therapists find game analysis beneficial (Vos & van Rijn, 2021c). Rather than endeavouring to name this type of interaction, it may be more helpful to understand the underlying individual dynamics. Therapists may identify games by observing recurring communication, behavioural patterns, ego-states and underlying motives, fostering awareness and insight into their dynamics. The therapist and the client may also enact/re-enact a game together. Game analysis may include the following steps:

- *Building Therapeutic Rapport:* The therapist creates a safe, empathetic, non-judgemental environment where clients feel comfortable sharing personal thoughts and behaviours.
- *Identification of Games:* The therapist observes the client's interactions and asks insightful questions to identify internal and behavioural patterns.

- *Awareness of Games:* The therapist reflects with the client recognise games that develop in their therapeutic encounter, which requires trust, authenticity, empathy and openness.
- *Analysis of Games:* Although games are unconscious, developing awareness of the process and flow of a psychological game can lead to analysis and a changing pattern.
- *Identify triggers:* The therapist may help the client recognise triggers and emotional responses associated with games, leading to increased awareness and regulation of their behaviours.
- *Understanding the Origin:* By examining the client's life script and exploring the origins of their self-limiting behaviours, the client may reframe their games as an activity from the past that no longer applies, and develop more authentic and adaptive relational patterns.
- *Developing Alternatives:* The therapist and client work together to identify more beneficial patterns of interaction. Psychological games are usually driven by genuine emotional needs, and their recognition can lead to finding more fulfiling ways of engaging with others.
- *Implementation:* The client is encouraged to apply these new behaviours in daily interactions. Ongoing support helps to adjust to these changes and reinforce positive outcomes.

Box 8.1

Components of Games

A psychological game is a series of unconscious transactions. Although painful, they are repetitive and lead to predictable outcome, usually ending with a 'payoff', a conformation of unconsciously held script-beliefs. For example, Jane often feels let down by her partners who abandon her, usually for someone else. A game typically involves the following components:

- *Confluence of Ego-states:* Games often involve specific ego-states interacting in predictable ways, leading to the game's conclusion.
- *Roles:* People engaged in a game take familiar positions/roles, such as Rescuer, Persecutor, and Victim in the Karpman Drama Triangle. Although players may switch roles as the game progresses, they usually take familiar roles. Jane is socially popular and felt outwardly confident when she met her partner, Andy, who was withdrawn. He felt grateful that someone like Jane was attracted to him. At this stage of the relationship, she took a role of a Rescuer, he of a Victim.
- *Switch:* Psychological games are often characterised by a sudden shift in the game's dynamics, which seems unexpected but is recognisable. This might involve a change in roles or a move that reveals the hidden psychological message of the transaction. As the relationship progressed, Jane was unable to sustain her cheerful, bright persona, started to binge eat and withdraw from their social circle. These were repeated patterns throughout her life. When she was at her most vulnerable, Andy told her that he did not

love her anymore and wanted to end their relationship. He was having an affair with her best friend. Retrospectively, the switch in roles was predicable, and she ended in a Victim position, he a Persecutor.

- *Payoff:* The ironically named payoff (Berne was an enthusiastic poker-player) is a familiar script reinforcing life script. It justifies the adverse script outcomes. Jane felt betrayed and unlovable and he that he was a bad person. This outcome maintained their familiar psychological position. She believed that everyone would betray and abandon her (similar to how she felt when her parents divorced), and he that women will deceive and use him (similar to caring for his mother who was chronically ill when he was growing up). The repetitive feeling Jane ended with was despair, whereas Andy felt anger.

Analysis of the Drama Triangle

The Drama Triangle is a helpful concept in analysing the process of psychological games with three roles (Karpman, 1971):

> *Victim:* usually in an I−/U+ life position (i.e., I am not OK, You are OK), and feeling helpless and in need of assistance.
> *Prosecutor:* usually in an I+/U− position and takes on a critical and blaming role.
> *Rescuer:* usually in an I+/U− position and attempts to save/fix the Victim.

It is often easily recognisable by therapists and clients and can be used for a recognition and exploration of the more complex and painful process underlying it. It is also helpful in not containing language that could be experienced as shaming by the clients, unlike some of the earlier terms used by Berne (such as 'gimmick' and 'con'). The Victim is usually in I−U+ life position, and feeling helpless and in need of assistance, the Prosecutor is in a I+/U− position and takes on a critical and blaming role, and the Rescuer attempts to save or fix the Victim from I+/U− position. We tend to have a most familiar role at the beginning and the end of the psychological games. An example of how a TA therapist examines a client's Drama Triangle involves observing the client's relational patterns and dynamics to identify recurring roles and interactions. Role Analysis consists of the client exploring their enactment of the Victim, Persecutor or Rescuer roles to foster awareness of their relational dynamics and the impact of these roles on their interactions. The drama triangle is helpful in not containing language that could be experienced as shaming, unlike some early terms used by Berne (e.g. 'gimmick' and 'con'). Through dialogue and exploration, the therapist helps the client recognise their tendencies to assume one or more of these roles in their relationships. By differentiating the client's ego-state, they may uncover motivations and emotional dynamics and promote more integrated and adaptive interactions. It is important to recognise that being vulnerable, helpful or potent, are not necessarily a role in psychological games; they only become that if they are repetitive and script-bound. In their explanation to clients, therapists may want to use a visual figure of Karpman's Drama Triangle which is widely available online.

Analysis of the Winner's Triangle

Acey Choy's Winner's Triangle (1990) is a model designed to promote healthier and more constructive interactions by transforming the roles in Karpman's Drama Triangle, including three roles:

Vulnerable (instead of Victim): The Victim role associated with feelings of powerlessness and resecure-seeking (strong Child ego-state) is transformed into the role of the Vulnerable which acknowledges needs and seeks solutions (strong Adult ego-state). This encourages individuals to acknowledge their feelings and needs without feeling helpless. They take responsibility for their situation and seek constructive solutions.

Assertive (instead of Persecutor): The Persecutor role with behaviours of blaming and criticising (strong Critical Parent ego-state) is replaced with the Assertive role with the respectful communication of needs and boundaries (strong Adult ego-state). This involves expressing one's needs and boundaries clearly and respectfully without resorting to aggression or blame.

Caring (instead of Rescuer): The Rescuer role associated with taking over other's problems and fostering dependency (strong Nurturing Parent ego-state), is transformed into the Caring role that offers support without fostering dependency (strong Adult ego-state). This means offering support and help without taking over or enabling dependency. It involves empowering others to solve their problems.

━━━━━━ 8.3 REFLECTIVE QUESTIONS ━━━━━━

- Remember an example of helping someone, needed help or complained/accused someone. Who were the Rescuer, Prosecutor and Victim? Were your actions realistic and proportionate to the situation? Did you shift roles? What triggered you to play this role? What made you and the other players stay in this game? How did you solve the drama? Do you recognise this role? Is this a recurrent pattern in your life, and if so, when and how did this start? What can you do to prevent getting stuck in a drama triangle? How could you transform the drama roles into winner roles?
- Answer the same questions for a client or person you know well.

ASSESSMENT OF SCRIPT-SYSTEMS ('RACKET')

The term 'Racket', coined by Berne, describes how we limit our expression and authentic needs to maintain psychological stability. Erskine and Zalcman (1979) renamed this concept to 'Script-system' for a more accurate and neutral term.

Script-system Analysis focuses on identifying and exploring habitual emotional responses containing script beliefs and emotional responses, as well as reinforcing memories, all maintaining our life script frame of reference and beliefs. They are usually experienced following an outcome of a psychological game. Still, they can be experienced internally without the bilateral competence of social interaction. In that sense, we can see the script-system as an intrapsychic script component.

Underlying the script-system are early-life experiences, unconscious motivations and needs. Historically, it is the way that a child adapts to their environment. The interactions that reinforce them are memories of previous painful experiences, leading individual to perpetuate these patterns without full awareness of their underlying dynamics. The importance of the script-system lies in its role as a defence mechanism and a means of fulfiling unmet emotional needs. Individuals develop it to cope with past experiences and navigate the world based on ingrained patterns of seeking validation, attention or control. Research on script-systems is limited, but studies suggest individuals may re-enact early-life patterns (Erskine & Zalcman, 1979; Zalcman, 1990).

Case Study 8.2

Jane

Jane, often ill and alone as a child, was praised for being bright and cheerful but felt unlovable and soothed herself with sweets. In her relationships, including with Andy, she believed she was unlovable, others would betray her, and life was unfair, leading to feelings of hopelessness. She recalled similar feelings with past partners, at school and with her parents, especially when hoping someone would come into her room. By examining her script-system, Jane reflected on her relationships and allowed herself to express her true self instead of always being cheerful. Her friendships deepened, and she felt more secure being herself.

8.4 REFLECTIVE QUESTIONS

- Think of a stressful or painful situation that occurs repeatedly in your life. At those times, what do you believe about yourself? What do you believe about other people and about quality of life? How do you feel in your body at those times?
- Think of a client/person you know well. Can you recognise when they enter into their script-system? What could be their underlying? How could this unmet need be fulfiled more beneficially?

Assessment of Strokes

Caregivers and authority figures convey their experiences, beliefs and expectations through repeated transactions rather than theoretical monologues. TA therapists analyse this process by examining an individual's stroke profile. A stroke is an experience of recognition or communication from one person to another.

Strokes can be positive, like verbal praise or compliments, non-verbal gestures like a smile, hug or pat on the back, active listening, encouragement, acts of kindness, recognition of effort and pointing out someone's strengths.

A stroke can also be harmful, like criticism, explicit or implicit disapproval, ignoring or dismissing a person, rejecting or refusing to engage with or exclude them from activities, blaming, gaslighting, sarcasm, undermining and invalidating feelings. A person gives a stroke conditionally if the stroke depends on a specific situation or outcome, such as a parent may praise their child only when they achieve an excellent school mark. Children may seek negative strokes if positive ones are unavailable, but an excess of negative strokes can harm self-esteem and behaviour patterns.

Strokes are essential for emotional and psychological development, and a lack of them can lead to feelings of isolation and developmental problems. Understanding and managing strokes is crucial for healthy relationships and emotional well-being. For example, Jane was praised for being cheerful despite her illness, leading her to believe she was only acceptable when cheerful. Research shows that a conditional sense of self is associated with worse mental health, while unconditional positive regard promotes well-being (Farber et al., 2018; Haines & Schutte, 2023; Kolden et al., 2018; Orth et al., 2018).

The evidence for the benefits of strokes is mainly indirect. Social support alleviates depression and promotes positive coping (Almeida et al., 2021; Almquist et al., 2017; Buchanan, 1995; Cacioppo et al., 2006; Cohen et al., 2004; Joiner et al., 1997; Marroquin, 2011; Segrin & Passalacqua, 2010; Shor et al., 2013; Uchino, 2006; Wang et al., 2017; Weeks et al., 1980). Individuals with mental health issues often face relational challenges, including relational bullying, which can have long-lasting effects (Brown et al., 1995). Mental health problems are linked to social withdrawal and negative communication styles, further straining relationships (Alfano & Perry, 1994; Hames et al., 2013; Joiner, 1993, 2000; Kazdin et al., 1985; Segrin, 2000). Addressing these patterns can improve relationships and well-being. Research on appreciation and compliments shows their positive impact on mood, self-esteem and interactions (Fredrickson, 2004; Gable et al., 2004, 2006; Singh, 2017; Zhao & Epley, 2019). Positive strokes lead to reciprocal interactions and a sense of significance and belonging (Kiesler, 1996; Prilleltensky, 2014; Ravitz et al., 2008; Vos, 2017, 2020). Self-affirmation, self-acceptance and self-compassion are crucial for mental well-being, whereas negative self-esteem and self-criticism are linked to mental health issues (Bagby et al., 1992; Beck et al., 1979; Blass & Blatt, 1996; Cox et al., 2004; MacBeth & Gumley, 2012; Neff, 2011; Wisco, 2009; Zessin et al., 2015).

8.5 REFLECTIVE QUESTIONS

- Identify in Table 8.1 how often you received and gave positive and negative strokes and how unconditional and conditional these strokes were as a child, and in your present life. What has remained unchanged in your stroking profile since you were a child; why have you continued this, and do you still want to continue this? What has changed, and if so, what may explain these changes, and do you still want to continue this? What stroking activities do you never/rarely or usually/always do? What could explain their frequency, such as early-life messages? Identify possible areas for improvement and the practical steps you may need to take to effectuate this change.

- When did you receive strokes as a child? Were most of the strokes given conditionally or unconditionally? How did this unconditional/conditional stroking impact your current conditional/unconditional sense of self-worth? How could you improve your self-worth, such as self-stroking or asking for unconditional strokes?
- Fill-in the stroke profile for a client/person you know, analysing the conditionality of strokes, development over their life-span, impact on their mental health and well-being, their strengths, areas for further development and possible steps to improve their stoking profile.

Table 8.1 Stroking Profile (Instruction: Insert a Cross on the Relevant Places on the Lines)

	How often?	Most of the time, unconditional or conditional?
Giving positive strokes	Never _____ Always	Always unconditional _____ Always conditional
Giving negative strokes	Never _____ Always	Always unconditional _____ Always conditional
Taking positive strokes	Never _____ Always	Always unconditional _____ Always conditional
Taking negative strokes	Never _____ Always	Always unconditional _____ Always conditional
Asking for positive strokes	Never _____ Always	Always unconditional _____ Always conditional
Asking for attention	Never _____ Always	Always unconditional _____ Always conditional
Refusing to give positive strokes	Never _____ Always	Always unconditional _____ Always conditional
Refusing to give negative strokes	Never _____ Always	Always unconditional _____ Always conditional

Assessment of Time Structure

Studying how individuals organise and allocate their time may offer valuable insight into their internal dynamics, relationship patterns and psychological needs. Time allocation and organisation are integral components of an individual's transactions. They can reveal underlying scripts, payoffs and script-systems within the TA framework. There is no specific research on time structure assessment, but TA therapists say time-structure analysis can be helpful (Vos & van Rijn, 2021c). By studying these diverse aspects of time organisation and allocation, TA therapists can better understand individuals' internal scripts, payoffs and script-systems, leading to greater insight and more effective interventions. Analysing time structure can help understand how much risk and strokes an individual takes (Figure 8.6).

Increasing level of risk and strokes

Withdrawal	Rituals	Pastimes	Activity	Games	Intimacy
(No social interaction)	(Familiar social interaction)	(Talking but no action)	(Energy directed towards outcome)	(Series of transactions with a psychological payoff)	(Expressing authentic feelings and wants without censoring)

Figure 8.6   Continuum of Activities to Structure Time

Topics to discuss with clients may include their stroking patterns and underlying beliefs about:

Work-Life Balance: How individuals prioritise and allocate time between work, personal life, and leisure activities can reflect their internal scripts and beliefs.

Social Interaction: Individuals' time socialising, seeking solitude, or engaging in meaningful connections can shed light on their relational patterns and emotional needs.

Leisure Pursuits: The type of activities individuals choose to engage in during their free time can indicate their unconscious motivations and emotional patterns.

Procrastination and Productivity: How individuals manage and structure their time regarding task completion, deadlines, and procrastination can reveal their coping mechanisms, anxieties, and avoidance patterns.

Self-Care Practices: The attention individuals allocate to self-care, relaxation, and personal development activities can reflect their self-worth, self-nurturing capacities, and emotional well-being.

Intimate relationships: Relationships with partner/relatives/friends that, for example, include expression of authentic feelings and needs.

8.6 REFLECTIVE QUESTIONS

- How do you structure your time? How much time do you spend on withdrawal, rituals, pastimes, games, intimacy and actions? What does this say about how much risk you take and your opportunities to exchange strokes? Have you always structured your time this way, or has anything changed, and if so, what made you change? Who taught you how to structure your time (this could be multiple individuals, such as parents, peers, and society)? What does this time-structure tell about your life script? What would you like to improve in structuring time, and what practical steps can you take to make this happen? If you were to give yourself a positive message about time, how would this sound, such as, 'It is OK to…'; 'You are allowed to…' Do you first need to process any underlying issues in your life script before making this change; if so, how could you process this?
- Answer the same questions for a client or person you know well.

TA ASSESSMENT TOOLS

Using questionnaires and standardised interview schedules in the assessment of clients in psychotherapy offers several benefits. Structured information gathering ensures that all crucial areas, as described in Chapters 4–7, are consistently assessed. Standardised assessment tools allow for more objective measurement of various psychological constructs, such as anxiety, depression and personality. This can provide valuable baseline data, and aid in tracking progress and comparing with norm-groups, allowing therapists to contextualise a client's experiences and identify areas of significant distress or improvement. Standardised tools can make the assessment process more time-efficient. Many standardised assessment tools have established reliability and validity, providing an evidence basis for tailoring interventions to individuals.

TA-Interview Schedules

Several TA-interview schedules have been developed; although most have poor to moderate quality due to a lack of research (Vos & van Rijn, 2021a):

> *Comprehensive Life script Interview* (McCormick & Pulleyblank, 1979). This interview includes a comprehensive life script interview and matrix including constructive and destructive messages, rewarding and self-defeating early-life decisions.
>
> *Decision Scale* (Woollams, 1979). With a 0-to-10 range, this scale assesses script information, the severity of decisions, favoured drivers, and clients' strengths.
>
> *Developmental Script Questionnaire* (Landheer, 1981). This structured interview examines a client's script in chronological stages and ego-states.
>
> *Ohlsson, Björk, & Johnsson's Script Questionnaire.* This script questionnaire has 43 questions and a scripted checklist, including Berne's (1972) script apparatus and Steiner's Script Checklist. This is the most comprehensive and studied interview schedule, and we have integrated this into our treatment manual.
>
> *Script Apparatus and Script Checklist* (Berne, 1972). This checklist aims to reveal the plot, characters, and course of events in their life script via questions about memories of favourite fairy tales, childhood and adolescent heroes, games, early memories and fantasies of death. This helps to identify early TA-concepts such as prescription/counterscript slogans, injunction stopper, script decision, parental pattern, script payoff, curse, demon, internal release, come-on, seduction, and permission. Steiner's Script Checklist (1975) extended Berne's work with banal scripts and a visual matrix, and this included, for example, counterscript, driver, counterinjunction, injunction attribution, decision, program, script-system, game, position, tragic ending, life course, pastime, payoff, sweatshirt, script-system, somatic component, therapist's role, mythical hero, and antithesis.
>
> *Other Tools.* For example, Parent-Adult-Child Projective Drawing Task (Turner, 1988), and Freehand Script Maze (Buryska, 1976).

TA-Questionnaires

Questionnaires can help assessment and case formulation (Prescott et al., 2017). We have conducted a systematic literature review and assessed the psychometric quality of all TA-questionnaires (Vos & van Rijn, 2021b). Below, we describe the two questionnaires in English with the most proven validity and reliability, and which were able to detect changes in our clinical trials (Vos & van Rijn, 2024a, 2024b, 2024c). Table 8.2 suggests other questionnaires (Vos & van Rijn, 2024a).

Life position Scale. This reliable, validated scale can be found in the appendix. Boholst (2002) developed this 20-item scale to operationalise positive or negative views towards themselves (I+/I−) towards others (U+/U−).

Schema Mode Inventory. This very well-studied questionnaire has good validity and reliability and was developed as part of Schema Therapy; their concept of 'schema-mode' resembles ego-states, and identifies more schema-modes. The 118-item questionnaire has the following scales: vulnerable child, angry child, enraged child, impulsive child, undisciplined child, happy child, compliant surrender, detached protector, detached self-soother, self-aggrandiser, bully and attack mode, punitive parent, demanding parent, and healthy adult. For sale via schematherapy.com

We have developed and validated three new tools, which can be found in the appendices (Vos & van Rijn, 2024a, 2024b, 2024c):

Systematic Case Formulation Form SCFF. This comprehensive form consists of all evidence-based components for the case formulation based on the research described in Chapters 4–5.

TA Goal Attainment Form TAGAF. This form helps clients identify therapy goals aligned with TA research outcomes, as explained in Chapter 6.

TA psychotherapy Competencies Scale TAP-SRCS. Therapists fill-in this scale to assess their key TA therapeutic competencies proven to improve TA outcomes: assessment, structuring, relational and experiential competencies.

Table 8.2 Questionnaires to Consider in TA psychotherapy

Construct	Primary Recommended Questionnaires	Alternative or Additional Questionnaires
Mental health issues	Patient Health Questionnaire/ PHQ-9 (depression)	Work and Social Adjustment Scale (impact of mental health problems)
	General Anxiety Disorder/GAD-7	WHOQOL-bref (quality-of-life)
	Trauma Checklist/PCL-5	
Client Interview	Ohlsson, Bjork&Johnsson (2011). (integrated in our treatment manual)	
Ego-states	Schema Mode Inventory/SMI* (comprehensive, well-studied overview of ego-states)	Tokyo University Egogram(Japanese only)
		Adjective Check List** (research-focused)

(Continued)

Table 8.2 Questionnaires to Consider in TA psychotherapy *(Continued)*

Construct	Primary Recommended Questionnaires	Alternative or Additional Questionnaires
		ANINT-A36** (Italian, integrating attachment and social-cognitive theories)
		Daley Ego-states Scale**
		Ego-state Inventory**
Life position	Life position Scale**	Rosenberg Self-Esteem Scale
	Self-Criticising/Attacking and Self-Reassuring Scale/SCASRS	ANINT-A36**
	Compassionate Resilience Scale/ CRS (using self-compassion in response to stressful events)	Transactional Behaviour Questionnaire**
	Inventory Interpersonal Problems/ IIP	
Stroking	n/a	Stroking Questionnaire
		Transactional Behaviour Questionnaire**
Injunctions/counter-injunctions/drivers	Early Memories of Warmth and Safeness Scale//EMWSS	Young Parenting Inventory YPI
		Drego Injunction Scale**
		ESPERO**
Therapeutic relationship (not specific TA)	n/a	Working Alliance Scale
		Agnew Relationship Measure-5
		Psychotherapy Relationship Questionnaire
Other TA-questionnaires	n/a	Transgenerational Script Questionnaire**
		Joines Personality Adaptation Questionnaire**
Questionnaires to measure fundamental psychological structures	Difficulties in Emotion Regulation/ DER	Kernberg's Interpersonal Psychological Organisation (questionnaire or interview)
	Dissociative Experiences Scale/ DES	Oxford Dissociative Experiences Measure
	Experiences in Close Relationships (attachment)/ECR	Adult Attachment Interview
	Psychological Mindedness Scale/ PMS	NEO-PI or MMPI (personality questionnaires)
Other questionnaires to consider	traumatic experiences/LEC-5	Stressful life events Screening Questionnaire (long; checks many life-events)
		Adverse Childhood Experience Questionnaire for Adults
		Trauma Related Shame Scale
		Conceptual Well-Being Scale (existential well-being, self-realisation, connections, meaning)
		Young Schema Questionnaire (maladaptive patterns of thinking, feeling, behaving)
		Brief Screening Complicated Grief
		COPE(coping-style)

Table 8.2 Questionnaires to Consider in TA psychotherapy *(Continued)*

Construct	Primary Recommended Questionnaires	Alternative or Additional Questionnaires
		Coping Flexibility Scale
		Acceptance&Action Questionnaire-II (experiential acceptance)
		World Assumptions Scale (basic assumptions about self, world, others)
		Existential Anxiety Questionnaire
		Meaning in Life Questionnaire
		Compass of Shame (coping with shame)
		Vos Sociodemographics and Life Situation Questionnaire (Vos, 2023)
Questionnaires to tailor TA-psychotherapy	Systematic Case Formulation Form for TA psychotherapy/ SCFF-TAP	n/a
	TA Goal Attainment Form/TAGAF	
	TA psychotherapy Competencies Scale/TAP-SRCS	

*Ego-states are called 'modes' in Schema-Therapy;
**Applicability, validation and/or translation uncertain

8.7 REFLECTIVE QUESTIONS

- Fill-in the questionnaires in the appendices of this book for yourself. If possible, also fill-in some other questionnaires in Table 8.2. How did it feel to fill-in these questionnaires? What was helpful? What was not helpful? What aspects of the results do you agree with, and what do you disagree with? How could you use these findings in your self-development?
- Which questionnaires could be helpful to use routinely in your therapy practice? What practical steps do you need to introduce these?

EVIDENCE-BASED TA CASE-FORMULATION

Overview

Based on research presented in Chapters 4–7, we developed a systematic assessment and case formulation, validated in our feasibility/pilot-studies (Vos & van Rijn, 2024b, 2024c).

Questionnaires at the start of therapy: Ask clients to fill-in the Life position Scale at home, and possibly questionnaires assessing ego-states (e.g. SMI), self-efficacy (SCASRS/ CRS), social functioning (IIP), psychopathology (PHQ-9/GAD-7/PCL-5), life events (LEC-5), injunctions (EMWSS) and in clients with more severe psychopathology questionnaires to measure fundamental psychological structures (DER/DES/ECR/PMS).

Systematic assessment sessions: We recommend having between one or three sessions to assess the client's main concerns, followed by two sessions to assess their aetiology/life script. This book's treatment manual gives step-by-step guidance on these assessment sessions, which includes the TA Goal Attainment Form (TAGAF) to identify therapy goals.

Case formulation: The questionnaires and sessions will yield much information; to organise this, use the comprehensive Systematic Case Formulation Form (SCFF-TAP). Therapists should book sufficient time to score questionnaires and develop the case formulation; the more frequent the therapist creates case formulations, the quicker formulating goes. We recommend discussing the SCFF-TAP with clinical supervisors or colleagues.

Case formulation sharing session: The therapist shares the case formulation with the client (verbally, although some clients also want a printed copy). Clients have described case formulation sharing as one of the most significant moments in therapy (Vos & van Rijn, 2024a). Therapists should avoid conveying this as a rigid label/diagnosis or in a condescending manner, and present this as hypotheses rather than absolute truths. The sharing of the case formulation should involve many questions and relational prompts, enabling clients to respond, inquire and contribute. This session aims to assist the client in gaining self-awareness, taking ownership of their circumstances and developing self-compassion for their life story.

Plan for interventions: The case formulation is a roadmap for targeted interventions in following sessions. For instance, if the case formulation reveals that an individual plays psychological games, starting as a Rescuer and ending up as a Victim, the interventions may centre around cultivating awareness, exploring its origins and alternative options. The client and therapist will collaboratively determine which areas to prioritise, and may in later sessions revisit the case formulation and therapy goals.

Overview of Systematic Case Formulation Form (see details in appendix)

i.   Field-specific case formulation: for example, DSM-V/ICD-11-diagnosis
ii. Phenomenological description: in client's own words
iii. Clinical model: for example, ego-states, life position, self-efficacy, social functioning (see Chapter 4); this may include secondary assessment of transactions, games, script-systems, stroking, time-structure (Chapter 8)
iv. Aetiology: for example, childhood context, fundamental psychological structures, early-life messages, responses/decisions in the past and present, including actions the clients have tried to improve their life (ask what worked and what not), and self-perpetuating mechanisms and feedback loops (Chapter 5)
v.   Treatment indicators: Suitability of the client for therapy (Chapter 6)
vi. Treatment aims: client's self-formulated therapy goals (e.g. TAGAF), and the therapist's formal translation into clinical or TA terms (Chapter 6).
vii. Therapeutic mechanisms: hypotheses about which TA-interventions may lead to the desired outcomes (Chapter 7).
viii. Risk assessment: assessment of risks of suicide, self-harm, harming others, and other risks.

ix. Critical self-reflection on assessment and case formulation

x. Interventions and treatment plan: practical interventions that may help achieve the client's goals, following logically from therapeutic aims, mechanisms, aetiology and clinical problems.

xi. Client response: client reactions and adjustments to case formulation; explicit agreement between therapist and client about therapy aims (vi.) and interventions/treatment plan (ix).

SUMMARY

- Systematic assessment and case formulation can improve therapy outcomes and the therapeutic relationship, and help tailoring evidence-based interventions.
- TA therapists primarily assess ego-states, life positions (self-efficacy, social functioning) and life scripts (there is much research evidence for these concepts). They may secondarily assess transactions, games, drama triangle, winner's triangle, script-systems/rackets, stroke-profiles, time structure (there is less direct evidence for these concepts).
- TA therapists may use assessment tools like Berne's, Ohlsson/Björk/Johnsson's Script Questionnaire (integrated into our treatment manual) and questionnaires like the Life position Scale and TA Goal Attainment Form (see appendices).
- The evidence-based TA case formulation systematically assesses all evidence-based aspects of the clinical phenomena, aetiology, therapy outcomes, goals and therapeutic mechanisms (Chapters 4-7). This may be developed with the Systematic Case Formulation Form template which includes: field-specific case formulation/diagnosis, phenomenological description in client's words, clinical model, aetiology, treatment indicators, treatment aims, therapeutic mechanisms, risk assessment and critical self-reflection.
- Assessment and case formulation are ongoing, which clients and therapists continuously monitor, review and improve. The case formulation should be regarded as hypotheses, which therapists check/verify sensitively with clients. The conversation about the case formulation can help the therapist improve the case formulation and give clients self-insight in their problems, and how their past influences their present.

9

RELATIONAL COMPETENCIES

How can a TA therapist develop a constructive therapist-client relationship? Research repeatedly shows how that clients can benefit from developing a positive therapist-client relationship (e.g., Norcross & Lambert, 2019). Similarly, TA therapists in our survey underlined the importance of the therapeutic relationship with many examples (Vos & van Rijn, 2021c). Statistical analysis of their answers revealed the following important dimensions of the therapeutic relationship in TA, as will be explained, supported with empirical evidence and exemplified in this chapter:

- Diversity and social justice
- Validating the client's autonomy
- Being non-judgemental
- Following the client
- Tailored (non)directiveness
- Stimulating the development of insight
- Working with transference and countertransference
- Working with resistance
- Working with impasses
- Repairing ruptures
- Real relationships and transactions

OVERVIEW OF RESEARCH ON THE THERAPEUTIC RELATIONSHIP

In their 2019 edition of '*Psychotherapy Relationships That Work*', Norcross and Lambert provided a comprehensive overview of research on the effectiveness of the client-therapist relationship across therapeutic approaches. Their meta-analyses showed that therapy is more successful when it establishes a positive alliance and collaboration between the therapist and the client. This involves empathy, positive regard and affirmation – similar to a position of 'I'm OK/You're OK' – and being genuine/congruent in the therapeutic relationship. The authors highlight the importance of addressing transference and countertransference, supporting clients to express their emotions, and repairing any ruptures in the therapeutic alliance. These findings align closely with humanistic values in TA, which emphasise equality, respect, empathy and the exploration of transactions and games within the therapeutic context.

Similar effective components of the therapeutic relationships were mentioned by TA therapists in our survey (Vos & van Rijn, 2021c). Our meta-analyses of 41 clinical trials also showed that TA treatments that explicitly focused on fostering a positive therapeutic relationship were more effective than those that did not (Vos & van Rijn, 2023); similarly, in our feasibility and pilot studies, we found that the therapeutic relationship predicted and mediated client improvements (Vos & van Rijn, 2024b, 2024c, 2024d).

DIVERSITY AND SOCIAL JUSTICE

Radical therapists such as Steiner have argued that working as a TA therapist is inherently political (Tudor, 2020). It seems impossible for a therapist to be completely neutral (Rowland & Cornell, 2021). For example, not actively addressing diversity and injustice may inadvertently give the message that the therapist approves and collides with the perpetrators. The therapist may function as a bystander in the client's drama. In this role, their passivity and silence may reinforce the client's experiences of injustice and unintentionally facilitate unhelpful or unjust social games (Gopakumar & Vaidik, 2024). Consequently, therapists should notice how the client's experiences of social injustice may be dissociated, enacted or re-enacted in the therapy room (Minikin, 2023). Therefore, TA-authors have argued that diversity and social justice are central TA-practice.

Minikin (2023) described how social alienation, structural oppression and transgenerational trauma can marginalise individuals through alienation and its impact on the psyche. TA therapists may help break this by acknowledging and validating their experiences, as research repeatedly shows:

> Acknowledgement means recognition by individual perpetrators and the complicity of all the people who enabled them. Survivors need many kinds of reparative action from their communities, ranging from immediate help and support in a crisis to broad education programs for prevention. They want bystanders to take a stand, recognise that a wrong has been done, and unambiguously denounce the crime, they want assurances that they did not deserve to be abused. (Herman, 2023)

Several authors have argued that social-justice-oriented TA should include a societal structural analysis (Campos, 2010), and that a client's impasses in social-justice may be broken by identifying the Parent, Adult and Child parts of society at a collective level in areas such as gender, ethnicity/race and sexual orientation (Campos, 2010).

> Victims of social injustice may never feel OK about themselves and others -regardless of how much therapeutic insight they gain- as long as the community does not actively validate their identity, albeit by the therapist as a symbolic representative

of that community. Healing from social injustice does not merely require work at an intrapsychic level in the therapy room or one-to-one between perpetrator and victim but also at the community level. Those who have been wronged might find it difficult to accept that obtaining validation from their offenders may never occur. Waiting for a genuine apology may keep victims trapped in a dependency role towards the perpetrator, who retains power over the victim by refusing a genuine apology, which may hinder the healing process and reconnection of the victim within society. Thus, the healing process should not hinge on the wrongdoers' acknowledgement of their experiences. Victims might have to grieve and regain their autonomy by letting go of unrealistic expectations about social-justice. Therapists may play a crucial role in exploring how clients may achieve some sense of justice, develop realistic expectations, and reclaim their agency. Alongside the individual healing process, therapists may help clients' recognition, healing, and reconciliation at the community level. (Vos, 2024, p. 6)

How therapists perceive and foster social-justice in their practice may reflect their personal, societal and professional context. For example, TA therapists may simplify their understanding of social-justice by seeing it as a binary concept: either one is the oppressor or the oppressed (Dhananjaya, 2022; Vos, 2024). Therapists may unconsciously engage in such processes of splitting, individualising complex socially unjust contexts or projecting their guilt and shame onto others, in response to their life script, unprocessed life experiences, feelings or traits they may struggle with (Vos, 2020). It may be emotionally easier to split the world into black-or-white, project unwanted feelings and play inauthentic games than to integrate the pains and complexities of social reality:

Offering psychological therapy to a victim of social injustice may be played as a superficial game that allows society to acknowledge social injustice without addressing its causes. However, (. . .) healing requires intimacy instead of games in an authentic therapeutic relationship. Therapists should, therefore, examine how they can offer true intimacy that facilitates the client to lower their need to play games and split. This requires that therapists acknowledge their own experiences and defence mechanisms. If therapists do not resolve their own experiences of injustice, they may, for instance, play the game of 'the rescuer' with clients; this game may function as a narcissistic defence against their own overwhelming emotions and bodily sensations. (Vos, 2024, p. 14)

To be able to do justice to their clients, TA therapists may want to engage in ongoing self-reflection and education to address personal biases and assumptions (Minikin, 2023), grounded in a supportive-empathic therapeutic relationship and an attitude of authentic curiosity, creativity and embracing uncertainty (Fowlie & Sills, 2018).

GENERAL RELATIONAL SKILLS IN TA

TA therapists use a range of relational techniques known to facilitate therapeutic relationships (Norcross & Lambert, 2019):

Empathy: Empathy is essential to effective treatments (Eklund & Meranius, 2021; Levitt et al., 2022; Nienhuis et al., 2018). This refers to the therapist's ability to understand and share the client's feelings, experiences, and perspectives. The therapist cultivates a compassionate and caring presence in the therapeutic relationship, demonstrating genuine concern for the client's well-being. The therapist enters the client's world, accurately comprehends their emotions, and communicates understanding and validation. Examples include listening actively, attentively and non-judgementally, via verbal and non-verbal communication. For example, a therapist may say, 'It sounds like you feel overwhelmed by work demands and struggle to find a balance. Can you tell me more about what that has been like for you?' The client may answer, 'Yes, it has been stressful, and I feel like I cannot keep up with everything.' Subsequently, the therapist reflects empathically, 'I hear that the pressure is taking a toll on you, and it has been challenging to cope with everything.'

Attunement: The client is attuned to the client's internal world and shares this, for example, via reflective statements conveying an understanding of the client's emotions and experiences. For example, a client may say, 'I am just so frustrated with myself for being unable to make any progress'. The therapist may reflect on their attunement, 'It seems you feel disappointed and discouraged about the lack of progress. It is understandable to feel that way given the difficulties you have been facing'.

Validation and normalisation: The therapist explicitly acknowledges and validates the client's emotions and experiences, expressing empathy for their struggles and challenges. The therapist may acknowledge that their client's emotions and responses are understandable within their circumstances, such as their life script and early-life context: these are normal responses to abnormal, adverse life events. Validation and normalisation aim to reduce feelings of isolation, shame, or self-blame by helping clients recognise that their struggles are not uncommon and can be addressed within the therapy-process. For example, a therapist normalises a client's feelings of sadness, anger, or confusion following the loss of a loved one by affirming that these emotions are typical responses; the therapist may explain that the grieving process involves a range of emotions and that there is no 'right' way to grieve. A therapist normalises a client's anxiety symptoms by explaining that many individuals experience stress and worries in response to life's challenges. A therapist normalises the challenges of interpersonal relationships by highlighting common communication difficulties, conflicts, and misunderstandings. A therapist normalises concerns about seeking therapy or discussing mental health challenges by addressing societal stigma and misconceptions surrounding mental health.

VALIDATING THE CLIENT'S AUTONOMY

Berne viewed the therapeutic relationship as a cooperative and egalitarian partnership between the therapist and the client, where the therapist assumes the role of a facilitator in the client's self-exploration and empowerment, and the client's input, insight and autonomy are recognised and honoured, ultimately promoting the client's capacity for self-directed change and personal growth. Examples include:

Openness: 'Practitioners create a positive context in which clients feel safe and open to express what is truly meaningful. Clients feel safe to unpeel the layers in their experiences and show their vulnerability. When practitioners are perceived as uninviting and unsafe, clients may focus more on superficial, inauthentic experiences. Empathy helps the practitioner to understand the client's lived experiences and offer better-tailored questions and suggestions. Thus, meaning is more likely to be explored in depth and totality when there is a positive relationship.' (Vos, 2017, p. 136)

Cooperative: Therapy goals, methods and organisational aspects are developed in collaboration between client and therapist.

Clear contracts: The therapist is clear about the therapeutic encounter's goals, methods and organisational aspects and reviews this regularly with the client.

Shared decision-making: The therapist explicitly invites the client's input, perspective, goals, and review of goals to foster a sense of ownership and autonomy in the therapy-process.

'This implies that the practitioner is transparent about the reason why certain questions are asked ("I would like to ask you this question, because. . ."), and any ideas should be tested as hypotheses and not as truths ("I wonder whether it might be the case that. . . How do you see this?")' (Vos, 2017, p. 138). Research shows the effectiveness of managing client expectations, for example, by explicating the treatment's aims, methods, and organisational aspects (Orlinsky et al., 2004; Tryon & Winograd, 2011; see goal-setting in Chapter 6).

Empowerment clients via psychoeducation/didactics: Instead of clouding therapeutic methods in mystery, Berne believed that clients benefit from learning about the therapy process. Therefore, he developed a language for his therapeutic model that is easy to communicate.

Strength-Based Approach: Therapists identify and build upon the client's strengths, resources, and resilience, emphasising their capacity for self-direction and self-growth, highlighting their resilience, creativity, and problem-solving abilities.

Facilitating Self-Reflection: Therapists encourage introspection, self-reflection, and mindfulness practices to foster self-awareness, insight, and the ability to make choices aligned with their values and aspirations.

Encouraging Self-Expression: Therapists create a safe and non-judgemental space for clients to express their thoughts, emotions, and needs, promoting self-advocacy and self-expression.

Promoting Self-Compassion: Cultivating self-compassion and self-acceptance to support the client in developing a kind and understanding relationship with themselves, fostering a sense of autonomy and agency in their self-care and well-being.

Belief in change: The therapist implicitly and explicitly expresses their belief in the client's abilities to change. However, this is not unfounded optimism; it integrates realistic limitations.

Realistic and sensitive to the client's context: The ideal of personal autonomy may be unrealistic and reflect Western bias (Campos, 2010; Car, 2013; Dhananjaya, 2022; Massey, 2007; Minikin, 2023; Sedgwick, 2020). Assess and adjust to the client's perceptions, wishes, and opportunities for autonomy. Bear in mind that some cultures may also have different expectations of healthcare professionals, such as expecting them to be an authority giving directive guidance (Paniagua & Yamada, 2013).

BEING NON-JUDGEMENTAL

Berne believed the therapist's role is to provide a safe, non-judgemental and supportive environment where clients can openly explore their thoughts, feelings and behaviours. Approaching the client's experiences with an open and non-judgemental attitude allows a deeper understanding of their unique perspective.

Cultural Sensitivity: The therapist recognises and respects the client's cultural, social, and individual differences and understands how these factors shape their experiences and emotional responses (Paniagua & Yamada, 2013).

Identity Affirmative: There is remarkably little literature on how TA therapists can work with LGBTQIA+ clients. In his early work, Berne hypothesised that homosexuality was a psychopathology caused by the individual's life script; this seems to have forced several TA therapists and clients back into the closet (Barnes, 2004; Shadbolt, 2004). It is vital to update TA theory and practices to integrate modern research and societal changes in norms regarding LGBTQIA+ (Trett, 2004). We, this book's authors, wholeheartedly embrace the call for developing a gay and transgender affirmative TA psychotherapy, and reject any pathologising of LGBTQIA+ experiences and conversion therapy (see also Shadbolt, 2004). TA therapists should explicitly and implicitly give the message of 'I'm OK, you're OK' (which may be a message LGBTQIA+ individuals may not have received from caregivers, relatives, friends and society). It may be argued that LGBTQIA+ affirmation aligns with Berne's humanistic values of autonomy and self-development and that his initial pathologisation was a product of his time. Despite an increased societal acceptance of a diversity of sexual orientations and gender identities, coming-out remains challenging on both the intrapsychic and transactional levels and TA therapists can have an essential supportive role in helping individuals to own and express their identity (Simerly, 2003). Affirmative therapy also extends to other topics within and beyond the LGBTQIA+ community, such as consensual nonmonogamy relationships, (a) sexual desires and struggles, BDSM, and sex work (Van Tol, 2017; Vos, 2023). Therapists should phenomenologically and non-judgementally explore these topics, without labelling these as psychopathological or explaining these topics away via lifescript analysis; although sexual and identity preferences may sometimes have some influences from one's early lifestory – including painful experiences –, clients may consciously choose, freely and healthily enjoy these preferences in the present (Vos, 2023). TA may offer many affirmative tools; for example, sexual and identity struggles may be explored from different ego-states, an 'I'm OK/you're OK' position, permissions, and the analysis of transactions, including how to give active consent in sexual/physically-intimate encounters -for example by strengthening the Adult when the Free or Adapted Child dominate disproportionally (Dalton et al., 2006; Parkin, 2002). In affirmative therapy, it seems vital to work with transference and countertransference. Therapists may also want to improve awareness, insights and competencies in how to work with sexual attraction that may happen in psychotherapy practice and supervision (van Rijn & Lukac-Greenwood, 2020).

FOLLOWING THE CLIENT

Although there is evidence for the effectiveness of using structures and treatment manuals, it is also important to remain relatively flexible and tailor therapy to the unique situation. (Vos, 2017, p. 138)

TA therapists follow the client by staying patient and following the client's change tempo. For example, the therapist will suppress their impatience to move to the next stage or topic in therapy. As described in Chapter 7, clients usually go through several stages of change. Although therapist may facilitate their progression, they cannot enforce this (Krebs et al., 2018; Prochaska & Norcross, 2001). They need to tailor and adjust their language and explanations to clients' stage, language and level of understanding.

TAILORING OF (NON-)DIRECTIVENESS

Directiveness refers to the extent to which the therapist provides guidance and instructions. In a directive approach, the therapist may actively steer the session, set goals and suggest specific strategies for the client. This approach can be beneficial in providing structure and clarity for clients seeking specific advice or struggling with decision-making. The advantages of a directive approach include quick decision-making, clear guidance and effectiveness in crisis or when addressing specific behavioural issues. Disadvantages include limiting the clients' autonomy and ownership of their therapeutic journey, and potentially creating imbalance in the therapeutic power dynamics.

Non-directiveness is characterised by therapists taking a more passive role, allowing clients to lead the course of the conversation. This approach emphasises the client's self-discovery and personal growth. The advantages include fostering independence, enhancing self-awareness and promoting clients' trust in their abilities. The disadvantages may include slower progression and potential difficulties in handling clients who require more structure, have less experience with therapy or are less verbally expressive.

An example where a client could benefit from directiveness is therapy for anxiety disorders, where structured interventions like exposure therapy may be necessary. Conversely, a client dealing with grief may benefit from a nondirective approach, where they need space to process and express their emotions in an open, non-judgemental environment. These examples show how the (non-)directiveness should be tailored to the client's unique situation, therapy goals and preferred approach. In the short-term, a client may benefit from a direct approach at the beginning of therapy if they have such a strong Adapted Child that they would feel helpless and may drop out from treatment if the therapist does not offer direction; in the long-term, a directive approach may reinforce their Adapted Child ego-state and hinder their development towards autonomy. This may be envisaged as the difference between macro-, meso- and micro-levels of the therapist-client relationship, where macro involves an explicit collaborative conversation planning about therapy goals and methods; meso applies chosen structured interventions as collaboratively decided; and micro operates phenomenologically, embracing clients' lived experiences; thus, therapists and clients may choose together to follow a structured and directive approach which does do justice to the client's preferences and their phenomenological flow of experiences (Vos, 2017).

STIMULATING THE DEVELOPMENT OF INSIGHT

A unique aspect of TA is helping clients to develop insight, for example, via explaining TA theories. This is generally known as 'psycho-education'. For instance, TA therapists provide information about transactions, ego-states and life positions and how life scripts may cause these. For example, by sharing the case formulation, the client may learn how TA theories apply to them. The therapist is transparent about their mental health, psychological processes, coping strategies, treatment and self-management options. Research shows that psychoeducation/didactics have positive effects (Donker et al., 2009; Lincoln et al., 2007).

WORKING WITH TRANSFERENCE AND COUNTERTRANSFERENCE

Transference and countertransference are essential tools for TA therapists, and many core concepts in TA such as lifescript and games, represent transferential phenomena and their enactment.

Transference in therapy refers to the unconscious redirection of a client's feelings and attitudes from current and past relationships with others and life script onto the therapist or other significant figures in their current life (Hayes et al., 2018; Høglend et al., 2012; Levy & Scala, 2012). This can include the client's emotions, desires and expectations towards the therapist, which are influenced by their previous experiences. Transference provides valuable insight into the client's inner world. It can be a powerful tool for exploration and understanding within therapy (Hayes et al., 2018; Yılmaz et al., 2024).

For example, a client may unconsciously project past dynamics onto the therapist, assuming roles like the Victim, Persecutor or Rescuer from the Drama Triangle. Victim Transference: A client may project feelings of helplessness and powerlessness onto the therapist, expecting the therapist to rescue them from their difficulties. They may seek constant reassurance and support, mirroring the Victim role from the Drama Triangle. Persecutor Transference: A client might perceive the therapist as critical or judgemental, reflecting their past experiences with authority figures or individuals who have been harsh or punitive. They may respond with defensiveness or resistance, assuming the role of the Persecutor within the therapeutic relationship. Rescuer Transference: A client may idealise the therapist as a saviour/fixer, seeking solutions and guidance without taking responsibility for their growth. They may unconsciously place the therapist in the Rescuer role, expecting them to alleviate their distress without active participation.

A TA therapist may use transference as a therapeutic tool by recognising and exploring the client's transference reactions to gain insight into their underlying relational patterns and unresolved emotions. They may encourage the client to reflect on their feelings and expectations towards the therapist, facilitating awareness of how past experiences influence their current interactions. The therapist may examine the client's communication and relational style to identify parallels with past relationships, shedding light on transference dynamics. Role-play and empty-chair exercises may help clients externalise and process transference dynamics, fostering a deeper understanding of their relational patterns. By addressing and working through transference within the therapy-process, a TA therapist can support the client in gaining awareness of their unconscious patterns and developing more adaptive and authentic relational dynamics.

Projective identification is a psychological phenomenon where an individual projects their unwanted feelings or traits onto another person, who then unconsciously identifies with and internalises these projections (Spillius & O'Shaugnessy, 2013). For example, a client feeling deep anger – even though they may not be consciously aware of this anger that they may be hiding behind a calm façade – might project this emotion onto the therapist, who then starts feeling and expressing anger themselves. A therapist may work with this by helping the client recognise and own their projected feelings, facilitating awareness and understanding of their internal states, and guiding them to healthier ways of expressing and managing these emotions.

Transferential phenomena are relational and are received, perceived and interpreted by the therapist who brings their own lifescript and experiences. Countertransference refers to the therapist's emotional and psychological responses to the client, which may be influenced by the therapist's unresolved feelings, experiences or conflicts, often following their life script. It involves the therapist projecting their emotions or attitudes onto the client, potentially impacting the therapeutic relationship and the quality of care. At most times, transferential experiences in therapy are co-created between the therapist and the client. It is essential that the therapist remains open to self-reflection and exploration and that this informs their interventions. This also allows the client to examine their unconscious experience during the therapeutic encounter. Research shows that managing countertransference significantly improves therapy effects (Hayes et al., 2018).

For example, a therapist seeks to accept and help all their clients to the extent of always perceiving them as Victims of their environment (van Rijn, 2023). This may lead to over-involvement in the client's issues and a reluctance to challenge the client. A therapist might also experience feelings of helplessness or powerlessness when confronted with clients who they perceive as critical and bullying, rendering them unable to engage with them (van Rijn, 2022).

We can expect to experience countertransference as therapists, more commonly so when we have reciprocal unresolved script issues. Sometimes, this can potentially impact the therapeutic relationship, as research on lifescript in supervision has suggested (van Rijn, 2023, 2022), and even lead to unsatisfactory endings. For this reason, therapists need to bring these issues to clinical supervision and engage in ongoing examination of their own personal processes. Working with transference safely can bring depth and intensity to complex therapeutic work.

9.1 REFLECTIVE QUESTIONS ABOUT TRANSFERENCE

Answer the following questions about a client or person you know well:

- How do I perceive the client's emotional reactions, communication and relational style within the therapeutic relationship? Are there consistent patterns that appear similar to relationships outside our therapeutic relationship, including the client's past?
- What emotions, desires or expectations do I sense from the client that may be influenced by their past experiences with significant figures in life?
- Do I notice idealisation or negative perceptions of me as the therapist that seem disproportionate to the current interactions? What could this say about how the client has learnt to relate with healthcare providers or authorities?
- To what extent are my emotions and perceptions realistic and mine, or are these the result from projective identification? How does projective identification influence the therapy-process, and what would be the best way to cope with this?

- How can I explore the client's communication/relational patterns and emotional reactions to develop a deeper understanding of their transference dynamics?
- How can I use reflective inquiry and empathic exploration to help clients become aware of and work through their transference within the therapy-process?

9.2 REFLECTIVE QUESTIONS ABOUT COUNTERTRANSFERENCE

Answer the following questions about a client or person you know well:
- What emotional reactions or biases do I notice arising within myself in response to the client?
- Are there specific themes or triggers in our interactions that may reflect unresolved feelings or relational dynamics from my own past or current experiences/relationships or lifescript?
- How do I perceive my countertransferential responses influencing the therapeutic relationship and potentially impacting the quality of care provided to the client?
- Can I identify any personal vulnerabilities or unmet needs contributing to my countertransference?
- What strategies can I implement to address and manage my countertransference, such as seeking supervision, engaging in personal therapy or setting clear therapeutic boundaries?

WORKING WITH RESISTANCE

Resistance in therapy is common and can manifest as reluctance to engage, skipping sessions, or defensiveness, possibly resembling a Rebellious Child (Drye, 1974). Lifescript patterns, developed over time, provide a sense of safety and meaning, even if they are no longer beneficial. Understanding and navigating resistance is crucial for therapeutic progress (Beutler et al., 2001; Beutler et al., 2002; Horner, 2005). The following are some strategies to address client resistance:

Normalise Resistance: Explain that resistance is a natural part of therapy and a protective mechanism. It offers an opportunity to explore underlying fears, beliefs, or past experiences.

Nondirectivity: Research indicates that resistance may reduce by therapists taking a more nondirective stance, and empower the client to take the lead (ibidem).

Revisit Goals/Contracts: Revisit therapy goals when resistance arises, and consider motivational interviewing (Moyers & Rollnick, 2002). Discuss if goal-adjustments are needed, reinforcing collaboration and client control.

Gentle Confrontation: Highlight discrepancies in a non-threatening way. For example, if a client avoids a topic, the therapist might say, 'I notice we change the subject when this topic arises. I am curious about that.' Ask what the client needs to feel safe and progress.

Supportive Relationship: Build trust through unconditional positive regard, empathy and consistency. Reflect on relationship dynamics, which can mirror patterns contributing to resistance.

Vary Methods: Use experiential or non-verbal methods for clients who struggle with direct discussions. For those who intellectualise emotions, provide psychoeducation about the importance of exploring emotions and defence mechanisms.

Explore the Function of Resistance: Understand resistance as a protective mechanism against painful emotions or traumatic memories. For example, individuals frequently seem to respond initially to shame by denial and avoidance of the topic, externalising by pointing at others (prosecutor-role), expressing anger towards others (aggressor-role), internalising and becoming depressed, helpless and fatalistic (victim-role), or withdraw socially and drop-out from therapy (Bradshaw, 2005; Elison et al., 2006). Some symptoms may be tied to their sense of self, and thus, letting go of these may feel like losing part of their identity, even if this part causes suffering. Therapists can work with clients to explore their identity beyond their issues, helping them envision a self that incorporates change while still feeling authentic; they may also invite the client to try out new activities and remind them that if this does not feel right, they can always return to their old life. Acknowledge the presence of pain and the role of resistance in protecting against it, including its benefits (at least in the past); create a safe environment to help clients gradually confront painful experiences. Try to understand what clients want to protect, and give them a sense that they may still change while protecting this essence.

Validate Control Needs: Resistance can be a way to keep control and autonomy, which may avoid vulnerability and protect self-image. Validate the client's need for control and this need's origins. Work collaboratively to review therapy goals and determine the next steps.

Foster Self-Compassion: Help clients differentiate accountability from guilt/self-blame. Highlight what was not in their control and explain practical steps they can take now.

Case Study 9.1

Mark

Forty-year-old Mark is unhappy in his career but resists exploring other options or taking steps towards change. The therapist uncovers that Mark's fear of the unknown and potential failure maintains the status quo. The therapist gently challenges Mark's assumptions about change and failure, encouraging tiny, manageable steps towards exploring his interests. They also work on building Mark's self-esteem and resilience to cope with potential setbacks.

Case Study 9.2

Brian

Brian, a 27-year-old IT-expert, resists forming close relationships due to a deep-seated belief that he is unworthy of love, protecting himself from anticipated rejection and hurt. Through a series of sessions focusing on Brian's self-esteem and past experiences, the therapist helps Brian identify and challenge his negative self-beliefs. This involves exploring Brian's family dynamics and past relationships to understand the origins of his beliefs.

WORKING WITH IMPASSES

An impasse refers to a point in therapy where progress seems to stall or stop altogether (Cornell & Landaiche, 2006; Leiper & Kent, 2001). It is a period of apparent standstill in the client's therapeutic journey. Despite efforts to change, old patterns persist, and new insights or behaviours seem out of reach. Impasses are crucial moments for therapeutic growth, as they often signify underlying issues or conflicts that must be addressed. These opportunities allow therapists and clients to explore deeper psychological structures and scripts that resist change.

A therapist can identify an impasse through several indicators. Despite ongoing efforts, the client does not seem to progress or achieve their therapy goals. The client repeatedly discusses the same issues without gaining new insights or changing perspectives. There may be increased resistance from the client, such as missing sessions, being late or displaying reluctance to engage in more profound therapeutic work. The client might seem emotionally withdrawn or disengaged during sessions, indicating a disconnect from the therapy process. The client and therapist may feel frustrated, despondent or stuck, sensing that the therapy is not yielding the expected results.

Overcoming an impasse requires patience, insight and sometimes creative therapeutic interventions. Addressing the impasse directly can be a powerful intervention. Asking the client about their feelings towards the current standstill can open new avenues for exploration. It might be helpful to revisit the therapy goals and case formulation, or gather additional information for example via questionnaires (Bram, 2015). This can clarify expectations and realign the therapy-process. Encouraging the client to express feelings or thoughts they might be holding back can uncover underlying issues contributing to the impasse. Introducing new therapeutic techniques or exercises can provide a fresh perspective and stimulate progress. This might involve more experiential work, such as role-playing, exploring aspects of the client's personality or scripts. Examining relational dynamics may increase insight, authentic communication and disclosure. Impasses often reflect transferential/relational patterns the client enacts in their life; exploring can lead to significant breakthroughs. Therapists might benefit from discussing impasses and countertransference with a clinical supervisor.

Case Study 9.3

Cathy

Cathy, a 54-year-old solicitor, attended weekly TA sessions for a year to address self-sabotage in her relationships and career. Despite initial progress, she hit an impasse, unable to move from acknowledgement to change, leading to repetitive sessions and increased frustration. The therapist noticed Cathy's disengagement and directly addressed the impasse, prompting Cathy to admit feeling stuck and hopeless. Recognising the impasse might be rooted in Cathy's life script, the therapist explored beliefs, and their origins, about her worthiness. They used creative role-playing exercises, allowing Cathy to 'speak' to her younger self, fostering emotional connection and self-compassion. This experiential technique helped Cathy emotionally connect with parts of herself frozen in past traumas and beliefs. The therapist also explored the possibility that Cathy's impasse reflected her relational patterns with authority figures, including enacting her script within the therapeutic relationship – by seeking and simultaneously fearing real change; authentic conversations about this revealed deeper fears about autonomy and success. This helped Cathy recognise how her behaviours maintained her life script and began challenging it by taking small risks in her relationships and career.

REPAIRING RUPTURES

Ruptures in a therapeutic relationship refer to disruptions or breakdowns in the trust, rapport or mutual understanding between the therapist and the client (Eubanks et al., 2018). These ruptures can occur when there is a mismatch in expectations, misunderstandings or conflicts hindering the therapy-process, or where there is game within the consulting room.

For example, the client may have specific expectations about the therapy-process or the therapist's role that are not aligned with the therapist's approach, leading to disappointment or frustration. The therapist's communication style or interventions may inadvertently create confusion, discomfort or feelings of being misunderstood by the client. Breaches of therapeutic boundaries may erode the client's trust and sense of safety. Differences in opinions, values or treatment goals may create tension, hindering collaboration and progress. An unconscious intersubjective process can also occur, where the therapist's own script issues are activated, and lead to a rupture of a familiar game payoff for both (Hargaden & Cornell, 2019). A therapist can be attentive to relational ruptures by paying attention to verbal and nonverbal cues from the client that indicate discomfort, resistance or dissatisfaction. They can engage in self-reflection and introspection to recognise moments of disconnection or tension within the therapeutic relationship and seek guidance and feedback from supervisors or colleagues. Research has shown that script-driven ruptures occur with both experienced therapists and novices, highlighting the importance of ongoing supervision.

Healing ruptures in the therapeutic relationship involves sensitive responsiveness, acknowledging and addressing the underlying issues that contributed to the breakdown. This can be achieved through encouraging open and honest dialogue with the client to explore the sources of tension or misunderstanding and collaboratively find resolutions. The therapist expresses their authentic understanding and empathy towards the client's experiences related to the rupture, fostering a sense of validation and support. The therapist takes deliberate steps to rebuild trust and rapport through consistent, genuine and empathic interactions with the client. Repairing relational ruptures in the therapeutic relationship can lead to significant improvements in the therapy-process and outcomes, for example, by enhancing trust and collaboration and deepening their understanding of the client's needs, relational patterns and areas for growth.

Psychological games may cause relational ruptures. Therapists try to prevent introducing transactions and games, via reflection on their own countertransference and script. When games develop , the therapist may remain non-defensive and open to talk through what happened, owning their part and apologising where needed. It is important to explore the client's experience and deal with it in the here-and-now. Making immediate interpretations is usually unhelpful (e.g. 'I didn't say that, you must be angry with your mother'); it is more helpful to be genuinely interested in what and how it happened from the client's perspective and look how to deal with it differently in future.

GENUINE RELATIONSHIP

Berne advocated a genuine, authentic bond with the client based on communicating honestly and transparently while upholding professional boundaries to ensure the client feels esteemed and appreciated. For example, a practitioner may express their own experiences of the relationship (e.g. by saying, 'I feel that. . .; I may be wrong. . . how do you feel about this?'). TA therapists do not adopt a neutral role as a blank canvas for the client's projections, like in some psychodynamic approaches. Authentic relationships allow clients to explore and experiment with real-life interactions, enabling the analysis and transformation of transactional patterns. Consequently, TA therapy aligns more closely with relational-humanistic approaches.

> Carl Rogers has suggested that congruence in the relationship between practitioners and clients helps clients to become more congruent with themselves (Atzil-Slonim et al., 2018; Kolden et al., 2018). You may also become authentic in everyday life when you learn to be authentic in the sessions. Thus, clients experience the relationship with the practitioner as a model for how relationships could be outside the consultation room. (Vos, 2017, p. 137)

SUMMARY

- Research shows that a positive therapeutic relationship improves therapy outcomes and reduces dropout.
- TA therapists may offer affirmative practice, validate the client's autonomy, work with resistance, impasses, transference and countertransference, being non-judgemental, following the client, stimulating insight development and repairing ruptures.
- TA therapists offer a genuine relationship and not merely a neutral role as a blank canvas. Genuine relationships allow clients to explore and experiment with real-life transactions.

10

STRUCTURING COMPETENCIES

How do we structure TA therapy? Research evidence shows that clients can benefit from having structure in therapy. Previous chapters have already described other structuring elements, such as working with therapy goals (Chapter 6) and psychoeducation to empower clients (Chapter 9); this chapter focuses on the stages across sessions and the structure of individual sessions. The semi-structured treatment manual in this book's last chapter provides a practical example.

- Stages in psychotherapies
- Stages in TA
- Structure of individual sessions

STAGES IN PSYCHOTHERAPIES

Many studies suggest that the changes that individuals experience happen through multiple stages. For instance, the Transtheoretical Model of Behaviour Change describes how individuals go through the stages of pre-contemplation to contemplation, preparation, action, maintenance and termination (Prochaska & DiClemente, 1997). Other models have focused on the role of motivational aspects of change, with potential implications for using motivational techniques/interviewing (Schwarzer, 2014).

Parallel to stages of individual change, psychological therapies also often follow a structured process; for example, most treatment manual progresses through stages of assessment, case formulation, intervention, application and evaluation (Vos, 2023). Research indicates that individuals experience gradual changes through such stages (Boswell, 2015). These therapeutic stages may be described as the different stages that clients go through in their relationship with the challenging experiences, painful memories, threatening emotions or destructive relationships that have brought them to therapy; many clients follow a predictable developmental sequence of recognising, reevaluating, comprehending and resolving these problematic experiences (Stiles, 2001). According to Stiles, these stages happen through the process of assimilating problematic communities of voices (similar to script-beliefs) until they become resources, rather than lead to detriment psychological health.

While some research suggests that change occurs in distinct stages (Prochaska & Norcross, 2001), with better outcomes associated with starting treatment at a higher stage (Krebs et al., 2018), the linearity of these stages is debated. Some argue that clients may not follow a rigid path and may even regress, necessitating a tailored approach (Bridle et al., 2005). Nonetheless, there is agreement that clients undergo successive shifts in their mind-set, leading to the potential benefit of offering distinct therapy stages (Katakis, 1989; Kiesler, 1996). Therefore, it is crucial to customise treatment stages to each client's needs, allowing for flexibility in applying therapeutic techniques to facilitate shifts in the client's frame of mind.

STAGES IN TA

Overview

Like other psychotherapies, clients undergo structured stages of change in the TA treatment manuals used in clinical trials (Vos & van Rijn, 2023). The TA survey also identified four distinct stages in the practices of most TA therapists:

1 *Preparation:* building a therapeutic alliance, creating a contract, an initial assessment of strengths and difficulties
2 *Assessment:* clinical and etiological analysis, strengthening the inner Adult
3 *Processing:* learning to accept and express experiences, working through past emotions and memories, developing insight and awareness, challenging unhelpful messages
4 *Decision-making and application:* making and applying decisions in daily life, and an ending therapy. (Vos & van Rijn, 2021c)

In classical TA, similar stages of treatment are commonly known as preparation, decontamination, deconfusion and redecision, consolidation or termination (Berne, 1961, 1966; Stewart & Joines, 1987; Woollams & Brown, 1978). Some TA therapists believe these stages occur linearly (Pulleyblank & McCormick, 1985; Woollams & Brown, 1978). However, other authors argue that deconfusion already starts in the first therapy session when the therapist responds empathetically to the client (Hargaden & Sills, 2014), because a supportive therapeutic relationship is needed before the therapist can challenge the client's irrational thoughts in a later stage (Clarkson, 1992; Hargaden & Sills, 2014). Despite many theoretical discussions and some case-studies, there is no systematic research on the effects and experiences of the specific TA-stages, their order and the therapeutic mechanisms of decontamination and deconfusion. Therefore, we assume that while most clients progress through these treatment stages, the boundaries of these stages often blur, and TA therapy must remain flexible and tailored to individual clients (Vos & van Rijn, 2021b). This is also reflected in our decision to use the neutral terms preparation, assessment, processing, decision-making and application stages.

Preparation Stage

The initial stage of therapy establishes the foundation for a positive therapeutic relationship by allowing clients to express their problems and needs freely. The therapist aims to be transparent, involve the client in decision-making and manage expectations by explaining general therapy goals and methods. This stage may include some initial work on decontamination, deconfusion and nurturing the integrating Adult, as therapist and client learn to work relationally and flexibly together. Motivational interviewing techniques, such as showing empathy, supporting self-efficacy and acknowledging resistance to change, can enhance the client's motivation for therapy. The therapist develops a basic treatment agreement with the client, with a detailed case formulation and a plan to follow later.

Some clients may find structured approaches challenging. It is crucial to empathically acknowledge their resistance while exploring underlying causes and life scripts (e.g. analyses may reveal a broader pattern of resistance against following authorities, a Rebellious Child or drama triangle). These frustrations may be reframed as opportunities to identify important patterns or messages in the client's life. The therapist should attempt to address practical causes of frustration where possible and help the client cognitively reframe their expectations to align with the structured format. The therapist may use frustrations to strengthen the therapeutic bond, authentically sharing their uncertainties while emphasising the collaborative nature of therapy. They can explain how structure, semi-standardised questions/questionnaires aid focusing the treatment on the most important problems, comparing it to a GP's diagnostic tools. The therapist may clarify that while initial sessions may be more structured, later sessions can be more flexible.

Assessment Stage (Traditional Terms: Decontamination Leading to Deconfusion)

The assessment phase aims to systematically assess the client's clinical phenomenon (ego-states, life position, self-efficacy and social functioning; see Chapter 4) and their possible underlying aetiology (see Chapter 5). This leads to the therapist formulating and sharing a case formulation that forms the foundations and justification of the plan for the subsequent therapy stages (Chapter 8). Throughout the assessment phase, the therapist should offer empathy and normalisation to create a supportive therapeutic environment (Chapter 9). This approach helps clients navigate the complex process of self-discovery, laying the groundwork for subsequent stages.

The client will be invited to explore and express their problems and possible causes in this stage. This can be a very emotional process for the client, triggering feelings of shame, guilt or helplessness. Therefore, the therapist should empathically engage with the client, acknowledge their suffering, normalise problems and provide hope. The assessment includes decontamination, and may move towards deconfusion, and nourishing the integrating Adult. The therapist should empathically engage with the client's resistance and explore the underlying protective needs (Chapter 9). Therefore, the therapeutic attitude focused on the three Ps of protection, permission and potency to the client. TA therapists have identified the three most important components in this stage: decontamination, evaluation and decision (crystallisation) and cognitive exercises.

Decontamination: In Classical TA, decontamination aims to clarify the Adult ego-state from the contaminating influences of the historical material deriving from Parent or Child ego-states. Decontamination may involve identifying and addressing unrealistic and unhelpful beliefs, separating current thoughts and behaviours from the life script and past conditioning, and developing a more autonomous and authentic sense of self. This process strengthens the Adult ego-state, through the development of insight enabling individuals to make conscious choices and effective problem-solving based on their needs and aspirations. For example, a client overwhelmed with work and experiencing anxiety and depression might have internalised messages about always appearing strong (Parental contamination) and fear of failure (Child contamination). Decontamination helps identify these outdated beliefs, promoting self-care and realistic self-evaluation.

Whereas there is limited direct research on the TA-concept of decontamination, other studies provide indirect support. It seems effective to address unrealistic/unhelpful beliefs and support developing more realistic/helpful beliefs (Hofmann et al., 2012), particularly if integrated with exploring addressing emotions (Aldao et al., 2010; Mergenthaler, 1996; Norcross & Lambert, 2019). It is also effective to explore how past experiences influence the client's present and foster self-insight (Allen, 2000; Bohlmeijer, 2007; Jennissen et al., 2018). Furthermore, clients benefit from learning to listen to their authentic self (Schlegel, 2013, 2009) and develop self-compassion (Gilbert, 2009; MacBeth & Gumley, 2012; Neff, 2011).

Evaluation and Decision (Crystallisation): At the end of each session, the therapist may summarise and shift the focus from past to present and future, connecting with therapy goals and helping the client make conscious decisions.

Cognitive Exercises or Adult Decontamination: The therapist may use cognitive-behaviour techniques (Chapter 12) to evaluate negative automatic thoughts by identifying beliefs, exploring contamination of Adult function, cognitive reframing, evaluating beliefs (e.g. how relevant, realistic, evidence-based and helpful is this belief?), formulating alternative beliefs (e.g. what would be a more relevant, realistic, evidence-based and helpful belief?), directly challenging and disconfirming with behavioural evidence, counter myths and negative injunctions (e.g. 'I cannot be happy until.'; 'I cannot change who I am'), positive reframing to counter helplessness or victim mentality reframing (e.g. What would you tell a friend?) and emphasising personal agency while acknowledging past experiences. However, it has been argued that such directive/confrontational interventions may only be feasible when there is a basic Adult functioning, and a trusting and supportive therapeutic relationship (Clarkson, 1992; Hargaden & Sills, 2014).

10.1 REFLECTIVE QUESTIONS

- Think of a client or person you know well. Which questions and interventions/exercises could help in their decontamination? What cognitive interventions could be helpful? How relevant and helpful would decontamination and cognitive interventions be in this stage?

Case Study 10.1

Isabella

Isabella, a 35-year-old solicitor, sought therapy to address persistent self-doubt and feelings of unworthiness affecting her personal and professional life. She did not recognise her achievements at work, and questioned the acceptance by her friends and her partner. These issues stemmed from childhood experiences and parental messages. In the decontamination stage, the therapist helped Isabella develop insight and challenge the influence of parental prejudices and childhood needs on her current thoughts and behaviours. Through reflective discussions and exercises, Isabella identified the origins of her self-critical beliefs. The therapist encouraged her to recognise moments when her thoughts echoed parental messages, particularly regarding self-worth and decision-making. This process allowed Isabella to understand how early parental conditioning influenced her present-day experiences. Through this insight, Isabella felt freer and more able to recognise her achievements at work, as well as love by the people close to her. This supported her in developing self-acceptance and autonomy.

Processing Stage (Traditional Terms: Working With Child Ego-State, Deconfusion Stage)

The processing stage focuses on experiential work in the here-and-now, re-experiencing and reformulating archaic material.

Prerequisites for this stage are:

- Assessment phase completion
- Clear case formulation agreed therapy goals and treatment plan
- Strong working alliances are needed as clients explore potentially painful emotions and memories that may be upsetting (Clarkson, 1992; Woollams & Brown, 1979).
- Safety Awareness: Careful monitoring of client distress during emotional processing.
- Adaptive Recognition: Understanding life script themes as historical coping mechanisms.

Following decontamination, TA therapists focus on work with the Child, or the deconfusion of the Child ego-state. The Child ego-state responds to introjected injunctive message that contradicts the inner need (e.g. a need to have a sense of agency and achievement, faced with the injunction 'Don't succeed') by adapting to their environment, usually by making an intuitive, often non-verbal decision, that balances their needs with the perceived limitations of the environment. These decisions are made by the Little Professor (A1) for example ('I'm ok, as long as I am not better than my father').

Objectives of deconfusion may include:

- Resolve the internal conflict and confusion originating from childhood experiences

- Clarify and untangle complex, often unconscious thoughts, feelings and behaviours
- Support clients in exploring underlying needs and suppressed feelings
- Guide clients through an experiential/reflective journey to understand the life script origins of their present problems, thoughts, emotions, behaviours, transactions
- Develop awareness of unconscious drivers and transactional patterns
- Empower clients to make conscious choices and challenge limiting beliefs
- Develop healthier, more adaptive ways of relating to themselves and others.

The deconfusion process may consist of multiple steps:

- *Identifying Conflicts*: Recognising contradictions between introjected messages and inner needs (e.g. need for achievement vs. injunction 'Don't succeed').
- *Revisiting Early Scenes*: Exploring suppressed memories and feelings.
- *Finding New Balance*: Discovering different options and clarity (Clarkson, 1992).
- *Developing Internal Safety*: Cultivating a sense of security (Clarkson, 1992; Woollams & Brown, 1979).

For example, imagine a client who had often attempted in her childhood to please her demanding mother by being the best at everything and suppressing her needs and experiences. Having realised that she was working excessively and not experiencing a sense of achievement during the decontamination stage, the client began to re-experience the distress of her childhood, fuelled by the attachment-based fear of losing her mother.

The sessions in this stage are less structured and tailored to the client's unique situation and needs, requiring both therapist and client creativity. The content of the sessions will follow from the case formulation, therapy goals and treatment plan. The therapeutic approach involves empathic Interactions to facilitate emotional understanding and exploration. Transference analysis may help examine the therapeutic relationship and past patterns (Hargaden & Sills, 2014; Widdowson, 2016). Deconfusion is primarily an affective process (Widdowson, 2016). Affective processing focuses on exploring and deepening emotional experiences and their meanings, which has proven effective, particularly when emotional processing is combined with cognitive understanding (Aldao, 2010; Bohart, 1993; Mergenthaler, 1996; Norcross & Lambert, 2019).

Case Study 10.2

George

In the previous case study, we followed Isabella, as she worked through decontamination identifying her script belief that she was not worthwhile, or successful unless she was perfect. The insight of the decontamination period led her to re-experience painful childhood experiences. She remembered her mother being critical of her messy appearance and dirty clothes, and being shouted at when she made mistakes. The beliefs she introjected were that she was worthless and unloved and her script decision to Be Perfect aimed to make her more acceptable to her mother. The deconfusion stage entailed revisiting the early scenes in her life, expressing feelings and developing new self-acceptance. She released that perfection was not achievable and that she could be loved and be successful as herself.

- Think of a client or person you know well. Which questions and interventions/exercises could help their deconfusion? How could your relationship help deconfusion?

Decision-Making and Change Stage

This stage involves clients deciding to change and implementing changes in their thinking, feeling, behaving, transactions, or life script patterns. In the broader realm of psychotherapy research, this idea resembles the Core Conflictual Relationship Theme (Luborsky & Crits-Christoph 1998), and the preparatory and action phases in the transtheoretical model (Prochaska & Norcross, 2001).

Prerequisites for this stage include:

- Understood the causes of their problems
- Explored hidden feelings and unmet needs
- Made sense of their past
- Developed internal safety (crucial for coping in daily life)

The Redecision Process has also been called 'changing a script decision'. This may involve the following objectives:

- Gaining awareness of alternative options and resources (e.g. in the Child ego-state)
- Modifying initial script beliefs and responses/decisions (e.g. in both Child and Adult ego-states)
- Creating conditions for structural life changes
- Establishing new personal decisions, goals and commitments
- Developing Adult ego-state
- Developing inner nurturing and self-efficacy
- Improving social functioning
- Experimenting with and evaluating changes in daily life
- Integrating cognitive and emotional processes in daily life
- Building robustness and autonomy.

Practically speaking, redecision involves helping clients set concrete daily life objectives. Research indicates that goals are most impactful when they are significant, meaningful, specific, straightforward, time-bound, challenging yet attainable, aligned with each other and focused on pursuing positive outcomes (Vos, 2017). The therapist supports clients in the planning, experimenting, evaluating and adjusting strategies to achieve the objectives. Finally, the therapist may stimulate the client to make long-term commitments.

Extensive research supports the effectiveness of goal-setting and developing life projects in therapy (Lindhiem et al., 2016; Lloyd et al., 2019; Tryon et al., 2018). Clients benefit from decision-making and trying out changes in therapy which may foster asense of hope

(Koehn & Cutcliffe, 2007; Larsen et al., 2007; Schrank et al., 2008; Snyder, 2003), self-efficacy (Corrigon, 2006; Maddux & Kleiman, 2006; Marks & Allegrante, 2005; Schwarzer, 2014) and the ability to live a meaningful and fulfilling life while embracing life's limitations (Vos, 2014b, 2016a, 2016b, 2017).

Case Study 10.3

You can already imagine Isabella starting to make changes throughout decontamination and deconfusion. These redecisions supported the development of her autonomy and choices. Following decontamination, she began to recognise that her friends appreciated her and made an effort to spend more time with them. She also spent more time with her partner and stopped filling their time with her anxieties about work. At work, she started to place healthy boundaries and was able to notice praise. Although these changes had a limited effect, they helped her focus on the early archaic experiences. Going through the deconfusion stage and recognising how these early adaptations impacted her life, she began to develop true-self acceptance. This was a life script redecision that enabled her to have intimacy in her relationships and a realistic version of success in her professional life.

10.3 REFLECTIVE QUESTIONS

- Think of a client or person you know well. How could you help them identify aspects of their life script that they want to change? Which questions and interventions/exercises could you suggest to help them script-redecision, decision-making and making changes? How could you motivate them, stimulate courage, skills and resources to make these changes actually happen?

Ending

The final sessions aim to evaluate and take stock of lessons learnt during TA, identify how the clients could continue their changes, develop contingency plans and cope with feelings of termination. As the end approaches, the client may experience existential feelings of 'ending' and 'finitude', resulting in emotions or difficulties in the therapeutic relationship (Adapted Child behaviour). It is essential to recognise these feelings and reflect on what relational ends mean for the client and how they could apply the lessons learnt in the previous sessions to cope with relational endings. The therapist should bring a copy of the original treatment aims and plan to evaluate the client's progress, celebrate achievements and prepare for future development.

Prerequisites before this stage involve the client and the therapist feeling that they have achieved the main treatment aims set in the assessment session. This means that the client has likely identified some new goals in life ('script change'), created conditions and inner safety to facilitate structural change ('facilitating script change') and has been experimenting and evaluating change in daily life. It could also be that the maximum number of sessions available for funding by the national health service or health insurance has been reached.

When a client presents with significant psychopathology or poses a risk to themselves or others in the last session, the therapist should explore options for the client to receive mental health support from another professional. This may involve referring the client to other healthcare services or recommending that they consult their family doctor. The therapist should avoid giving the impression in previous sessions that they could endlessly continue providing therapy to this client. Such an indication could potentially lead clients to become dependent or exaggerate their need for help, manipulating the therapist into prolonging therapy.

STRUCTURE OF AN INDIVIDUAL SESSION

Therapists may use different structures for sessions tailored to specific clients and urgent needs. The following is a potential overview of a session (Vos, 2017).

Step 1: Emotional Check-in

Check-in: The check-in aims to establish a connection, inquire about significant life events and explore psychological development, for example, via questions like 'How are you feeling today?' or 'Since our last session, how have you been?' When clients find it challenging to respond to broad inquiries, a more specific question may be posed, such as 'Could you share three meaningful moments from the past week?' (Vos, 2017). Some clients tend to provide extensive responses during the emotional check-in, so clarifying the purpose of this exercise and requesting that the client focus on, for example, their top three most impactful experiences can be beneficial.

Session goals and wishes: The therapist asks whether the client has any specific goals and wishes for today's sessions. The therapist will help the client relate their needs/wishes to the overarching therapy goals they may have agreed on.

Step 2: Bridging Between Sessions

Memory: To maintain a sense of continuity, it can be beneficial to encourage the client's reflection on the previous session via questions such as, 'What do you recall from our last session?' or 'Have you been pondering our session during the past week? If so, what has been on your mind?'

Refresher: The therapist may ask the client to summarise key points from the last session, or give their summary.

Connecting sessions: Following this refresher, the therapist may establish a connection between the previous and current sessions, highlighting their interrelation. For instance, they could say, 'In our previous session, we explored your current challenges. In today's session, we could delve into how these challenges originated in the past. How do you feel about this?' It is crucial to be transparent about the rationale behind this approach, emphasising that the client is seen as autonomous and has the power to influence the course of treatment.

Contract/goals: It can be helpful to reiterate the therapy contract/goals with the client, reminding them of their active participation and reinforcing their agency in shaping their therapeutic journey.

Step 3: Evaluating Homework

Homework can improve outcomes (Mausbach et al., 2010). The therapist's approach to discussing and reinforcing homework assignments is essential for maximising their effectiveness.

When reviewing homework, the therapist emphasises positive aspects of the client's efforts, acknowledging that even attempting the task is a significant step forward. This positive reinforcement is crucial, especially when clients feel they may have failed. The therapist recognises that learning new skills takes time and assures the client that challenges will be addressed in future sessions. Suppose the client perceives their efforts as a failure. In that case, the therapist skillfully reframes this as a success, highlighting the valuable information gained about what doesn't work. This perspective shift allows for the development of better strategies in subsequent sessions.

Analysing challenges faced during homework assignments, or incomplete homework, is an integral part of the process. The therapist avoids criticism or punishment. Instead, they explore the reasons empathetically, identifying potential issues with the homework formulation, the client's internal resources, practical constraints or social factors. This non-judgemental approach maintains a supportive therapeutic environment and encourages open communication about obstacles. This approach turns every experience, whether perceived as successful or not, into a learning opportunity. The overall process of addressing homework in therapy is one of continuous improvement, as insights from each homework experience refine future homework and therapeutic approaches.

Step 4: Session Goal

The therapist and client decide together on the goal and methods of the session. The therapist can give a proposal, particularly in the first sessions when it may be more appropriate to be more directive and function as a role model; the therapist must provide the rationale, show how this fits within the broader agreed therapy goals/contract and ask the client for consent about this structure for this session. The therapist explains that this session structure does not need to be rigid and that they could decide together to deviate from this agenda if something else arises.

Step 5: Content

This step contains this session's specific content.

Step 6: Ending

The practitioner checks how the clients evaluate the session. For example, the therapist may ask about the three most significant lessons, messages or decisions that the client takes away from this session (crystallisation). The client can be asked for any wishes for the next session(s); it is crucial that the therapist writes this down in their notes and comes back to this in the next session to show their reliability. The therapist and client may decide to assign some tasks/homework to prepare for the upcoming session.

SUMMARY

- Research indicates that clients go through stages of change in therapies and benefit from specific therapeutic stages.
- TA therapies often consist of the following stages: preparation to build the initial therapeutic relationship and initial therapeutic contract; assessment of clinical and aetiological phenomena, leading to a case formulation and treatment (traditionally described as decontamination leading to deconfusion); processing to explore, express and deepen experiences and work through past emotions (traditionally defined as working with the Child and deconfusion); decision-making and application of change (traditionally described as script-redecision) and ending therapy.

11

EXPERIENTIAL COMPETENCIES

How do you work with the client's experiences in the present? After a generic overview of experiential skills in psychotherapies and TA, this chapter will explain several evidence-based ways to help clients accept, explore, deepen and express their experiences. These experiential competencies seem particularly important for the TA therapeutic stage of processing/deconfusion.

- Experiential acceptance exercises
- Mindfulness exercises
- Body-oriented exercises
- Imagination exercises

EXPERIENTIAL SKILLS IN PSYCHOTHERAPIES

Research indicates that experiential processing skills assist clients in embracing, expressing and delving into their experience and emotional processing levels, which are pivotal components of effective psychotherapy (Diener et al., 2007; Norcross & Lambert, 2019). The more profoundly and deeply clients scrutinise their experiences, the more effective psychotherapy becomes (Greenberg et al., 2007; Hendricks, 2002; Orlinsky et al., 2004; Pos et al., 2008; Sachse & Elliott, 2002). Nonetheless, some studies propose that emotional processing in isolation may not be efficacious or detrimental (Mohr et al., 1990), but is effective when combined with cognitive understanding (Bohart, 1993). For instance, Mergenthaler (1996) discovered that therapy is most effective when there are elevated levels of emotion and cognitive abstraction during a session, as TA therapists often do.

Engaging in experiential depth in the present moment implies that therapists encourage clients to embrace, express and explore their experiences. This involves employing mechanisms to assist clients in liberating themselves from inhibitions, cultivating insight and fostering a constructive relationship with the past. Clients are encouraged to focus on their present experiences rather than solely dwelling on the past. Therapists explicitly concentrate on and deepen clients' experiences and foster self-insight, such as engaging in emotional-physiological work with Child ego-states, stimulating inner Child-Parent dialogue, alleviating pressure from the inner Parent, promoting trust and tolerance of emotions, focusing on specific examples and replacing inner inhibitions with freedom.

This approach aims to help clients transcend themselves and their past, creating a pathway for personal growth and self-discovery.

Let us take a step back. What do we mean by emotion and feeling? According to modern cognitive behaviour therapy (CBT) research, thoughts, emotions, behaviour and physical sensations are interconnected and influence one another: we cannot disconnect them (Beck, 2020). This understanding aligns with modern CBT theory, which asserts that these elements are linked and that changes in one can lead to changes in others. When individuals experience distress or worry, their thinking patterns and emotional responses can exacerbate negative feelings, similar to TA therapists claiming how transactional core messages can impact the behaviour and emotions of the ego-states (Chapter 4). Therefore, modern CBT-therapists claim that by altering how a person thinks, therapists aim to change how individuals interpret the world around them, addressing unhelpful thinking styles and laying the groundwork for addressing neurotic symptoms, similar to TA therapists helping clients to rewrite their life script (Chapter 5). Furthermore, when you feel bad, you are more likely to think about negative examples in your past (mood-congruent memory retrieval bias), which shows that our emotions also impact our thinking; similarly, when a client is in a particular ego-state, they will mainly access memories and parts of their life script associated with that ego-state. For example, a client's Critical Parent ego-state may reinforce their symptoms of depression by primarily focusing on negative memories or by refusing to go entirely into details in their past; a therapist may need to help the client shift to other states, such as the realistic Adult ego-state, to access different parts of the client's life script; the therapist may suggest a role-play or empty-chair exercise with the Critical Parent and Adult dialoguing with each other about the past.

EXPERIENTIAL SKILLS IN TA

Awareness requires living in the here-and-now, and not in the elsewhere, the past or the future. (Berne, 1964, p. 90)

In our survey, TA therapists said the following about experiential-therapeutic competencies:

Therapists stimulate clients to accept, express, and explore their experiences. This involves using mechanisms to help clients become free from inhibitions, transcend the self and develop self-insight and a constructive relationship with the past. Clients are also stimulated to focus on their experiences in the here-and-now, not merely on the past, and to take risks to fulfil their potential in the present. (Vos & van Rijn, 2021c, p. 39)

TA psychotherapy emphasises the importance of present experiences in facilitating client change and understanding. It suggests that individuals can alter their life scripts by becoming aware of and modifying their transactions, focusing significantly on the here-and-now. This approach is crucial for understanding and addressing current behavioural and emotional patterns, allowing for direct exploration and work through real-time interactions, feelings and responses. Emphasising the present moment aids in developing self-awareness, emotional insight and the ability to make conscious choices, fostering personal growth and improved relational dynamics.

> The moment a little boy is concerned with [categorising the specific birds as] a jay and a sparrow, he can no longer see the birds or hear them sing. (Berne, 1964, p. 89)

This quote highlights the importance of focusing on immediate experiences without overanalysing, promoting full engagement and appreciation of the present. The concept of the Somatic Child is integral, as it involves attuning to clients' physical and emotional experiences, enhancing awareness of bodily responses and their impact on thoughts, feelings and behaviours. This holistic approach contributes to a deeper understanding of internal processes and personal growth within the TA framework.

- *Authenticity and Awareness:* Present-focused work aligns with TA's here-and-now principle, fostering authenticity and awareness of current experiences rather than being controlled by past scripts (Berne, 1961). Clients may, for example, be able to identify how particular situations, beliefs, emotions or behaviours give a constricting or uneasy bodily sensation because they are associated with a negative life script. In contrast, self-chosen authentic values may lead to liberating bodily sensations.
- *Emotional Access:* Enables real-time emotion processing, crucial for emotional regulation (Greenberg & Paivio, 1997).
- *Ego-State Work:* Facilitates identification and adaptation of ego-states for healthier interactions (Stewart & Joines, 1987).
- *Problem-Solving:* Develops effective skills through the Adult ego-state's rationality (Malouff et al., 2007).
- *Therapeutic Alliance:* Strengthens client–therapist collaboration, critical for successful outcomes (Baier et al., 2020; Johnsson & Stenlund, 2010; Martin et al., 2000).
- *Personal Responsibility:* Encourages clients to take responsibility for current experiences, a central TA goal (Berne, 1964).
- *Behavioural Change:* Facilitates lasting change by modifying present behaviours (Hayes et al., 1999).
- *Psychological Distress Reduction:* Reduces anxiety and depression by preventing rumination, for example, via mindfulness (Segal et al., 2012).
- *Mindfulness:* Promotes non-judgemental observation of present experiences (Kabat-Zinn, 2018).
- *Changing the Cycle:* Transactional processes can be self-perpetuating. A strong Critical Parent in a client's life script can lead to constant self and other criticism, focusing on flaws. This triggers negative thoughts, uncomfortable bodily sensations, avoidance, withdrawal and negative interactions, reinforcing a low mood and negative thoughts (see left cycle in Figure 11.1). However, if a therapist encourages mindfulness or

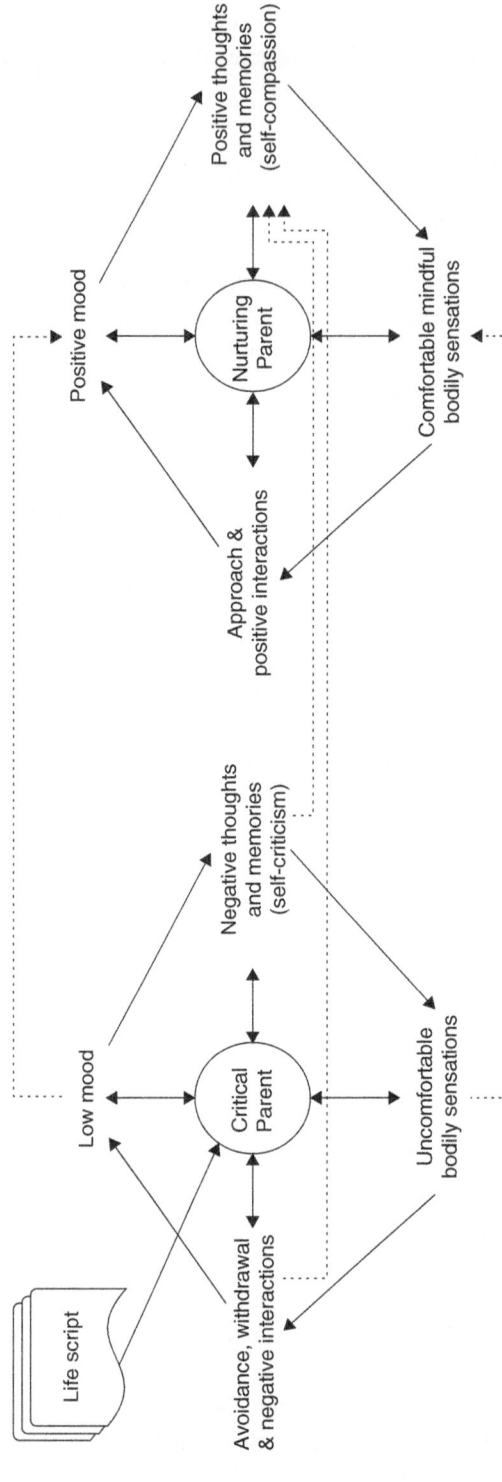

Figure 11.1 Example of How Experiential Exercises/Interventions May Break Self-Perpetuating Cycles

self-compassion, it can initiate a Nurturing Parent cycle, which fosters positive thoughts, comfortable bodily sensations, an approach attitude, positive interactions and improved mood (right cycle in Figure 11.1). Interestingly, clients don't need to initially believe in their or others' 'OK-ness'. By focusing on bodily sensations and treating it as a role-play, they can break the Critical Parent cycle and start the Nurturing Parent cycle. This 'fake it till you make it' approach (Vos, 2018) can sometimes shift the client from negative to positive transactional processes.

EXPERIENTIAL ACCEPTANCE EXERCISES

Therapists often assume clients can easily explore their feelings for self-discovery. However, without guidance towards accepting these experiences, clients may disengage or engage superficially. This aligns with 'experiential acceptance', a key component of psychological resilience that involves recognising experiences as they are and using them to reveal potential paths forward. Experiential acceptance involves approaching life's experiences openly and without judgement, countering the impulse to avoid discomfort. As Hayes et al. (1999, 2006) highlighted, acceptance promotes psychological flexibility and better mental health outcomes. It is a deliberate choice to welcome one's entire experience, mitigating avoidance cycles and fostering a kinder self-relationship.

Several factors may contribute to avoiding experiences:

- *Critical Parent:* Internalised judgement and criticism can lead to harsh self-dialogue.
- *Adult:* Overshadowed by overactive Parent or Child states, hindering neutral assessment.
- *Adapted Child:* An overly dominant Adapted Child may, for example, be the result of a strict upbringing, narcissistic caregivers and/or a lack of mirroring and validation by caregivers in early-life, which gives the individual the idea that their authentic emotions and needs do not matter and that they are only allowed to experience and express socially desirable emotions.
- *Dysfunctional Fundamental Psychological Structures:* Past traumas may cause emotional dysregulation or experiential avoidance (Schore, 2003, 2015).
- *Life Script:* Deep-seated beliefs and injunctive messages, such as helplessness or unworthiness, can hinder acceptance of triggering experiences.
- *Transactions:* Crossed or ulterior transactions can create internal and external conflicts.
- *Script-Systems:* These involve expressing socially acceptable feelings to mask genuine, perceived unacceptable emotions (Erskine & Zalcman, 1979; O'Reilly-Knapp & Erskine, 2010; Zalcman, 1990). Feelings typically masked by script-systems include vulnerability, fear or sadness and are substituted with more socially palatable emotions like anger or indignation. This emotional sleight of hand distorts self-perception and complicates interpersonal relationships, as a facade obscures the genuine emotional state. For example, a person who frequently resorts to anger (a script-system feeling) to avoid feeling hurt or vulnerable is not fully accepting their genuine emotional experiences.

This lack of acceptance can lead to repeated conflict, misunderstanding in relationships and an inner disconnection from one's authentic self.

TA therapists may help clients accept experiences through:

1 *Identification:* Recognising patterns of experiential avoidance.
2 *Learning Practical Emotion-Regulation Skills:* See next sections (e.g. mindfulness, breathing).
3 *Strengthening Adult:* Promoting objective processing of experiences.
4 *Strengthening Nurturing Parent:* Promoting a more kind, compassionate approach to oneself and one's experiences.
5 *Revising Life scripts:* Exploring origins of avoidance and rewriting narratives.
6 *Improving Transactions:* Engaging in clearer, more reciprocal communication.
7 *Experiential Acceptance:* Clients are encouraged to practice experiential acceptance via various exercises, as explained in the following sections.

TA therapists may also use a phenomenological approach to help clients accept and explore their experiences more fully, leading to more authentic and fulfilling lives (Nuttall, 2006; Summers & Tudor, 2000). Phenomenology focuses on exploring and understanding individuals' lived experiences and the interpretations/meanings they derive from them (Vos, 2017). Key phenomenological concepts include *epoché (bracketing)*, which means setting aside one's judgements and preconceptions to accept experiences as they come (let experiences reveal themselves). *Equalisation* means treating all aspects of a client's experience as equally important. *Horizontalisation* means examining experiences side-by-side without assuming hierarchy. Phenomenological-therapeutic methods can foster experiential acceptance in several ways:

- *Non-Judgemental Exploration:* By creating a space free from preconceptions, clients can examine their experiences without the burden of self-criticism or societal expectations. This can lead to greater self-acceptance and compassion.
- *Validating All Experiences:* Treating all aspects of a client's experience as equally important helps them acknowledge and accept parts of themselves they may have previously ignored or devalued.
- *Recognising Patterns:* Laying out experiences side-by-side can help clients see recurring themes in their lives. This awareness can lead to acceptance of these patterns as part of their lived experience, rather than as flaws to be eliminated.
- *Uncovering Authentic Values:* By peeling away layers of external expectations, differentiating what feels more meaningful from less meaningful, clients can discover and accept deeper, possibly suppressed wishes and meanings.
- *Embracing Complexity:* Phenomenology acknowledges the multifaceted nature of experiences, helping clients accept the complexity of their lives rather than seeking simplistic solutions.

Box 11.1

Experiential Avoidance in Religion

Strict religious upbringing or cult involvement can significantly impact an individual's relationship with their body and their ability to accept, feel, deepen and express their authentic experiences. These environments may teach that the body is sinful, leading to disconnection from bodily sensations and emotions as a defence against guilt and shame (Pargament et al., 2004). This hinders experiential acceptance—the ability to embrace thoughts, feelings and bodily sensations without judgement.

While religion can offer psychological benefits, it can also cause stress when personal experiences conflict with religious teachings (Pargament, 1997). Individuals may learn to suppress or deny experiences deemed unacceptable or sinful (Pargament & Ano, 2004). Marlene Winell describes the Religious Trauma Syndrome (RTS) as a condition experienced, for example, by those leaving authoritarian religions, manifesting as anxiety, depression and difficulty accepting experiences (Winell, 2008).

Therapists can help by creating a non-judgemental space for clients to explore experiences and beliefs. Techniques include:

- Ego-state analysis to challenge internalised critical voices
- Explaining experiential acceptance as a healthy practice
- Reframing harmful beliefs
- Teaching mindfulness for reconnection with bodily experiences
- Life script analysis and two-chair work to explore religious background
- Encouraging independent exploration of beliefs and values
- Re-decision work to revise early decisions influenced by strict religious beliefs
    This approach fosters compassion, openness and curiosity in clients' experiences.

MINDFULNESS EXERCISES

Therapists can stimulate experiential acceptance through various techniques. Research supports the effectiveness of mindfulness exercises (Goldberg, 2018; Khoury et al., 2013), which integrates organically and effectively within TA (Shepherd, 2020; Žvelc et al., 2011). Mindfulness involves focusing on the present moment, accepting thoughts, feelings and sensations without judgement. It transitions individuals from a goal-oriented 'doing' state to a present-focused 'being' state. This practice, rooted in Buddhism, has been adapted for therapeutic contexts, showing significant reductions in stress, anxiety and depression (Grossman et al., 2004; Kabat-Zinn, 2003). Clients may need to have developed stable fundamental psychological structures – such as sufficient emotion regulation skills – to do these self-distancing exercises, as otherwise, these exercises may worsen their well-being, such as reinforcing dissociation. Although research has focused on complete mindfulness-training programmes such as mindfulness-based stress reduction (Stahl & Goldstein, 2019) and mindfulness-based CBT (Segal et al., 2012), therapists may select and apply specific mindfulness techniques:

- *Emotional Awareness Meditation:* Guiding clients to identify and accept current emotions without changing them.
- *Cognitive Defusion:* Treating thoughts as temporary experiences and hypotheses, rather than absolute truths (Hayes et al., 1999; Masuda et al., 2004; Powers et al., 2009). For example, the therapist may ask clients to envision their thoughts as leaves floating down a stream, observing them pass without attachment.
- *Present Moment Awareness:* Populist authors such as Tolle and Brown encourage regular practice of present moment awareness, urging readers to notice when their mind wanders to the past or future and gently bring their focus back to the present. Similarly, Brown (2010) teaches readers to observe their emotional reactions to situations without immediately acting on them, allowing space for a more conscious response. This approach seems effective in therapy (Schneider, 2015).
- *Emotion Charts and Mapping:* Tracking feelings to identify script-systems and understand emotional processing within the body.

Box 11.2

Focusing

Focusing is a powerful tool for clients to explore deep feelings and find healing (Gendlin, 1996). This technique helps clients notice how life issues resonate within their bodies without becoming overwhelmed. The steps involves:

1 *Creating a Safe Space:* Help clients find a comfortable, quiet area, ideally with eyes closed, to minimise distractions.
2 *Relaxation and Clearing:* Guide the client to take deep breaths and relax. Ask them to scan their body for any areas of tension mentally and to visualise releasing this tension with each exhalation. This process helps clear a space where emotional and physical sensations can be observed without immediate involvement.
3 *Getting a Felt Sense:* Direct attention inward to notice bodily sensations, emotions or thoughts without changing them. Ask to identify an area in their body where feelings about a specific issue are most noticeable, often in the chest, stomach or throat.
4 *Finding a Handle:* Encourage clients to identify a word, phrase, image or sound that resonates with the felt sense.
5 *Resonating and Checking:* Ask clients to hold the felt sense and handle together, checking for congruence.
6 *Asking:* Encourage the client to ask the felt sense, 'What is it about the whole of this issue that makes me feel this way?'. This is an invitation for more profound insight, not an analytical question. The client should wait for the felt sense to respond, which might deepen or shift the sensation.
7 *Receiving:* Accept whatever emerges in response with curiosity—images, words, insights or shifts in feeling.
8 *Deepening Contact:* Stay with the felt shift, allowing insights to unfold and integrate.
9 *Closure:* Gradually return attention to the room, discussing and reinforcing insights gained.

BODY-ORIENTED EXERCISES

If you're not petted, your spinal cord will begin to dry up. (Berne, 1972, p. 67)

Emotions are not merely in the mind but also in the body; it seems that traditionally, TA therapists may have overlooked this embodied dimension, although more studies are getting published on the embodied nature of TA-processes (Cornell, 2018; Ligabue & Tenconi, 2021; Waldekranz-Piselli, 1999). Research shows the effectiveness of body-oriented exercises (Rosendahl et al., 2021).

- *Grounding Techniques:* Grounding techniques help clients stay present and manage anxiety, dissociation or overwhelming emotions. These include:
  - *5-4-3-2-1 Technique:* Naming five things they can see, four things they can touch, three things they can hear, two things they can smell and one thing they can taste.
  - *Focused Breathing:* Deep, slow breaths with emphasis on exhaling.
  - *Object Focus:* Concentrating on an object's qualities, such as texture or colour.
  - *Mindful Walking:* Paying attention to physical sensations during movement.
  - *Safety Checking:* Check surroundings, for example, the four walls or corners of the room, to rationally confirm one is safe, even though the body may feel unsafe.
  - *Grounding Objects:* Using tactile items for focus.
  - *Strong Smell:* Use a strong smell that is ideally associated with positive memories.
  - *Visualisation:* Imagining roots or energy flow through the body.
  - *Shaking:* Vigorous body movement to release tension.
- *Body Scan:* This involves attentively moving one's focus through different body parts, noticing sensations without trying to change them.
- *Mindful Breathing:* Clients focus on their breath, bringing attention back when the mind wanders, thereby practising moment-to-moment acceptance.
- *Somatic Experiencing* (SE): This body-focused therapeutic approach helps with trauma and other stress disorders (Levine, 1997). It draws upon the idea that traumatic experiences can lead to disruptions in the autonomic nervous system and that the body holds onto this trauma through physiological symptoms, often reinforced via avoidance/denial of the bodily sensation. A therapist asks a client to bring their attention and describe the bodily sensations associated with a stressful memory, such as tightness in the chest. SE assumes that by bringing the attention to the bodily sensation, the tension may naturally release. By alternating between positive/neutral body sensations and traumatic body sensations, individuals do not need to feel overwhelmed, gradually learn to tolerate their physical discomfort, develop affect regulation via alternating attention and resolve automated trauma responses. For example, clients may be asked to focus on a specifically located physical sensation and its edges, subsequently focus on the area around and then come back to learn to tolerate these feelings and break the habit of hyperfocusing or avoiding one location. Dissociation is addressed by letting awareness drift outside the body, with caution towards speed and comfort. For example, slight movements are encouraged to

promote thawing and return to normal sensation when stuck in a freeze state. SE is supported by a growing body of research, suggesting its benefits in PTSD and emotional dysregulation (Kuhfuß et al., 2021).

- *Progressive Muscle Relaxation:* This involves tensing and relaxing muscle groups sequentially (McCallie et al., 2006). Starting from the feet and moving up, it increases awareness of physical sensations associated with tension and relaxation. This is often combined with deep breathing, helps reduce physical tension and is used to alleviate anxiety, stress and insomnia.

IMAGINATION EXERCISES

Research suggests the effectiveness of imaginary techniques (Hall et al., 2006; Tozzi, 2023).

- *Imagery:* A client may relax by imagining they are at a location that evokes positive emotional reactions, like a beach, a mountain or relaxing with a pet or friend. Detailed instructions prompt the individual to vividly imagine each sensory experience (what do you see/hear/touch/taste/smell).
- *Guided fantasy:* Therapists lead clients through imaginative journeys tailored to their needs. For example, a client with low self-esteem might visualise a joyous setting, life as a path or their own commemorative service, exploring their significance to others. Strive for specific details, engaging all sensory experiences.
- *Magic Want and Science Fiction:* Clients are encouraged to think beyond their life script limitations by imagining they have a magic want, or write a Sci-Fi about a perfect future, perhaps centuries ahead, focusing on positive experiences.
- *Empty Luggage:* Clients symbolically discard unwanted traits or beliefs by writing them on paper and placing them in a container, helping to release oppressive aspects of their life narrative.
- *Rituals:* These aid emotional closure and future envisioning. Examples include writing letters to the departed, burning painful memories, planting trees or celebrating life events (Goodwyn, 2016).
- *Art:* Clients express themselves through drawing, painting, collage-making or photography.
- *Safe Space Exercise:* This exercise creates a mental refuge clients can return to whenever they need to feel safe and calm, providing a powerful coping mechanism for managing stress, anxiety and traumatic memories. The process involves:
  1 *Preparation:* Begin by finding a comfortable and quiet environment where the client can relax without interruption. Encourage the client to adopt a comfortable posture, sitting or lying down, and to close their eyes.
  2 *Guided Breathing:* Initiate the exercise with a few deep, controlled breaths to help the client relax. Instruct them to inhale slowly, hold their breath for a moment and then exhale gently, releasing tension with each breath.
  3 *Visualisation:* Ask clients to imagine where they feel safe, peaceful and happy. This could be a real place they have visited, a childhood memory or an imagined setting.

Encourage them to envision this place in as much detail as possible, using all their senses—what they see/hear/smell/touch/taste.

4 *Deepening the Experience:* Encourage exploration of details in the imagined space, like the quality of the light, temperature and how their body feels in this place. Encourage noticing the feelings of relaxation, safety and peace.

5 *Anchoring the Safe Space:* Anchor this feeling, for example, by connecting this with a physical gesture, a word or an image they can use to quickly return to this sense of safety in times of need.

6 *Returning:* Gently guide clients back to the present while maintaining the sense of peace.

7 *Integration:* Discuss the experience and encourage its use during overwhelming moments.

SUMMARY

- This chapter has explained how clients may struggle to accept and stay with their genuine experiences, often caused by their life script. TA therapists may help clients connect with their flow of experiences, tolerate, deepen and express these.
- TA therapists can use various techniques to stimulate experiential acceptance, such as analysing and challenging the role of the Critical Parent and Adapted Child, strengthening the Adult, revising the Life script, improving Transactions and Script-systems and using a non-judgemental/phenomenological approach.
- Mindfulness exercises include emotional awareness meditation, cognitive defusion, present moment awareness, responding instead of reacting, emotion charts, emotion mapping and focusing.
- Body-oriented exercises include grounding, body scan, breathing, somatic experiencing and progressive muscle relaxation.
- Imagination exercises include safe space, imagery, guided fantasy, telling science fiction, empty luggage projection, rituals and art.

12

INTEGRATIVE-THERAPEUTIC COMPETENCIES

How do TA therapists integrate exercises from other therapeutic approaches into their practice? Most TA therapist use skills from different therapeutic modalities in their TA-work (Vos & van Rijn, 2021c), which seems nowadays common across many therapies (Vos, 2023). This chapter includes some of the most frequently integrated evidence-based interventions/ exercises that originated in other therapeutic schools, such as those we identified in TA clinical trials (Vos & van Rijn, 2023).

- Role-play exercises
- Diary exercises
- Autobiographical writing exercises
- Cognitive exercises
- Behavioural exercises
- Self-compassion exercises

ROLE-PLAY EXERCISES

Role-play techniques allow clients to explore thoughts, feelings and behaviours in a safe, structured environment, gaining flexibility in roles, transactions and ego-states (King & Temple, 2018). These techniques are central to TA for understanding and changing inter-personal dynamics. Role-play techniques empower clients to express unspoken feelings, understand diverse perspectives, resolve internal conflicts and improve communication skills by externalising internal dialogues, while simultaneously gaining insights into past experiences, connecting with their potential for change and exploring authentic self-expression. While some clients may feel uncomfortable due to self-consciousness or fear of judgement, therapists should build a strong alliance and offer safety procedures. Research supports the effectiveness of role-play (Corsini, 2017; Kipper & Ritchie, 2003). Key role-play techniques include:

- *Empty-Chair Method:* One of the most well-known role-play techniques, the Empty-chair, involves placing an empty-chair opposite the client, associated with positive outcomes if used in several sessions (Pascual-Leone & Baher, 2023). The client is then invited to imagine someone (e.g. a parent, partner or even a part of themselves) sitting in the chair. The client engages in a dialogue with the imagined person, alternating between their role and the role of the other by physically moving to the empty-chair to respond. This technique can help clients in TA express unspoken feelings, understand others' perspectives and resolve internal conflicts (McNeel, 1976).

- *Parent–Child Dialogue:* A variation using two chairs to represent different ego-states, helping externalise internal conflicts between Parent and Child.
- *Two-Chair Conflict Resolution:* Clients move between chairs representing conflicting parts of themselves, exploring internal dilemmas.
- *Rehearsal Role-Play:* Clients practice challenging situations with the therapist playing the other role or observing, improving communication skills and confidence.
- *Historical Role-Play:* Re-enacting significant past experiences to gain insights, challenge beliefs and heal emotional wounds. Experimenting with different endings provides a sense of control.
- *Future Self Role-Play:* Clients are invited to embody their future selves, imagining how they would think, feel and act after achieving their therapy goals. This can involve speaking from the future self's perspective, offering advice, encouragement or insights to their present self. This clarifies goals and strengthens motivation.
- *Script-System Role-Play:* Clients re-enact situations where they typically use script-systems but express genuine feelings, revealing potential outcomes of authenticity.

DIARY EXERCISES

Research shows the effectiveness of working with diaries and writing exercises (Bohlmeijer et al., 2003; Pennebaker, 2012; Reinhold et al., 2018; Ruini & Mortara, 2022).

- *Emotions Diary:* Clients may be asked to keep a diary of emotional experiences, noting when they felt a particular way, what situation triggered the emotion and which ego-state they believe they were in. This practice increases emotional awareness, mindfulness and self-reflection.
- *Ego-State Diary:* At the end of each day, clients record the most challenging situations and identify how strong each ego-state was, and how this made them feel/think/behave; after several weeks, the diary may reveal a pattern; clients may want to reflect when this pattern started and what has caused this (e.g. life script early-life); clients may decide to develop a new response to challenging situations, and record how these made them feel better
- *Life Position Diary:* The same as the ego-state diary, but to record and change life positions in the most challenging daily.
- *Life Script Diary:* This diary identifies the messages that they can identify in their responses to difficult situations; they identify patterns, and the start/cause of these;

they may decide to tell themselves a different message, and record how this makes them feel.

- *Script-System Diary:* Clients write about daily experiences and emotions, helping differentiate between genuine feelings and script-based ones, encouraging introspection and self-acceptance.
- *Gratitude Diary:* Clients keep a daily or weekly journal of things they are thankful for, shifting focus from problems to joys, fostering well-being and contentment, potentially facilitating a shift from Critical Parent to Nurturing Parent and Free Child.
- *Past Self Letter:* From their Adult and Nurturing ego-state, clients may write a letter to themselves as a child, and in their Child ego-state, they compassionately acknowledge the injustices and unfair life messages they have received. This may help emotional processing, self-compassion and an Adult/Nurturing Parent approach towards their past.
- *Future Self Letter:* Clients write from their future self's perspective, offering encouragement, insights and advice. This exercise connects clients with long-term goals and aspirations, providing motivation and perspective.

AUTOBIOGRAPHICAL WRITING

Autobiographical and expressive writing can be a powerful therapeutic tool that can reduce symptoms of depression, anxiety and stress, while enhancing emotional well-being, self-esteem and mood (Pennebaker, 2012). Writing one's autobiography may help:

- Explore and understand how their life scripts/experiences have shaped them
- Cultivate self-compassion and a kinder attitude towards their life-story and their past responses/decisions
- Emotionally process events
- Identify patterns and recurring themes
- Understand the influence of their past on current beliefs and behaviours
- Facilitate emotional catharsis
- Find coherence and meaning in their life story
- Develop sense of control

Therapists can guide autobiographical writing by:

- *Setting the Stage:* Introduce the concept of life scripts and potential benefits of autobiographical writing. Emphasise that this is a non-judgemental space and that there is no right or wrong approach.
- *Structured Prompts:* Provide clients with structured prompts to guide their writing. These can include phases of life (childhood, adolescence, adulthood), significant relationships, pivotal moments, challenges faced and achievements. This can be tailored to their situation.

- *Encourage Detail:* Ask clients to include sensory details (what they saw, heard, felt) and emotional responses to events. This can deepen the process of reflection and emotional processing.
- *Intergenerational Script:* Clients may consider writing the transgenerational story of their family, and their unique position within this, which may help them understand the intergenerational origins of their individual life script (Noriega, 2010).
- *Regular Review:* Schedule sessions to discuss what the client has written. Use these discussions to explore insights, clarify life scripts and reinforce self-compassion.
- *Privacy and Pace:* Assure clients that their writings are private and that they can share as much or as little as they feel comfortable with. Encourage them to take the process at their own pace.

COGNITIVE EXERCISES

TA therapists may use cognitive techniques (Bergmann, 1981), as research shows the effectiveness of various cognitive techniques (Hoffman, 2012).

Cognitive Reframing

Cognitive reframing is the process of deliberately shifting one's perspective to view a situation, person or experience in a different and often more positive or constructive light (Beck, 2020). TA therapists may use cognitive reframing to help a client transition from a limiting Child or Critical Parent ego-state to a more balanced and resourceful Adult ego-state, or from an I−/U− position to I+/U+, encouraging a more adaptive and empowering interpretation of events and relationships. For example, a person reacting defensively during work conflicts from the Free Child ego-state can, with a therapist's help, identify this pattern, understand its origins, learn to reframe/reinterpret this and activate the Adult ego-state for logical assessment and problem-solving.

Clarifying, Specifying and Concretising

Therapists ask clarifying questions to understand the client's experience better and move from abstract to specific, concrete examples, facilitating deeper understanding and exploration of their assumptions and reasons. Example questions include 'Can you explain this further?' 'Could you elaborate?' 'Could you give some everyday-life examples?' 'How precisely did this happen?' 'What happened then? What did you feel/think/do?' 'If I had a video camera, what would this camera have recorded?' 'If we return to my opening question, how does this specific example answer this question?' The therapist may explore underlying reasoning/assumptions: 'Is this always the case?' 'When is this the case, and when not?' 'How is this possible?' 'What is needed for this to happen/to be true?' 'Why do you think this assumption holds here?' 'Why do you say that?' 'Is this always true?' 'How do you know this?' 'Is there reason to doubt this evidence?' 'Is this logical to say?' 'So you say that when X happens, Y follows: is this logical? What evidence do you have?' (Vos, 2017).

Specify Memories

Memories are often tainted by the current emotional state (mood-congruent memory retrieval bias); therefore, ask specific questions: 'Describe a specific example of a precise moment in time. Where were you? Who were you with? What did you see/hear/smell/taste/feel?' (Vos, 2017).

Multisensory Questions

Note that clients give different answers to questions using different words: 'What do you think about…?' 'How do you feel about…?' 'How do you remember…?' 'How do you interpret…?' 'What did you do…?' 'What do others say…?' (Vos, 2011, 2017). Individuals could be asked to explore differences and similarities: 'Is there a difference between how you feel and think about this?' Questions about 'how do you feel' seem to be associated more with the body, engrained life scripts, the Somatic Child and early-life affect regulation – questions about 'what do you think' appeal more to the Adult or Critical Parent.

Life Script Questions

Therapists may explore where experiences originate and what they are influenced by, for example, 'When was the first time you felt this?' 'How did this experience/idea start and develop over time?' 'Where does this experience/idea come from?' 'Is this your idea, or did this come from someone else?' 'Has anything or anyone influenced the development of this experience/idea, and, if so, which influences did you experience?' 'Is this something you can(not), must (not) and/or (do not) want?' (Vos, 2017).

Prioritising: If clients feel overwhelmed or mention many concerns or topics, give a summary or ask them to prioritise: 'What is the most important?' 'What are the three most important points/lessons?' 'What are highlights?' 'Rank these examples from most important to least important.' It may be helpful to repeatedly ask why questions to identify the essence: 'why is this meaningful/important?' 'what makes this meaningful/important?' 'what is the most important/meaningful aspect?' (Vos, 2017).

Socratic Questioning

This method helps clients identify inconsistencies in their thinking, understand the origins of their beliefs and consider alternative perspectives. A TA therapist might use this to explore the roots of a client's script beliefs or ego-state responses, encouraging the client to critically examine how these patterns were learnt and whether they serve a beneficial purpose in the present. A therapist might ask, 'What evidence supports your belief that you are unsuccessful?' 'How does this belief affect your daily actions and decisions?' 'Can you recall a time when you felt competent and successful, and what was different about that situation?' 'How might someone who cares about you describe your successes and strengths?' 'What would be the impact on your life if you shifted your focus from perceived failures to acknowledged successes?' 'In what ways does this belief serve you, and in what ways does it hinder you?' 'How might your life change if you viewed your efforts and outcomes through a lens of learning rather than failure?' and 'What steps can you take to start challenging this belief in your everyday life?', all aimed at unravelling and reconstructing the client's self-perception and belief systems to foster a more positive and empowered mindset. A therapist may ask a client who frequently experiences inadequacy from a Child ego-state: 'What experiences led you to believe you are not good enough?' 'How do these beliefs affect your behaviour and relationships now?' 'What evidence do you have that contradicts this belief?' This process can help the client recognise that their feelings of inadequacy are based on past experiences rather than present reality, facilitating a shift towards more Adult ego-state–based perspectives grounded in current evidence and rationality. By applying Socratic questioning, a TA therapist can guide clients towards self-discovery and cognitive restructuring, promoting healthier, more adaptive ways of thinking and relating to the world.

Strengthen Adaptive Ego-States and Transactional Core Messages

The therapist may highlight positive examples in the client's stories, ask clients at the start of the session 'What positive things have happened?', point out the advantages of focusing or believing in adaptive ego-states and transactional core messages, point out evidence, make a list of examples, refer to other people and role-models, use a chart to collect evidence, induce images of current and historical positive experiences and act as if it were true (Beck, 2020).

Dual Attitude

Therapists may help clients accept that conflicting aspects of life can coexist (Vos, 2015). This approach encourages individuals to stop viewing their desires and obligations as mutually exclusive, allowing for a more integrated and fulfilling life. By acknowledging that one can simultaneously be successful in one's career and be a good parent, clients learn to navigate the complexities of life without succumbing to the pressure of choosing one path over another. This mindset shifts the focus from an either/or perspective to a both/and outlook, challenging false dichotomies and the fear of paradoxical feelings. This can foster tolerating paradoxical feelings and offers an opportunity for training frustration tolerance, which may benefit clients inclined to split.

Dereflection

Hyper-reflection refers to an individual's obsessive self-focus on their problems, creating a debilitating cycle where the more they reflect on their issues, the worse they seem to become (Vos, 2017). This cycle is often exacerbated by hyper-intention, where the intense desire to solve a problem (such as the need to sleep) paradoxically increases anxiety and further impedes the ability to find a solution. Such patterns are common in conditions where letting go of controlled thinking is necessary, like insomnia or hypochondria, and can be triggered or worsened by sudden adverse life events. Viktor Frankl suggests that the solution lies in de-reflection, which shifts focus away from self and problems towards more meaningful external activities and experiences. This approach encourages individuals to engage in actions without overthinking, breaking the cycle of hyper-reflection and hyper-intention by immersing themselves in the real world and its possibilities for meaningful engagement. The clients' cycle of hyperreflection/hyperintention may be broken, and they may be connected with their flow experiences by engaging in activities, particularly those that they deem meaningful and that involve physical activities, preferably outside. Examples include sports, hiking, gardening, playing a musical instrument, meeting friends or volunteering. The key is to become absorbed in the activity, redirecting the focus from self-preoccupation to the task.

Guided Discovery

Therapists encourage clients to examine their beliefs and assumptions and discover alternative ways of thinking and acting. Therapists facilitate insight by enabling clients to reach their conclusions, fostering deeper understanding and lasting change. For instance, a therapist might challenge a client's belief of incompetence by having them list recent successes and reflect on these examples. This process encourages clients to question and re-evaluate their beliefs, leading to a more balanced self-view. The steps include identifying an unhelpful/unrealistic belief, developing open-ended questions to encourage evidence for and against the belief, exploring more realistic/helpful alternative perspectives, encouraging evaluating the difference in the impact of the original and alternative belief and applying new insights in real-life situations.

Automatic Thought Record

This key CBT tool helps individuals identify, challenge and change negative, unrealistic, or unhelpful thoughts (Beck, 2020). These spontaneous thoughts, triggered by specific events, can significantly impact emotions and behaviours. This exercise aims to develop a more balanced and realistic way of thinking, improving emotional well-being and decision-making. It helps clients become aware of their automatic thoughts, especially negative ones, and identify patterns contributing to their problems. Therapists practice this in the session before they give this as homework. By examining evidence for and against these thoughts, clients can challenge and modify them, managing emotions more effectively and enhancing problem-solving skills. A typical record includes several columns that clients fill-in for several challenging moments at the end of each day; clients usually start with only a few columns (a-d), which they extend in a later session (a-g), and try to change later (a-j):

a. *Date and Time:* When the event or thought occurred.
b. *Situation:* Describe the specific situation leading to the negative/unrealistic/unhelpful thought, including details like location, activity and people involved. This may help identify triggers.
c. *Emotion:* Note the emotions felt during the situation and rate their intensity on a 0–100 scale.

d. *Automatic Thoughts:* Write down the automatic thoughts, including any cognitive distortions/biases.

e. *Evidence Supporting the Thought:* List facts that support the automatic thought.

f. *Evidence Against the Thought:* Identify facts that contradict or challenge the thought, including the identification of logical errors/biases such as black-or-white thinking or over-generalisation.

g. *Helpfulness of the Thought:* Rate how helpful or unhelpful the thought is.

h. *Alternative Thought:* Develop a more realistic and helpful thought based on the evidence.

i. *Outcome:* Record changes in mood after considering the alternative thought and rate the new emotion's intensity on a 0–100 scale.

j. *Behavioural Outcome:* Note any behaviour changes resulting from shifting thoughts and emotions.

Cognitive Restructuring

This technique aims to identify and challenge unhelpful/unrealistic beliefs and scripts, replacing them with more adaptive, realistic ones. This technique helps individuals examine how childhood beliefs, often absorbed from parental figures and stored in the Parent ego-state, influence their thoughts and behaviours. For instance, a person might internalise the belief that 'mistakes are unacceptable', leading to perfectionism and fear of failure. This belief, manifesting in the critical Parent ego-state, can cause anxiety and self-doubt. The individual learns to identify this script and its impact, then challenges it by exploring evidence that mistakes can lead to growth and learning. The therapist helps reframe this belief, fostering a nurturing internal dialogue rooted in the Nurturing Parent or Adult ego-state, acknowledging mistakes as part of the learning process. This can reduce anxiety, improve self-esteem and promote a balanced approach to challenges. Key steps include:

- *Identification:* Identify the problematic thought patterns, beliefs or scripts influencing the client's current behaviour and emotions.

- *Awareness:* Identify which ego-states are activated during these thoughts and emotions.

- *Examination:* The client examines the origin and validity of these beliefs, questioning how they were formed and whether they are based on facts or outdated perceptions.

- *Assessment:* The impact of these beliefs on the client's current life is assessed, focusing on how they affect feelings, behaviours and relationships.

- *Challenge:* The therapist and client work together to challenge unhelpful or irrational beliefs by looking for evidence against them and considering alternative perspectives. Self-challenging questions may include: Have I confused a thought with a fact? What would I tell a friend if they had this thought? What would a friend say about my thoughts? How many times has it happened in the past? Am I confusing a possibility with certainty? It may be possible; is it likely? If I was not feeling low or anxious, would I see the situation differently? Can/did anyone see this another way? If you played devil's advocate, what would you say? Imagine yourself on your deathbed, which option feels most meaningful? (Vos, 2017).

- *Alternatives Creation:* New, more adaptive beliefs and scripts are created, grounded in the Adult ego-state, which is realistic, helpful, and based on current evidence. Helpful questions in this creation process may include: Based on the evidence I have listed for and against, is there an alternative way of thinking about this situation? Write one sentence which summarises evidence for and another for evidence against; when you combine these sentences with the words 'and' or 'but', does it create a more balanced thought? If a friend was in a similar situation, what would I say to them? Can a friend or family member think of other ways to understand the situation?
- *Integration:* These new beliefs are then integrated into the client's thought patterns, replacing the old, unhelpful ones.
- *Practice:* The client responds to situations using these new beliefs, reinforcing them through repetition and real-world application.
- *Evaluation:* The effectiveness of these new beliefs in reducing distress and improving behaviour is evaluated, with further adjustments made as necessary.

Identifying Cognitive Bias

Unhelpful thinking patterns and biases are often rooted in early life scripts and reinforced through ego-states. This may significantly impact a client's emotional well-being and interpersonal relationship and be self-reinforcing as this can lead clients to interpret situations through a skewed lens, fostering negative emotions and behaviours that do not accurately reflect reality. A therapist may help increase awareness, explore origins in the life script and recognise how their distorted thinking influences their feelings and behaviours, often leading to self-fulfilling prophecies that reinforce the original unhelpful belief, challenging distortions, for example, via Socratic questioning, developing new scripts grounded in the Adult ego-state and practising new behaviours. Common unhelpful thinking patterns and biases include:

- *Confirmation Bias:* The tendency to search for, interpret, favour and recall information in a way that confirms one's pre-existing beliefs or hypotheses, leading to a skewed perception of reality.
- *Negativity Bias:* The propensity to give more weight to negative experiences or information than positive, which can reinforce negative scripts and affect emotional well-being.
- *Self-Serving Bias:* The common habit of attributing positive events to one's own character but attributing negative events to external factors, impacting personal growth and self-awareness.
- *Availability Heuristic:* Overestimating the importance of information that is readily available, often recent or emotionally charged, which can distort understanding of the likelihood or importance of events.

- *Anchoring Bias:* The tendency to rely too heavily on the first piece of information seen (the 'anchor') when making decisions, even if that information is irrelevant or misleading.
- *Overgeneralization:* Making broad interpretations from a single or few events, leading to a distorted perception of reality and potentially reinforcing harmful scripts.
- *Catastrophizing:* The inclination to assume the worst will happen, often leading to heightened anxiety and avoidance behaviours.
- *All-or-Nothing Thinking:* Viewing situations in only two categories instead of on a continuum, such as 'I am either a success or a failure', which can limit flexibility in thinking and responding.
- *Emotional Reasoning:* The bias of assuming that because we feel a certain way, it must be true, which can lead to decisions based on emotions rather than facts.
- *Labelling*: Assigning labels to oneself or others based on limited information or single events, which can reinforce negative self-concepts and hinder personal growth.

Identifying Transactional Core Messages Via the Downward-Arrow Technique

TA therapists can use the downward-arrow technique from CBT to delve into the transactional core messages or life scripts that clients developed in childhood. These messages often manifest as injunctions, drivers, counterinjunctions, permissions, allowances, programmes and other early-life messages that guide behaviour and emotional responses. Here's how TA therapists might use this technique:

1 *Identify Distress:* Clients often come to therapy for concerns about psychopathology, psychological distress, lack of self-realisation, general well-being, quality of life, behaviour, self-efficacy and social functioning.
2 *Identify Coping and Avoidance Techniques:* Explore clients' coping or avoidance strategies, which may involve games, an imbalanced stroke profile, conditional strokes and time structured mainly with withdrawal, rituals, pastimes, games and rare intimacy.
3 *Identify Dysfunctioning Ego-States or Life Positions:* Pinpoint recurring ego-states or life positions causing distress but perceived as genuine or beneficial by the client. This could emerge from diary entries, repetitive themes or specific thoughts and behaviours.
4 *Uncover the Underlying Message in the Present:* The therapist probes to uncover the message this state or position seems to respond to, often articulated as a rule or command such as 'Do not...' or 'It is OK to...', aiming to phrase it in a generalised or third-person form like 'You should...'.
5 *Explore the Message's Core:* Through questioning, the therapist explores the essence and implications of this message, its meaning about the self, others and life; the fears it harbours; and its importance and meaningfulness to the client. For example, 'If this message is true/valid/applicable: so what? What does this say about you? What does

this say about other people, the world or life? What is so bad about. . .? What is the worst part? What makes this so important to you? Why does this feel meaningful? What is the most meaningful part?'

6 *Reformulate the Message:* Together, the therapist and client work to refine the message to capture its essence better. For example, 'How would you describe the message this most meaningful part tells you?' This is followed by further questions to explore the message's core (Step 4).

7 *Identify the Transactional Core Message:* The process of questioning (Step 5) and refining the formulation of the message (Step 5) continues until a transactional core message is revealed, often indicated by a change in the client's emotional state, a moment of insight or the client's consistent repetition of the message.

8 *Identify the client's Responses/Decisions in the Past Towards the Message:* Identify how the client has responded/decided towards the transactional core message, such as accepting, rejecting or transforming this or having another affective, cognitive or behavioural response and its emotional and behavioural impact. For example, 'How have you responded to this core message as a Child?' The therapist guides the client to assess the message's historical relevance, realism and helpfulness. 'How did it help you follow this message when you started saying this? To what extent has this message helped you in life?'

9 *Reflect on the Impact of Accepting the Transactional Core Messages:* The therapist helps the client reflect on the impact of their transactional core message on their underlying message in the present, dysfunctioning ego-states and life positions, coping and avoidance and distress/outcomes. The therapists also acknowledge feelings of shame, hurt or frustration alongside relief or insight. The therapist promotes a sense of understanding and self-compassion.

10 *Trace the Message's Aetiological Origins in the Life Script:* The therapist asks questions about the first time the client internalised this message, its source and the context of its adoption to help trace its origins. This exploration includes examining the message's role as a response to others' messages and differentiating between the voices of others and the client's own developed voice. When was the first time or period that you started saying this message to yourself? Could you describe this time/period? Was there anything specific in that situation that made you start saying this message? Who was the first person ever to give this message to you? Who were they, and why was their message important to you? Was this message a response to another message that someone gave, like turning their message around or rebelling, such as saying "Be yourself" when someone said "Do not be yourself"? How does it feel to say this message to yourself? Does this feel like your own voice or someone else's voice? If multiple people gave this message to you, how would they specifically say this, for example, in which tone and voice; try to remember how they sounded, and differentiate this sound from your voice that you have now developed yourself?' The therapist stimulates understanding and self-compassion.

11 *Redecide in the Present:* The therapist guides the client to assess the message's current relevance, realism and helpfulness and emotional and behavioural impact. 'How helpful is the message now? How does this message make you feel? How does this message make you behave and interact with others, and how helpful is this to yourself/others? How true/realistic is this message; what evidence do you have for this? Would you say this message to a person you love, and if so, why (not)?' The therapist focuses on differentiating the relevance/realism/helpfulness in the past from the present and challenging unhelpful thought patterns and biases. Based on this evaluation that aims to strengthen the client's Adult functioning, the therapist asks the client how they want to respond now to this message: do they still want to follow this? The redecision may involve the client formulating a new, more realistic, helpful core message (Step 4). This alternative message may be written down, repeated and integrated into daily life as a form of homework. For example, 'Do you want to continue giving this message to yourself, or would you like to replace this with an alternative? If you were to replace this original message with a realistic and helpful alternative message, how would that message sound?'

BEHAVIOURAL EXERCISES

Research shows the effectiveness of using various behavioural techniques to help clients accept their experiences (Bennett-Levy et al., 2004; Ekers et al., 2008).

Behavioural Experiment

A behavioural experiment tests beliefs in real-life situations to gather evidence and challenge unhelpful, unrealistic transactional core life messages. This method allows clients to gather evidence about their thoughts and beliefs through their own experiences rather than relying solely on theoretical discussion or introspection. Behavioural experiments provide concrete evidence that can challenge and modify clients' long-held, unhelpful, unrealistic transactional core life messages; by actively testing these beliefs in real-world scenarios, clients can see first-hand when their expectations do not align with reality, facilitating a shift in perspective. By confronting feared situations or outcomes in a controlled and systematic way ('desensitisation'), clients can gradually reduce the anxiety associated with these scenarios. Behavioural experiments encourage clients to explore alternative behaviours and perspectives, develop more adaptive coping and problem-solving skills and improve self-efficacy. Behavioural experiments can help clients operate more from their Adult ego-state, which is characterised by being rational, objective and able to assess reality accurately. An experiment is usually done in multiple steps:

- *Identify the Irrational Thought:* Begin by helping the client identify a specific irrational thought or belief impacting their behaviour and emotional state. This thought should be clearly defined and related to their scripts/transactions causing distress or dysfunction.

- *Develop a Hypothesis:* Work with the client to develop a hypothesis related to the identified thought. This hypothesis should predict what the client expects will happen if the irrational thought were true in a specific situation.
- *Plan the Experiment:* Together, plan an experiment that can test the hypothesis in the real world. Ensure that the experiment is realistic and achievable and that it directly challenges the irrational thought in question. The plan should include a clear description of the behaviour/action to be taken, the setting/context in which the experiment will occur and specific criteria for what will be observed/measured.
- *Set Expectations:* Discuss and document what the client expects will happen during the experiment based on their current irrational belief.
- *Conduct the Experiment:* Encourage the client to experiment as planned. It is crucial that the client approaches the experiment with an open mind and is observant of their reactions and outcomes.
- *Review the Results:* Review the outcomes with the client after the experiment. Discuss what happened, focusing on any discrepancies between their expectations and the real-world results.
- *Reflect on the Experience:* Encourage the client to reflect on how the experiment challenges their original thought. Discuss how the evidence gathered through the experiment contradicts their irrational belief.
- *Formulate New Beliefs:* Based on the experiment's outcomes, work with the client to formulate new, more rational and helpful beliefs. These beliefs should be grounded in the evidence collected during the experiment.
- *Plan for Future Application:* Finally, discuss how the client can use the insights gained from the experiment to challenge similar irrational thoughts. Plan additional experiments if needed to reinforce these new, healthier thinking patterns.

Improving Frustration Tolerance and Embracing Uncertainty

Frustration tolerance is the ability to manage feelings of frustration without becoming overwhelmed or resorting to unproductive behaviours (Leyro et al., 2010). Clients with low frustration tolerance often switch to the Child ego-state, responding impulsively or with avoidance. These techniques help clients tolerate discomfort, realise uncertainties are less threatening than feared and become more resilient and flexible in navigating life's complexities. Therapeutic strategies include:

- *Incremental Steps:* Encourage clients to try small new activities or make minor routine changes to increase comfort with uncertainty. Examples include delegating tasks or visiting a new restaurant without reading reviews.
- *Positive Reinforcement:* Highlight successful encounters with uncertainty to build self-confidence and adaptability.
- *Adult Ego-State:* Encourage clients to stay in the Adult ego-state during stress, using role-playing to practice rational, solution-focused responses.
- *Coping Strategies:* Reinforce positive self-talk and coping mechanisms to manage frustration.

Breaking the Vicious Cycle of Rumination

Rumination involves repetitive focus on distress and problems without seeking solutions, leading to increased anxiety, depression and helplessness. In TA, this may manifest as clients revisiting past negative scripts. Therapists may guide clients to stay in the Adult ego-state, focusing on current reality and problem-solving. Therapists may use behavioural experiments to challenge and change unhelpful thought patterns. Encourage clients to move towards action and new, favourable resolutions. These strategies help clients break the cycle of rumination, fostering a more solution-focused mindset.

Promoting Sleep Hygiene

Sleep hygiene refers to the habits and practices conducive to sleeping well regularly (Irish et al., 2015). An individual might have poor sleep hygiene due to their ego-states and life script by engaging in behaviours or thought patterns that disrupt sleep, such as staying up late to fulfil a part of their 'Adult' ego-state that demands productivity, or being kept awake by 'Child' ego-state fears and anxieties stemming from their life script. A TA therapist may give psychoeducation on sleep hygiene by helping clients understand how their ego-states influence their sleep habits and offering strategies to promote a healthier balance. They might suggest establishing a calming pre-sleep routine to soothe the 'Child' ego-state and setting firm bedtime boundaries to satisfy the 'Adult' ego-state's need for structure. Examples of sleep hygiene practices a therapist may recommend are maintaining a consistent sleep schedule, creating a restful environment (cool, dark and quiet), limiting screen time before bed to reduce exposure to stimulating blue light and encouraging relaxing activities before bedtime, such as reading or meditation, to help transition from the 'Parent' or 'Adult' ego-states to a more restful 'Child' state. These practices aim to support balanced ego-states for improved sleep quality.

Graded Exposure

Graded exposure helps individuals gradually face and overcome their fears or anxieties (Abramowitz, 2019; Smits et al., 2022). It is particularly beneficial for clients who experience intense anxiety or phobias, where direct confrontation with the feared object or situation might be overwhelming. A TA therapist might first work with the client to identify the fear's origins within their ego-states or life script narratives, understanding how these fears are maintained or reinforced. The therapist and client together would then develop a hierarchy of fear-inducing situations, ordered from least to most anxiety-provoking. Starting with the least threatening situation, the client is gradually exposed to the fear in a controlled and supportive environment, allowing them to practice coping strategies and challenge negative beliefs within their Adult ego-state. As the client becomes more comfortable at each level of exposure, they move to more challenging situations, fostering resilience and adaptive responses within their ego-states. Throughout this process, the TA therapist provides guidance, support and reinforcement, helping the client reinterpret and integrate these experiences into a healthier life script free from the constraints of their fears.

Interoceptive Exposure

Interoceptive exposure is a therapeutic technique aimed at reducing fear of bodily sensations by deliberately inducing and allowing clients to habituate to these sensations, breaking the cycle of avoidance and fear (Boettcher et al., 2016). A TA therapist might use this with clients by guiding them through exercises that elicit physical symptoms associated with anxiety, such as rapid heartbeat or shallow breathing, to reframe these sensations in the Adult ego-state as non-threatening. Examples include running in place to increase heart rate or spinning in a chair to induce dizziness, helping clients learn to manage and interpret these sensations more adaptively.

Eye Movement Desensitisation and Reprocessing

Eye Movement Desensitisation and Reprocessing (EMDR) is a psychotherapy treatment designed to alleviate distress associated with traumatic memories, effectively treating PTSD, anxiety, depression and other psychological issues by having clients recall traumatic memories while engaging in bilateral stimulation activities, such as eye movements, tapping or auditory stimulation. Body-oriented EMDR is considered more effective for many clients because it acknowledges and directly engages with the physical manifestations of trauma, focused on the underdeveloped fundamental psychological structures such as affect dysregulation and the memories stored in the Somatic Child, thus facilitating a more holistic and integrated healing process. TA therapists may train in EMDR to incorporate this in their work to help clients process and integrate traumatic memories more fully. By doing so, they address both cognitive and somatic components of trauma, facilitating deeper psychological and emotional healing and enhancing the effectiveness of the therapy-process by leveraging the body's role in storing and releasing traumatic memories. Scientific studies and meta-analyses have supported the efficacy of EMDR (Davidson & Parker, 2001; Rodenburg et al., 2009; Torres-Giminez et al., 2024).

Behavioural Activation

An example of social withdrawal in the context of TA could be a client who, operating out of a fearful Child ego-state, avoids social interactions due to beliefs developed from past experiences, leading to isolation and depression. However, the client may feel less in control due to the lack of positive experiences. Behavioural activation helps clients engage in activities that they find enjoyable or that give them a sense of accomplishment to combat depression, anxiety or other emotional difficulties (Cuijpers et al., 2007). It is based on the principle that positive activity can improve mood and reduce negative thought patterns. A TA therapists may follow these steps:

1 *Identify Activities:* Together with the client, the therapist identifies activities that the client used to enjoy or might bring a sense of achievement, factoring in social components.
2 *Set Goals:* The therapist works with the client to set realistic, achievable goals for engaging in these activities, perhaps starting with low-intensity social interactions.

3 *Action Planning:* The client and therapist detail an action plan, which gradually increases social engagement (e.g. starting with saying hello to a neighbour and then having a coffee with a friend).

4 *Ego-State Analysis:* Discuss how these behaviours can be supported by the Adult ego-state, providing rational and encouraging self-talk to overcome withdrawal tendencies of the Child state.

5 *Monitor Progress:* The therapist helps the client monitor their feelings and thoughts after attending social activities, reinforcing the connection between action and improvement in mood.

6 *Reinforce and Adjust:* Using insights gained, the therapist reinforces positive outcomes and helps adjust the action plan to challenge social withdrawal and improve frustration tolerance and engagement.

SELF-COMPASSION EXERCISES

Research shows the effectiveness of using various behavioural and experiential techniques to help clients accept their experiences (Chawla & Ostafin, 2007; Duffy et al., 2024; Elliott et al., 2021; Hendricks, 2002).

- *Conditions of Worth:* Conditions of worth are standards we believe we must meet to be considered valuable or worthy of love and acceptance by others. These conditions often develop early in life, stemming from our interactions with parents, caregivers and significant others. They are internalised through experiences where love or approval is contingent upon behaving in certain ways or meeting specific expectations. Over time, these conditions can profoundly influence our self-esteem and how we relate to others, leading us to believe that our worth is conditional upon external validation or achievements. Conditions of worth are externally imposed criteria stored within the Parent, which can dominate the Child need for unconditional acceptance and the Adult's capacity for objective evaluation. These conditions can lead to a disconnection from true self-awareness and self-compassion as individuals strive to meet these external standards at the expense of their genuine feelings and needs. A TA therapist can challenge conditions of worth and help clients develop more unconditional self-love by:
  - *Creating Awareness:* Help clients understand their conditions of worth and their impact on feelings, thoughts and behaviours.
  - *Encouraging Critical Examination:* Guiding clients to critically examine the origins and validity of these conditions. This may involve questioning whether these standards are indeed their own or if they have been adopted from others (e.g. parents, society).
  - *Promoting Self-Compassion:* Introducing self-compassion and mindfulness practices to help clients treat themselves with kindness and understanding rather than judgement.

- ○ *Reframing Self-Concept:* Assisting clients in developing a new self-concept based on their intrinsic worth rather than external achievements or the approval of others. This might involve identifying and reinforcing their inherent qualities and values.
- ○ *Encouraging Autonomy:* Supporting clients in making choices that reflect their true self rather than choices aimed at fulfilling conditions of worth. This autonomy strengthens the 'Adult' ego-state, enabling clients to evaluate their worth independently of external standards.

- *Self-Care:* Self-care involves engaging in activities that nurture physical, mental and emotional health. It can be hindered by life scripts emphasising constant achievement over personal well-being. Common examples include exercising, maintaining a nutritious diet, getting enough sleep, practising mindfulness or meditation, pursuing hobbies and seeking social support. Individuals may not engage in self-care due to their life script. For example, a person with a life script emphasising the need to constantly prove their worth through achievement might neglect self-care, seeing it as unproductive or selfish. A TA therapist can stimulate a client to engage in self-care by:
  - ○ *Identifying Script Beliefs:* Helping the client uncover and understand the beliefs within their life script that hinder self-care, such as feelings of unworthiness or the need to prioritise others.
  - ○ *Promoting Autonomy:* Encouraging clients to make autonomous decisions reflecting their needs/desires, rather than adhering to their life script.
  - ○ *Reframing Self-Care:* Working with the client to reframe self-care not as a selfish act but as a responsible choice enabling them to be their best self for others.
  - ○ *Setting Small, Achievable Goals:* Assist clients in setting small, achievable self-care goals.
  - ○ *Mindfulness and Self-Compassion Practices.*

- *Self-Compassion:* As introduced in Chapter 6, self-compassion (Gilbert, 2010; Neff, 2011; Schwartz, 2021) involves treating oneself with kindness, understanding and support during times of failure, perceived inadequacy or suffering. It encourages individuals to be gentle and forgiving towards themselves, recognising that imperfection and difficulties are part of the human experience. In TA, self-compassion can help clients challenge and reframe critical internal dialogues often found within the Critical Parent, encouraging a more Nurturing Parent. Self-compassion may reduce self-criticism and harsh internal dialogues, often stemming from introjected parental or societal messages. It can enhance emotional resilience, allowing clients to better cope with negative emotions and setbacks. It encourages a more balanced and compassionate Adult ego-state, which can objectively assess situations without undue influence from Critical Parent or vulnerable Child. Examples include:
  - ○ *Mindful Self-Compassion Breaks:* Teach clients to pause during moments of distress, recognise their feelings with mindfulness, extend kindness to themselves and remember the common humanity in their experiences.

○ *Making a List of Strengths and Qualities:* This may include three examples for each of the following starting with 'I am. . .': things I am good at, compliments I have received, what I like about my appearance, challenges I have overcome, I have helped others by, things that make me unique, what I value the most and times I have made others happy.

○ *Self-Compassion Letter Writing:* Guiding clients to write letters to themselves from a compassionate and understanding perspective, addressing their struggles, feelings and needs.

○ *Positive Self-Affirmations:* These statements can help individuals focus on their strengths and values, fostering a mindset of self-acceptance and compassion. Examples include 'I am worthy of love and respect', 'I am capable of overcoming challenges' and 'I treat myself with kindness and patience'. These affirmations can rewire negative thought patterns, encouraging clients to view themselves more positively and cultivate a compassionate relationship with themselves. An individual may write these down and repeat them daily.

○ *Reparenting Techniques:* Helping clients develop and internalise a Nurturing Parent voice, which offers compassion and understanding rather than criticism.

○ *Reframing Exercises:* Assisting clients in recognising and challenging their critical inner dialogue, encouraging them to reframe these thoughts in a more compassionate and supportive way.

○ *Role-Playing:* Engaging clients in role-plays that allow them to practice responding to themselves or imagined others with compassion and understanding, enhancing their ability to apply these skills in real-life situations.

SUMMARY

This chapter has given a broad toolkit with tools from other therapeutic modalities that TA therapists often use.

- Role-play exercises include Empty-Chair Method, Parent–Child Dialogue, Two-Chair Conflict Resolution, Rehearsal Role-Play, Historical Role-Play, Future Self Role-Play and Script-System Role-Play.
- Diary exercises include ego-state, life position, voices and messages, emotions, script-system and gratitude diaries. Individuals may write an autobiography, life review or letter to their future or past self.
- Cognitive exercises include keeping an automatic thought record, cognitive restructuring, identifying unhelpful thinking patterns and cognitive biases, identifying core transactional messages, reframing, clarifying, specifying, concretising, specifying memories, multisensory and life script questions, prioritising, Socratic questioning, strengthening adaptive ego-states and fostering a dual attitude and dereflection. Transactional core messages may be identified via the Downward-Arrow Technique.

- Behavioural exercises include behavioural experiments, improving frustration tolerance and embracing uncertainty, breaking the cycles of rumination, promoting sleep hygiene, graded and interoceptive exposure, EMDR and behavioural activation.
- Self-compassion exercises explore conditions of worth and promote unconditional self-worth, self-care and self-compassion.

PART IV
TA PSYCHOTHERAPY FOR SPECIFIC DISORDERS

13

DEPRESSIVE DISORDERS

DIAGNOSIS AND PSYCHOTHERAPIES

A depressed client might enter therapy feeling overwhelmingly sad, losing interest in activities they once enjoyed and struggling with a sense of worthlessness and fatigue. Clinical criteria for a depressive disorder include experiencing these feelings most of the day, nearly every day, for at least two weeks, along with significant weight change, sleep disturbances, restlessness or slowed behaviour, fatigue or loss of energy, feelings of worthlessness or excessive guilt, impaired concentration or indecisiveness and recurrent thoughts of death or suicide. These symptoms must cause significant distress or impairment in social, occupational and other areas of functioning and not be caused by substance use or medical condition. The diagnosis is clarified by the absence of a manic episode, distinguishing it from bipolar disorders.

The primary evidence-based psychotherapeutic treatments for depression, as highlighted by clinical guidelines, include CBT, Inter-Personal Therapy (IPT) and Problem-Solving Therapy (PST) (Cuijpers, 2020). CBT is renowned for its efficacy in evaluating, challenging and modifying dysfunctional thoughts and behaviours, making it the most studied and supported psychotherapy for depression. IPT focuses on addressing social issues that maintain depression, and PST emphasises developing and implementing problem-solving skills. TA therapists may want to integrate some of these therapeutic competencies in their work with depressed clients (see Chapter 12).

TA PSYCHOTHERAPY FOR DEPRESSION

Berne posited that recurrent depression often stems from unexpressed or unresolved issues in one's life script, leading to internal conflict within the individual's ego-states. This conflict consumes energy needed for current emotional experiences, manifesting as depression. Berne's approach involves identifying and addressing these repressed emotions and conflicts to change the individual's life script. This process includes analysing past responses/decisions, understanding their present impact and encouraging autonomous decisions to fulfil one's true desires and resolve depressive symptoms.

Research confirms that depressive disorders often involve a dominant, vulnerable Child state overwhelmed by sadness and a Critical Parent state perpetuating feelings of worthlessness. Strengthening the Adult ego-state can foster a balanced perspective, mitigating depressive feelings by enabling objective and compassionate self-assessment. Depressed individuals often live out harmful scripts filled with expectations of failure or inadequacy. TA therapy helps identify and rewrite these scripts towards positive, self-affirming narratives, empowering individuals to change their life stories into ones of hope and self-actualisation.

Depressive disorders can be exacerbated by dysfunctional transactions that reinforce negative self-views or unhealthy relational dynamics. Therapeutic work aims to modify these patterns, encouraging constructive interactions that improve mood and self-esteem. Depression can involve script-systems and games that confirm negative self-beliefs or maintain the depressive state. Identifying and interrupting these patterns can help individuals break free from self-defeating cycles, opening up new possibilities for emotional well-being. TA therapy also focuses on increasing awareness and acceptance of positive strokes, enhancing self-worth and reducing depressive symptoms.

In practice, depression is effectively treated by TA therapists, with research showing large therapeutic effectiveness similar to CBT, IPT and PST. (Vos & van Rijn, 2023). The TA-manual developed for depression has shown significant effects in feasibility and pilot studies (Vos & van Rijn, 2024a, 2024b, 2024c) (Table 13.1).

Table 13.1 Evidence-Based Formulation for Depression

Component Name	Research Evidence and Common Findings
Common TA-clinical presentation	Clients often report sadness, lack of interest, low life satisfaction and social withdrawal. Some individuals may hide depression behind a script-system or game, e.g. acting-out or workaholism.* Time structures may include withdrawal, rituals, pastimes, games and limited intimacy.*
Common TA-clinical model	Strong: CP, AC, U−, I−; taking/asking negative/conditional strokes*
	Weak: A, NP, FC, U+, I+; taking/asking positive/unconditional strokes*
Common TA-aetiology	Various aetiological factors may contribute/interact with depression:
	Childhood contextual factors increasing the likelihood of depression
	• Genetic factors, heritability
	• Socioeconomic context and injustice
	• Adverse Childhood Experiences, e.g. abuse, bullying, family role
	• Upbringing/parenting style
	Fundamental psychological structures increasing the likelihood
	• Underdeveloped or problematic ego-boundaries, separation/individuation, splitting, mentalisation, attachment
	• Ineffective coping and affect regulation skills
	• Unrealistic ideas about life, e.g. due to denial of existential givens (e.g. sheltered/spoiled/neglected/traumatic upbringing), may decrease resilience to respond effectively to later life-events.
	Transactional core messages increasing the likelihood
	• Restricting injunctive messages (Don't...) and drivers (e.g. Be Perfect, Please, Be Strong, Try Hard) and lacking important allowers and permissions ('It's OK to...').

Table 13.1 Evidence-Based Formulation for Depression *(Continued)*

Component Name	Research Evidence and Common Findings
	Responses/decisions increasing the likelihood
	• At some point in life, the client started accepting/following the transactional core messages from their life script. If there is a long pattern of depressive episodes, this response/decision may have started earlier in life. If this is a first depressive episode, it may be worthwhile exploring what made them recently respond/ decide to accept the life script.
	Self-perpetuating mechanisms and feedback loops
	• Negative self-beliefs ('I am worthless'), high standards ('If I do not achieve the highest mark, I have failed') and inability to achieve standards/satisfaction ('Nothing I do is good enough'); withdrawal which reduces the opportunity for pleasure/ achievement and the chance to find out that their negative beliefs may be false; a lack of positive experiences may increase hopelessness, negative self-perception and negative thinking
Common TA-goals	Foster self-insight: life script, ego-states, games, script-systems, strokes, time structure
	Strengthen: A, NP, FC, U−, I−, taking/asking positive/ unconditional strokes, self-compassion/self-efficacy
	Weaken: CP, AC, U−, I−, taking/asking negative/conditional strokes
Tips and tricks	• This book's treatment manual has been validated for clients with depression.
	• Regularly check suicide/self-harm risk (Chapter 25)
	• Focus therapeutic relationship on empathy/compassion
	• Prevent reinforcing the Critical Parent during the assessment; foster self-understanding and self-compassion towards their life story*
	• Depressed clients benefit from: psychoeducation; self-compassion exercises; imagination exercises to feel safe; behavioural activation to break withdrawal; role-play to practice new skills; some clients benefit from mindfulness exercises although sometimes this reinforces emotional dissociation (check fundamental psychological structures); identify/improve unrealistic/biased/unhelpful thoughts, e.g. via automatic thought record, cognitive restructuring and other behavioural/cognitive exercises (Chapters 11–12)

CP = Critical Parent, NP = Nurturing Parent, A = Adult, AC = Adapted Child, FC = Free Child; U+/− life position 'You're OK/not OK' and social functioning, I+/I− life position 'I'm OK/not OK' and self-efficacy.
*Suggestions based on clinical/theoretical expertise.

Box 13.1

Bipolar Disorder

Bipolar disorder is characterised by significant mood swings, including emotional highs (mania or hypomania) and lows (depression), affecting behaviour, energy levels and daily tasks. Diagnosis involves identifying at least one episode of mania/hypomania and depressive episodes, with symptoms like extreme mood swings, changes in sleep, energy, thinking and behaviour. Therapists diagnose this through detailed history, including family history, and long-term observation. It is important not to label clients too quickly with mania or bipolar disorder:

> The more intensely a person lives, the easier it is for their mood to swing between extremes. A fundamental clinical task is to accept patients' unpredictability, welcome their vitality, and harness it as a valuable resource in the therapeutic relationship rather than confusing it with mania. (Terlato, 2023, p. 222)

Evidence-based psychotherapeutic treatments for bipolar disorder include psycho-education, CBT and family-focused therapy, aimed at improving understanding, managing symptoms and enhancing family communication and support. These therapies are recommended alongside medication.

There are few TA-studies on bipolar disorders, although case studies suggest benefits (Carter, 2018); the following should be interpreted tentatively. TA may help clients understand their ego-state responses, managing relational dynamics during mood swings. Recognising when operating from a Critical Parent or Free Child state can help manage interactions that might escalate due to mood variability. Clients can learn to respond more appropriately to their emotions and thoughts by becoming aware of their operating ego-state. Therapists can work with clients to develop strategies for staying in the Adult ego-state. By analysing transactions between the client and others, therapists can identify patterns contributing to conflict or misunderstanding, which is crucial during mood episodes. The goal is to facilitate more harmonious transactions. Identifying and addressing games can help clients break harmful patterns, particularly in relationships. Effective communication strategies are crucial for maintaining relationships affected by mood swings. Ensuring positive strokes and reducing negative ones can improve self-esteem and reduce feelings of rejection or isolation. Understanding and re-scripting harmful life scripts can foster positive outlooks and healthier interpersonal relationships.

14
ANXIETY DISORDERS

The body, which was previously anxious, unpredictable, and insecure, gradually becomes a source of needs, desires, and resources that can be understood and addressed (Ligabue & Tenconi, 2021, p. 335).

DIAGNOSIS AND PSYCHOTHERAPIES

Clients coming to therapy for anxiety often report feeling constantly on edge, overwhelmed by worries and physical anxiety symptoms they cannot control. Anxiety disorders encompass a range of conditions characterised by excessive and persistent fear or worry in situations where most people would not feel threatened, alongside a variety of physical symptoms such as heart palpitations, sweating, restlessness, muscle tension and disturbances in sleep and concentration. The clinical criteria include excessive fears/anxieties disproportionate to the actual danger, lasting for six months or more, and causing significant distress or impairment in social/occupational/other areas of functioning. The paragon of evidence-supported therapeutic strategies for anxiety chiefly lies in CBT, often outshining pharmacotherapy (Bandelow et al., 2015; Cuijpers et al., 2013). Therefore, TA therapists working with anxiety should train themselves in CBT techniques (Chapter 12).

TA PSYCHOTHERAPY FOR ANXIETY

Although few scientific studies specifically focus on TA treatments of anxiety disorders, overall, TA-clients report significant reductions in their anxiety symptoms (Vos & van Rijn, 2022). Even though the critical therapeutic interventions for anxiety may focus on CBT techniques, the therapeutic process may be facilitated by TA's focus on developing self-insight and finding alternative responses in specific transactions/games, strengthening the Adult and Nurturing Parent and offering a supportive, safe therapeutic relationship.

TA therapists rarely specifically address anxiety as a distinct category, possibly as there may be various underlying aetiological causes and subsequent different clinical models and therapeutic mechanisms. In an early stage of treatment, a client may develop safety via the supportive therapeutic relationship and improving the Nurturing Parent through self-compassion. Anxiety disorders often seem linked to the dominance of an overly critical or overprotective Parent ego-state or vulnerable Child ego-state feeling overwhelmed or scared. Therapeutic work may focus on strengthening the Adult, promoting rational thinking and calmness. Anxiety can be triggered or worsened by dysfunctional transactions, especially those that reinforce a person's fears or self-doubts; TA can help individuals recognise and alter these patterns, fostering healthier exchanges. Anxiety disorders can be maintained through games and script-systems that serve to avoid deeper fears or keep oneself in a familiar, though uncomfortable, psychological state; TA could focus on identifying and breaking these cycles, helping individuals to express their needs and emotions more authentically. Anxiety disorders might be part of a person's life script predisposing them to react to situations with anxiety; therapeutic efforts can aim to rewrite this script, encouraging more adaptive responses to stress. For example, some individuals with anxiety disorders might have a script that seeks out negative strokes, which can validate their anxious thoughts or feelings; TA therapy might involve learning to seek and accept positive strokes, thus building self-esteem and reducing reliance on anxiety as a means of gaining attention or recognition (Table 14.1).

Table 14.1 Evidence-Based Case Formulation

Component Name	Research Evidence and Common Findings
Common TA-clinical presentation	Anxiety may show in various life domains and transactions. Some individuals may hide anxiety behind a script-system or game, including unrealistic strong self-presentation, acting-out or workaholism.* Out of fear, they may structure their time with withdrawal, rituals, pastimes or games and avoid intimacy.*
Common TA-clinical model	Strong: CP, I–*
	Sometimes strong: CP, U–, taking/asking negative/conditional strokes*
	Weak: A, NP, FC, I+
	Sometimes weak: U+, taking/asking positive/unconditional strokes*
Common TA-aetiology	Various aetiological factors may contribute/interact with anxiety:
	Childhood contextual factors increasing the likelihood of anxiety
	• Genetic factors, heritability • Socioeconomic context and injustice • Adverse Childhood Experiences, e.g. abuse, bullying, family role • Upbringing/parenting style
	Fundamental psychological structures increasing the likelihood
	• Underdeveloped or problematic ego-boundaries, separation/individuation, splitting, mentalisation, attachment • Ineffective coping and affect regulation skills • Unrealistic ideas about life, e.g. due to denial of existential givens (e.g. sheltered/spoiled/neglected/traumatic upbringing), may decrease resilience to respond effectively to later life events.
	Transactional core messages increasing the likelihood
	• Restricting injunctive messages (Don't. . .) and drivers (e.g. Be Perfect, Try Hard, Hurry) and lacking important allowers and permissions ('It's OK to. . .').

Table 14.1 Evidence-Based Case Formulation *(Continued)*

Component Name	Research Evidence and Common Findings
	Responses and decisions increasing the likelihood
	• At some point in life, the client started accepting/following the transactional core messages from their life script. If there is a long pattern of anxiety, this response/decision may have started earlier in life. If this is a first episode, exploring what made them recently respond/decide to accept the llife script may be worthwhile.
	Self-perpetuating mechanisms and feedback loops
	• Vicious cycles often strongly contribute to the development and reinforcement of anxiety. For example, avoiding a feared situation may give a temporary sense of relief, reinforcing the belief that avoidance is helpful; avoidance increases the internal threshold, as the feared situation may start to feel more threatening, and the sense of self-efficacy and self-control may decrease due to a lack of positive experiences in coping with the feared situation.
Common goals	Foster self-insight: life script, ego-states, games, script-systems, strokes, time structure
	Strengthen: A, NP, FC, I+
	Possibly strengthen: U+, taking/asking positive/unconditional strokes*
	Possibly weaken: CP, I−, U−, taking/asking negative/conditional strokes*
Tips and tricks	• Focus therapeutic relationships on empathy/compassion to create a sense of safety.
	• The main focus should be CBT techniques, focused on psychoeducation, behavioural experiments, graded exposure, building frustration tolerance and embracing uncertainty, behavioural activation, identifying/transforming unrealistic/biased/unhelpful thoughts and behaviours, cognitive restructuring/reframing and breaking rumination cycles (Chapter 12).
	• Clients may benefit from analysing transactions/games and role-play to experiment with feared situations.
	• Some body-oriented exercises may be very effective, e.g. teaching grounding and breathing techniques. Mindfulness exercises sometimes reinforces hyperfocus and worsen anxiety.
	• It is recommended first to treat anxiety and improve the client's affect regulation skills before the life script is rigorously analysed and/or other problems addressed, as script-analysis often increases anxiety levels (Vos & van Rijn, 2024b-d).

Note: CP = Critical Parent, NP = Nurturing Parent, A = Adult, AC = Adapted Child, FC = Free Child; U+/− life position 'You're OK/not OK' and social functioning, I+/I− life position 'I'm OK/not OK' and self-efficacy.
*Suggestions based on clinical/theoretical expertise.

Box 14.1

Obsessive-Compulsive Disorder

Obsessive-Compulsive Disorder (OCD) is characterised by persistent, unwanted thoughts (obsessions) and repetitive behaviours (compulsions) aimed at reducing anxiety or preventing feared events, causing significant distress or impairment. Clinical criteria include obsessions, compulsions or both that are time-consuming or cause significant distress or impairment in daily functioning.

A TA therapist can identify OCD by observing rigid, ritualistic behaviours and thought processes aimed at controlling anxiety, indicating an overactive Critical Parent or Adapted Child ego-state. The primary treatment for OCD is CBT with Exposure and Response Prevention, often combined with medication (SSRI).

There are few TA-studies on OCD; the following should be interpreted tentatively, and therapists may want additional training and work in a multidisciplinary team. Individuals with OCD may exhibit overactive Critical Parent and Adapted Child ego-states, characterised by internalised rules driving obsessive thoughts and compulsive behaviours. The Adult ego-state may become contaminated by irrational beliefs from the Parent or Child ego-states, leading to distorted risk evaluation and reliance on compulsions. The TA therapist may strengthen the Adult ego-state, promoting rational thinking and problem-solving. Techniques include reality testing, rational analysis of fears and developing adaptive coping strategies. Compulsions may serve as emotional script-systems/rackets, providing temporary anxiety relief. The therapist may focus on the client's transactions, identifying patterns that trigger or worsen OCD symptoms. By analysing transactions, healthier interaction patterns can be developed. Games in OCD involve rituals to avoid bad outcomes, perpetuating anxiety cycles. The therapist helps the client recognise and interrupt these, replacing them with healthier behaviours. Reparenting techniques address the overactive Parent ego-state, providing nurturing responses to reduce self-criticism and obsessive thoughts. The goal of treatment may involve promoting autonomy, increasing the client's capacity for awareness, spontaneity and intimacy, leading to a more integrated self.

Case Study 14.1

John

John, a 42-year-old IT manager, sought therapy for persistent anxiety affecting his job performance, decision-making and social interactions. Early sessions with his TA therapist fostered a supportive relationship, enhancing his Nurturing Parent ego-state through self-compassion exercises. The therapist identified an overactive Adapted Child and Critical Parent ego-state, fuelling John's anxiety. They focused on strengthening his Adult ego-state to promote thinking and self-soothing that made him feel calmer. Dysfunctional transactions at work and personal relationships were explored and altered to foster healthier exchanges. For example, leading up to regular meetings with his manager, John recognised that he usually expected criticism, felt anxious and sought reassurance by the manager, which made him feel even more insecure and resulted in few positive strokes. John learnt to ground himself, identify the areas he wanted to talk to his manager about and contribute to setting the agenda for the meetings. He felt empowered through this and also received more positive strokes by his manager. He learnt to identify and break away from games and script-systems/rackets that maintained his anxiety, such as seeking validation through negative strokes. When his anxiety had sufficiently reduced, they worked on rewriting his life script, seeking and accepting positive strokes, thereby building self-esteem and reducing anxiety. Over time, John reported significant reductions in anxiety.

15

TRAUMA DISORDERS

DIAGNOSIS AND PSYCHOTHERAPIES

Post-Traumatic Stress Disorder (PTSD) involves persistent re-experiencing of traumatic memories three months or more after a traumatic event, avoidance of trauma-related stimuli, negative alterations in cognition and mood and marked changes in arousal and reactivity, starting at least one month post-trauma. Acute Stress Disorder (ASD) features similar symptoms – intrusive memories, negative mood, dissociation, avoidance and heightened arousal – occurring between three days and one month after the event. Complex PTSD (C-PTSD), often resulting from prolonged trauma like childhood abuse, includes additional symptoms such as emotional regulation difficulties, a persistent sense of threat and self-concept issues

Clients with PTSD, ASD or C-PTSD may also experience dissociation, such as not feeling in touch with reality or themselves (derealisation, depersonalisation). Diagnostic criteria emphasise symptom duration, onset, impact on functioning and exclusion of symptoms caused by substances, medical conditions or other psychological disorders. Research highlights the importance of differentiating between those who develop these disorders later in life, with fully developed psychological structures, and those who develop them early, for example, developmental trauma disorder, often with immature coping, affect regulation skills and insecure attachment (Van der Kolk, 1994).

Evidence-based psychotherapeutic treatments for ASD, PTSD and C-PTSD include EMDR, CBT, Prolonged Exposure Therapy and Narrative Exposure Therapy (Bisson et al. 2007; Jericho et al., 2022; Lewis et al., 2020; Mavranezouli et al., 2020; Mahoney et al., 2019; Watts et al., 2013). These therapies are preferred for their long-term benefits and lower risk of adverse side effects compared to pharmacological treatments. TA therapists working with ASD/PTSD/C-PTSD may seek additional training in these approaches, especially EMDR. Those working with C-PTSD may benefit from learning somatic/experiential skills for affect regulation (Novak, 2008; Schwartz, 2021). Children may require specific approaches (Morena, 2014).

TA PSYCHOTHERAPY FOR TRAUMA

Several TA-publications focus on trauma disorders (Novak, 2013; Stuthridge, 2006). Several TA core techniques, such as script-analysis, explicitly focus on how adverse life experiences may impact the present. Some clinical trials suggest that TA can be effective in treating

PTSD, for example, in veterans (Vos & van Rijn, 2023). Research indicates the importance of treating PTSD/ASD/C-PTSD clients in specific phases (Herman & Van der Kolk, 2020), which is an extension of typical TA-stages (Chapter 10).

Stage 1: Creation of Safety

The therapist creates a safe environment where the client feels secure by offering a supportive, compassionate relationship (Chapter 9), body-oriented, imagination and mindfulness exercises like breathing, orienting, grounding and safe space visualisation (Chapter 12). The aim is to let the client know, not only rationally but also experientially, that the current factual situation is safe and that this is not the past that was threatening and harmful. These skills strengthen the Adult to orient and regulate themselves. The therapist may use analysis/exercises in transactions to help the client return to the present. Psychoeducation often plays a vital role in strengthening the Adult, for example, by explaining the diagnosis, the role of healthy eating, sports and physical exercise and sleep hygiene. As the therapist may unintentionally engage in the client's enactment and re-enactment, they should remain aware of relational/transference processes and games (Novak, 2015).

Therapists may motivate clients to use their social support network if this is not abusive or reinforcing traumas and avoidance. Traumas often trigger the life position that everyone and oneself are not-OK (U−/I−), and positive social encounters can disprove this belief, as well as stimulate the Adult function and affect regulation. Socially isolated individuals may benefit from connecting with other victims of similar traumas, as they often feel better understood and at ease with them, such as specific therapy groups for war veterans or victims of domestic violence. As research indicates that social relationships and other forms of meaning may stimulate affect regulation via the vagus nerve (Dana, 2018; Dang et al., 2021; Porges, 2011), it may be helpful to ask the client what they find meaningful in life, find more ways to experience these meanings and become more aware of meaningful moments, for example, via a meaningful moments diary (Chapter 5) (Vos, 2017). Withdrawn clients may benefit from behavioural activation (Cuijpers et al., 2007) and role-play exercises to gradually rebuild confidence in mildly stressful situations.

Stage 2: Skills Training

In clients with underdeveloped fundamental psychological structures, such as clients whose C-PTSD is grounded in early-life neglect and abuse, it is crucial to improve basic skills, such as affect regulation and overcoming/integrating splitting. Later-life traumatic events or triggers may also cause a re-enactment of early developmental dramas, even though these seemed to have been resolved for most of life: after experiencing a severe psychological trauma, an individual may regress to a childlike state as a coping mechanism, re-enacting early-life emotional experiences and relying on immature affect regulation and splitting. This regression can occur as a way to seek safety and comfort, especially when the trauma triggers overwhelming emotions that the individual may not have learnt to regulate effectively. Despite functioning well in daily life, the trauma may activate unresolved emotional patterns from childhood, leading to a temporary regression to less mature coping strategies. It may support the client's nurturing self-compassion and Adult functions to explain that the recent traumatic/stressful experience seems to have put them under so much emotional pressure that any vulnerabilities in their fundamental psychological structure become visible, even though these cracks and tears in their foundations are almost invisible and have relatively little impact on their everyday functioning when they are not under such amount of stress. Evidence-based training of fundamental psychological structure skills may, for example, be found in STAIR training (Cloitre et al., 2020) and Dialectical Behaviour Therapy (Kothgassner et al., 2021; Panos et al., 2014). Clients may also benefit from somatic therapies or mindfulness training (Goldberg et al., 2023, 2018; Khoury et al., 2013). Stroke analysis may reveal that victims of childhood abuse have long-lasting issues around self-compassion and self-efficacy; the therapist may, therefore, integrate a range of self-compassion techniques (Chapter 11).

Clients with dissociative symptoms may particularly benefit from somatic and affect regulation-focused interventions; as their affect regulation may be structurally underdeveloped, their treatment may require long-term multidisciplinary specialist treatment, particularly if associated with severe dissociation such as psychosis. These clients may quickly switch between ego-states or get stuck in an ego-state as a defensive response to guard against anxiety; it may be helpful for clients to develop insight into these ego-states and how to find more valuable alternatives. Only when the client seems strong enough should a therapist offer a client processing; it may be that the client needs to wait or is never ready for deep processing.

Stage 3: Experiential Processing

All evidence-based ASD/PTSD/C-PTSD treatments involve a stage of processing of the traumatic events. They often have the following sub-stages (Cloitre et al., 2020; Herman & Van der Kolk, 2020).

3A: Identifying How the Trauma Affects the Present

TA therapists may use their usual primary and secondary assessment tools, particularly script-system analysis, while being aware that a critical symptom of ASD/PTSD/C-PTSD is avoidance and denial. Analysis of transactions may reveal games re-enacting parts of the trauma. A client may, for example, come to a therapist for a problem that seems unrelated to their deep-rooted traumas, such as work-related problems or burnout, which may result from playing script-systems or games that prevent the client from addressing and solving their underlying traumas.

> Trauma interferes with this integrative capacity, creating excluded ego-states and a disorganised self. The child's experience of abusive caregivers is internalised in a series of toxic Parent/Child ego-states. This inner world shapes the child's view of the world outside, leading to patterns of transferential enactment that reinforce a traumatic script. (Stuthridge, 2006)

Transactions are often skewed by the individual's trauma lens, interpreting neutral or positive interactions as threatening. Therapy may cognitively challenge and recalibrate these transactions to be more reality-based and less influenced by past trauma.

A common phenomenon in victims of childhood abuse is a deep sense of shame and vulnerability, whereby this sense of shame and vulnerability is so overwhelming that they may respond by complete denial/avoidance, projection onto others via anger, internalisation such as depression and withdrawal; thus, individuals may play these games or script-systems to avoid their shame/vulnerability, but by this avoidance, they may reinforce these feelings and prevent new positive experiences (Bradshaw, 2005; Elison et al., 2006; Erskine, 1994). Note that, in line with Karpman's Drama Triangle, guilt and self-blame, such as survival guilt, seem to be familiar games in trauma survivors, even though the clients did not have a realistic option other than doing what they did and developing the symptoms they have.

> Shame is comprised of the script belief "Something is wrong with me," formed due to messages and decisions, conclusions in response to impossible demands, and defensive hope and control. In addition, from an ego-state perspective, shame involves a diminished self-concept in compliance with criticism, a defensive transposition of sadness and fear, and a disavowal of anger. Furthermore, archaic shame may be either a Child or a Parent ego-state fixation. The suggestion is made that self-righteousness denies a need for relationship. A contact-oriented relationship psychotherapy that emphasises methods of inquiry, attunement, and involvement is [recommended]. (Erskine, 1994, p. 86)

As these games of self-blame or self-victimisation validate the client's negative life position towards self/others, the therapist may want to identify and disrupt these games and encourage more genuine, healthy interactions. Cognitive techniques may help determine how realistic and helpful feelings of guilt and self-blame are, and analysis may identify the psychological payoff of creating an artificial sense of control in a situation where they had very little power.

It can help clients to develop insight into these mechanisms, as long as the therapist shows empathy and fosters a sense of self-compassion by allowing the client to understand that it is understandable that they developed these script-systems and games and that many ASD/PTSD/C-PTSD sufferers report these. Clients may be supported by creating more realistic and helpful alternatives to these script-systems and games, which can sometimes be grounded in efficient solutions; however, clients may find it challenging to stop these at this stage altogether.

Many trauma therapists argue that it can be difficult for clients to come to the core of their traumatic experiences because of having developed strong avoidance/denial mechanisms (Dana, 2018; Gendlin, 1996; Van der Kolk et al., 1994). Therefore, trauma therapists often use their variations of phenomenological methods to unpeel the layers of the client's experiences (Chapter 12; Vos, 2017). Usually, the client will first present a secondary emotion to the therapist (e.g. script-system, game), which may be analysed to identify the underlying primary emotion; however, this primary emotion may still not be fully experientially integrated and, therefore, the therapist may ask the client to focus on the underlying somatic experience, and the memories and situations they associate this with (Chapter 11).

For example, a client may oscillate between showing anger or helplessness towards the therapist (secondary emotion), which may be caused by an underlying feeling of vulnerability or shame (primary emotion). Even if the client can name the emotion of vulnerability, this may sound rational and with a cognitive distance; therefore, the therapist may ask the client to identify the somatic component, such as, 'Where does this feel in your body?'. As soon as the client becomes aware of the underlying bodily movements and sensations, they often respond strongly as these are core experiences they may have been suppressing and avoiding. At this point, the therapist may ask what memories come up when they focus on these bodily sensations, when they started, or in which situations these physical sensations are usually the strongest and when they were in such situations for the first time. When the client can connect memory with these sensations, the therapist may start exposure-therapy or EMDR (see Stage 3C) to process the memory.

3B: Analysing Life Script

Depending on when and how the trauma happened, the therapist may focus on different periods in their life. Script-analysis may be led by the presenting traumas, possibly concentrate on one at a time and/or by patterns identified in diaries or previous analyses. Clients may not be consciously aware of traumas (amnesia) or feel emotionally disconnected (dissociation). Therefore, sometimes the therapist may need to read between the lines of what a client says and does, and this is where secondary assessment of transactions, games and script-systems may be insightful. Again, this analysis should be done with much (self) compassion, not to increase feelings of shame or guilt, and not to make reductionistic/ essentialistic claims about having found the sole and only cause of life's problems. The word 'decision' may need to be avoided, as individuals usually develop ASD/PTSD/C-PTSD as they had no other alternative response option. It is essential to highlight that even though they may not have had a choice in the past, they may now be able to decide to heal.

3C: Exposure to Trauma and Avoided Feelings

Evidence-based trauma treatments usually include some exposure to traumatic experiences and avoided feelings, such as trauma-based CBT, EMDR, Narrative Exposure Therapy or the increasingly empirically-supported body-oriented EMDR (Schwartz, 2021). This should not be done by a therapist without additional trauma training. There are several theoretical explanations of why exposure may work, such as stimulating affect tolerance, habituation and extinction or reconditioning by connecting the feared stimulus with an alternative response in a safe context. In this stage, the client's active imagination often automatically emerges, similar to cognitive rescripting, coming up with symbolic solutions, metaphors and fairy tales that may give them a sense of safety and a language to express their inner emotional shifts, like Jung wrote about the healing power of our 'active imagination' (Rubinstein & Lahad, 2023).

Stage 4: Recovery

Many trauma therapists seem to stop the treatment when the client has sufficiently processed the trauma experientially and the psychopathological symptoms have adequately decreased. However, many clients report struggling with other outcomes, such as self-realisation, well-being, quality-of-life, behaviour and relationships; therefore, several existential and positive-psychology treatments have been developed to help with these issues (Vos, 2024a). TA therapy can play an essential role in this stage by assisting clients formulating new positive transactional core messages, re-scripting the narrative of victimhood or powerlessness towards empowerment and resilience, further improving their ego-states (particularly Adult, Nurturing Parent and Free Child), improving their life position (I+/U+), formulating and achieving new self-determined life goals (see Vos, 2017, to help clients learn how to live a meaningful and satisfying life). Often, clients struggle with transactions and games, particularly with individuals who were directly/indirectly associated with the trauma; the therapist may help them develop insight into this and strengthen their Adult particularly if the client decides to be/stay in contact or go for a process of mediation or reconciliation. This stage requires a continuing focus on self-compassion, existential/meaning-oriented exercises (Vos, 2017) and a sense of justice and reconciliation in the community (Herman, 2023) (Table 15.1).

Table 15.1 Evidence-Based Case Formulation for Trauma Disorders

Component Name	Research Evidence and Common Findings
Common TA-clinical presentation	Clients often present with anxiety, although they may try to avoid these feelings, e.g. via emotional disconnection/dissociation. Their symptoms affect many life domains, such as sleeping, work, self-care and social relationships. ASD/PTSD/C-PTSD may be shown as dysfunctional ego-states (such as quick shifts or rigid stuckness), transactions, games (e.g. regression to a Child state; Drama Triangle; reliving a script reinforcing victimhood or powerlessness) and script-systems suppressing or overexpressing but rarely showing true feelings. Clients seem to regress to a Child state when experiencing triggers of flashbacks, feeling as vulnerable and helpless as they did during the traumatic event. Individuals may have a pattern of negative strokes, reinforcing a negative self-image. Out of fear, they may structure their time with withdrawal, rituals, pastimes or games and avoid intimacy. Some individuals show internalised symptoms such as withdrawal, whereas others may externalise via risk-taking, acting-out and aggression.*
Common TA-clinical model	Strong: I−, U−, AC (when triggered/flashbacks)
	Sometimes strong: CP, taking/asking negative/conditional strokes*
	Weak: A, NP, FC, I+, U+
	Sometimes weak: taking/asking positive/unconditional strokes*
Common TA-aetiology	Various aetiological factors may contribute/interact with PTSD/ASD/C-PTSD, such as a traumatic experience; C-PTSD seems more likely than PTSD/ASD to include multiple interacting factors.

Table 15.1 Evidence-Based Case Formulation for Trauma Disorders *(Continued)*

Component Name	Research Evidence and Common Findings
	Childhood context increasing the likelihood of PTSD/ASD/C-PTSD
	• Genetic factors, heritability
	• Socioeconomic context and injustice
	• Adverse Childhood Experiences, e.g. abuse, bullying, family role
	• Upbringing/parenting style
	Fundamental psychological structures increasing the likelihood
	• Trauma disorders may involve problems in affect regulation, attachment, ego-boundaries and splitting; these problems seem like a temporary re-enactment or regression. Victims of severe early-life childhood abuse and neglect are more likely to have underdeveloped fundamental psychological structures, which makes them more likely to develop ASD/PTSD/C-PTSD in response to stressful/traumatic life events as they have never developed the skills to cope with stress. The functioning of these fundamental psychological structures may first need to be strengthened before clients may be able to safely process their traumatic memories and affects.
	Transactional core messages increasing the likelihood
	• Sometimes restricting injunctive messages (Don't…) and drivers (e.g. Be Perfect, Try Hard, Hurry) and lacking some crucial allowers and permissions ('It's OK to…')
	Responses/decisions increasing the likelihood
	• Often, in traumatic situations, individuals have little choice other than doing what they did; however, they may develop unrealistic self-blame to develop a sense of control retrospectively and, via the Drama Triangle, avoid their true feelings of helplessness and vulnerability. It can be helpful to help clients develop a realistic sense of what was and what was not in their power. Avoid blaming language such as using the word 'decision'. Clients may struggle with moral injury, which is the psychological distress that results from actions, or the lack of them, violating their moral/ethical code (e.g. hurting/killing a person, albeit as self-defence, or soldiers in war/battle).
	Self-perpetuating mechanisms and feedback loops
	• ASD/PTSD-C-PTSD is often associated with many vicious cycles, which are important to analyse and create alternatives for.
Common TA-goals	Foster self-insight: life script, ego-states, games, script-systems, strokes, time structure
	Strengthen: A, NP, FC, I+, U+
	Possibly strengthen: taking/asking positive/unconditional strokes*
	Possibly weaken: CP, I−, U−, taking/asking negative/conditional strokes*
Tips & and tricks	See this chapter.

CP = Critical Parent, NP = Nurturing Parent, A = Adult, AC = Adapted Child, FC = Free Child; U+/− life position 'You're OK/not OK' and social functioning, I+/I− life position 'I'm OK/not OK' and self-efficacy.
*Suggestions based on clinical/theoretical expertise.

Box 15.1

Dissociative Disorder

Dissociation is often observed in ASD/PTSD/C-PTSD but can also occur independently. Dissociative Disorder involves disruptions in consciousness, memory, identity, emotion, perception, body representation, motor control and behaviour. Symptoms include memory lapses, depersonalisation, derealisation and fragmented identity. TA therapists can identify Dissociative Disorder through inconsistencies in the client's narrative, sudden mood or identity shifts and feelings of detachment. Evidence-based treatments for Dissociative Disorders include CBT, EMDR and DBT, which aim to integrate dissociated experiences into a cohesive self-concept. Stage-oriented treatment, progressing from safety and stabilisation to trauma processing and integration, is recommended. Clients in cults/sects may need specific attention (Hyams, 1998).

There are few TA-studies on dissociation; the following should be interpreted tentatively. Erskine (2017) highlights that dissociation may occur during traumatic experiences lacking reparative relationships. Contact-oriented relationship therapy, involving enquiry, attunement and involvement, may help dissolve dissociation and integrate trauma. Therapeutic engagements should include acknowledgement, validation, normalisation and presence, described as permission, potency, protection and intrapsychic punishment. There is a risk of (re)enactment (Minikin, 2023).

In Dissociative Disorders, there may be a pronounced disruption in ego-state integration, leading to significant dissociation. TA therapists can help clients map their ego-states, enhancing integration and fostering a cohesive self-identity. Dissociative individuals might engage in games and emotional script-systems to manage internal conflict, often leading to further dissociation. TA therapists can help clients understand the payoffs and costs of these behaviours, motivating change and healthier emotional management. Clients may have developed life scripts based on early trauma, contributing to dissociation. When clients have sufficient self-insight and affect regulation skills, therapists may help clients uncover and re-evaluate these scripts, promoting healthier patterns of relating. Strengthening the Adult and fostering a compassionate internal dialogue between ego-states can promote autonomy, helping clients gain control over their thoughts and actions, reducing dissociative experiences.

Case Study 15.1

Bill

Bill came to therapy with severe PTSD symptoms following a recent car accident, including panic attacks, agoraphobia and withdrawal. The therapist suspected deeper issues and provided a supportive relationship, teaching Bill grounding, breathing and orienting techniques to help him regulate his emotions. Somatic exercises helped Bill reconnect with his body and manage tension. Social activities and hobbies were encouraged, leading to quick progress. The therapist then used EMDR on the car accident memories, but some symptoms persisted. Exploring Bill's life story revealed unresolved grief from losing a childhood friend at age ten, which the car accident had re-triggered. Grief work allowed Bill to express his feelings, including anger, and understand the validity of his emotions. Reconnecting with childhood friends provided additional support. The combination of affect regulation, processing the car accident, grief work and new social connections significantly reduced Bill's symptoms. In the final sessions, they focused on Bill being more authentic and expressive in his interactions.

16

CLUSTER-A PERSONALITY DISORDERS (PARANOID, SCHIZOTYPAL, SCHIZOID)

DIAGNOSIS AND PSYCHOTHERAPIES

Clients presenting with Cluster-A personality disorders may come to therapy describing feelings of extreme social discomfort, distrust in others or disconnection from reality, often feeling isolated or misunderstood. Cluster-A personality disorders, encompassing Paranoid, Schizoid and Schizotypal Personality Disorders, are characterised by odd or eccentric behaviours, significant social anxiety not limited to specific situations, distrustful and suspicious perceptions of others' motives and peculiar ways of thinking and perceiving the world. Therapists may identify these disorders by carefully observing the client's interpersonal behaviour, communication style and emotional expression, looking for persistent patterns that deviate from cultural expectations and impair social or occupational functioning. Clinical criteria include pervasive patterns of social detachment, acute discomfort in close relationships, cognitive or perceptual distortions and eccentricities in behaviour, beginning by early adulthood and present in various contexts.

Evidence-based psychotherapeutic treatments for Cluster-A personality disorders primarily focus on tailored approaches that address the unique aspects of these disorders. Dialectical Behaviour Therapy (DBT), Schema Therapy and Mentalisation-Based Treatment (MBT) are among the therapies that have shown effectiveness for personality disorders in general and are applied for Cluster-A disorders (Katakis et al., 2023; Stoffers-Winterling et al., 2022; Verheul & Herbrink, 2007).

TA-FRAMEWORK FOR CLUSTER-A PERSONALITY DISORDERS

Studies on TA for Cluster-A personality disorders are scarce; therefore, use the following tentatively, and TA therapists may seek additional training and work in a multidisciplinary team. These disorders often involve underdeveloped fundamental psychological structures, such as splitting, blurred or rigid ego-boundaries and problematic separation/individuation and attachment. These early-life structural issues impact the client's ego-states and life position, potentially requiring a different therapeutic approach than TA.

However, TA may still offer a relevant framework alongside other interventions. Individuals with Cluster-A personality disorders seem to operate from a distorted Parent or Child ego-state, leading to paranoid thoughts or eccentric behaviours rather than the rational, present-oriented Adult ego-state. A dominant Parent ego-state may include rigid or suspicious beliefs inherited from parental figures, while a dominant Child ego-state may involve feelings of isolation, fear or confusion about social interactions. Schizoid disorders may be regarded as a withdrawn Child (Little, 2001). Strengthening the Adult ego-state can help these individuals assess reality more accurately and make healthier decisions.

Transactions in Cluster-A individuals might frequently be characterised by mis-interpretations or miscommunications, often due to projecting fears and anxieties onto others, leading to a breakdown in meaningful social exchanges. Their stroke economy may heavily favour negative strokes due to distrust or discomfort with others, reinforcing isolation and social anxiety. They might engage in psychological games that keep others at a distance or validate their paranoid or schizoid views.

The concept of script-systems can help understand how individuals with these disorders manage their emotional expressions and needs, often reinforcing their isolation or paranoia. Maladaptive scripts based on early experiences of mistrust, isolation or ridicule may add to eccentric or paranoid behaviours and thoughts in adulthood. A study on individuals with paranoia revealed drivers such as 'Be strong' (76%) and 'Be perfect' (65%), along with a sense of 'stuckness' in the first stage of the development, with many experiencing script prohibitions like 'Do not be close' (74%) and 'Do not have feelings' (72%); the prevailing combinations of the 'personal adaptations' were 'schizoid' (92%) and 'paranoid' (81%) (Mruh, 2020). Mellacqua (2020, 2014) offers a paradigm for TA treatment of individuals with schizophrenia and Cluster-A personality disorders, though focused on extreme cases. The question remains whether TA can help people change unconscious decisions that are subtle, are ego-syntonic and feel familiar. Haimowitz (2000) and Yontef (2001) provide affirmative answers based on work with schizoid clients.

TA may contribute to the treatment of this population, though more research is needed. The therapist may help the client become aware of which ego-state they are operating from, especially in social situations, and how this affects their interactions. Encouraging the use of the Adult ego-state can foster a more balanced and less paranoid view of others' intentions. TA can involve re-parenting, challenging dysfunctional beliefs from the Parent ego-state and replacing them with healthier ones. TA therapists may help identify and rewrite scripts of rejection or betrayal, aiming to increase autonomy and the capacity to make new decisions not bound by historical script beliefs. Through role-play and other techniques, therapists can help clients improve social skills, understand social cues and recognise the impact of their behaviour on others. Building a trusting therapeutic relationship is crucial, as trust is often a core issue for people with these disorders.

Case Study 16.1

William

William, a 32-year-old software developer, exhibited symptoms of Schizotypal Personality Disorder, including intense social anxiety, feelings of disconnection and interpreting others' actions as hostile. His life was marked by isolation and a sense of being different. Being part of William's multidisciplinary treatment team, his TA therapist focused on increasing awareness of his Child and Parent ego-states, which were dominated by social fear and rigid, suspicious beliefs from his upbringing. The therapist aimed to strengthen William's Adult ego-state to foster a more rational approach to social situations. Role-play exercises helped William challenge his paranoid thoughts and odd beliefs. The therapist also addressed his negative life scripts, such as 'Do not be close' and 'Do not have feelings', encouraging him to rewrite these scripts for healthier social interactions. Improving William's stroke economy was another focus, encouraging him to accept positive feedback and reduce distrust. This approach aimed to break down psychological games that reinforced his isolation. Through these strategies, William gradually improved his social skills, understanding of social cues and overall sense of connection with others.

Box 16.1

Schizophrenia

Schizophrenia is a severe mental disorder marked by disruptions in thinking, language, perception and self-awareness, often with hallucinations, delusions and disordered behaviour. Symptoms may include persistent delusions, hallucinations, disorganised speech, catatonic behaviour and negative symptoms like reduced emotional expression, significantly impacting social and occupational functioning. TA therapists may identify schizophrenia by noting difficulties in coherent conversation, disconnection from reality and disrupted ego-states. Treatment guidelines emphasise a multidisciplinary approach, primarily focused on symptom management, combining pharmacologic and non-pharmacologic treatments. Evidence-based psychotherapies include CBT, Family Therapy, Social Skills Training, Assertive Community Treatment and Cognitive Remediation (Pfammatter et al., 2006; Turner et al., 2014).

There are few TA-studies on schizophrenia (Mellacqua, 2020, 2014, offers insightful studies); the following should be interpreted tentatively, and TA therapists may seek additional training and work in a multidisciplinary team. TA therapists may view schizophrenia as disruptions in ego-state structures (contamination of the Adult by Parent/Child), particularly a breakdown in the Adult functions, leading to dominant archaic Parent and Child states that distort reality. Therapy aims to strengthen the Adult ego-state through exercises and dialogues to clarify ego-state roles, reduce contamination and confusion and enhance reality engagement, grounded in present moment awareness and self-compassion. Clients may struggle with explicit transactions due to ego-state disturbances, leading to misunderstandings. TA therapy may improve transactional clarity by helping clients recognise and adjust their ego-state communication, improve interpersonal interactions and reduce conflict, for example, via role-play and cognitive/behavioural exercises/interventions. These ego-state disruptions may stem from unmet early childhood needs, leading to fragmented ego-states and impaired thinking, and schizophrenic experiences may be linked to early-life experiences and life scripts. In clients with sufficient self-insight and stability, TA therapists may help clients uncover and challenge these early life-experiences, life scripts and responses/decisions, promoting more adaptive thinking patterns; some clients, who have sufficient fundamental psychological structures such as affect regulation, may benefit from trauma treatment (be careful as trauma treatment too early in the process may trigger severe responses/symptoms). TA therapists focus on strengthening the Adult ego-state through dialogue and TA techniques, aiming to enhance reality differentiation, communication skills and healthier transactions, thereby promoting adaptive coping mechanisms and greater reality congruence.

17

CLUSTER-B PERSONALITY DISORDERS (NARCISSISTIC, ANTISOCIAL, BORDERLINE, HISTRIONIC)

DIAGNOSIS AND PSYCHOTHERAPIES

Clients with Cluster-B Personality Disorders might come to therapy expressing intense emotions, unstable relationships and impulsive actions, often feeling overwhelmed by their behaviour and its impact on their lives. These disorders are characterised by dramatic, overly emotional or unpredictable thinking or behaviour and include Antisocial, Borderline, Histrionic and Narcissistic Personality Disorders. Clinically, symptoms across these disorders vary but commonly include a marked disregard for others (Antisocial), fear of abandonment and unstable relationships (Borderline), excessive emotionality and attention-seeking (Histrionic) and a grandiose sense of self-importance (Narcissistic). Therapists may identify these disorders by carefully assessing these symptoms, considering the client's history and current functioning, and noting persistent patterns of behaviour that significantly impair social, occupational or personal functioning. Even though these personality disorders may include extreme presentations, therapists should not over-pathologise or identify clients with their labels, as this may reinforce feelings of isolation and stigma (Aldridge, 2021).

The main evidence-based psychotherapeutic treatments for Cluster-B Personality Disorders include DBT, Schema Therapy and Mentalisation-Based Treatment (Cristea et al., 2017; Keefe et al., 2020; Klein et al., 2023; Leichsenring & Leibing 2003; Stoffers-Winterling et al., 2022; Verheul & Herbrink, 2007; Wilson 2014).

TA-FRAMEWORK FOR CLUSTER-B PERSONALITY DISORDERS

For all personality disorders, TA therapists should first and foremost follow the general guidelines in their field (Hoyt, 1989), and they may follow additional training and contribute to a multidisciplinary team. There are few studies on TA and Cluster-B

Personality Disorders. Noteworthy are Eva Horn (Horn, 2015) and Moniek Thunissen (Thunnissen, 2015, 2010), who conducted clinical trials on TA for personality disorders, with a primary focus on Cluster-B. They showed how clients had large improvements comparable to or better than other psychological treatments. TA therapists interested in working with this population should familiarise themselves with their publications.

The publications of these authors suggest similar aetiological and clinical models, as well as therapeutic mechanisms as outlined in this book, although tailored to this specific population and individual clients. For example, individuals with Cluster-B personality disorders may exhibit imbalances in their ego-states, such as an overactive Child leading to impulsive and emotionally driven behaviours prevalent in Borderline and Histrionic Personality Disorders or an overactive Parent ego-state leading to the control and disdain seen in Narcissistic Personality Disorders.

The assessment of transactions may be helpful in this population. There may be many crossed transactions, where communication breakdowns occur because the message's sender and receiver operate from different ego-states, leading to conflicts and misunderstandings. Ulterior transactions often underlie the manipulative and deceitful behaviours associated with some Cluster-B personality traits, where the social message differs from the psychological message. People with Cluster-B personality disorders may frequently engage in games, seeking attention, validation or power in ways that are ultimately self-defeating or destructive to relationships. Individuals with Cluster-B personality disorders may have an insatiable need for strokes, manifesting as excessive attention-seeking behaviour in those with Histrionic Personality Disorder or as a demand for admiration and respect in those with Narcissistic Personality Disorder. Script-systems can be seen in the emotional turbulence and manipulative behaviours characteristic of Cluster-B disorders.

Individuals with Cluster-B personality disorders have sometimes been associated with adverse childhood experiences, such as abuse or neglect, causing not only traumatic experiences but also unhelpful/underdeveloped fundamental psychological structures, such as issues in ego-boundaries, splitting, mentalisation, affect regulation, attachment and discounting of existential givens (Fruzzetti et al., 2005). The client's life scripts seem marked by drama and intensity, stemming from early life-experiences and responses/decisions; these scripts may lead to repetitive and self-perpetuating patterns of dysfunctional relationships and self-image issues. Therefore, some therapists focus on helping clients develop fundamental psychological structures, and if they have sufficiently developed these, they process their traumas (Chapter 15; Cloitre et al., 2020; Herman & Van der Kolk, 2020). If clients have sufficient basic skills and the therapeutic relationships is sufficiently strong, a TA therapist may help clients identify scripts and support them in scripting new narratives that encourage healthier choices and outcomes. A central goal of TA is to promote autonomy, defined as the capacity to make new decisions unencumbered by unresolved past experiences; for these clients, achieving autonomy can mean breaking free from the destructive patterns that have dictated their relationships and self-concept, leading to a more integrated and fulfilling life.

A TA therapist may help a client with a Cluster-B personality disorder through a multifaceted approach addressing the client's unique challenges. By helping clients understand their ego-states, a TA therapist can increase self-awareness regarding how these states influence their thoughts, feelings and behaviours. Strengthening the Adult ego-state can promote more balanced and reflective responses. Clients may learn to analyse, recognise and alter these transactions leading to miscommunication or conflict to foster healthier relationships. Given the interpersonal sensitivities and challenges common in Cluster-B personality disorders, such insights can be particularly transformative, as well as triggering and leading to drop out from therapy. Clients are often unaware of the psychological games they play, which can perpetuate cycles of conflict, victimisation or manipulation; by bringing these games into consciousness, a TA therapist helps clients stop engaging in these patterns, leading to more authentic and fulfilling interactions. The Drama Triangle may show extreme examples in this population, and, for example, clients with antisocial personality disorder may benefit from a drama triangle analysis to shift (Sigmund, 1999). Borderline individuals may show a triad of 'I am a helpless person', 'It is a hostile world' and 'Everything is all or nothing' (Alden & Osti, 1989). For clients with Cluster-B personality disorders, learning to experience and express genuine emotions rather than script-systems can improve emotional regulation and interpersonal dynamics. A treatment focused on the here-and-now with a positive stroking system and separation individuation may benefit histrionic clients (Birnbaum, 1987).

Note that given the games of several of these personality disorders, the therapist is likely to be pulled into games and transference/countertransference transactions, such as projective identification (Chapter 8); it is crucial to be aware of these games, set clear boundaries and use these in the treatment process (Divac-Jovanoic & Radojkovic, 1987).

Case Study 17.1

Archie

Archie, a 56-year-old physical scientist with a successful career but a tumultuous personal life, was diagnosed with Borderline Personality Disorder. He exhibited symptoms like emotional instability, intense fear of abandonment and unstable relationships. Recognising that the therapeutic relationship would be particularly significant for this client, his TA therapist was careful to establish a consistent therapeutic environment to counteract his fear of abandonment and focused on identifying his predominant Child ego-state, which drove his impulsive behaviours. Initially, Archie idealised his therapist. They worked on strengthening his Adult ego-state for balanced responses. They explored crossed and ulterior transactions in his interactions, leading to misunderstandings and conflicts. By becoming aware of these patterns, Archie learnt to adjust his communication for clearer exchanges, reducing interpersonal friction. However, after the period of decontamination, the therapeutic relationship changed and his early-life decisions games became apparent in their therapeutic relationship. Archie often struggled during the therapist's absences. He was frequently angry with him for the many perceived slights and ruptures. This was very challenging for the therapist, who often felt powerless and incompetent. With the help of supervision, he succeeded in continuing his steady, accepting, non-defensive presence and maintaining clear boundaries. During this time, Archie was often late or much too early for appointments, attempted to make contact between sessions and missed payments. Each time, they talked through each rupture and boundary violation. Gradually, Archie developed a more secure sense of self; he engaged with people in his life from a I+/U+ life position and could reflect on the times when he couldn't do so. His relationship with the therapist also became less conflictual.

18

CLUSTER-C PERSONALITY DISORDERS (OBSESSIVE-COMPULSIVE, DEPENDENT, AVOIDANT)

DIAGNOSIS AND PSYCHOTHERAPIES

Clients with Cluster-C Personality Disorders may come to therapy feeling extremely anxious, fearful of rejection or showing an excessive need for control and order in their lives. Cluster-C personality disorders encompass Avoidant, Dependent and Obsessive-Compulsive Personality Disorders, each characterised by pervasive anxiety and fear. Avoidant Personality Disorder is marked by feelings of social inadequacy, hypersensitivity to negative evaluation and avoidance of social interaction. Dependent Personality Disorder presents through a pervasive need to be taken care of, leading to submissive and clinging behaviour and fears of separation, while Obsessive-Compulsive Personality Disorder (not to be confused with Obsessive-Compulsive Disorder) features a preoccupation with orderliness, perfectionism and control, at the expense of flexibility, openness and efficiency. Therapists may identify these disorders by carefully assessing these symptoms, understanding the client's history and observing their interpersonal behaviour and emotional responses during therapy sessions. Often, these disorders are associated with adverse childhood events (Crisan, 2023).

The main evidence-based psychotherapeutic treatments for Cluster-C Personality Disorders include Schema Therapy, Short-Term Psychodynamic Supportive Psychotherapy and Affect Phobia Therapy. These therapies have been studied for their effectiveness in treating the pervasive anxiety, fear and maladaptive coping mechanisms that are characteristic of Cluster-C disorders (Leichsnering & Leibing, 2003; Verheul, 2007).

TA-FRAMEWORK FOR CLUSTER-C PERSONALITY DISORDERS

There are few articles on TA and Cluster-C personality disorders; the following should be interpreted tentatively, and TA therapists may seek additional training and work in a multi-disciplinary team. Several studies have examined transactional principles in dependency disorders (Wouters & Smale, 1990; Zivkovic, 2023). One study suggested the positive effects of mindfulness-integrated TA on interpersonal dependency (Sharifi et al., 2019), and some authors speak highly of TA's relevance for avoidant personality disorder (Kantor, 2003).

Individuals with Cluster-C personality disorders may have a weakened Adult state, leading to behaviours driven by Parent or Child states. For example, the Child state might dominate in Dependent Personality Disorder, seeking care and reassurance. The internalised Parent state might be overly critical in Obsessive-Compulsive Personality Disorder, leading to perfectionism and control. Strengthening the Adult ego-state can help individuals analyse situations more objectively, reducing anxiety and dependence on others for their self-esteem and decision-making. Identifying and addressing script systems and games may help understand and change how they manipulate their emotional expressions and interactions based on their script beliefs, thus enabling them to change these patterns and engage in more genuine and satisfying relationships. People with Cluster-C disorders often live out life scripts that reinforce their fears and avoidance of rejection or failure. These scripts are unconscious pathways formed in childhood that dictate an individual's feelings, thoughts and behaviours. If clients have sufficient self-insight and fundamental psychological structures, TA therapy may help individuals recognise and rewrite these scripts, enabling them to make new, healthier choices that are not dictated by past fears or expectations. Some clients may have a script limiting their stroke economy, either by accepting negative strokes as their norm or avoiding situations where positive strokes could be received due to fear of rejection. Therapy may expand the client's capacity to accept and seek out positive strokes, improving their self-esteem and reducing their reliance on maladaptive coping mechanisms.

Case Study 18.1

Willow

Willow, a 24-year-old marketing specialist, sought therapy for symptoms of Dependent Personality Disorder, including a pervasive fear of being alone, difficulty making decisions without excessive reassurance and low self-confidence. These symptoms caused significant distress in both her personal and professional life, as she relied heavily on approval from colleagues and friends for even minor decisions. Her TA therapist assessed Willow's ego-states and found that her Child ego-state was predominantly driving her behaviours, seeking constant care and reassurance, while her Adult ego-state was weakened, leading to difficulties in making independent decisions. The therapist strengthened her Adult ego-state using mindfulness-integrated TA techniques, helping Willow pause, observe her responses and make more rational, self-supported decisions. By identifying Willow's life scripts and script systems, the therapist helped her understand how she manipulated her emotional expressions to elicit care from others. This awareness allowed Willow to start changing these patterns, focusing on engaging in more genuine and fulfilling relationships. They also worked on expanding her stroke economy, encouraging her to recognise and seek out positive affirmations and interactions. Gradually, Willow was exposed to situations where she could make decisions independently, reinforcing her self-esteem and reducing her reliance on others for validation. Through therapy, Willow began to rewrite her life script, moving away from those early-life messages that reinforced her fears and dependency. This enabled her to make healthier choices, boosting her confidence in her ability to function independently and engage in more balanced relationships.

19

NEURODIVERSITY

Participants all reported a sense of frustration, sadness, and shame regarding how others have responded to their neurodivergence and neurodivergent behaviours historically. (Bowers & Widdowson, 2023)

DIAGNOSIS AND PSYCHOTHERAPIES

Clients coming to TA psychotherapy may present with difficulties in social interactions, repetitive behaviours and a strong preference for routine, which can be indicative of Autism Spectrum Disorders (ASD). ASD is characterised by a range of symptoms that include persistent deficits in social communication and social interaction across multiple contexts. Additionally, individuals with ASD may show restricted, repetitive patterns of behaviour, interests or activities. Therapists may identify ASD by observing these symptoms, understanding the individual's developmental history and noting any atypical communication patterns or challenges in making and maintaining connections with others. Over the last decade, there have been many advances in research on ASD diagnosis and treatment. At this moment, the most frequently used evidence-based psychotherapeutic treatments include CBT and Early Start Denver Mode; CBT may address issues such as anxiety (Hartman et al., 2023; Rosenau et al., 2024; Spain et al., 2015).

Clients coming to TA psychotherapy might display an inability to focus, hyperactivity and (sometimes) impulsive behaviours, which may suggest Attention-Deficit/Hyperactivity Disorder (ADHD). ADHD is defined by inattention and/or hyperactivity-impulsivity patterns that interfere with functioning or development. The clinical criteria require these symptoms to be present long term and inappropriate for the individual's developmental level. A therapist may identify ADHD by carefully evaluating the client's behavioural history, ability to maintain attention during sessions, impulsive interruptions and difficulties in organising tasks or following through on therapeutic assignments. The main evidence-based psychotherapeutic treatments for ADHD include behavioural therapy and parent training in behaviour management. Most guidelines recommend a multimodal approach; for example, CBT helps individuals with ADHD develop coping strategies and problem-solving skills (Fullen et al., 2020; Moriyama et al., 2013). Note that some clients may present a combination of ASD/ADHD and other frequent comorbid problems such as dyspraxia, dyscalculia and auditory processing disorder.

TA-FRAMEWORK FOR NEURODIVERSITY

Where does TA fit in the story of neurodiversity? More research is needed; that is a clear conclusion. Several authors have argued that TA may not be able to help or cure the underlying neurocognitive functions. TA therapists working with this population may want to update their knowledge, get relevant training and work in a multidisciplinary team.

TA therapists may be able to help with psychological comorbid issues and side effects, such as coping with feeling different from neurotypical people, reducing negative self-image, improving self-compassion and improving coping skills and social functioning particularly in high-stress situations. Furthermore, many neurodiverse individuals have a history of masking their struggles, thanks to which they may be able to achieve the highest academic and professional levels. Masking means that they have learnt coping and compensatory mechanisms; however, masking may have side effects, such as feeling misunderstood, exhaustion, burnout, masking their authentic self and negative self-image, and their masking strategies may fail under intense stress. TA may support them in their journey towards self-acceptance, self-compassion, self-expression and authenticity.

Autism Spectrum Disorder

Understanding Ego-states (Parent, Adult, Child) may help individuals with Autism Spectrum Disorder (ASD) recognise and differentiate their own and others' states, which is beneficial in social situations. Therapists can assist individuals in identifying their operating ego-state during interactions and encourage accessing the Adult ego-state for rational problem-solving. This approach aids in making informed decisions and organising life effectively.

Recognising types of transactions (complementary, crossed, ulterior) can improve social interactions and communication skills. Teaching individuals with ASD to engage in complementary transactions reduces misunderstandings and enhances social relationships. Therapists can help identify and understand emotions linked to different ego-states, guiding clients in healthy emotional expression. By interpreting social cues and emotional expressions within the framework of ego-states and transactions, therapists can help clients navigate social situations more comfortably, using role-playing and social stories for practice.

Individuals with ASD may have developed specific patterns of emotional expression to protect themselves from social threats. Identifying and understanding these patterns may lead to more authentic and effective emotional expression. Therapy may also focus on improving the ability to recognise and express positive strokes, enhancing social connectivity and emotional exchange. Exploring and revising life scripts that include feelings of isolation or misunderstanding can empower individuals with ASD to develop self-compassion and form healthier self-concepts and relationships.

The therapeutic relationship, based on TA principles of mutual respect and validation, provides a safe environment for individuals with ASD to explore their thoughts, feelings and behaviours without judgement. TA therapists can also educate families on effective communication strategies and supportive environments encouraging positive transactions. Studies suggest that TA may support individuals with ASD (Heyrat & Feshakari, 2021).

Case Study 19.1

Roger

Roger, a 36-year-old copywriter with ASD (a diagnosis he had received two years ago), asked for therapy due to difficulties in social interactions, particularly in understanding and expressing emotions and organising his daily life due to challenges with planning and decision-making. His situation was further complicated by feelings of isolation and being misunderstood. The TA therapist worked with Roger on identifying which ego-state he was operating from in various interactions and encouraged him to access his Adult ego-state more frequently. This promoted Roger's rational thinking and problem-solving abilities. Understanding transactions helped Roger decode social interactions and improve his communication skills. Through role-playing and social stories, the therapist provided practical tools to practice and prepare for various social scenarios. By exploring emotions linked to different ego-states, Roger began to recognise and express his feelings, improving his ability to give and receive positive strokes and enhancing his social connectivity. They explored Roger's life scripts, including feelings of isolation and misunderstanding, which increased his self-compassion. The therapist's engagement with Roger's family was also crucial, providing them with effective communication strategies and understanding Roger's behaviours and needs, thereby creating a supportive environment that encouraged positive transactions.

Attention-Deficit/Hyperactivity Disorder

Understanding the distinct ego-states may help individuals with ADHD manage impulsivity and develop more appropriate responses in various situations. For instance, fostering the Adult ego-state can aid in improving decision-making and reducing impulsive actions. Therapists can work with clients to strengthen their Adult ego-state, characterised by rational thinking and problem-solving, to help them respond more effectively. By analysing transactional patterns, therapists may help recognise and adjust their patterns of interaction that may be influenced by impulsivity or inattention, enhancing their relationships and social functioning. Individuals with ADHD might unknowingly participate in psychological games, such as 'Why Don't You, Yes But' or 'Uproar'; recognising and understanding games may help individuals with ADHD and their therapists work towards more authentic and constructive ways of meeting their needs for attention and interaction. Script-systems and payoff may be used for dealing with frustration or unmet needs in ADHD; identifying and addressing these patterns can help individuals with ADHD express their emotions in more helpful ways and reduce misunderstandings/conflicts in relationships. People with ADHD may have developed harmful life scripts based on experiences of failure, criticism or misunderstanding, which can affect their self-esteem and motivation. TA offers the opportunity to explore and challenge these life scripts, encouraging individuals with ADHD to adopt more positive and empowering narratives about themselves and their capabilities.

Stop Neuronormativity!

Several authors have argued that TA therapists may want to be aware of possible ableism in the disproportionate assumption that 'My "I'm OK, you're OK" could differ from yours' (Oates, 2021). The criteria for OK'ness that some TA therapist seem to assume may not apply to ASD individuals. Furthermore, several authors have argued that neuronormativity may impact relational material and drive adaptive masking patterns, creating script-systems and script formation; this neuronormativity may increase inner tensions and dissatisfaction in neurodivergent individuals (Leong & Graichen, 2024). Emerging research suggests how different neurocognitive developments and functionality may lead to different subjective ego-state experiences, such as the Adult (Keenan, 2024). Consequently, several authors have called for decentering neuronormativity in TA psychotherapy (Moores & Oates, 2024). This underlines the importance that we, as authors of this book, put on conducting a systematic assessment and tailoring the therapy to the client's unique needs, wishes, goals and strengths.

Case Study 19.2

Joe

Joe, a 44-year-old CBT therapist, asked a TA therapist to help him with his long-standing struggles with ADHD, manifested as difficulties in maintaining focus, organisational challenges, impulsive behaviour and emotional dysregulation. Despite his professional background, Joe struggled personally and professionally, often overwhelmed by daily tasks and interpersonal interactions. His TA therapist introduced the concept of Ego-states, allowing Joe to recognise when his Child ego-state was dominating, leading to impulsivity and emotional reactions, versus when his Adult ego-state could be harnessed. Through TA therapy, Joe worked on identifying which ego-state he was operating from in various situations, particularly during moments of distraction or impulsivity. The therapist encouraged Joe to engage his Adult ego-state more frequently, offering practical problem-solving strategies to enhance his executive functioning skills, such as planning, organising and completing tasks. Analysing transactions helped Joe understand how his interactions with others could be influenced by his ADHD symptoms, including some relational games. A significant part of the therapy focused on Joe's life scripts that had developed around his ADHD, including feelings of inadequacy and fear of failure. By exploring these scripts and understanding their impact, Joe began to rewrite them, adopting a more positive self-image and setting realistic goals. The therapeutic relationship provided a model of clear, respectful communication and positive reinforcement, which Joe found empowering. This supportive environment enabled him to explore new ways of thinking and behaving, improving his daily functioning and relationships.

20
BEHAVIOUR PROBLEMS AND DELINQUENCY

DIAGNOSIS AND PSYCHOTHERAPIES

The previous chapters already described some behavioural struggles/problems that may, for example, be caused by personality disorders or ADHD. Another disorder involving behaviour problems is conduct disorder, which is a mental health condition characterised by a persistent pattern of behaviour that violates the rights of others or major societal norms, including aggression, deceitfulness, theft and serious rule violations. Oppositional Defiant Disorder is characterised by a persistent pattern of angry/irritable mood, argumentative/defiant behaviour or vindictiveness lasting at least six months, significantly impairing social, educational or occupational functioning. Individuals with behaviour problems are more likely to have run-ins with authorities and are overrepresented in prisons. Although research on conduct disorder and oppositional defiant disorder seems scattered, frequently reported psychotherapeutic treatments include parent management training, Multisystemic Therapy, Functional Family Therapy, CBT, social skills training, collaborative problem-solving and some school-based interventions (Alexander et al., 2013; Henggeler et al., 2009; Kazdin, 2021).

TA-FRAMEWORK

In the 1970s and 1980s, TA was frequently applied in forensic settings and schools to prevent or treat individuals with behavioural problems, such as externalising behavioural problems, oppositional defiant, disruptive and impulse control disorders and delinquency (Vos & van Rijn, 2023). When we examined these studies, it seemed that some individuals in these studies may nowadays receive a different or a more specific diagnosis, or their behaviour problems may be comorbid with other disorders, such as ADHD or personality disorder (Vos & van Rijn, 2022). This is why this chapter follows after the previous chapters on different diagnoses, which may first need to be considered.

The lack of clinical differentiation may explain the broad range of effects of TA treatments in prisons and schools, but the overall effects were still positive (Vos & van Rijn, 2023). For example, after TA in prisons, prisoners reported small to medium positive improvements in self-efficacy, social functioning, psychopathology and general well-being. The TA treatment manuals focused on behaviour modification for externalised behaviour problems, delinquency, violence, oppositional defiant disorders and people in prison (Jeness, 1975), preventing conflict escalation and violence on micro- and macro-levels (Morris, 2006). Over the last few years, several successful intervention studies focused on the parent–child relationship to reduce the child's behaviour problems, aggression and other externalising behaviours (Honarparvaran et al., 2017; Kulashekara & Kumar, 2014; Saberinia & Niknejadi, 2019). However, more research is needed on TA's relevance, experiences and effectiveness for individuals presenting with behaviour problems and/or delinquency. In the meantime, how could TA therapists tentatively use their skills, possibly in addition to additional training and working in a multidisciplinary team?

Analysis of ego-states may help this group of clients. For example, actions stemming from the Child ego-state might be impulsive or emotionally driven. In contrast, those from the Parent ego-state might be overly critical or authoritarian. Encouraging the development and strengthening of the Adult ego-state may enhance rational thinking, problem-solving and decision-making, reducing reliance on less adaptive responses. Associated with this is the effectiveness of training distress tolerance (Jabbari et al., 2019; Rahmati et al., 2020).

Analysing transactions, or the communication exchanges between people, may reveal patterns that escalate conflicts or contribute to misunderstandings. Dysfunctional transactional patterns may reinforce negative behaviours and relationships. Teaching individuals to engage in complementary (rather than crossed or ulterior) transactions can improve communication skills, reduce conflicts and foster positive interactions. Individuals with behaviour problems might engage in games reinforcing their view of the world as hostile or unjust. Identifying and interrupting these games can help individuals break free from destructive cycles and engage in more authentic and constructive relationships. Individuals can learn to express their needs and emotions directly and constructively by recognising and addressing packets and payoff collection patterns, reducing reliance on script-systems and payoff collecting.

Even though their externalising behaviour may suggest strong self-esteem, there may be underlying self-concept issues, which TA may address (Peek, 1975; Torkaman et al., 2020). Redirecting the pursuit of strokes towards positive behaviours can fulfil the need for recognition in healthier ways. Many individuals with externalised behaviour problems may be acting out negative life scripts developed in childhood, which can include themes of violence, victimisation or defiance. Through TA, individuals can explore and rewrite these life scripts, adopting positive narratives that lead to healthier choices and behaviours.

Case Study 20.1

Tom

Tom, a 15-year-old schoolboy, was brought to therapy by his 37-year-old mother, due to his oppositional defiant behaviours that included frequent temper outbursts, argumentativeness with adults, deliberate annoyance of others and blame-shifting for his mistakes. These behaviours were causing significant distress at home and school, impacting Tom's academic performance and social relationships. Tom's TA therapist began by assessing his ego-states, noting a dominance of the Child ego-state, manifesting as impulsive and emotionally driven behaviours, and an underdeveloped Adult ego-state, which hindered his problem-solving and decision-making abilities. The therapy focused on strengthening Tom's Adult ego-state, enhancing his capacity for rational thinking and effective problem-solving. This involved exercises to increase his distress tolerance and engage in more constructive communication patterns, moving away from dysfunctional transactional patterns that escalated conflicts or contributed to misunderstandings. The therapist worked with Tom on identifying the games he played that reinforced his view of the world as hostile or unjust. By interrupting these games and addressing Tom's grievances, the therapy aimed to help him express his needs and emotions more directly and constructively, reducing reliance on negative behaviours to fulfil his need for recognition. Tom was also encouraged to explore and rewrite his life scripts, which had developed themes of defiance and victimisation, recognise vulnerabilities and develop self-compassion. Tom adopted positive narratives, leading to more helpful choices and behaviours and improving interactions with family and peers.

21

PROBLEMATIC USE OF ALCOHOL OR DRUGS

DIAGNOSIS AND PSYCHOTHERAPIES

A client coming to TA therapy with problematic use of alcohol or drugs might describe feeling unable to cope without substances, experiencing mood swings, neglecting responsibilities or having trouble maintaining relationships. Problematic use of alcohol or drugs spans a spectrum from mild to severe. It is characterised by a cluster of cognitive, behavioural and physiological symptoms indicating that an individual continues substance use despite significant substance-related problems.

This includes an intense craving for the substance, the development of tolerance, withdrawal symptoms when not using and considerable impairment or distress in daily functioning. Formal diagnoses include, amongst others, Substance Use Disorder and Substance-Induced Disorders, with specific criteria for different substances based on patterns of use, impact on daily life and physical symptoms. Note that a large number of individuals with problematic use of alcohol or drugs are also diagnosed with other disorders, such as trauma. As a consequence of the alcohol/drug use, individuals may also report medical or cognitive problems, issues in work performance and absenteeism, financial problems, social disturbances, domestic abuse and homelessness; therefore, helping these individuals may require additional training and work in a multidisciplinary team.

TA therapists may identify problematic use of alcohol or drugs by observing patterns of transactions that suggest a reliance on substances to manage emotional states, along with alterations in the client's ego-states and life scripts that revolve around substance use. Clinical guidelines recommend assessing potential problematic use of alcohol/drugs, exploring safeguarding issues such as the impact on children, providing empathy, giving feedback and psychoeducation on risks, increasing self-efficacy and identifying and advising strategies to support reduction, including potential referral to their GP, specialist services and community recovery programmes such as Alcoholics/Narcotics/Cocaine Anonymous. Therapeutic case formulations may include predisposing/vulnerability factors (e.g. life script, socioeconomic context, genetics/heritability, trauma, abuse, neglect, negative transactional core messages), precipitating factors (e.g. triggers), self-perpetuating factors (e.g. unhelpful thoughts/behaviour/coping) and protective factors (e.g. social network, employment, meaningful activities). Drink/drug usage diaries and questionnaires may help in the assessment (e.g. AUDIT-C, ASSIST-Lite, FAST, M-SASQ, SADQ, LDQ, APQ).

The main evidence-based psychotherapeutic treatments include CBT, motivational interviewing, contingency management, acceptance and commitment therapy and mindfulness-oriented interventions. These treatments are grounded in an empathic/non-judgemental, collaborative, relation-focused, stigma-reducing, strength-based, goal-oriented, structured and trauma-informed approach. They may focus on changing behavioural habits – for example, via realistic goal-setting, rewards and skills training, coping with withdrawal symptoms and reducing harm, improving unhelpful thought processes, negative self-talk and self-compassion, building motivation and skills for change, improving distress tolerance and problem-solving abilities, involving their social network who may reinforce their behaviour, sometimes in addition to medication-assisted treatment. Increasingly, treatments focus on recovery, which helps individuals to build positive benefits from sustaining abstinence or moderate use and to live a meaningful and satisfying life (see Vos, 2017, for meaning-centred interventions). Ideally, treatments happen in confidential, multidisciplinary, recovery-oriented care systems, ideally close to their living situation.

This section is based on the UK NICE committee and *Orange Book* guidelines for the clinical management of problematic use of alcohol/drugs.

TA-FRAMEWORK

TA therapists have historically recognised the spectrum of problematic use of alcohol and drugs as a multifaceted issue that necessitates a comprehensive approach, focusing on the individual's unique needs and tailoring the therapy accordingly. Several clinical trials suggest the benefits of TA (Etemadi-Charadh et al., 2017; Forghani, Rajaei & Bayazi, 2021; Ohlsson, 2002; Williams & Glarino, 2023). These studies strongly contest Berne's labelling of alcoholism as a game, as he seemed to oversimplify the multidimensional and biophysical components, which may require therapeutic interventions in addition, or sometimes in contradiction, with analysing and modifying games (Selavan, 1990).

Several TA-concepts may hypothetically be relevant to problematic use of alcohol or drugs. A client might rely on substances as a response to their Child's ego-state, which seeks comfort or escape, or they might be stuck in a Critical Parent state filled with self-blame. TA therapists may strengthen the Adult, to assess reality and make healthy decisions, thus helping the client engage in problem-solving behaviours and self-care without substance use. Dysfunctional transactional patterns, such as conflicts or miscommunications with significant others, can influence problematic use of substances. A TA therapist can help the client identify and modify these patterns, promoting more effective communication and reducing relational triggers for substance use. The therapist may work with the client to identify possible games and script-systems surrounding their substance use, helping them to stop these patterns and develop more authentic and constructive ways of meeting their needs. A TA therapist might explore how substances serve as a substitute for healthy strokes the client is missing in their life. The therapist may guide clients towards healthier behaviours and social interactions by identifying alternative, positive ways to fulfil their need for strokes, for example, by developing more fulfilling social relationship and a meaningful life (Vos, 2017). Problematic alcohol/drug use may be part of a negative life script, which may be explored, to write a new, healthier script aligning with their recovery goals.

22

PHYSICALLY ILL CLIENTS

DIAGNOSIS AND PSYCHOTHERAPIES

Chronic or life-threatening physical illnesses can significantly impact mental health, leading to increased rates of depression and anxiety as individuals cope with the uncertainty, pain and potential disability associated with their condition (Vos, 2016b). The stress of managing a chronic illness may lead to feelings of frustration, hopelessness, guilt, isolation, low self-esteem and a diminished sense of control over one's life, exacerbating other mental health struggles. Furthermore, the fear of mortality and the existential questions that arise from facing a life-threatening illness can trigger profound psychological distress, including episodes of acute stress, PTSD or suicidal ideation. Additionally, the physical limitations and the constant need for medical care can disrupt daily routines, identity, meaning and social relationships.

Since the turn of the millennium, many health guidelines recommend evidence-based psychosocial support and psychotherapy for individuals with chronic or life-threatening physical illnesses. Although the recommended treatments may vary per illness, many approaches seem to include a therapeutic approach focusing on a positive therapeutic relationship, practical problem-solving, exploring how to live a meaningful and satisfying life despite the physical challenges, strengthening inner resources and social network, increasing self-compassion and self-care activities and if needed treating other mental health problems and unresolved issues in their life script that may be triggered. Chronic or life-threatening illnesses can lead to existential crises and a search for meaning in life; Vos's research (2014, 2016a, 2017, 2021a, 2021b, 2002) suggests that meaning-centred therapies can be particularly effective for individuals facing physical illnesses, significantly improving their quality-of-life and reducing psychological stress by helping them find meaning and hope amidst their conditions.

TA-FRAMEWORK

From a TA therapist's perspective, identifying the psychological impact of a chronic or life-threatening illness can involve observing shifts in the client's life script and transactions that may indicate struggles with meaning, existential concerns or maladaptive coping mechanisms. As TA-studies seem to suggest (Vos & van Rijn, 2021a), in the context of physical disease, clients might regress to a Child ego-state, feeling vulnerable and in need of care, or might adopt a Parent ego-state, trying to instruct themselves or others on what should be done. By recognising these ego-states, a therapist may tailor their approach, offering guidance and support in the Adult ego-state to encourage more adaptive Adult ways of coping with illness and its psychological impact.

Someone with a physical disease might have a script that influences how they view their illness, perhaps as a form of punishment, a challenge to overcome or a factor that defines their identity. Clients may explore how their life script influences their response to illness. By bringing unconscious scripts into awareness, clients can rewrite parts of their script to foster a more positive and proactive approach to managing their disease and overall life.

Therapists should not pathologise or label the client's responses to their illness; instead, clients may benefit from explicitly acknowledging that their response may be normal in abnormal situations, that everyone responds uniquely and that there is not one universally best approach; this may foster self-compassion. Clients are already suffering from a physical illness, and therapists should not add another illness by telling them their responses/coping styles are wrong (Vos, 2017). Although their responses should never be completely reduced or labelled as a game or conscious decision, individuals might unknowingly participate in psychological games or responses that may not be beneficial in the long-term. For example, it may be unhelpful to get stuck on the question, 'Why me?', or the beliefs, 'I am helpless' and 'My life is over' (although in the short term these seem normal responses), as this may reinforce feelings of victimhood or helplessness; the therapist may help the client reframe these questions/beliefs, and focus on what they can still do, and how they may still live a meaningful and fulfilling life despite their physical challenges (Vos, 2016a, 2016b, 2017).

Physically ill clients often report a shift in relationships and transactional patterns with their loved ones; this could create confusion, uncertainty and stress in the clients and their loved ones. Physically ill individuals often say that they 'have learnt who their real friends are'; some individuals in their network find it challenging to cope with these relational/transactional changes, may not know how to respond and may withdraw from their relationship. The response of their social network, or lack thereof, may trigger disappointment and loneliness. Clients may benefit from exploring these changes and realistic opportunities in their transactions, learning to express needs for practical and socioemotional support, finding new support networks, breaking unhelpful patterns such as getting stuck in a Patient/Child role, fostering authentic communication and intimacy and exploring and improving how they give and receive strokes.

Case Study 22.1

Bernard

Forty-five-year-old Bernard was diagnosed with prostate cancer, which profoundly disrupted his life narrative and self-identity. He reported symptoms of depression, anxiety and difficulty adjusting to his medical condition, indicative of an existential crisis and a diminished sense of purpose. Bernard showed frequent responses from a Child ego-state and victim-role, where Bernard felt vulnerable, demanding care from others. Recognising this, the therapist engaged him from an Adult ego-state, providing guidance and support to foster more adaptive coping mechanisms, differentiating realistic needs from things he could realistically take responsibility for. Script-analysis revealed that Bernard had learnt in early-life to view illness as a form of punishment, significantly influencing his current responses. The therapist helped Bernard explore and bring this unconscious script to awareness. By exploring his responses and transactions from this aetiological perspective, Bernard learnt how his responses unintentionally reinforced feelings of victimhood. The therapist guided him in breaking these maladaptive patterns and encouraged him to communicate his needs and emotions healthily. Furthermore, the therapist worked on increasing Bernard's awareness of his stroke economy, helping him seek and create more fulfilling exchanges of recognition and attention, thus addressing his isolation and enhancing his sense of meaning and purpose amidst his condition. Through these interventions, Bernard began to rewrite parts of his script, adopting a more self-compassionate, proactive approach to managing his disease and improving his psychological well-being.

Box 22.1

Somatic Symptom Disorders

Somatic Symptom Disorder (SSD) is characterised by an excessive focus on physical symptoms like pain or fatigue, causing significant distress or functional problems without a fully explanatory medical condition. Clinical criteria include persistent thoughts, feelings or behaviours related to these symptoms for over six months. Conversion Disorder, a subtype of SSD, involves neurological symptoms such as blindness or paralysis, with criteria emphasising the incompatibility between the symptom and recognised medical conditions, causing significant distress or impairment. The primary treatment for SSD is CBT, focusing on examining and adapting health beliefs, reducing stress and symptom preoccupation and improving daily functioning. Supportive treatments include psychoeducation, stress management techniques like progressive muscle relaxation and sometimes physical therapy and hypnosis.

Despite the potential relevance of TA to SSD, no studies exist on its application; the following should be interpreted tentatively, and therapists may want additional training and work in multidisciplinary teams. TA therapists may offer an empathic, compassion-focused relationship, avoiding confrontation, as clients often feel disbelieved by others. It is important not to give clients the idea that they receive therapy because the therapist does not believe them; a therapist may explain that TA therapy may not aim to cure the somatic symptoms, but help clients cope better with their symptoms and secondary impact such as emotional and social problems caused by their illness. Individuals with SSD may report disruptions in their ego-states, operating from a Child ego-state, feeling helpless over their symptoms. A

TA therapist may help strengthen the Adult ego-state, promoting a rational approach to symptom management. Analysis of transactions may help, although this should be done sensitively. Therapists have reported the game of the 'Wooden Leg', where symptoms are used to avoid difficult situations. Identifying and compassionately interrupting these games is crucial. Therapists may help clients recognise these patterns and encourage other ways to meet their needs. Improving the client's stroke economy can reduce reliance on somatic symptoms. Life scripts may predispose individuals to interpret physical sensations in a way that reinforces the disorder. Therapists can help clients uncover and rewrite these scripts, fostering a more adaptive narrative and promoting autonomy in responding to stress and bodily sensations.

23

EATING DISORDERS

DIAGNOSIS AND PSYCHOTHERAPIES

Eating disorders, such as Anorexia Nervosa, Bulimia Nervosa and Binge Eating Disorder, are characterised by abnormal or disturbed eating habits stemming from emotional and psychological distress. The clinical criteria include excessive preoccupation with food, body weight and shape, leading to severe eating or exercise behaviours that significantly impair physical health and psychosocial functioning. TA therapists may identify eating disorders by observing a client's transactions and ego-states that reveal patterns of control, avoidance or distorted self-image related to food and body perception. The main evidence-based treatments for eating disorders include medical treatment, CBT, which focuses on identifying and changing distorted beliefs about weight, body image and food, and Interpersonal Psychotherapy, which addresses interpersonal issues that contribute to the development and maintenance of eating disorders. Additionally, Family-Based Therapy is particularly effective for adolescents with Anorexia Nervosa, involving the family in supporting the individual to regain control over their eating behaviours healthily (Hay, 2013; Kotilahti et al., 2020; Monteleone et al., 2022).

Eating disorders, particularly anorexia, can lead to dangerous undernourishment, and therapists must work alongside the health professionals to ensure client's safety.

TA-FRAMEWORK

There are few TA-studies on eating disorders, although case studies suggest benefits (e.g. Atkinson, 2023; Brunt, 2005; Rasulova, 2022); the following should be interpreted tentatively, and TA therapists may want additional training and work in a multidisciplinary team. TA therapists seem to view eating disorders as manifestations of deeper psychological issues, often related to early-life decisions and scripts, related to obsessive perfectionism and underlying feelings of shame. The obsessive behaviours, particularly in anorexia, include their relationship with food and body image. We could consider eating disorders from the perspective of a psychological game where the payoff is a sense of control and, in extreme cases, the physiological experiences linked to starvation, suppressing the underlying psychological pain. TA therapists may focus on identifying and working with these games and the underlying script issues leading to the deconfusion of the underlying traumatic experiences. By helping clients to experience and express genuine emotions within a respectful and consistent therapeutic relationship, therapists may support individuals in letting go of the cycle of disordered eating. It is worth noting that cultural influences play a part in developing disordered eating.

Case Study 23.1

Lisa

Lisa, a 26-year-old woman, presented with symptoms of Anorexia Nervosa, including severe restriction of food intake, an intense fear of gaining weight and a distorted body image, believing she was overweight despite being underweight. Her professional performance declined recently, and she isolated herself from friends and her partner, showing signs of depression. Her TA therapist began by exploring Lisa's background and life script. She grew up in a chaotic household with an alcoholic father and a controlling mother. Her older sister rebelled against her parents, but Lisa was quiet and a 'good girl'. She initially became anorexic at the age of 15 and was briefly hospitalised. Since then, she continued to control her eating and occasionally binged and purged when under stress but maintained safe levels of body weight. She was a perfectionist in her dress and performance at work and worked long hours to achieve her tasks to the highest standard. Through therapy, they identified that Lisa's perfectionism overlaid her deep fear of failure and feelings of worthlessness and shame. Controlling her food intake was a strategy she used to have some self of self-efficacy and control in her childhood environment; the physiological impact of self-starvation, alongside the elation of the experience of self-control, suppressed her feelings of worthlessness and shame. The first task in therapy was the development of an accepting therapeutic relationship and trust, and the gradual strengthening of Lisa's Adult ego-state. Gradually, they started the exploration of her Child ego-state and deconfusion, including accepting her feelings and what she described as her 'inner mess'. Throughout this time, the therapist did not focus on Lisa's food habits but worked instead on self-acceptance and the expression of emotion. Lisa was knowledgeable about nutrition, and the therapist acknowledged her expertise and agreed that they would jointly monitor her health. This maintained their working alliance and meant the therapist did not become an overwhelming authoritarian presence. During this time, the therapist also had contact with the GP. There was a three-cornered contract between the GP, Lisa and the therapist, that if her weight fell below safe levels, the GP would refer her to the hospital. This agreement created sufficient security for Lisa, and she did not have to use it throughout therapy. This was one of the achievements she was proud of. She gradually learnt to take care of herself and limit her own expectations of herself and others, thus using her Adult state to support her vulnerable.

24
SEXUAL DISORDERS

DIAGNOSIS AND PSYCHOTHERAPIES

Sexual dysfunctions are characterised by a persistent disturbance in sexual desire, arousal or response, significantly impacting an individual's ability to engage in or enjoy sexual activity, often rooted in psychological, relational or situational factors. Clinical criteria and symptoms vary across specific dysfunctions but commonly include lack of sexual interest, inability to achieve or maintain sexual arousal and pain during intercourse. A TA therapist may identify sexual dysfunctions by observing how clients' transactions, ego-states and life scripts influence their sexual behaviours and attitudes, potentially uncovering dysfunctional patterns that contribute to their sexual issues. The main evidence-based psychotherapeutic treatments for sexual dysfunctions include CBT, which is effective across various sexual dysfunction disorders by helping individuals identify and restructure maladaptive cognitions related to sexuality, and Mindfulness-Based Cognitive Therapy, which has been associated with improvements in sexual function and well-being. CBT strategies often encompass sex education, cognitive restructuring, exposure, systematic desensitisation and sensate focus exercises, aiming to improve sexual function and satisfaction. See examples in LoPiccolo and LoPiccolo (2012), Peterson (2017), and Vos (2022a).

TA-FRAMEWORK

There are few TA-studies on sexual disorders; the following should be interpreted tentatively, and TA therapists may want additional training and work in a multidisciplinary team. Clinical supervision and reflection may help coping with potential erotic transference and countertransference (Chapter 9).

TA therapists may begin by phenomenologically exploring the clients' subjective experiences of sexuality, moving beyond mere symptomatology to understand the deeper meanings and personal narratives surrounding sex via open questions such as, 'What does intimacy mean to you?' or 'How do you experience desire for physical intimacy, touch and sex and the lack thereof?'. The therapist adopts a non-judgemental, open stance, inviting clients to describe their experiences, without resorting to preconceived notions or diagnostic labels. The TA therapist pays attention to historical, cultural and social narratives that may have shaped the client's understanding, experiences and expression of sexuality, such as societal taboos, norms and values.

Sexual problems may be caused by deeper relational and psychological issues, possibly tied to unresolved past traumas, dysfunctional life scripts and impaired ego-states that disrupt intimacy and sexual function. Sexual dysfunctions may, for instance, stem from negative parental messages internalised in the Child ego-state or harsh self-criticisms from the Parent ego-state, leading to anxiety and avoidance of sexual activity. TA therapists may identify and reframe maladaptive scripts and transactions, facilitating the integration of a healthier Adult ego-state. The more balanced, rational approach by the Adult may help mitigate shame or fear instilled by the Critical Parent or the unmet needs of the Free Child, fostering a healthier sexual self-image with clear boundaries. Individuals with sexual disorders might seek negative strokes due to their problems, reinforcing unhealthy patterns. Therapists may assist clients in recognising and expressing genuine emotions rather than relying on inauthentic script-system feelings or behaviours. Some may also need to work on problematic fundamental psychological mechanisms, such as developing more realistic and helpful ego-boundaries, attachment and affect regulation skills; for example, clients may need to learn how to differentiate sexual needs from physical needs for non-sexual intimacy, emotional needs or distraction from avoided/suppressed emotions, and to develop healthy strategies to regulate their various needs and emotions. Ultimately, TA therapy may help empower clients to live more authentically in their sexual lives, making choices that reflect their true desires and values rather than acting out of fear, shame or compulsion, and engage in fulfilling sexual relationships/transactions involving intimacy, mutuality and consent.

Case Study 24.1

James

James, a 35-year-old gay IT specialist, presents with a history of BDSM (Bondage, Dominance, Sadism and Masochism) fantasies tracing back to his early childhood. He expresses a desire to explore these interests further within his current relationship but feels conflicted due to a history of sexual abuse by his brother during childhood. James seeks therapy to reconcile his past trauma with his desire for a healthy, consensual BDSM relationship with his partner. The TA therapist begins by creating a safe, non-judgemental space for James to discuss his BDSM interests and past experiences. The therapist emphasises the validity and normalcy of BDSM desires, distinguishing between non-consensual abuse and consensual kink practices (see Chapter 9). The therapist helps James explore how his Adult, Parent and Child ego-states interact in the context of his BDSM fantasies and past trauma. The therapist introduces the concept of redecision therapy to help James rewrite the script that conflates his abuse with his BDSM interests. By acknowledging the autonomy and consent present in his current relationship, James begins to see his BDSM fantasies as a valid form of sexual expression, separate from his childhood experiences. To address the trauma, the therapist works with James on integrating his Child ego-state, providing the care and validation it lacked during his childhood. This process involved therapeutic techniques such as chair work, where James dialogues with his younger self, offering compassion and understanding. Simultaneously, the therapist encourages James to communicate openly with his partner about his desires, boundaries and fears, fostering boundaries such as a consensual and safe exploration of BDSM via safe words, aftercare and ongoing consent. Over time, James feels more at peace and views BDSM as a healthy part of his sexual identity. He realises that, even though the origins of his BDSM fantasies may lie in early-life traumatic experiences (negative), these fantasies may have become inherently meaningful (positive). James and his partner establish a trusting and communicative BDSM dynamic, respecting their boundaries and desires. This case study illustrates the affirmative role a TA therapist can play in helping clients like James navigate complex feelings around BDSM and past trauma, promoting a healthy, consensual and fulfilling exploration of their kink interests. See Ferenchak (2022), and Shahbaz and Chirinos (2016), for information on working as a therapist with BDSM, and Davies, 1996, for working with LGBTQIA+ clients.

25

EXISTENTIAL CONCERNS AND SELF-DEVELOPMENT

DIAGNOSIS AND PSYCHOTHERAPIES

Many individuals ask existential questions at several points in life, such as, 'What is my meaning in life?'. Questions may be latent in everyday life, but may surface and manifest as an active search for meaning, or evolve into a crisis. A lack of meaning in life, and/or a meaning-oriented, existential, spiritual or identity crisis can increase the development of depression, suicidal ideation and other psychopathology (Vos, 2017, 2023, 2016a, 2016b); this highlights the mental health impact of existential questions and the importance of addressing these concerns in therapy. Research shows that existential and meaning-centred therapies can have large effects on helping clients with existential concerns and self-realisation (Vos et al., 2014; Vos & Vitali, 2018).

Crises in Life

Researchers have differentiated various types of crises in life (Vos, 2017).

Existential crisis: This refers to a period of profound questioning about the nature of existence and one's place in the world, often triggered by a significant event or realisation that leads to feelings of uncertainty, meaninglessness and questioning of fundamental beliefs about life. Clients may benefit from explicating these existential struggles, and overcoming possible denial/avoidance of existential givens (Vos, 2017).

Identity crisis: This involves a profound questioning or uncertainty about one's sense of self and place in the world. This can be triggered by significant life changes, challenges to one's self-perception or conflicts between personal values and external expectations, leading to confusion, instability and a search for a new sense of identity.

Spiritual crisis: This involves a deep questioning or loss of faith in one's spiritual beliefs, a sense of emptiness or disconnection from one's spiritual or religious community (Agrimson & Taft, 2009; Pargament et al., 2013, 1997). Individuals may benefit from exploring and revisiting the impact of religious/spiritual upbringing, and make autonomous, realistic decisions in the present (Winell, 2008).

A crisis in meaning: Individuals may struggle to find or maintain a sense of meaning, purpose or significance in life. This can result from life transitions, personal losses or confronting life's limitations, leading to emptiness and questioning the value of one's pursuits and existence.

Furthermore, individuals may struggle with feelings of meaninglessness when they cannot achieve their meaningful life-goals; therapists may invite clients to systematically explore all possible types of meaning, so that clients develop a broader range of meaning-centered (therapists recommend individuals to have six or more important meanings in life, so that they have some meaningful goals if one meaningful goal becomes unattainable) (Vos, 2025). Clients may want to dominantly focus on social and larger types of meaning as these are associated with better mental and physical health than materialistic, hedonistic, self-oriented types (Vos, 2017, 2023a). Therapists may also want to stimulate clients to critically listen to their experiences/intuitions to discover their sense of meaning in life (Vos, 2017, 2023, 2024); for example, a therapist may start with an experiential or mindfulness exercise followed by systematic questions about each of the six possible types of meaning: 'let your intuition remind you of any examples in the past, present or future of this type of meaning' (Vos, 2017). In contrast to using our experiences/intuition, in early life, individuals often follow the traditions and conform to social expectations, values and norms of upbringing (Vos, 2023a); this may be described as following one's life script/injunctive-messages/drivers. During adolescence, individuals may develop a mechanistic/functionalist approach to life, for example, by trying to (unrealistically) rationally control their life and rigidly strive in the most linear way possible to ambitious self-set goals; this may be described as inflexible or contaminated ego-states. During midlife, individuals often revisit the traditional and mechanistic/functionalist approaches to life, and may develop a critical-intuitive/phenomenological approach; that is, individuals may learn to use their experiences and listen to their intuitions (see Chapter 11) while remaining realistic, critical and self-reflective (see Chapter 12); this may be described as an integrated self, flexibly accessing all ego-states. The traditional and mechanistic-functionalistic approaches are associated with less fulfilling meanings and more mental and physical health problems than the critical-intuitive approach (ibidem).

Boundary Situations

Questions and crises about life may be a response to boundary situations in life, such as traumatic events, chronic illness, the loss of a loved one, divorce or experiences of discrimination. Such questions/crises are often a normal response to an abnormal response to the confrontation with existential givens (Vos, 2017, 2016a, 2016b).

An evidence-based concept related to the TA-concept of discounting existential givens regard world assumptions. Janoff-Bulman (2010) conducted comprehensive research illuminating how individuals shape their daily existence by relying on a core set of underlying beliefs about themselves, others and the surrounding world. These assumptions include beliefs about our invulnerability, the world's benevolence, the meaningfulness of our actions and the predictability of our environment; these seem to be existential core transactional messages.

Assumptions about self-worth, trust in others and the controllability of one's life are fundamental to how individuals perceive and interact with the world. These assumptions are the foundations of our ego-states and life positions in our everyday-life. We begin forming these assumptions early on in life, influenced by the explicit and implicit messages our caregivers and authority figures imparted. Our early-life interactions tell us that the world is predictable, people are benevolent, and our actions matter.

Life events, such as sudden loss, trauma, betrayal or significant failures, can shatter our world assumptions. These events challenge individuals' core messages about themselves and the world, leading to profound disorientation and fundamental uncertainty. The world does not seem to make sense anymore; even worse, we may no longer find a sense of stability in ourselves. Our ego-states and life positions, which were built upon these shattered assumptions, undergo a sudden transformation, resulting in behaviour and transactions that seem unusual for a person. This may lead to symptoms of anxiety, depression and a sense of detachment from our surroundings, loss of meaning, eroding our trust in others and ourselves.

In the face of existential givens and shattered assumptions, individuals may reflect on the origins of these assumptions in their early-life experiences. Suppose caregivers and authority figures have denied a child's inherent truths about existence. In that case, it may leave them vulnerable to developing unrealistic or unhelpful assumptions that are prone to being shattered. For instance, if a child grows up without experiencing any adversity, they may create unrealistic expectations of their invincibility. However, these assumptions will likely be shattered when encountering life's challenges, suffering, illness and death. In therapy, adults who have had their unrealistic assumptions shattered may wish to revisit the beliefs they formed in their early years and cultivate more realistic assumptions about their vulnerability. Since these assumptions are deeply rooted in early-life experiences, this process can be emotionally intense for the client, involving feelings of anger and sadness towards their caregivers and authority figures who deny them these fundamental truths. Addressing the impact of shattered assumptions is crucial in therapeutic interventions to help individuals reconstruct their beliefs, restore a sense of security and regain a coherent understanding of themselves and the world.

TA FRAMEWORK

Research underscores the multidimensional nature of an individual's subjective experience of meaning in life, encompassing motivation, values, practical skills and existential coping strategies, all of which contribute to an individual's overall experience of meaning in life (Vos, 2017, 2025). Individuals develop their sense of meaning in life through a complex interplay of personal experiences, values and existential givens. This process involves integrating their life story, generational influences and subjective ethical norms to create a coherent sense of direction and purpose. TA emphasises the role of autonomy, communication and script-redecision, highlighting the importance of making choices congruent with one's current desires and needs rather than being driven by past traumas or societal expectations.

Several TA-concepts are associated with existential questions and crises. For example, the life script, which represents an individual's unconscious decisions about themselves, others and life, can be deeply intertwined with existential concerns. A TA therapist can help clients by exploring and understanding their life script, identifying existential themes or conflicts and supporting them in making conscious choices to reframe their script to align with their current needs and desires. Additionally, life positions influence an individual's perception of themselves and their place in the world; developing a position of I'm OK/You're OK may foster a more balanced and authentic view of themselves and others. Furthermore, drivers, such as 'Be perfect' or 'Hurry up', may contribute to existential crises by shaping an individual's motivations and behaviours. A TA therapist can help clients identify and re-evaluate these drivers. A TA therapist may support clients with existential questions and crises by using TA concepts to explore and reframe their life script, life positions and drivers, ultimately promoting personal growth, self-awareness and a more fulfilling life.

Therapists may want to integrate TA and existential approaches to psychotherapy, combining their strengths, particularly in the work with clients struggling with existential questions, such as individuals struggling with traumatic life-experiences, and chronic or life-threatening illnesses (Nuttall, 2006). In addition to TA, existential therapies may offer explicit theories, competencies and interventions that help therapists support clients in exploring and making sense of their existence, values and human challenges, addressing topics such as freedom, authenticity, responsibility and the search for meaning in life (Vos, 2023a). In addition to existential therapies, TA may offer a comprehensive clinical and aetiological framework that may help understand how past experiences and script beliefs may influence the client's current existential position and questions, and their ability to live a meaningful and fulfilling life despite life's challenges. Reflective questions 5.7. give some example exercises. See Vos (2017) for an evidence-based approach to help clients live a meaningful and fulfilling life that can easily be integrated with other methods such as TA.

DEVELOPMENTAL CRISES

Existential questions and crises often seem related to an individual's psychosocial development stages. Berne's trainer Erik Erikson (Erikson, 1994; Schlein, 2016) described that individuals develop through the stages Trust/Mistrust (infancy), Autonomy/Shame-and-Doubt (toddlerhood), Initiative/Guilt (early childhood), Industry/Inferiority (school age), Identity/Role Confusion (adolescence), Intimacy/Isolation (young adulthood), Generativity/Stagnation (middle adulthood) and Ego-Integrity/Despair (late adulthood). Erikson's framework complements TA by highlighting the importance of social transactions and the influence of early experiences on an individual's identity and behaviour. Erikson's model is supported by research and, for example, shows the impact of stages on existential well-being and mental health (Casey et al., 2008; Bosma & Kunnen, 2001; Marcia, 2010). Psychotherapy literature identifies additional stages:

Quarterlife-Crisis

Quarterlife transitions, typically occurring in one's mid-20s to early 30s, often involve significant life changes such as starting a career, forming long-term relationships and establishing independence (Robbins, 2004; Stapleton, 2012). Researchers identify common symptoms as feeling lost, confused, anxious or trapped, alongside the pressure to meet societal expectations and the fear of missing out. Therapists are recommended to encourage self-exploration, reflect on personal values and goals and build resilience and flexibility in facing life's uncertainties. It is also beneficial to foster a supportive social network that encourages open discussion about these experiences, helping to normalise the quarterlife crisis as a common developmental phase. Seen from a TA-perspective, a quarterlife-crisis may be associated with life scripts, ego-states and transactions. Life scripts from childhood may come under scrutiny during a quarterlife crisis as individuals question whether their current path aligns with their desires and values. A TA therapist may help clients by exploring these scripts and making active decisions for potentially new, more fulfilling life paths. Therapists may help individuals stuck in unhelpful patterns from Parent or Child states, possibly caused by restricting drivers and lack of permissions and allowances; they may strengthen the Adult functioning and autonomy.

Midlife-Crisis

Midlife transitions, experienced around the ages of 40–60, are characterised by reflections on achievements, legacy and mortality, experiencing a desire for change or renewal in aspects such as career, relationships or life-goals, and dealing with feelings of regret, stagnation or the fear of ageing. These transitions may impact mental health through feelings of dissatisfaction, depression and a re-evaluation of life goals, identity and values. In terms of TA, a midlife-crisis may involve the following (Setiya, 2014). Life scripts, patterns in ego-states, time-structure, transactions and games may be revisited as individuals question their path and consider changes. TA therapists may help clients by exploring and revisiting scripts, facilitating script-redecision to embrace more fulfilling choices resonating with their current self-understanding and aspirations. Therapists may strengthen the Adult ego-state, flexibly using positive elements of the Parent and Child states, such as nurturing qualities, freedom, joy and creativity.

This journey towards autonomous functioning means that individuals move beyond scripted behaviours and ego-states to access a more authentic Adult ego-state, which may consciously integrate previously repressed, undesired, challenging or frightening aspects of the self (script-system/racket). The psychoanalyst which Carl Gustav Jung has described this as the process of individuation and work with one's shadow (Jacoby, 2016). For instance, a persistent operation from the Critical Parent ego-state might mask insecurities or fears residing in the shadow; by contrasting behaviours and attitudes of the different ego-states, TA therapists may assist clients in identifying what aspects of themselves they might be rejecting or ignoring, thus giving clues to the shadow's/script-system's contents. Therapists may recognise the value of these shadow aspects, encourage reflection and acceptance and find ways to express them constructively. In this process, individuals may revisit their earlier individuation-separation stages, re-enact (regress) earlier needs and merge/symbiosis, which the therapist can be aware of via clear therapeutic boundaries and analysis of transference and transactions. The therapist can help the client to become aware of these relational processes, which may lead to an investigation into the shadow side of their ego-states and unresolved aspects of their life script. Integrating their shadow may foster empathy and self-insight in their transactions and help clients find more intimacy and authenticity in relationships. By challenging and re-evaluating these life scripts, clients may begin confronting and integrating their shadows, leading to more authentic and fulfilling lives.

Retirement

Retirement transitions mark a period of adjustment to a post-work life, which, while potentially offering freedom and opportunities for personal growth, can also pose challenges to mental health and existential well-being, including loss of identity, social status, purpose and social connections, leading to risks of depression and isolation. The informal diagnosis of 'empty nest syndrome' regards the experience of parents when their children leave home, leading to feelings of sadness, loss and identity crisis. In TA-terms, individuals may struggle with changes in their pattern of transactions, roles, games, such as parents may struggle decreasing their parent role when their children become more independent. The loss of work and care-tasks may shift one's time-structure, creating a sense of loss. TA therapist may strengthen the Adult ego-state, enable clients to make rational, autonomous decisions about their future while finding healthy ways to express and enjoy their Child ego-state, fulfil unmet emotional needs and rediscover passions or hobbies. Clients may explore new ways to receive and give strokes and break loneliness, such as engaging in community activities, volunteering or developing new social networks. Therapists may help clients explore and revisit their, for example, unresolved traumas and unrealistic expectations about life they may have developed in childhood. Achieving autonomy means finding new purposes and making choices congruent with their current desires and needs rather than being driven by past roles or societal expectations.

Case Study 25.1

Peter

A TA therapist encountered Peter, a client in his midlife crisis, exhibiting signs of existential questioning and dissatisfaction with his current life trajectory. Peter grappled with feelings of stagnation, re-evaluation of personal values, and a desire for greater fulfilment. The client explored his life script, identified and changed limiting beliefs and expectations about life. Via experiential exercises, Peter learnt to listen to what his intuition told him is meaningful in life; he identified clear life-goals, which he translated into practical steps and experiments to improve his daily-life.

Box 25.1

Complex Grief

Clients may present symptoms of persistent longing, intense sorrow and difficulty accepting the loss of a loved one. Recent research suggests no specific stages in the grief process, challenging previous notions of linear grief progression. Complex grief, unlike normal grief, may involve prolonged and intense symptoms, such as persistent yearning, disbelief and difficulty moving on, often leading to impaired daily functioning. A TA therapist may identify complex grief by observing persistent and intense grief symptoms that significantly impact the client's daily life and well-being. The main evidence-based psychotherapeutic treatments for complex grief include integrative meaning-centred therapy and narrative therapy, both of which have been shown to address the complexities of grief effectively (Neimeyer, 2011, 2015, 2021). The dual model of grief encompasses both loss-oriented and restoration-oriented processes, emphasising the oscillation between confronting the reality of the loss and adapting to life changes. This model aligns with TA-concepts by acknowledging the interplay between the Child, Parent and Adult ego-states in processing grief and the influence of life scripts and relational patterns on the grief process. TA therapists may work with the dual model of grief by utilising ego-state work, script-analysis and relational techniques to help clients navigate the loss-oriented and restoration-oriented aspects of grief, ultimately promoting healing and integration. TA therapists have highlighted that stagnations and other problems in the grief process may stem from unresolved conflicts and unfinished business related to the deceased. TA therapists may address these issues through ego-state work, script-analysis and relational techniques to help clients process their grief and resolve underlying conflicts. By exploring the client's internal dialogue and relational patterns, TA therapists aim to facilitate a deeper understanding of the grief process and support the client in achieving a more adaptive and integrated response to loss.

PART V
EVIDENCE-BASED TA TREATMENT MANUAL

26

OVERVIEW OF
TA TREATMENT

Part V comprises the TA psychotherapy manual, an evidence-based guide designed following clinical trials in clients with mild to moderate depression (Vos & van Rijn, 2024a, 2024b, 2024c). Recognising the diverse needs of individuals, the manual is adapted beyond depression treatment, aiming to serve a wide array of clients with varying disorders. It is structured to provide a fundamental 16-session framework, informed by dose-response research indicating significant client improvement within thirteen to eighteen sessions (Vos et al., 2019). This flexibility makes the manual suitable for various settings, including training institutes, inpatient and outpatient mental healthcare and private practice. It proves especially beneficial for trainee therapists, offering a solid base that can be integrated into TA training.

The manual emphasises customisation, urging therapists to tailor their approaches to the specific conditions and individual needs as detailed in Part IV of this book. It advocates for applying the general treatment philosophy over strict adherence to the manual's text, recognising and valuing the unique insights and skills therapists bring; research indicates that the therapists's competencies and integrity may be more important than strict adherence to a treatment manual (Power, 2022). This approach underscores the necessity of reading the entire book to fully grasp the integrated, evidence-based components from various TA schools, as highlighted in Chapter 3. For example, Chapter 10 explains the therapy stages. While this manual is an evidence-based common denominator across different TA methodologies, its greatest strength lies in its adaptability, allowing therapists to provide personalised, effective care (Table 26.1).

Table 26.1 Overview of the Sessions in the Treatment Manual of Evidence-Based Transactional Analysis Psychotherapy

Therapy Stage Name	Stage Aims	Session Number(s)	Name of Session(s)	Steps in Sessions
1. ESTABLISHING RELATIONSHIP, INITIAL ASSESSMENT AND INITIAL TREATMENT CONTRACT	• offer the opportunity to the client to share their problems, needs and wishes • lay the foundations for a positive therapeutic relationship • inform the client about TA's aims and methods • develop a basic agreement/ contract about the treatment • check the client's eligibility	1–2	Establishing relationship, initial assessment and initial treatment contract	1 Welcome 2 Explaining session aim/ method 3 Exploring client's motivation 4 Exploring triggers of problems 5 Exploring coping with problems 6 Identifying general therapy goals 7 Filling-in TA Goal Attainment Form Informing about TA 8 Exploring the life context 9 Checking eligibility 10 Explaining TA's aim and method 11 Explaining organisational issues 12 Deciding together 13 Ending
2. SYSTEMATIC ASSESSMENT	• assess the client's current problems (clinical phenomenon) • assess possible causes of the client's problems (aetiology) • develop a case formulation based on which a plan is agreed upon for the next stage	3–4 (some content may carry-over to a next session)	Assessment of clinical phenomenon (see Chapter 4)	1 Emotional check-in 2 Bridging between sessions 3 Session goal 4 Discuss homework/ questionnaires 5 Systematic examination of ego-states and life positions under challenging situations 6 Examine self-perception of ego-states

7 Examine the client's life position of 'You're OK/not-OK' and social functioning

8 Examine self-efficacy and life position 'I'm OK/not-OK'

9 Examine stroke balance

10 Optional: an initial exploration of transactions, games, and fundamental psychological structure

11 Summary of clinical phenomenon

12 Ending

5–6

(some content may carry-over to a next session)

Assessment of aetiology (see Chapter 5)

1 Emotional check-in

2 Bridging between sessions

3 Session goal

4 Discuss homework/questionnaires

5 Examine the development of the problems in the subjective experience of the client

6 Life story in the client's own words

7 Systematic examination of the client's life-history

8 Examine transactional core messages

8 A. Follow-up questions

(Continued)

Table 26.1 Overview of the Sessions in the Treatment Manual of Evidence-Based Transactional Analysis Psychotherapy *(Continued)*

Therapy Stage Name	Stage Aims	Session Number(s)	Name of Session(s)	Steps in Sessions
				8 B. Systematic analysis of injunctions/counter-injunctions/drivers
				8 C. Connect early-life messages with the present
				9 Summary of Aetiology
				10 Ending
		7 (some content may carry-over to a next session)	Sharing case formulation and developing treatment plan	NB: Therapist creates case formulation before the session.
				1 Emotional check-in
				2 Bridging between sessions
				3 Session goal
				4 Discuss homework
				5 Share case formulation
				6 Agreement on treatment 'contract'
				7 Summary
				8 Ending
3. EXPERIENTIAL PROCESSING IN THE HERE-AND-NOW	In session 6, the therapist and client have agreed on a unique treatment plan for the unique client. Within each of these five sessions, the therapist will use their therapeutic competencies (mainly Chapters 11–12) to facilitate the experiential processing.	8–12 (some content may carry-over to a next session)		1 Emotional check-in
				2 Bridging between sessions
				3 Discuss homework
				4 Session goal
				5 Work with the chosen method to achieve the session goal
				6 Summary
				7 Ending

4. MAKING DECISIONS AND CHANGES IN DAILY LIFE	13.	Setting new life goals and making plans	1 Emotional check-in 2 Bridging between sessions 3 Discuss homework 4 Session goal 5 Identify experiential learning and impasses 6 Identify new goals in life ('redecision') 7 Reflection on the conditions for structural change and creating a plan of action 8 Creating the conditions for structural change in therapy 9 Summarise/evaluate 10 Creation of safety 11 Homework 12 Ending
	• decide new goals in life (script-redecision) • create conditions and inner safety for structural change in life (facilitating script-change) • experimenting and evaluating change in the session and trying it in daily life • identify and overcome impasses and resistance		
	Session 16:	14–15	Application in daily life	1 Emotional check-in 2 Bridging between sessions 3 Discuss homework 4 Identify new goal 5 Experimenting within the session 6 Creation of safety 7 Homework: experimenting in daily life 8 Ending
	• evaluating and taking stock of lessons learnt during TA. • identifying how the clients could continue their changes and developing contingency plans. • saying goodbye and coping with feelings of termination.		

(Continued)

Table 26.1 Overview of the Sessions in the Treatment Manual of Evidence-Based Transactional Analysis Psychotherapy *(Continued)*

Therapy Stage Name	Stage Aims	Session Number(s)	Name of Session(s)	Steps in Sessions
		16	Ending	1 Emotional check-in 2 Bridging between sessions 3 Discuss homework 4 Identify learning and re-assess therapy goals 5 Develop contingency plans 6 Explore feelings of ending 7 Creation of safety 8 Evaluation and saying goodbye

Note that this manual integrates citations from manuals by Vos, 2017, marked with one asterisk*, Ohlsson, Björk & Johnsson, 1992 marked with**, and Widdowson, 2013, with***.

27

ESTABLISHING RELATIONSHIP, INITIAL ASSESSMENT AND CONTRACT (SESSIONS 1–2)

Aims of therapy stage:

- offer the opportunity for the client to share their problems, needs and wishes
- lay the foundations for a positive therapeutic relationship
- inform the client about TA's aims and methods
- develop a basic agreement/contract about the treatment
- check the client's eligibility.

Recommendations:

- Bring a copy of the TA Goal Attainment Form for the client to take home, reflect on the goals and bring this to the next session.

SESSIONS 1–2: ESTABLISHING RELATIONSHIP, INITIAL ASSESSMENT AND CONTRACT

Step 1: Welcome

- The therapist welcomes the client and shares their information about the client as transparency can build trust.

Step 2: Explaining Session Aim/Method

- The therapist communicates the objectives and procedures of today's meeting, being mindful of the session's time constraints. The therapist clarifies that this session touches on many topics, which may feel like jumping between topics and not going deep. The focus is on getting to know each other initially, exploring whether this therapy is suitable and if the client and the therapist can foster a good relationship.

Step 3: Exploring Client's Motivation

- The therapist asks the client about their motivation for receiving TA and their psychological needs at this stage. This may, for example, involve the following questions:
  - Why do you ask for my help and/or are referred to me?*
  - What are the main issues that you are struggling with at this moment in your life?*
  - Could you give some examples of difficult situations in your life?*
  - What would you like to change in your life?*
  - How do these problems impact your daily life? For example, do they influence your emotions, relationships, work, hobbies, physical well-being, etc.?*

Step 4: Exploring Triggers of the Problems

The therapist asks questions about the specific context of the problems:

- Why do you ask for help at this specific moment in your life (any specific triggers)?*
- Are there any specific situations where your problems seem worse?*
- Are there any specific situations where your problems seem better?*

Step 5: Exploring Coping With the Problems

The therapist asks questions about how the client copes with the problems:

- What have you already done to improve your situation? What was helpful and what was not helpful?*
- Have you asked for help from friends or family? What did they say? What was helpful and what was not helpful?* How do people around you (family, friends, neighbours, community) generally see and cope with such problems? If people around you knew that you were coming to therapy, how would they respond? (These questions help understand the (sub)cultural assumptions and expectations about mental health and health care. Be aware of stigmatisation of mental health problems, and validate their decision to come to therapy.)
- Have you had any counselling or therapy before, and if so, what changes did it make in your life? What was helpful and what was not helpful?*
- In all these things you have tried, what have you learnt about the problems and their possible solutions?

Step 6: Identifying General Therapy Goals

The therapist asks questions about what it would look like if the problems were no longer there:

- What do you hope to achieve with TA? How would your life look like if therapy is successful?*

- If you could wish for three things to change in your life, what would these be (imagine you have a magical want and can wish for anything)?*
- What do you need to be able to live an authentic, fulfiling and meaningful life?*

Step 7: Filing-in the TA Goal Attainment Form

The therapist introduces the TA Goal Attainment Form (see Appendix) to the client, identifying any goals already mentioned and brainstorming about any additional goals. The therapist emphasises that not all sections/goals need to be completed, and that inauthentic objectives should be avoided. The importance of setting genuine, meaningful goals is stressed, with the understanding that these can be revised at any time, particularly by session 6, which marks the end of the assessment and case formulation stage. Clients are advised to set at least three goals. The therapist may need to help the client formulate and reformulate the goals to ensure these goals are important, specific, achievable, timely, challenging, mutually conducive and positive. These criteria, drawn from various research findings, underscore the value of setting well-defined, realistically attainable goals within a reasonable timeframe and oriented towards positive outcomes rather than avoiding negative states (Vos, 2017). The therapist may suggest the client takes the form home to consider and complete it more thoroughly in their own time and discuss this in the next session. The therapist and client each keep a copy. The form includes the following headings (connecting with other concepts in Chapter 6):

- Emotional goal (e.g. emotions, psychopathology, psychological distress)
- Goals about self-beliefs (e.g. life position 'I'm OK/not-OK', self-efficacy; exploring, accepting and expressing one's identity and coping with social norms and restrictions about oneself)
- Social goal (e.g. life position 'You're OK/not-OK', social functioning, behaviour, coping with social injustice)
- Living in the present (e.g. develop realistic insight and freedom from life script)
- Life goal (e.g. self-realisation, general well-being, quality-of-life)
- Other goal

Step 8: Exploring the Life Context

The therapist asks some general questions to understand the life situation and strengths of the client, as research indicates that merely asking about what is problematic in the client's life can be counter-effective ('iatrogenic harm'; Vos, 2017, 2023). This could involve some of the following.

- **General:** Could you tell me anything about your life situation that may be relevant to me?*
- **Self:** Describe yourself briefly as you are now.**
- **Housing:** How is your housing situation? How and with whom do you live now?**

- **Children:** Do you have children? If yes, who are they, and who is the other parent? Who looks after them? Do your problems impact them, and if so, how?** (Explore any possible safeguarding risks for young children.)
- **Social life:** Could you tell me something about your social life? Do you have friends and relatives? How is your relationship with them? Any intimate relationships? Any difficult relationships? Partner? Who helps you? Do your problems impact them?*
- **Time structure:** What are your main activities in everyday life? For example, do you work, study, care for others, or are you retired, sick, etc.? How do you pass your time if you are not working or studying?* How is your work/life balance? What leisure activities do you do, and how often? How much time do you spend alone, and what do you do then? How much time do you spend with others? Could you give me a general idea of the types of relationships these are; for example, do you mainly engage in rituals, passing the time (talk, but no action), playing games, goal-oriented action, or do you feel some emotional closeness and intimacy? How many people do you feel real emotional closeness or intimacy with? How does it feel to be emotionally close or intimate; how do you usually respond to feeling closeness/intimacy? Has any of these social and everyday activities changed or become more difficult due to your problems? How satisfied do you feel about how you usually spend your time? Would you like to change anything in your everyday and social activities, or are you satisfied with these? (These questions may help to get an idea of how clients structure their time, e.g. via withdrawal, rituals, pastimes, activities, psychological games, and intimacy. Notice risk-taking and intimacy, or a withdrawal thereof, in their activities.)
- **Diversity and social-justice:** Could you tell me about your education? How do you earn your living; if you have a job, how satisfying or stressful is this? Are you OK financially, without worrying too much? How would you describe your position in society? For example, how do you see your culture, gender, sexual orientation, racial and ethnic identity, social class, economic status and family educational levels? To what extent do you feel you can accept and express who you truly are with the people around you, your community and society? If not, what prevents you from accepting and expressing yourself authentically? What personal experiences do you have of societal injustice, discrimination or unfair treatment; could you give some examples, which could be big traumatic experiences, structural problems or small everyday annoyances or micro-aggressions (if you have many examples, could you describe the most recent and most impactful ones)? To what extent are these experiences of injustice, discrimination or unfair treatment unique to you, or more structural in society (how much power do you have in society)? How do these experiences of injustice, discrimination, unfair treatment or power differences impact you; what feels particularly threatening in society to you or your loved ones? How do you make sense of these experiences of injustice, discrimination, unfair treatment or power differences (what is the meaning of these experiences to you)? What do you have to do to survive (what kinds of threat response are you using)? (Note that the latter questions explore the client's perceptions of powers, threats, meaning and responses, as described in the

Power-Threat-Meaning Framework by Johnstone & Boyle, 2018) How do you feel that the problems for which you have come in therapy are caused by society or bad luck in life?

- **Self-realisation:** When have you felt most authentic, autonomous or free in your life; what were you doing, and who were you with? Can you think of a time when you felt you were your most authentic self? What factors contributed to this feeling of authenticity? What makes you come out of bed in the morning? What do you find meaningful in life?* Are you satisfied with how much time you spend on activities that feel authentic and meaningful? Are you satisfied with what you have achieved in life? Do you feel there is more to life that you have not tried out or achieved yet; what is stopping you? Has this changed due to your problems? (This helps understand the impact on self-realisation, well-being and quality-of-life.)

- **Strengths/resilience:** What are your strengths? What helps you to get through a difficult day?* Think back about a previous difficult moment in your life; what helped you get through this period? How could these strengths help you with your current problems?

Step 9: Checking Eligibility

- **Urgent problems:** Are there any problems in your life that need to be solved before we can start therapy? For example, do you have any social, financial, work, housing or other urgent concerns?*

- **Severe health problems:** How is your health at this moment? Do you have any disabilities or issues I should be aware of? If any diagnosis, what is the prognosis and treatment, and are you receiving all the medical care you need? How does your health impact your daily life and the problems for which you have come to me? How could your health issue impact our sessions? Do you need any adjustments in our sessions, and if so, what could I do to make the sessions more accessible and comfortable?*

- **Other severe issues:** Has anyone diagnosed you with psychosis or addiction to alcohol and/or drugs? Do you have difficulties talking or understanding, or a severe learning problem? Do you have issues in reading or writing that may, for example, make it difficult to fill-in a questionnaire? If so, how do you currently manage this, and do you think this may influence therapy?

- **Suicide Risks:** Have you had any thoughts about hurting yourself or ending your life? Do you find yourself thinking about death or wishing you were dead? (If at risk, continue with questions from the text box below.)

- **Legal responsibility:** Are you under eighteen years, under custody, sectioned or has anyone told you that you do not have the legal right to make decisions for yourself?

- **Self-reflection:** As part of therapy, I will ask you to reflect on yourself, your thoughts, emotions, behaviour, relationships and life history. Looking into the past may bring up feelings or insights that may initially feel uncomfortable but often help to feel better in the long term. Of course, I will support you, and we will not discuss anything you do not want to do. In general, are you willing to do this?

- **Additional questions:** (If relevant, check psychological mindedness, capacity for reflection, introspection and honesty, willingness to participate actively, curiosity and interest in developing self-understanding, realistic expectations of therapy, realistic goals and desire to make reasonable sacrifices as part of the change process.)
- **Medication:** Do you receive any medication, and if so, what is the name, what is this for, and who has prescribed it? The therapist may want to explain*** 'Sometimes, clients might want to stop taking their medicine or take less of it during therapy. It is important not to do this until you've made enough progress in therapy, meaning you are feeling better in a way that can be measured. It is a good idea to keep going to therapy even if you start taking less medicine to make sure you stay on track and don't start feeling down again. If you are thinking about changing how much medicine you take, you should always talk to the doctor who gave it to you first. They need to oversee any changes. Changing your medicine while in therapy can make it tricky to know what's helping you get better, so it is usually best to wait a bit before making any changes.'

Step 10: Explaining TA's Aim and Method

The therapist gives a realistic overview of TA's aims and methods, tailored to the client, and checks how relevant this is for the client. This may include some psychoeducation about TA concepts, but make sure this is not too theoretical or off-putting to the client. Consider the following points:

- **Aims:**
  - the client's self-determined therapy goals
  - improve your emotions and stress (e.g. emotions, depression, anxiety, distress)
  - feeling better about yourself ('I'm OK', self-efficacy)
  - feeling better about and around others ('You're OK', social functioning)
  - feel more spontaneous, authentic, autonomous, free and capable of living a meaningful and fulfiling life despite life's inevitable struggles (self-realisation, well-being, quality-of-life).
  - understanding and improving your role in relationships (transactions, games, behaviour)
  - (usually) become less critical and more nurturing towards yourself (Critical and Nurturing Parent)
  - (usually) become more realistic, balanced, rational and logical (Adult)
  - (usually) less automatically adapt to others if you do not want, and feel freer (Adapted and Free Child)

- **Method:**
  - assessment of your current life and problems (analysis of clinical phenomenon/ structural analysis; assessment competencies)
  - analyse the cause of your current problems, which may involve looking at your life-story (analysis of aetiology/life script)

○ focus on what you are experiencing and feeling now in your life (experiential competencies)

○ I will be supportive, authentic and empathetic so you can feel safe talking or working on anything you'd like. Our focus is trying to achieve your therapy goals; we will regularly check whether our sessions are still helpful in achieving these goals and whether we need to change any of our methods or adjust the goals. I work collaboratively and honestly; for example, I find it helpful to hear what is going on for you and what you like and do not like. I will give as many explanations, guidance and direction as you want. Usually, I may be more active in the first sessions, and in the later sessions, I may take more of a backseat. Let me know if you need more explanations or help or if we need to change the direction of our therapy, as this is your time! (relational competencies)

○ In the first sessions, we will focus on getting to know each other and examining your problems and life story. This may help us to get a complete understanding of your problems and causes based on this. In the fifth or sixth session, we will conclude what we think is the core of what is going on and causing this, and we will brainstorm the logical next steps. In the next stage, we will decide together what we could do to solve the underlying causes of the problems and try out new ways to deal with the problems. In the last sessions, you may want to start making some active changes in daily life, and I can help you with this. How does this sound to you? (structuring competencies)

Step 11: Explaining Organisational Issues

Discuss organisational procedures, such as:
- Contact details
- Session length
- Contact outside sessions
- Appointments
- Cancelation
- Holidays
- Payment
- Parking/transport
- Confidentiality and data-protection
- Note-taking
- Professional guidelines and complaint procedures

Step 12: Deciding Together

The therapist summarises previous steps and collaboratively decides with the client on pursuing TA, focusing on a pressure-free, informed choice that empowers the client, potentially marking a new, autonomous decision-making experience. The therapist may want to write down any agreements.

Step 13: Ending

- Homework (e.g. fill-in questionnaires)
- Session summary
- Wishes
- Summarise agreements

Box 27.1

Examining Suicide Risks

When a psychotherapist aims to assess a client's risk of suicide, it is essential to approach the subject with sensitivity and empathy, ensuring the client feels supported and understood, emphasising that help is available and that they are not alone in their struggles. The therapist needs to examine the role of suicidal ideation; for example, is thinking about death merely a wish that the problems are over, or are these active plans? What does it mean for the therapeutic relationship and transaction that the client shares this, and if the client has shared their suicidal thoughts or attempt with others, what does that mean for their relationship and transactions? Depending on the client's responses, immediate action may be required, including developing a safety plan or referral to emergency services to ensure the client's safety. Know relevant protocols from your organisation or professional body. The following questions are framed to open a dialogue and allow the client to share their experiences and feelings without fear of judgement.

- **Direct Questions:** Have you had any thoughts about hurting yourself or ending your life? Do you find yourself thinking about death or wishing you were dead?
- **Frequency, Duration and Intensity:** How often do you have these thoughts, and how long do they last? Would you say these thoughts are intense or hard to control?
- **Plans and Means:** Have you thought about how you might hurt yourself? Do you have access to the means to carry out this plan?
- **Previous Suicide Attempts:** Have you ever acted on these thoughts or attempted to harm yourself before? Can you tell me what happened during your previous attempt(s)?
- **Reasons for Living and Dying:** What has stopped you from acting on these thoughts? Can you tell me about the things you feel are worth living for?
- **Hopelessness and Burdensomeness:** Do you feel there's no way out of your current situation? Do you ever feel like you are a burden to others?
- **Support System:** Who can you talk to when feeling down or thinking about hurting yourself? How supported do you feel by the people around you?
- **Coping Strategies:** What helps you feel better when having these thoughts? How do you look after yourself when unwell (Nurturing Parent)? What practical steps can you do when you feel this way (Adult)? Have you been able to use any strategies to cope with these feelings?
- **Immediate Safety:** Do you feel safe right now? Is there someone you can be with to help you feel safer?
- **Willingness to Accept Help:** How do you feel about getting help with these feelings? Are you open to exploring options to keep you safe?

Case Study 27.1

Tara

Tara, a 35-year-old marketing manager, seeks TA therapy due to her struggles with depression. In the initial session, Tara expresses her psychological struggles, detailing feelings of hopelessness, lack of motivation and overwhelming daily tasks. She provides examples of difficult situations, such as struggling to get out of bed in the morning and feeling emotionally drained at work. Tara's depression impacts her daily life, affecting her emotions, work performance and relationships with colleagues and family. She strongly desires to change her life, aiming to find joy in daily activities and improve her relationships. Tara's primary motivation for therapy is to regain a sense of purpose and fulfilment in her personal and professional life. During the session, she also discusses her difficulty in maintaining work-life balance and the impact of her depression on her physical well-being. Tara's depression impacts her transactions by causing her to withdraw socially, leading to a lack of genuine intimacy and closeness in her interactions with others. She struggles to structure her time well, often spending excessive amounts of time alone, engaging in withdrawal and avoidance of intimacy, which further exacerbates her feelings of isolation and disconnection. Tara's introspective nature and willingness to actively participate in therapy indicate her psychological mindedness and capacity for reflection.

28

SYSTEMATIC
ASSESSMENT
(SESSIONS 3–7)

AIMS OF STAGE

- assess the client's current problems (clinical phenomenon, Chapter 4).
- assess possible causes of the client's problems (aetiology, Chapter 5).
- develop a case formulation based on which a plan is agreed upon for the next stage (Chapter 6, Appendix).

RECOMMENDATIONS

- Ask the client to fill-in relevant questionnaires, and bring these in before the next session (at least before you make the case formulation). In the next session, ask about their experiences, for example: 'How was it like for you to complete them?'; 'Did you have any problems filling this in?'; 'Were there any unexpected questions or new things you may have learnt about yourself?' Explore whether completing questionnaires has brought up any themes and memories. If the client has forgotten to fill-in some questionnaires, kindly ask them to complete them before the next session. Explain the aim of the questionnaires; for example, it is essential to fill these in because they will help identify the possible causes of the client's problems, which will help to find possible interventions/solutions; like a GP uses a thermometer and stethoscope to make a quick and reliable diagnosis so that a tailored treatment could be started quickly. If clients struggle to fill-in, ask them what this struggle was about and explore practical solutions; explore possible transactional meanings and scripted responses as some clients may see questionnaires as homework and a Critical Parent judging them; therefore, be transparent about the motivation and procedures, focusing on an egalitarian, collaborative relationship.

SESSION 3–4: ASSESSMENT OF CLINICAL PHENOMENA

Session Aims

- Analysis of dominant ego-states in difficult or problematic situations, for example, via game analysis, drama triangle analysis, stroke analysis, analysis of non-verbal behaviour and specification
- Analysis of social functioning and underlying position regarding others (You're OK/not-OK)
- Analysis of self-efficacy and underlying position regarding self (I'm OK/not-OK)

Step 1: Emotional Check-In

- Check-in
- Session goals/wishes

Step 2: Bridging Between Sessions

- Memory
- Refresher
- Bridging
- Contract

Step 3: Session Goal

Step 4: Discuss Homework/Questionnaires

Step 5: Systematic Examination of Ego-States and Life Positions Under Challenging Situations

The therapist asks for one or multiple examples to analyse the dominant ego-states, possible games and possible dramas in these problematic situations. The therapist can move to the next step when they have a generic understanding of the dominant ego-state in situations representative of the main problem.

- **Multiple examples of the client's main problem:** Can you give an example of a situation when you struggled a lot with your main problem? Could you describe this in detail, such as where you were, who was there, what you saw, what happened, how you responded, what happened next, etc.? If possible, could you tell the story about what happened before, at the start, in the middle, at the end and after?
- **Other examples:** Can you recall a recent situation where you reacted strongly? Could you also describe this in detail, including what happened before/start/middle/end/after?
- **Evaluation (initial exploration of scripts):** Looking back, can you identify recurring themes or 'scripts' in your life that dictate how you respond to challenges or opportunities?

Step 6: Examine Self-Perception of Ego-States

The therapist may consider examining how the participant views each ego-state. This may only be recommended for clients with sufficient self-insight. This only regards the client's *explicit self-understanding*, not their less-reflected or possible underlying conflicts. Particularly in this and the next step, be aware of possible cultural bias and reflect on what may considered normal, realistic or helpful in their community; do not impose your ego-state label onto a client, but help the client self-identify their ego-states. The therapist may want to explain a basic TA model of Critical Parent, Nurturing Parent, Adult Free Child and Adapted Child.

- **Psycho-education:** In TA, therapists often talk about ego-states. Ego-states are like different versions or parts of ourselves that come out in various situations: the Parent part that taught us, the Adult part that thinks and decides and the Child part that feels and experiences. We all experience these different ego-states, but some can be stronger than others.
- **Critical Parent:** The 'Critical Parent' is a part of us that criticises and sets high standards, often echoing the judgemental or controlling voices we've heard from authority figures in our past. Can you share some moments when you felt like you were in a Critical Parent state? For example, I am interested in hearing about times when you might have been particularly judgemental, strict, demanding or punitive, either with yourself or others. Are there any particular situations or persons that trigger this state?
- **Nurturing Parent:** The 'Nurturing Parent' is the part of us that offers care, support and encouragement to ourselves or others, much like a loving parent would. Can you share some moments when you felt like you were in a Nurturing Parent state? Are there any particular situations or persons that trigger this state?
- **Adapted Child:** The 'Adapted Child' is the part of us that adjusts behaviours and responses to meet the expectations and rules of others, often shaped by early experiences and conditioning. Can you share some moments when you felt like you were in an Adapted Child state? Are any particular situations or persons triggering this state?
- **Free Child:** The 'Free Child' is the part of us that embodies spontaneity, creativity and play, free from the constraints of learnt behaviour and societal expectations. Can you share some moments when you felt like you were in a Free Child state? Are any particular situations or persons triggering this state?
- **Adult:** The 'Adult' is the part of us that processes information rationally, makes decisions based on current reality and mediates between the demands of the Parent and the Child's impulses. Can you share some moments when you felt like you were in an Adult state? Are any particular situations or persons triggering this state?
- **Other ego-states:** Even though this treatment manual follows the structural model research has shown to apply to most people, it is essential to leave the possibility open that other ego-states may better apply to the client or that the client prefers other

terminology (Chapter 4). The evidence-based structural model seems to mainly apply to individuals with neurotic problems combined with a relatively developed fundamental psychological structure; individuals with problematic development of their fundamental psychological structure may require a different, tailored conceptualisation.

- **Frequency and intensity:** Thanks for giving me these examples of the different ego-states. When you look at your life in general, which ego-state feels the strongest and the most frequent? Has this ego-state always dominated? When did this become more dominant, and was there anything particular about the situation or persons around you that triggered that change? Which ego-state feels the weakest and the least frequent? How easy is it for you to go from one state to another ego-state, or can you stay in one state for very long?

- **Problems:** If we now look at the problems you came in therapy for, how does this relate to ego-states? For example, think about a moment when your problem was extreme: which ego-state was strong and which was weak?

- **Message:** If you think about the ego-state that you seem to find the most difficult, what message does this seem to give, for example, articulated as a rule or command such as 'Do not...', or 'It is OK to...', aiming to phrase it in a generalised or third-person form like 'You should...'. (This may help identify core messages. Ask follow-up questions to explore and identify the message's core even better, and if needed reformulate this more precisely; for example, ask 'what makes this message so difficult/strong/meaningful; what is its essence; could we formulate this message more precisely?' (See Identifying Transactional core messages via the Downward-Arrow Technique in Chapter 12.))

Step 7: Examine the Client's Life Position of 'You're OK/Not-OK' and Social Functioning

- **Social life (if not already explored):**
  - Could you tell me about your social life or relationships with friends, relatives and colleagues?
  - How extensive is your social network?
  - Do you sometimes feel alone or socially withdrawn? If so, how often; what do you do to prevent or break loneliness?
- **Positive relationships:** Who are the most important people to you? Could you describe your relationships and what makes them positive?
- **Negative relationships:**

  (The therapist may use this as an initial analysis of transactions and games, as described in Chapter 8, although there may not be enough time in this session to go into much depth; you may analyse their transactions in more detail later).
  - Who are the people you do not like, hate or find challenging to relate with?
  - Are there any relationships you find particularly difficult now? Could you tell more about them, your relationship and what you find challenging? Could you give some examples?

○ Could you give an example of a challenging encounter and what happened; talk me through the start, middle and end of that meeting? (This involves a first analysis of transactions; consider initial ego-state, shift in ego-states, repeated patterns, complementary, crossed, ulterior or duplex transactions, emotional outcome for everyone involved; how often, with which people and in which situations does this pattern usually happen; when did this start, and has this changed over time).

○ In your current relationships, do you notice patterns in communicating or responding to others that remind you of your childhood interactions with people? Reflecting on your relationships, can you identify any 'games' you play in conflicts or stress; what do you think you gain from these interactions? If there is one pattern or 'game' you could change in your life, what would it be and why; what do you think stops you from changing it? (This is an initial analysis of transactions and games; consider payoffs, roles, confluence of ego-states, switch, antithesis).

- **Self-evaluation:**
  ○ Looking at these positive and difficult examples, if you listen to your gut feeling, do most people usually feel OK or not-so OK to you?
  ○ Do you feel that you have enough positive relationships in your life? Do you typically trust people; what makes you (not) trust people, and have you always felt this way?
  ○ Do you feel you have enough emotionally close, intimate and partner relationships; if not, what would you like to be different, and what is stopping you?
  ○ Do you feel you have enough people with whom you can be yourself and authentic; if not, what stops you from being yourself or authentic?
  ○ Is there anything you want to change in your relationships and social life, or how you relate and communicate with people in general?

Step 8: Examine the Client's Life Position of 'I'm OK/Not-OK' and Self-Efficacy

- **Positive self:** What do you like most about yourself?** Could you give some examples of when you felt good about yourself; how did you respond or behave in this situation?
- **Negative self:** What do you dislike most in yourself?** Could you give an example of when you felt bad about yourself; how did you cope with feeling bad? What would you want to conjure up in yourself if you were a magician?** What do you think you can achieve even though you are not a magician?**
- **Self-evaluation:** Looking at these positive and difficult examples, if you listen to your gut feeling, do you usually feel OK or not-so OK about yourself? Do you typically feel capable, in control and know how to cope with most situations; if not, are there any specific situations in which you do not feel this way, or is this a generic feeling? How would you describe your self-esteem? What activities do you do to look

after yourself or to relax (self-care), and how often? Do you feel you take responsibility for yourself, or do you usually lean on others to make decisions for you; could you give some examples?

Step 9: Examine Stroke Balance (This Could Be Skipped)

- **Psychoeducation**: A stroke is a form of recognition or communication between individuals.

Strokes can be positive, like praise, smiles or acts of kindness. They can also be negative, such as criticism or dismissal. Conditional strokes depend on specific situations, like a parent praising a child only for good marks. Strokes significantly impact interpersonal relationships and personal well-being (Chapter 8).

- **Fill-in the Stroking Profile Exercise:** this can be found in section '8.4. Reflective questions' and 'Table 8.1. Stroking profile'. Ask for examples.

Step 10: Optional: Exploring Fundamental Psychological Structures

At this stage, the therapist may have started to form initial impressions of the client; based on this, they may want to explore some initial hypotheses. Not all questions may be relevant for each client.

Mentalisation

- Can you describe a recent interaction in which you felt completely understood and responded positively? What was going through your mind? What do you think made this communication successful? Do you feel you can usually be yourself in your current relationships, or do you often conform to others?
- Can you describe a recent argument or misunderstanding in which you felt not-understood or upset? What was going through your mind? Can you identify what they might have been feeling or thinking? How do you usually react when encountering behaviour you cannot immediately understand?

Splitting

- Can you think of a time when your initial impression of someone's motives turned out to be incorrect; how did you come to understand their intentions?
- Do you often find yourself swinging between idealising and devaluing people in your life; can you give me an example?
- How do you typically feel about someone after they disappoint or upset you; are there times when you struggle to hold onto positive feelings about someone if they have done something to upset you?
- How do you reconcile different emotions or views about a person or situation?
- Do you notice patterns in your relationships where you start by feeling very close and positive about a person but then feel betrayed or let down by them?

- When thinking about people who have been important in your life, how do you integrate the good and the bad aspects of your experiences with them?
- How do you think your way of seeing people as all good or all bad has affected your relationships; are there recent examples where this way of thinking has led to challenges in understanding or relating to others?

Separation-Individuation

- Do you hold back from expressing emotions or thoughts to avoid conflict or keep peace in your relationships? How comfortable do you feel pursuing interests or goals not shared by your close family or friends?
- How do you set boundaries with others; can you give an example of a boundary you've set recently? Have there been times when your boundaries were not respected; how did you handle it?
- How do you typically handle disagreements or conflicts? Is there a pattern in how these situations unfold for you? In moments of conflict, do you find it easy to maintain your viewpoint, or do you often concede to avoid tension?
- When faced with major life decisions, how much do you rely on the input of others compared to your judgement? Can you think of a situation where you struggled to decide because it meant going against the advice or wishes of someone close to you?
- Where do you usually seek validation for your achievements or decisions? Is it more from within yourself or from others? How does it affect you when others do not agree with or support your choices?

Step 11 Summary of the Clinical Phenomenon

- **Summary:** When the systematic explorations do not bring up any new significant problems, the therapist may propose to summarise the problems that the client has reported. As this is accessible language, it may be helpful to start this summary with the core message from their ego states and life positions (I/You're OK/not-OK). Ideally, the client summarises the issues but often finds this difficult. If the therapist does the summary, this should be formulated as close to the original formulations and words of the client, and check with the client whether this is correct and how the summary could be improved. If multiple problems are mentioned, the therapist will ask what the most important problems are. The therapist may consider summarising the problems in TA-terms (e.g. ego-states, life position, games).
- **Optional: evaluation and decision (crystallisation; Chapter 9)**
- **Optional: cognitive exercises (decontamination of Adult; Chapter 9)**

Step 12 (Each Session): Ending

- Homework (e.g. fill-in any questionnaires not filled in yet; possibly let the client keep a daily diary describing the most difficult moments and identify the ego-states in these moments, and the impact this had on their emotions and behaviours; this ego-state diary may be used in next sessions to identify patterns, triggers and core transactional messages)

- Session summary/key-lessons
- Wishes
- Summarise agreements

Case Study 28.1

Tara

Tara expressed her struggles with feeling capable and in control, often leaning on others to make decisions for her. She shared that she feels not-so-OK about herself in many situations and has difficulty practicing self-care regularly, and seems to be mainly receiving/asking negative and conditional strokes but asks for few positive strokes, and gives many unconditional positive strokes to others. She reported a frequently strong Critical Parent ego-state, characterised by harsh self-criticism and perfectionist tendencies; she recognised this as stemming from her upbringing with a highly critical and demanding mother. This internal voice echoing her mother's disapproving remarks seem to lead to feelings of inadequacy and self-doubt. Additionally, Tara expressed a dominant Adapted Child ego-state, manifesting in compliant and self-sacrificing behaviour, stemming from her childhood experiences of feeling responsible for her parent's emotional well-being; this led her to a pattern of neglecting her own needs and prioritising others, resulting in emotional exhaustion and a lack of fulfilment. These ego-states seem to impact her transactions with people. For instance, in her interactions with her manager at work, who she perceives as a Critical Parent, she continuously conforms to perceived expectations, seeking approval and validation, often leading to internal conflict, emotional suppression and self-doubt. Sarah's tendency to prioritise others' needs over her own, influenced by the Adapted Child ego-state, also seems to impact her relationships and interactions, potentially leading to challenges in asserting her boundaries and expressing her authentic self. Tara seems to be frequently playing the 'Please Don't Reject Me' game with her manager; she continuously seeks validation and approval from her manager, adapting herself to conform to perceived expectations to avoid rejection or disapproval. This seems to lead to a cycle of seeking external validation and feeling depressed when she perceives her manager's feedback as critical or disapproving.

SESSIONS 4–5: ASSESSMENT OF AETIOLOGY

Step 1: Emotional Check-in

- Check-in
- Session goals/wishes

Step 2: Bridging Between Sessions

- Memory
- Refresher
- Bridging
- Contract

Step 3: Session Goal

Step 4: Discuss Homework/Questionnaires

Step 5: Examine the Development of the Problems in the Subjective Experience of the Client ('phenomenological analysis')

- When did you, for the first time, become aware of your problems?
- How were the problems in the beginning?
- How did the problems develop?
- How are the problems now?
- Where would you like the problems to go?

Step 6: Life Story in the Client's Own Words

This step does not aim to get a comprehensive life history but is a loose exercise that helps to identify the most influential life event. The therapist may give a maximum number, for example, ten (dependent on how talkative the client is). The client may write each event with a keynote on a Post-it and put the Post-its to develop a sense of coherence in life.

- **Important life events:** Could you identify the most important moments that have shaped who you are today? Think about positive events and difficult situations. For each, please describe what happened, what it meant to you then, and its lasting impact on your life. This does not need to be very detailed as this is just a starting point to discuss your life story, and I am sure we will look at other events and details today and in future sessions.
- **Diversity and social-justice (note that some of the questions may already have been answered):** How would you describe the position or role of your family/community in society when you grew up? Has this changed, and if so, how and what may have caused this? For example, how do you see your culture, gender, sexual orientation, racial/ethnic identity, social class, economic status and family educational levels? How much power did you or your family have in society; what felt threatening in society to you or your family; what could you do to cope with these threats, and what resources did you have; how did you make sense of this and how did this impact you (Johnstone & Boyle, 2018)? How did the social position or role of you and your family impact the life that you have led? What personal experiences do you have of societal injustice, discrimination or unfair treatment in life; could you give some examples, which could be big traumatic experiences, structural problems or small

everyday annoyances or micro-aggressions (if you have many examples, could you describe the most recent and most impactful ones)? To what extent do you feel that you could accept and express who you truly are in your community and society in general that you grew up in? If not, what prevented you from accepting and expressing yourself authentically? Has anything changed in how you accept and express who you are; if so, what has changed, and what has possibly caused these changes? How do you feel that the problems for which you have come in therapy are caused by your position or role in society, or by bad luck in life?

- **Core message:** If you were to summarise the core message you received from these life events and experiences of diversity and social injustice, how would you formulate this (e.g. Don't. . ., Do. . ., It's OK to. . .)? Sometimes this is clear, sometimes not. (Ask follow-up questions to explore and identify the message's core more precisely, e.g. ask, 'What makes this message so difficult/strong/meaningful; what is its essence; could we formulate this message more precisely?')
- **Important decision points**: Can you think of a moment in your life when you made a significant decision that set the course for your future? What was happening around you? What role did your internal 'Parent', 'Adult' or 'Child' play in making that decision?
- **Follow-up questions**: Check any life event questionnaires you may have administered. Ask any follow-up questions about important life events, particularly adverse childhood events, that have not been fully addressed.

Step 7: Systematic Examination of the Client's Life-History

The therapist may use these questions to explore the client's life history, but they may skip questions that the client has already disclosed or may be irrelevant. This section gratefully integrates many (reformulated) questions from Ohlsson (2002), who built their formulations on Berne. Notice that the therapist may not always need to ask the client to formulate the core message, although this sometimes helps to boil down complex information into one sentence.

Introduction to Life (0–6 Years)

- What does your name mean?
- How old are you?
- Tell us what you know about your birth?
- Were there any special medical circumstances around your birth, did you have any disability, or did you have to undergo any surgeries in your early-life?
- How did you experience your welcome into life in terms of love and support from your family and those around them in your first years in life?
- What dreams or expectations do you think your parents had for your future in that period?
- Who are your biological parents?
- Where and with whom did you live as a baby?

- What do you know about the first years? For example, how did your parents/caregivers look well after you? Were there any worries or concerns about you or your parent's life situation? What parenting style did your parents/caregivers have? How did they respond to your needs? For example, did they let you cry for a long time or immediately respond?
- If you were to summarise the core messages you received in the first years of life, how would you formulate this (e.g. Don't..., Do..., It's OK to...)? (Sometimes this is clear, and sometimes not; it is OK if you cannot formulate this. Ask follow-up questions to identify the essence of the message and if needed, formulate a more specific/precise message).

FAMILY DURING CHILDHOOD (0–18 YEARS)

The following questions are about the parents/caregivers. Do not assume that there was a father and mother around; ask about who looked after the client; adjust the names and pronouns, if needed, and ask the following questions about each important parent/caregiver, which can be more or fewer than two.

Parent/caregiver (answer these questions for each of them, e.g. mother, father)

- Describe your parent/caregiver briefly, as they were when you were little.
- What did you like best about them? What is the best memory of them?**
- What did you like the least? What is the worst memory of them?**
- What did they do when they were displeased with you?
- What did they do when they were pleased with you?
- How did they help or make you better or more independent?
- How did they hinder or make you a worse or less independent person?
- Was there any bullying or any form of abuse, – emotional, physical or sexual; did they respect your boundaries and privacy?
- In what way would you have liked them to have been different?**
- What dreams, hopes or expectations did they have about you?
- If you were to summarise the core message they have given you in life, how would you formulate this (e.g. Don't..., Do..., It's OK to...)? (Ask follow-up questions to identify the essence of the message and if needed, formulate a more specific/precise message).

Siblings (answer these questions for each of them)

- Did you have siblings or other children you grew up with together?
- What are their names, and what was your age difference?
- How would you describe your relationship with them?
- What did you like in your relationship with them?
- What did you not like in your relationship with them?
- Did you feel equally treated?

- Was there any bullying or any form of abuse, – emotional, physical or sexual? Did they respect your boundaries and privacy?
- What were your social roles or positions in your family (e.g. being the joker, the helper, the silent one, etc.)?
- If you were to summarise the core message they have given you in life, how would you formulate this (e.g. Don't. . ., Do. . ., It's OK to. . .)? (Ask follow-up questions to identify the essence of the message and if needed, formulate a more specific/precise message).

Grandparents (answer these questions for each of them)

- What kind of a life did your grandparents live?
- How important were your grandparents for you? If they were important, how would you describe your relationship?
- How did they influence your development? What expectations and dreams did your grandparents have about your future when you were little?
- If you were to summarise the core message they have given you in life, how would you formulate this (e.g. Don't. . ., Do. . ., It's OK to. . .)? (Ask follow-up questions to identify the essence of the message and if needed, formulate a more specific/precise message).

Extended family (only discuss if significantly crucial to the client's development)

- Are there other relatives who have been particularly important to you and your development? What is their name and familial relationship to you (e.g. uncle, aunt, cousin)?
- How did they influence your development? What expectations and dreams did they have about your future when you were little?
- What were your social roles or positions in your extended family (e.g. being the joker, the helper, the silent one, etc.)?
- Were there any family secrets or topics nobody dared to discuss that influenced everyone? Have there been any big traumatic life experiences in previous generations?
- If you were to summarise the core message that your extended family has given you in life, how would you formulate this (e.g. Don't. . ., Do. . ., It's OK to. . .)? (Ask follow-up questions to identify the essence of the message and if needed, formulate a more specific/precise message).

Other important adults (only discuss if significantly crucial to the client's development)

- Are there other important adults who have been particularly important to you and your development? What is their name and relationship to you (e.g. teacher, family friend)?
- How did they influence your development, such as becoming a better or worse person? What expectations and dreams did they have about your future when you were little?

- If you were to summarise the core message they have given you in life, how would you formulate this (e.g. Don't..., Do..., It's OK to...)? (Ask follow-up questions to identify the essence of the message and if needed, formulate a more specific/precise message).

OPTIONAL: FUNDAMENTAL PSYCHOLOGICAL STRUCTURES (1–12 YEARS)

(The therapist may NOT need to ask all these questions, as they focus on fundamental psychological structures that the therapist may already have a good idea about.)

Individuation-Separation and Attachment

- To what extent did you feel seen and loved by your family?
- How did you react to separations from your parents or primary caregivers as a child, like during school drop-offs or stays with relatives?
- At which moments in your early-life did you feel as if you were doing the tasks of an adult? (An adult task could be as practical and mundane as helping in the household, but this could also be about giving emotional support to your parents or trying to solve problems in a relationship.) How did the real adults respond to you doing this adult task even though you were not an adult yet? How did it feel to act like an adult? Did you feel you were allowed to be a child?

Affect-Regulation

- Can you describe your earliest memories of being soothed or comforted when you were upset as a child? How were you usually comforted in times of distress, and what impact do you think this has had on you?
- Can you remember your earliest memories, or stories that others may have told you, about when you started to explore the world around you, such as crawling or walking around? How did your parent/caregivers react to you exploring the world, for example, when you were upset or excited; did they see you, soothe or compliment you, or ignore you? Did you explore a lot, or were you more shy staying close to your caregivers or adults? (These questions may help identify attachment, separation-individuation and the development of early affect regulation skills.)
- In your family, how were conflicts or differences of opinion handled? Was there space for complexity in feelings and opinions?
- Looking back, how were emotions expressed in your family? Was there space for all emotions, or were some emotions discouraged? (Happiness, sadness, anger, shame and anxiety are key emotions.)
- How were you taught to handle anger, sadness, shame, or fear during childhood?
- Can you think of a time in your early-life when you felt overwhelmed by your emotions? What did you do to cope with that feeling?

- Can you share a time when you felt your opinions or interests significantly differed from those of your family; how was this received? How comfortable do you feel pursuing interests or goals not shared by your close family or friends?
- Can you share an experience when you needed support during childhood; how was it handled?
- Were there particular strategies you used as a child to manage difficult feelings? What coping strategies have you developed over time for managing intense emotions? Do you consider these helpful or unhelpful? Can you identify any emotional response patterns you would like to change? What steps have you taken, if any, towards this change? What goals do you have for enhancing your emotional regulation skills? Are there specific areas you wish to improve? How comfortable do you feel experiencing a wide range of emotions, and what support do you need to navigate them better?

How do you see your early experiences influencing your current ways of regulating emotions?

Splitting/Integration

- Can you recall any specific instances from your childhood where you felt a strong sense of being either good or bad? How did those perceptions change over time, if at all?
- Can you recall any instances from your childhood where you felt someone was completely good or bad, or can you describe a situation where you felt torn between seeing someone as good or bad? How did those perceptions change over time, if at all?
- Have you noticed any patterns in your relationships with others where you tend to see them as good or bad; how does this impact your interactions with them?
- Have you ever felt that others were projecting negative or positive traits onto you? How did this make you feel, and how did you respond to it?
- Do you find yourself projecting certain traits or emotions onto others that you may have difficulty acknowledging within yourself? Can you provide examples of when this has occurred?
- Can you identify recurring themes or patterns in your relationships that may be influenced by your early experiences and internalised beliefs about yourself/others?

SCHOOL EXPERIENCES DURING CHILDHOOD (APPROX. 4–18 YEARS)

- When did you begin school?
- How was your learning experience at school? For example, did you get good marks or was learning difficult? How did your achievements make you feel about yourself? How did your parents and other adults respond to your intellectual achievements?
- How were your relationships with other children during childhood? For example, what social position or role did you have in your class and groups of friends?

How were your relationships with other children and friends? Do you have experience being bullied or bullying, or any form of abuse, emotional, physical or sexual? What did you do to make friends or to feel accepted by others? How did your peers or friends make you feel about yourself?

- Suppose you were to summarise the core message that your school experiences during early childhood (both regarding achievements and social relationships) have given you in life. How would you formulate this (e.g. Don't. . ., Do. . ., It's OK to. . .)?
- When do you think that you started puberty? How was it to become a teenager? Did this change anything in your relationships with your parents and siblings, and if so, how?
- If you were to summarise the core messages that your teenage years have given you, how would you formulate this (e.g. Don't. . ., Do. . ., It's OK to. . .)?

CULTURAL AND SPIRITUAL BACKGROUND DURING CHILDHOOD AND TEENAGE YEARS

- Reflecting on your childhood and teenage years, can you identify moments when you felt most authentically yourself? What about times when you thought you had to behave differently from how you felt inside? To what extent have you continued these patterns of being yourself or adjusting to others? How independent have you become since then?
- When you were a child or teenager, who was your hero? What made them heroes in your eyes? What fairy tale, story, movie, imagination or game did you like best as a child? Tell me about the story. What is it that appeals to you in the story?** If you were to summarise the core message they have given you in life, how would you formulate this (e.g. Don't. . ., Do. . ., It's OK to. . .)?
- How would you briefly summarise your family's religion, spirituality or political opinions? Did your family attend religious or ideological meetings, such as churches, mosques or political groups? Were you allowed to have your own beliefs and opinions? If you were to summarise the core message they have given you in life, how would you formulate this (e.g. Don't. . ., Do. . ., It's OK to. . .)? What have you kept from your family's religion, spirituality or politics as an adult?

REFLECTING ON LIFE'S JOURNEY

- Could you briefly describe the highlights or best moments in your life?
- What have been the most challenging situations or periods in your life?
- Who have been your most important friends and family members? What did they mean to you, and how did they influence you? If you were to summarise the core messages they have given you in life, how would you formulate this (e.g. Don't. . ., Do. . ., It's OK to. . .)?

- Can you describe any recurring patterns in your relationships since adolescence? (Analyse possible transactional patterns and games).
- Can you think of any moments since adolescence when you reacted strongly to a situation and, in hindsight, felt your reaction was out of proportion? (Analyse ego-states and the possible preceding transactions or game).
- Briefly describe any unfair or unjust situations or periods in your life. How did others around you respond to this injustice? How did you respond? Do you feel that over the years, this injustice has stopped or that justice has been done? How do you feel now about this injustice? If you were to summarise the core message these situations have given you, how would you formulate this (e.g. Don't..., Do..., It's OK to...)?
- What would the title and subtitle be if someone would make a movie of your childhood and teenage years? What genre would this movie be (e.g. comedy, tragedy, thriller, drama)? What would be the climax of this movie? The same for your twenties and thirties? The same for your later life?**
- Think about the four most important groups you have been a member of, such as an extended family, groups of friends or colleagues. What makes them so important to you (e.g. something they do or give to you, or something you do or give to them)? How would you describe your usual social position or role in these groups (e.g. being a joker, leader, follower, a silent one, etc.)? Is your position or role different in different groups? Have your positions and roles changed over time? How autonomous and free do you usually feel in social situations? How much do you feel other people usually try to control you or make you submit? What would this be if you would change something in your usual role or position in groups? What has stopped you from making this change?
- We are now at the end of exploring your life story. Are there any other life events or experiences that have influenced the person you have become that I should know about?

Step 8: Examine Transactional Core Messages
Step 8A: Follow-up Questions

The therapist checks whether they have enough information about the following or whether they need to ask any additional questions:

- Childhood context
  - Genetics/temperament
  - Life events/socioeconomic context
  - Sources of early-life messages
- Fundamental psychological structures
  - Ego-boundaries and separation/individuation
  - Splitting and integration
  - Mentalisation
  - Example: coping and affect regulation mechanisms
  - Example: discounting of existential givens
  - Example: attachment

Step 8B: Systematic Analysis of Injunctions/ Counter-Injunctions/Drivers

The previous questions identified many core messages from childhood. The following questions help to synthesise and prioritise amongst the many messages.

- **Most important messages:** I have asked you what messages you received several times during your life story. What messages have influenced you the most to become the person you have become today?
- **Explicit reflection:** Show Tables 4.1. and 4.2 to the client, and ask: What were the most important injunctions (don't be/exist, be you, be a child, grow-up, make-it/success, do anything), permissions (it's OK to be, to be you, to be child, grow-up, make-it/succeed, two yesses for every no), drivers (be perfect, please others, be strong, try hard, hurry-up) and allowers (you are good enough as you are, please yourself, be open and express your wants, do it, take your time)) you learnt early on?

Step 8C: Connect Early-Life Messages with the Present (if Not Already Discussed)

- Which life messages (injunctions, permissions, drivers and allowers) are not present in your life today? Could you give an example? How did this change? What decision did you make about this?
- What life messages (injunctions, permissions, drivers and allowers) remain today? Could you give an example? Were you ever at a crossroads where you could change this? Did you ever decide to continue this, and if so, could you tell me more about it? (NB: Ensure you speak about this compassionately, non-blamingly).
- How do your current problems -the reason that you came to therapy possibly-relate to these messages you learnt in early-life?

Step 9: Summary of Aetiology

- **Summary:** When the systematic explorations do not bring up any new significant aetiological topics, the therapist may propose to summarise the problems that the client has reported. As this is accessible language, it may be helpful to start this summary with the core messages from their ego-states and life positions (I/You're OK/ not-OK). Ideally, the client summarises the issues but often finds this difficult. If the therapist does the summary, this should be formulated as close to the original formulations and words of the client, and check with the client whether this is correct and how the summary could be improved. If many transactional core messages are mentioned, the therapist will ask about the most important ones. The therapist may consider summarising the aetiology in TA-terms, and connect this with previously explained terms such as ego-states, life position and games.
- Optional: evaluation and decision (crystallisation; Chapter 9)
- Optional: cognitive exercises (decontamination of Adult; Chapter 9)

Step 10: Ending

- Homework (e.g. fill-in any questionnaires that have not been filled in yet; consider letting a motivated client keep any of the diaries in the Appendix, such as the Voices and Messages Diary)
- Evaluation (e.g. key lessons)
- Wishes
- Summarise agreements

Case Study 28.2

Tara

Tara described several life events, such as the death of her father when she was fourteen and leaving her alone with her mother (she has no siblings). Consequently, her mother became an even more enormous influence on her life. Tara feels as if her mother is trying to let her step in her father's shoes, but whatever Tara does is not good enough in her mother's eyes. Her mother gave her several core messages: 'Don't be you', 'Don't be a child', 'Be Perfect', 'Be Strong' and 'Try hard'. As a child and teenager, her relationships were usually about helping and looking after others, trying to get their validation, although she often felt unseen. There was an adult family friend who gave her an initial feeling of being seen for who she was, but one day, when drunk, he touched her breasts as a young teenager; this experience reinforced her belief that other people are not-OK and cannot be trusted and that her opinion does not matter.

SESSION 7: SHARING CASE FORMULATION AND DEVELOPING A TREATMENT PLAN

Session Aims

- Before this session, the therapist develops a case formulation with the help of the Systematic TA Case Formulation Form in the Appendix (explained in Chapter 8). The therapist may wish to consult a supervisor or colleague for input/feedback. Some clients want to receive a paper copy of the case formulation.
- The therapist shares the case formulation with the client, tailored to their language and level of understanding.
- Based on the case formulation, the therapist and client decide the goals and methods of the next sessions (therapy contract).

Step 1: Emotional Check-in

- Check-in
- Session goals/wishes

Step 2: Bridging Between Sessions
- Memory
- Refresher
- Bridging
- Contract

Step 3: Session Goal

Step 4: Discuss Homework/Questionnaires

Step 5: Share Case Formulation
- The therapist shares the case formulation with the client. This may overlap with the summaries in previous sessions; repetition may help the deeper processing of information.
- This should be formulated as hypotheses and not as absolute truths. The therapist will ask whether the summary is correct and how the summary could be improved.
- The therapist focuses on the most important aspects, if the case formulation is complex.
- This could include empathic recognition and compassion for their journey (nourishing the Nurturing Parent; e.g. 'Given your life story, it is understandable that you struggle'), validation of strengths (nourishing the integrating Adult) and confrontation/contamination ('These are the parts where you may improve').
- The therapist may share a reflection on the transaction/transference how this could be related to the life script, and how this could be managed in the next stage of the treatment.

Step 5: Agreement on Treatment Contract
Following the treatment goals discussed in the previous session and from the case formulation, the therapist and the client agree on a specific plan for next sessions. They will re-evaluate this plan at the start and/or the end of the following sessions to ensure they still follow their agreed plan or determine whether they would like to adjust it. The more specific the plan is, the easier the subsequent sessions will go.

Step 6: Summary
- Optional: evaluation and decision (crystallisation; Chapter 9)
- Optional: cognitive exercises (decontamination of Adult; Chapter 9)

Step 7: Ending
- Homework (e.g. diaries to record ego-states, life positions or transactional messages that may arise in difficult situations; record the situation details/trigger and impact on behaviours and emotions)
- Session summary
- Wishes
- Summarise agreements

When to Move to the Next Stage?

The client is ready to advance to the next stage when their problems have been systematically examined and possible causes assessed, leading to a jointly developed and agreed-upon systematic case formulation and therapy plan. Not all problems may be identified at this stage; perfectionism is discouraged, and the focus is on prioritising the most significant issues for the next stage. The transition to the next phase may also include discussions on the dynamics of perfectionism within the therapy process, such as resistance, impasse, transference or projective identification.

Case Study 28.3

Tara

This was a very emotional session for Tara, in which she cried a lot, as she started to see the connections between these early-life experiences and the internalisation of these transactional core messages that impact her current mental health, ego-states and transactions. Tara said that she had never really grieved over the loss of her father and that she has never acknowledged the injustices that happened to her during her teenage years; she says that she feels seen and acknowledged by the therapist.

29

EXPERIENTIAL PROCESSING IN THE HERE-AND-NOW (SESSIONS 8–12)

AIMS OF STAGE

In session 7, the therapist and client have agreed on a unique treatment plan for the unique client. Within the next five sessions, the therapist will aim to achieve the client's goal by using their therapeutic competencies, particularly their experiential competencies (Chapter 11) and integrative-therapeutic competencies (Chapter 12). This will mainly focus on the experiential processing, deepening and expressing of their life experiences and life script messages and their impact on their everyday functioning, such as the problems that brought them to TA therapy. This may include additional assessments of the clinical phenomenon or aetiology (Chapters 4–5). From session seven onwards, there is less structure and more freedom as these sessions are tailored to the unique situation and the unique needs of the client. This is where the therapist and client must become creative and tailor the treatment, as Carl Jung said: 'develop a unique therapy for each unique client'.

SESSIONS 8–12

Step 1: Emotional Check-in

- Check-in
- Session goals/wishes

Step 2: Bridging Between Sessions

- Memory
- Refresher
- Bridging
- Contract

Step 3: Discuss Homework

Step 4: Session Goal

The client and therapist decide the session's goal and method, considering the client's therapy goals. The therapist should already have some possible topics/interventions in mind that they could work on based on the case formulation.

Step 4: Work With the Chosen Method to Achieve the Session Goal

Step 5: Summary

- Optional session summary/key-lessons
- Optional evaluation and decision (crystallisation; Chapter 9)
- Optional cognitive exercises (decontamination of Adult; Chapter 9)

Step 6: Ending

- Homework (e.g. following Chapters 11–12)
- Wishes for next session
- Summarise agreements

Case Study 29.1

Tara

Session 7–10 focused on grieving the loss of her father. This included talking about her father, mindfulness and experiential exercises. Tara was also asked to write a letter to her father, which she brought to her father's grave to burn there as a ritual. Sessions 11–12 focused on expressing her anger towards her mother. Writing a letter to her mother (which she never sent but burned in a favourite picnic spot as a child) helped her accept and deepen her feelings and become more self-compassionate. The therapist did several self-compassion exercises, such as writing positive self-affirmations.

30

MAKING DECISIONS AND CHANGES IN DAILY LIFE (SESSIONS 13–16)

AIMS OF STAGE

- Decide new goals in life (script-redecision)
- Create conditions and inner safety for structural change in life (facilitating script-change)
- Experimenting and evaluating change in the session and trying it in daily life (see Chapter 12 on experiments)
- Identify and overcome impasses and resistance (Chapter 9)

SESSION 13: SETTING NEW LIFE GOALS AND MAKING PLANS

Step 1: Emotional Check-In

- Check-in
- Session goals/wishes

Step 2: Bridging Between Sessions

- Memory
- Refresher
- Bridging
- Contract

Step 3: Discuss Homework

Step 4: Session Goal

Step 5: Identify Experiential Learning and Impasses

- *Evaluation of lessons learnt:*
  The therapist invites the client to review the last stage and summarise what they have learnt. For example, the client could be asked to mention the three

important lessons. To stimulate experiential acceptance and autonomy, the client is stimulated to formulate this in personal and experiential terms: 'I feel that...' The therapist can use this evaluation for complimenting (positive strokes and self-stroking by the client) and developing a sense of self-efficacy.

- *Evaluation of needs and wishes*:
  Based on the evaluation of the lessons learnt, the therapist invites the client to express their deeper wishes and needs in life, which have not (not completely or not always) been fulfilled in life (yet).

- *Evaluation of lessons not learnt*:
  The therapist and the client may want to examine which lessons have not been learnt in the last sessions, for example, by comparing the therapy progress with the treatment aims and plan made in the assessment stage. What keeps the client from moving under challenging areas (impasse)? What does the client fear? What would happen if the client did not have this problem/symptom? How could this impasse relate to the client's history (TA-models may help to explain this)?

- *Checking the application of lessons in daily life*:

  The therapist may ask the client to visualise a scene (real or imagined) where the client experiences his symptom and then verbalise his implicit learning statement. It is helpful to use heighteners to increase the level of emotional arousal. Following this, the therapist creates a juxtaposition experience by asking the client to bring to mind the experiences that contradict the original implicit learning. Then, the therapist asks the client what it is like for him to have both sets of knowledge simultaneously.***

- *Identify and overcome impasses and resistance (Chapter 9)*

Step 6: Identify New Goals in Life ('Redecision')

Based on the previous step and in line with their general therapy goals, the client identifies the next goals they want to learn. The client can be recommended to formulate three to five goals fulfilling the following criteria:

- important
- specific and simple
- not too far in the future
- challenging
- attainable
- mutually conducive (in the case of multiple goals)
- focused towards something positive

Step 7: Reflection on the Conditions for Structural Change and Creating a Plan of Action

- *Reflection on required conditions*
  The therapist invites the client to reflect on what is needed to achieve the new goals in life. This could be practical issues (e.g. increasing assertiveness) or more emotional (e.g. improving self-esteem or grieving about the past).
- *Creating a plan of action to create the required conditions*
  Based on the reflection on the required conditions, the client and therapist make a plan of action. This plan will most likely start with doing (imaginary) experiments within the therapy session (see next step) before the clients try experimenting with a change in daily life.

Step 8: Creating the Conditions for Structural Change in Therapy ('Facilitating Script-Change')

The therapist may consider conducting experiments in the safe setting of the therapy session before the client experiments in their daily life, such as (Chapters 11–12):

- *Experiments in imagination ('in-vitro')*
  The client could be asked to imagine a situation where they would try new behaviours, thoughts or feelings. Research shows that imaginary 'in-vitro' experiments increase clients' likelihood of experimenting in daily life, 'in-vivo'. The in-vitro experiment can identify any challenges that may emerge, including negative self-talk. Cognitive challenging – for example, the therapist playing the devil's advocate – could help the client develop effective coping strategies to deal with any challenges they may face when they try changes in daily life outside of the therapy setting.
- *Experiments in the therapeutic relationship*
  The therapeutic relationship could be used for experiments, such as analysing relational issues (e.g. transference, countertransference, projective identification).
- *Experiments with ideas about the past in imagination ('in-vitro')*
  The client could do imaginary experiments with life-defining moments in their past. For example, they re-enact a scene from the past, or they could be interviewed by the therapist while in their parent's role. This could help the client to develop deeper insight into how their past still influences them in daily life, to break experiential avoidance about the past or to imagine alternative, more positive endings to negative life events. This could give them a sense of self-efficacy and freedom and undermine feelings of hopelessness and determinism by their life script (e.g. 'if I can to some extent feel free towards the past, I could also be free towards the present'). The client could also take time to grieve over lost opportunities in the past, develop a symbolic

ritual about the past or write a letter to people from their past (which could or could not be sent in reality).

- *Experiments with overcoming the Drama Triangle*
Client may explore and experiment their role as victim, rescuer or prosecutor, or may have biased, Black-or-white ideas about influential figures in their past (Chapter 8).

- *Experiments with functional fluency in the session*
Functional fluency is the ability to change between emotions or ego-states (Temple, 2002). This also includes the use of different coping styles in different situations; research shows that there is not one best coping style that fits each situation, but it is the flexibility of coping styles that matters; coping flexibility is significantly impaired in individuals with depression, and helping clients to become more flexible in their coping could improve their symptoms (Kato, 2015). Learning to switch is an important aspect of effective psychotherapy (Vos, 2014). The therapist could develop experiments to help the client shift from one emotion/ego-state/coping-style to another. It could be helpful to use the terminology of the TA models. For example, the therapist could mention a range of (imaginary) emotionally challenging situations, and the therapist asks the client to respond to each situation first as Child, then as Parent and finally as Adult.

- *Experiments with being in the present moment*
The therapist could stimulate the client to be in the present moment of the therapy. This could be as simple as asking the client whether they experience that they are in the present moment and what has caused them being or not-being in the present. The therapist could also give feedback when the client is not in the present (e.g. 'I can see you are now not in the present moment'). The therapist could do skills exercises to help the client be in the present moment, such as focusing or mindfulness exercises.

Step 9: Summary

The client is asked to summarise and evaluate the experiments in the session. The therapist should stress positive aspects (e.g. 'You may say that you feel you have failed in this experiment, but I see that you have taken a huge step by trying to do this experiment. Trying this out is already a positive first step. Anything new takes time to learn. We will continue this in next sessions'.). Challenges could be analysed to identify learning points for next sessions.

Step 10: Creation of Safety

Clients can feel anxious/resistant about change. Therefore, it can be helpful for the therapist to follow the summary with therapeutic interventions to create a sense of inner safety.

Step 11: Homework

Homework is important role in this therapy stage, and should logically follow from the treatment goals/plan and experiments in the session. The homework needs to be provided in the following ways*:

- Clear rationale and relationship with treatment goals and methods.
- Specific terms (when? where? with whom? what?) and preferably steps (step 1, step 2,...).
- Clear, attainable and challenging goals
- Describe in terms of an 'experiment'; even if the client feels that they 'fail' the experiment is still successful (reframe failure as having learnt what does not work).
- Write down to take home
- Use terms that work for the client, as the word 'homework' may have unhelpful associations, such as 'applying at home what we have explored in the therapy session', 'playing with this in your daily life' and 'experimenting'.

Step 12: Ending

- Session evaluation/key-lessons
- Wishes
- Summarise agreements

Case Study 30.1

Tara

Session 13 focused on analysing the transactions and games that Tara repeatedly plays, particularly with her manager. Her new insight into her life script and increased self-compassion helped her change her part in the game process and gradually built her self-confidence at work. The following sessions focused on developing her insight and exploring and trying out alternative responses.

SESSIONS 14–15: APPLICATION IN DAILY LIFE
Step 1: Emotional Check-In

- Check-in
- Session goals/wishes

Step 2: Bridging Between Sessions

- Memory
- Refresher
- Bridging
- Contract

Step 3: Discuss Homework

The therapist asks about the client's experience with the homework. The therapist should empathically and positively reframe reported challenges, failures, resistance and mis-understandings, such as having learnt what does not work or design/instruct homework better.

Step 4: Identify New Goal

The therapist invites the client to identify any next steps or learning goals that they may want to focus on in this session based on the homework experience and the new life goals identified in the first session of the application/script-change stage. The therapist and client may want to re-assess the progress regarding the overall treatment goals and plan.

Step 5: Experimenting Within the Session

There may be some experiments within the therapy session (see session 13), but in the later sessions, the focus should be on the client doing experiments and creating structural change in daily life. The experiment's aim within the session is to prepare the client to conduct experiments in daily life.

Step 6: Creation of Safety (See Session 13)

Step 7: Homework: Experimenting in Daily Life

The following are examples of many possible types of homework a therapist may give the client, as session 13 explained:

- Experiments with ideas about the past in real life
- Experiments with functional fluency in daily life
- Personal experiments in daily life
- Interpersonal experiments in daily life

Step 8: Ending

- Session evaluation/key-lessons
- Wishes
- Summarise agreements

When to Move to the Next Stage?

A client can progress to the next stage when they have established new life goals, created conditions for structural change through inner nurturing and improved Adult functioning and actively experimented with and evaluated these changes in their daily life, with significant achievement of the treatment goals set during the assessment stage. This transition may also be prompted by reaching the maximum number of sessions, highlighting that therapy is an ongoing process rather than a quest for perfection, emphasising defining what is 'good enough'. In cases of perceived perfectionism within the therapeutic relationship, the therapist may address and explore these dynamics through discussions of transference;

therapists may want to reflect on their therapeutic relationship, countertransference and perfectionism.

Case Study 30.2

Tara

The therapist helped Tare brainstorm more helpful alternative responses to triggering situations, which they practised in role plays. Tara started experimenting with tiny changes in daily life, such as successfully saying no to her manager and not automatically doing overwork when that was not needed. She also dedicated more time to her friends and joined a volleyball club.

SESSION 16: ENDING

Aims of Session

1 evaluating and taking stock of lessons learnt
2 identifying how the clients could continue their changes and developing contingency plans
3 saying goodbye and coping with feelings of termination

Step 1: Emotional Check-In

- Check-in
- Session goals/wishes

Step 2: Bridging Between Sessions

- Memory
- Refresher
- Bridging
- Contract

Step 3: Discuss Homework

Step 4: Identify Learning and Re-assess Therapy Goals

- *Evaluation of lessons learnt:*
  The therapist invites the client to review all sessions and summarise what they have learnt. For example, the client could be asked to mention the three most important lessons. To stimulate experiential acceptance and autonomy, the client is stimulated to formulate this in personal and experiential terms: 'I feel that…' The therapist can use this evaluation for complimenting (positive strokes and self-stroking by the client) and developing a sense of self-efficacy.

- *Evaluation of therapy goals*
  The therapist and the client may want to compare the progress with the treatment aims and plan made in the assessment stage. The focus of this evaluation lies in the positive achievements. Most likely, there will be aims that have not been achieved; this should be reframed positively (e.g. 'you have learnt many skills during TA so that you can further develop yourself now on your own with these skills') or expectations about the treatment could be cognitively challenged (e.g. 'how realistic is it to be expecting to achieve all aims in brief therapy?'; 'what would you say to a friend who would have achieved what you have achieved?')

Step 5: Develop Contingency Plans

- *Identify aims and plans for self-improvement*
  The therapist may invite the client to identify aims and plans they may want to develop further. Like providing homework, it is important to make these aims and plans specific, particularly for short term goals.
- *Contingency plans*
  The therapist may invite the client to identify what they would do if they encounter difficult situations in future (Who? What? Where? When? How?). The therapist could offer some imaginary experiments with difficult situations.

Step 6: Explore Feelings of Ending

- *Identify feelings about therapy ending*
  The therapist asks the client to express how they feel about ending therapy. The therapist empathically engages with the client and may ask the client to use any of the lessons learnt to cope with these feelings of ending. The therapist may mirror the client by sharing some feelings about ending.
- *Identify feelings about ending relationships and life in general*
  The therapist pays attention to emotions, wishes and fears about dependency and autonomy, memories of previous relational endings and losses, and coping with one's death/mortality. The client may need time to express grief. The therapist may stimulate a dual attitude: acknowledge the fundamental reality of finitude in life while stressing that despite this finitude, people can live a meaningful and satisfying life; our finite period could even make our experiences and relationships more intense and meaningful*. The focus of this exploration is to help the client look towards the future with a sense of hope, freedom and opportunities instead of being stuck grieving over the loss of the past or the finitude of life.

Step 7: Creation of Safety

Step 8: Evaluation and Saying Goodbye

During the last 15 minutes, the therapist may invite the client to say/ask anything. Most likely, the client will be thanking the therapist; the therapist needs to acknowledge the client's gratitude while stressing that the client has done all the work (e.g. via a Bull's Eye Transaction).

Case Study 30.3

Tara

Already since session 10, Tara's mood and energy levels started increasing. By session 16, she seemed happier and content with herself and life. She had treated herself with a new haircut and new clothes that she liked; this seemed to show her strengthened inner Free Child. In session 16, Tara looked back on her therapy journey. The therapist validated the inner work and resilience. The TAGAF form showed that Tara had achieved her therapy goals largely or entirely. They agreed on a practical plan if Tara would experience a relapse, which she wrote down as an agreement with herself. Ending the therapy triggered memories about the loss of her father. Still, Tara said that she feels 'strong and OK now' thanks to the grieving work they had done together; to help her overcome her projection and foster psychological integration, the therapist highlighted how despite a loss, our love or appreciation for the person can remain, as well as the memories. The therapist said Tara could always contact them for follow-up, refresher or additional sessions.

APPENDICES

Instruction:

Write down any specific goals you may want to achieve in psychotherapy. Try to be as specific as possible, and ensure these goals are achievable. You do NOT need to formulate each goal. If you cannot think of a goal, do NOT create artificial or inauthentic goals. During the final session, we will ask you to mark the extent to which you have achieved each goal.

Emotional goal

Example:	I want to feel less sad, sleep better, feel less anxious and better cope with stressful situations.
Write one or more goals at the start of therapy:	-- -- -- --
Rate when evaluating progress or outcomes:	1 2 3 4 5 6 7 (1. Goal not at all achieved – 7. Goal completely achieved)

Goals about my self-beliefs

Example:	I would like to feel more 'OK' about myself, for example, by developing more self-esteem, accepting my identity who I really am, being more independent from others, loving myself more, being more compassionate with myself, understanding my motivations better, being able to plan activities and goals in life and to achieve these.
Write one or more goals at the start of therapy:	-- -- -- --
Rate when evaluating progress or outcomes:	1 2 3 4 5 6 7 (1. Goal not at all achieved – 7. Goal completely achieved)

Social goal

Example:	I would like to feel more 'OK' with others by developing more friendships, trusting others more, having more intimate relationships, being more authentic in my relationships with others and knowing how to deal with difficult people. This may include learning to be more myself, expressing myself in relationships and coping with discrimination or unjust societal situations.
Write one or more goals at the start of therapy:	-- -- -- --

(Continued)

Rate when evaluating progress or outcomes: 1 2 3 4 5 6 7 (1. Goal not at all achieved – 7. Goal completely achieved)

Living in the present

Example:

I would like to live more in the here-and-now, understand better how I have become the person I am now, understand how my experiences earlier in life influence my current thoughts feelings and behaviour, be more authentic, become more honest with myself, feel more in control in how I respond to situations and people, feel more like an Adult in how I live my life, feel less pressure from my inner Critical Parent, develop self-care by my inner Nurturing Parent, give more attention to my inner Free Child, act less often like a Rebellious Child, less automatically conform to the expectations from others like an Adapted Child.

Write one or more goals at the start of therapy:

Rate when evaluating progress or outcomes: 1 2 3 4 5 6 7 (1. Goal not at all achieved – 7. Goal completely achieved)

Life goal

Example:

I would like to be able to feel more energy and flow in my life, find out what I find meaningful in life, learn how to achieve goals in life, be more spontaneous, experience the freedom to make my own independent decisions in life, live a meaningful and satisfying life despite life's challenges and limitations.

Write one or more goals at the start of therapy:

Rate when evaluating progress or outcomes: 1 2 3 4 5 6 7 (1. Goal not at all achieved – 7. Goal completely achieved)

Any other goal

Example:

Here, you can write any other goals.

Write one or more goals at the start of therapy:

Rate when evaluating progress or outcomes: 1 2 3 4 5 6 7 (1. Goal not at all achieved – 7. Goal completely achieved)

Source: Adapted from Vos & van Rijn (2024a).

Table A.2 Systematic TA Case Formulation Form

Component name	Include at least the following	Tips and tricks
i Field-specific case formulation	Client name, pronoun A Formulation of DSM/ICD-diagnosis B Physical diagnosis if relevant C Impact of symptoms on daily life	Use questionnaires (PHQ-9/GAD-7/PCL-5) as a hypothesis; confirm this in conversation. Check relevant disorder-specific chapter in Part IV.
ii Phenomenological description of concerns.		Summary of the problem in the client's words.
iii Description of clinical TA model (Chapter 4)	1 Ego-state structure and functioning: Critical Parent, Nurturing Parent, Adult, Adapted Child and Free Child 2 Life position 'You're OK/not-OK' and social functioning 3 Life position 'I'm OK/not-OK' and self-efficacy	Describe the client's symptoms/concerns in TA-terms. Justify the clinical model with examples; if no clear evidence, write this is a hypothesis. Facilitate this by using standardised interviews/questionnaires. This description might include other aspects (not required) (Chapter 8): • Transactions • Games • Script-systems • Stroking • Time-structure
iv Description of aetiology (Chapter 5)	Childhood context • Genetics and temperament • life events and socioeconomic context • Sources of early-life messages Fundamental psychological structures • Ego-boundaries and separation/individuation • Splitting and integration • Mentalisation • Example: coping and affect regulation • Example: discounting of existential givens • Example: attachment Transactional core messages • Injunctions • Drivers and counterinjunctions • Permissions • Allowances • Payoffs • Programs • Other early-life messages Responses and decisions	How has the client developed the clinical concerns in life? This includes a description of the history of the main clinical problem, the duration of the concerns, specific situations in which the concerns are experienced as more present or less present and whether anything has helped the client to deal with these concerns in the past. Explores the general development of the current problems in TA themes in the client's life. Consider using standard interview schedule and questionnaires.

(Continued)

Table A.2 Systematic TA Case Formulation Form *(Continued)*

Component name	Include at least the following	Tips and tricks
	• In the past • In the present • What has the client tried; what worked, and what did not work Self-perpetuating mechanisms and feedback loops	
v Treatment indicators (Chapter 6)	Reflect whether TA is indicated/ contra-indicated.	Consider the following points (not required to describe each point): • willing/able to change • willing/able face emotional pain • not merely a passive recipient of help • contain feelings • basic Adult ego-state functioning (e.g. no active psychosis, psychoactive substances or severe cognitive disabilities), • motivated, committed • positive expectations • realistic expectations • sufficiently secure attachment to trust and confide in their therapist • sufficient daily-life psychological and social support to create change • attend all sessions • Other eligibility criteria from institution/service • No urgent socioeconomic or physical concerns that need to be addressed before starting • Other arguments pro and contra TA
vi Treatment aims (Chapter 6)	Formulate therapy goals/aims: 1 Formulated by the client (copy TA Goal Attainment Form TAGAF) 2 Formulated in clinical-diagnostic terms of psychopathology (e.g. reduce symptoms of depression) 3 Formulated in TA-terms	Examples of goals in TA-terms (Chapter 6): • Improve ego-states • Improve life positions, social functioning, self-efficacy • Gain insight in life script and its influence on present issues • Improve self-realization, general well-being and quality-of-life • Improve behaviour (e.g. insight and improved transactions, games, script-systems, time structure, stroking, intimacy)

Table A.2 Systematic TA Case Formulation Form *(Continued)*

Component name	Include at least the following	Tips and tricks
vii Therapeutic mechanisms (Chapter 7)	A Therapeutic mechanisms in TA-terms: • Analysis and change of dominant ego-states • Improving life position 'You're OK' and social functioning • Improving life position 'I'm OK' and self-efficacy B Therapeutic mechanisms for specific clinical diagnosis (check Part IV) C Hypotheses about of how specific therapist skills could help achieve the treatment goals (Chapter 9): • assessment and aetiological analysis • experiential work in here-and-now • positive relationship • offering a structure in the treatment • transference/countertransference	Focused on therapeutic aims, the therapist formulates how the client could benefit from TA. Therapists should not only describe WHAT therapeutic mechanisms or specific interventions they will use, but also justify HOW they expect that this can help the client achieve the treatment goals.
viii Risk assessment	This should include any possible thoughts, plans and actions regarding: A suicide; B self-harm; C harming others; D harming the therapist; E other risks. Include plans to prevent or reduce risks, and what to do in an emergency.	
ix Interventions and treatment plan		If not already mentioned in vii, this may include specific examples (see examples in Chapters 11–12).
x Self-reflection and reflexivity	The therapists reflect on their position and possible biases.	For example, countertransference, embodied sensations, clinical intuitions, therapeutic relationship, cultural, religious and sexual differences, reflections from third parties (e.g. supervisor).
xi Response from the client when sharing the case-formulation		Describe client's response and how the case formulation was adjusted and explicit agreement about therapy aims (vi) and interventions/treatment plan (ix).
xii Other information		

Table A.3 TA Psychotherapeutic Self Report Competencies Scale (TAP-SRSC)

For the following TA core competence below, please rate how well you feel you applied them in this session:

1 Much improvement in application needed: I felt like a beginner, as if I did not have the concept
2 Moderate improvement needed: I felt like an advanced beginner, who is beginning to do this, but needs to work on the concept more
3 Slight improvement in application needed: I need to make a focused effort to do more of this
4 Adequate application of competence: I did enough of this, but need to keep working on improving how well I do it
5 Good application of competence: I did enough of this and did it skilfully
6 Excellent application of competence: I did this consistently and even applied it in a creative way
7 N/A

Competence	Examples	
Analysing clinical and aetiological phenomena	Conducting an explicit/systematic assessment or case formulation; analysing ego-states, social functioning or self-efficacy; analysing etiological development/life story/life script.	1 2 3 4 5 6 N/A
Offering a structure in the session	Following treatment manual, specific therapeutic stages, explicitly discussing the session structure with the client, explicitly discussing or following treatment contracts, using psycho-education and didactics.	1 2 3 4 5 6 N/A
Working at experiential depth in the here-and-now	Examining the current feelings of the client, deepening emotions, behavioural experiments triggering emotions, systematic desensitisation, stimulating clients to tolerate emotions	1 2 3 4 5 6 N/A
Creating and using a constructive client-practitioner relationship	Positive therapist-client alliance and collaboration; showing empathy, positive regard, affirmation, genuineness and congruence; having a real relationship; working with transference/countertransference; appropriately responsive to the client; tailoring treatment; repairing alliance ruptures if needed.	1 2 3 4 5 6 N/A
How do you think that you can improve your TA therapist competencies?	Based on the previous scores, how can you improve your skills and improve future sessions? What practical steps do you need to do to improve your skills and sessions?	open question

Life Position Scale

Instructions to Client

Please to which extent the following statements apply to you for the last two weeks.

Question	All of the time	Most of the time	Half of the time	Sometimes	Never
1. I like myself	4	3	2	1	0
2. I don't feel good about myself	4	3	2	1	0
3. I am proud of who I am	4	3	2	1	0
4. I feel helpless	4	3	2	1	0
5. I feel confident about myself	4	3	2	1	0
6. I am aware of my positive traits	4	3	2	1	0
7. I wish I hadn't been born into this world	4	3	2	1	0
8. I feel I won't reach my dreams	4	3	2	1	0
9. I think others dislike me	4	3	2	1	0
10. I believe I am basically good	4	3	2	1	0
11. I wish some people were dead	4	3	2	1	0
12. I find it easy to appreciate others	4	3	2	1	0
13. Others are basically OK	4	3	2	1	0

14. I get irritated with other people	4	3	2	1	0
15. I distrust people	4	3	2	1	0
16. I feel suspicious of other people's intentions	4	3	2	1	0
17. I am impatient with other people's mistakes	4	3	2	1	0
18. Most people can be trusted	4	3	2	1	0
19. People can do a good job	4	3	2	1	0
20. I look forward to meeting other people	4	3	2	1	0

End of questions

Figure A.1 Life position Scale

SCORES

The sub-scales do not have norm groups. The following is a rough interpretation:

- I+ sum-scores 5–8 = never
- I+ sum-scores 8–12 = sometimes
- I+ sum-scores 13–17 = half of the time
- I+ sum-scores 18–22 = most of the time
- I+ sum-scores 23–25 = all of the time

REFERENCES

Aburn, G., Gott, M., & Hoare, K. (2016). What is resilience? *Journal of Advanced Nursing, 72*(5), 980-1000.

Abramowitz, J. S. (2019). *Exposure therapy for anxiety: Principles and practice*. Guilford Publications.

Agrimson, L. B., & Taft, L. B. (2009). Spiritual crisis: A concept analysis. *Journal of Advanced Nursing, 65*(2), 454-461.

Ahn, H. N., & Wampold, B. E. (2001). Where oh where are the specific ingredients? A meta-analysis of component studies in counseling and psychotherapy. *Journal of Counseling Psychology, 48*(3), 251.

Aldao, A., Nolen-Hoeksema, S., & Schweizer, S. (2010). Emotion-regulation strategies across psychopathology. *Clinical Psychology Review, 30*(2), 217-237.

Alden, M., & Osti, J. (1989). Cognitive distortions in borderline personality disorder. *TAJ, 19*(1), 51-52.

Aldridge, B. (2021). Core self, sense of self, and whole self. *TAJ, 51*(1), 49-62.

Alexander, J. F., Waldron, H. B., Robbins, M. S., & Neeb, A. A. (2013). *Functional family therapy for adolescent behavior problems*. American Psychological Association.

Alfano, M. S., & Perry, M. (1994). Attributional style. *Journal of Research in Personality, 28*(3), 287-300.

Allen, J. R. (1999). Biology and TA. *TAJ, 29*(4), 250-259.

Allen, J. R. (2000). Biology and TA II. *TAJ, 30*(4), 260-269.

Almeida, I. L. D. L., Rego, J. F., Teixeira, A. C. G., & Moreira, M. R. (2021). Social isolation and its impact on child fand adolescent development. *Revista Paulista de Pediatria, 40*(1), e2020385-e2020399.

Almquist, Y. B., Landstedt, E., & Hammarström, A. (2017). Associations between social support and depressive symptoms: social causation or social selection—or both? *The European Journal of Public Health, 27*(1), 84-89.

American Psychological Association. (2006). Evidence-based practice in psychology. *American Psychologist, 61*(4), 271-285. https://doi.org/10.1037/0003-066X.61.4.271

Angus, L., Watson, J. C., Elliott, R., Schneider, K., & Timulak, L.(2015). Humanistic psychotherapy research 1990-2015. *Psychotherapy Research, 25*(3), 330-347.

Anne, M., & Boholst, F. A. (2021). Life positions and depression. *Psychological Reports, 124*(3), 1015-1030.

Arndt, J., Schimel, J., Greenberg, J., & Pyszczynski, T. (2002). The intrinsic self and defensiveness. *Personality and Social Psychology Bulletin, 28*(5), 671-683.

Arntz, A., & Van Genderen, H. (2020). *Schema therapy for borderline personality disorder*. Wiley.

Atkinson, M. (2023). Nourish: A framework for nourishing eating-disordered clients using a structural and relational methodology. *TAJ, 53*(2), 147-161.

Atzil-Slonim, D., Bar-Kalifa, E., Fisher, H., Peri, T., Lutz, W., Rubel, J., & Rafaeli, E. (2018). Emotional congruence between clients and therapists and its effect on treatment outcome. *Journal of Counseling Psychology, 65*(1), 51.

Baier, A. L., Kline, A. C., & Feeny, N. C. (2020). Therapeutic alliance as a mediator of change: A systematic review and evaluation of research. *Clinical Psychology Review, 82*, 101921.

Bär, A., Bär, H. E., Rijkeboer, M. M., & Lobbestael, J. (2023). Early Maladaptive Schemas and Schema Modes in clinical disorders: A systematic review. *Psychology and Psychotherapy: Theory, Research and Practice, 96*(3), 716-747.

Bagby, R. M., Cox, B. J., Schuller, D. R., Levitt, A. J., Swinson, R. P., & Joffe, R. T. (1992). Diagnostic specificity of the dependent and self-critical personality dimensions. *Journal of Affective Disorders, 26*(1), 59-63.

Bakermans-Kranenburg, M. J., & VanIjzendoorn, M. H. (2011). Differential susceptibility to rearing environment depending on dopamine-related genes. *Development and Psychopathology, 23*(1), 39-52.

Bandelow, B., Reitt, M., Röver, C., Michaelis, S., Görlich, Y., & Wedekind, D. (2015). Efficacy of treatments for anxiety disorders. *International Clinical Psychopharmacology, 30*(4), 183-192.

Barnes, G. (2004). Homosexuality in the first three decades of TA. *TAJ, 34*(2), 126-155.

Barr, J. (1987). The therapeutic relationship model: Perspectives on the core of the healing process. *TAJ, 17*(4), 134-140.

Bateman, A. W., & Fonagy, P. (Eds.). (2019). *Handbook of mentalizing in mental health practice.* American Psychiatric Pub.

Baumrind, D. (1991). The influence of parenting style on adolescent competence and substance use. *Journal of Early Adolescence, 11*(1), 56-95.

Beblo, T., Fernando, S., Klocke, S., Griepenstroh, J., Aschenbrenner, S., & Driessen, M. (2012). Increased suppression of negative and positive emotions in major depression. *Journal of Affective Disorders, 141*(2-3), 474-479.

Beck, A. T., Rush, A. J., Shaw, B. F., & Emery, G. (1979). *Cognitive therapy of depression.* Guilford.

Beck, J. S. (2020). *Cognitive behaviour therapy.* Guildford.

Beebe, B., & Lachmann, F. M. (2013). *Infant research and adult treatment: Co-constructing interactions.* Routledge.

Benjamin, J. (1992). *Recognition and destruction.* Analytic.

Benjamin, J. (2018). *Beyond doer and done to.* Routledge.

Bennett, R. (1999). A TA approach to the categorization of corporate marketing behavior. *Journal of Marketing Management, 15*, 265-289.

Bennett-Levy, J., Westbrook, D., Fennell, M., Cooper, M., Rouf, K., & Hackmann, A. (2004). Behavioural experiments: Historical and conceptual underpinnings. *Oxford Guide to Behavioural Experiments in Cognitive Therapy*, 1-20.

Bergmann, L. H. (1981). A cognitive behavioral approach to transactional analysis. *Transactional Analysis Journal, 11*(2), 147-149.

Berne, E. (1957). Ego-states in psychotherapy. *American Journal of Psychotherapy, 11*(2), 293-309.

Berne, E. (1958). Transactional analysis. *American Journal of Psychotherapy, 12*(4), 735-743.

Berne, E. (1961). *TA in psychotherapy.* Grove.

Berne, E. (1962). Intuition. VI. The psychodynamics of intuition. *Psychiatric Quarterly, 36*, 294-300.

Berne, E. (1964). *Games people play.* Penguin.

Berne, E. (1966). *Principles of group treatment.* OUP.

Berne, E. (1971). Away from a theory of the impact of interpersonal interaction on non-verbal participation. *TA Bulletin, 1*(1), 6-13.

Berne, E. (1972). *What do you say after you say hello?* Grove.

Besharat, M. A., Dehghani, S., & Tavalaeyan, F. S. (2014). Mediating role of early maladaptive schemas on the relationship. *Journal of Family Psychology, 1*(1), 3-18.

Beutler, L. E., Moleiro, C., & Talebi, H. (2002). Resistance in psychotherapy: What conclusions are supported by research. *Journal of Clinical Psychology, 58*(2), 207-217.

Beutler, L. E., Rocco, F., Moleiro, C. M., & Talebi, H. (2001). Resistance. *Psychotherapy: Theory, Research, Practice, Training, 38*(4), 431.

Birnbaum, J. (1987). A replacement therapy for the histrionic personality disorder. *TAJ, 17*(2), 24-28.

Bisson, J. I., Ehlers, A., Matthews, R., Pilling, S., Richards, D., & Turner, S. (2007). Psychological treatments for chronic post-traumatic stress disorder: Systematic review and meta-analysis. *British Journal Psychiatry, 190*(2), 97-104.

Blass, R. B., & Blatt, S. J. (1996). Attachment and separateness in the experience of symbiotic relatedness. *Psychoanalytic Quarterly, 65*(4), 711-746.

Blizard, R. A. (2001). Masochistic and sadistic ego-states. *Journal of Trauma & Dissociation, 2*(4), 37-58.

Bøe, T., Sivertsen, B., Heiervang, E., Goodman, R., Lundervold, A. J., & Hysing, M. (2014). Socioeconomic status and child mental health: The role of parental emotional well-being and parenting practices. *Journal of Abnormal Child Psychology, 42*, 705-715.

Boettcher, H., Brake, C. A., & Barlow, D. H. (2016). Origins and outlook of interoceptive exposure. *Journal of Behavior Therapy and Experimental Psychiatry, 53*, 41-51.

Bohart, A. C. (1993). Experiencing. *Journal of Psychotherapy Integration, 3*(1), 51-67.

Bohart, A. C. (2005). Evidence-based psychotherapy means evidence-informed, not evidence-driven. *Journal of Contemporary Psychotherapy, 35*, 39-53.

Bohlmeijer, E., Smit, F., & Cuijpers, P. (2003). Effects of reminiscence and life review on late-life depression. *International Journal of geriatric psychiatry, 18*(12), 1088-1094.

Bohlmeijer, E., Roemer, M., Cuijpers, P., & Smit, F. (2007). The effects of reminiscence on psychological well-being in older adults: A meta-analysis. *Aging and Mental Health, 11*(3), 291-300.

Boholst, F. A. (2002). A life position scale. *Transactional Analysis Journal, 32*(1), 28-32.

Boholst, F. A., Boholst, G. B., & Mende, M. M. B. (2005). Life-positions and attachment styles. *TAJ, 35*(1), 62-67.

Bokanowski, T., & Lewkowicz, S. (Eds.). (2018). *On Freud's splitting of the ego in the process of defence.* Routledge.

Booth, L., & Booth, J. (2016). The impact of transaction types on interpersonal communication effectiveness. *Journal of Social Psychology, 42*(3), 178-192.

Bornstein, M., Hahn, C. S., & Haynes, O. M. (2010). Social competence, externalizing, and internalizing. *Development and Psychopathology, 22*(4), 717-735.

Bosma, H. A., & Kunnen, E. S. (2001). Determinants and mechanisms in ego identity development: A review and synthesis. *Developmental Review, 21*(1), 39-66.

Boswell, J. F. (2015). Psychotherapy: Process, mechanisms, and science–practice integration. *Psychotherapy, 52*(1), 38.

Boszormenyi-Nagy, I. K. (2013). *Between give and take.* Taylor Francis.

Bowers, C., & Widdowson, M. (2023). TA psychotherapy with clients who are neurodivergent. *International Journal of TA Research and Practice, 14*(1).

Bowlby, J. (1982). *Attachment and loss*. Hogarth.

Bowlby, J. (1998). *Attachment and loss*. Random House.

Bradley, S. J. (2003). *Affect regulation and the development of psychopathology*. Guilford.

Bram, A. D. (2015). To resume a stalled psychotherapy? Psychological testing to understand an impasse and reevaluate treatment options. *Journal of Personality Assessment, 97*(3), 241-249.

Bradshaw, J. (2005). *Healing the shame that binds you: Recovery classics edition*. Health Communications.

Bremner, J. D., & Marmar, C. R. (2002). *Trauma, memory, and dissociation*. APA.

Bridle, C., Riemsma, R. P., Pattenden, J., Sowden, A. J., Mather, L., Watt, I. S., & Walker, A. (2005). Systematic review of the effectiveness of health behavior interventions based on the transtheoretical model. *Psychology & Health, 20*(3), 283-301.

Brown, G. W., Harris, T. O., & Hepworth, C. (1995). Loss, humiliation and entrapment among women developing depression. *Psychological Medicine, 25*(1), 7-21.

Brown, M. (2010). *The presence process*. Namaste.

Brunt, M. (2005). The use of TA in the treatment of eating disorders. *TAJ, 35*(3), 240-253.

Buchanan, J. (1995). Social support and schizophrenia: A review of the literature. *Archives of Psychiatric Nursing, 9*(2), 68-76.

Burt, K. B., Obradovic, J., Long, J. D., & Masten, A. S. (2008). The interplay of social competence and psychopathology over 20 years. *Child Development, 79*(2), 359-374.

Buryska, J. (1976). The freehand script maze. *Transactional Analysis Journal, 6*(2), 160-166.

Cacioppo, J. T., Hughes, M. E., Waite, L. J., Hawkley, L. C., & Thisted, R. A. (2006). Loneliness as a specific risk factor for depressive symptoms. *Psychology and Aging, 21*(1), 140-151.

Calati, R., Oasi, O., De Ronchi, D., & Serretti, A. (2010). The use of the defence style questionnaire in major depressive and panic disorders. *Psychology and Psychotherapy, 83*(1), 1-13.

Caldwell, J. G., Shaver, P. R., Li, C. S., & Minzenberg, M. J. (2011). Childhood maltreatment, adult attachment, and depression as predictors of parental self-efficacy in at-risk mothers. *Journal of Aggression, Maltreatment & Trauma, 20*(6), 595-616.

Campbell, S. B. (1995). Behavior problems in preschool children. *Journal of Child Psychology and Psychiatry, 36*(1), 113-149.

Campbell-Sills, L., Barlow, D. H., Brown, T. A., & Hofmann, S. G. (2006). Effects of suppression and acceptance on emotional responses of individuals with anxiety and mood disorders. *Behaviour Research and Therapy, 44*(9), 1251-1263.

Campos, L. P. (2010a). Beyond script destiny. *TAJ, 40*(3-4), 278-287.

Campos, L. P. (2010b). Redecision therapy and social justice. *TAJ, 40*(2), 85-94.

Casey, B. J., Getz, S., & Galvan, A. (2008). The adolescent brain. *Developmental Review, 28*(1), 62-77.

Castonguay, L. G., & Beutler, L. E. (Eds.). (2005). *Principles of therapeutic change that work*. Oxford University Press.

Cantwell, S. (2018). *Talk about what might be helpful*. University of Roehampton.

Car, K. B. (2013). *Reconstruction of Autonomy in transactional analysis*. Tilburth University.

Carl, J. R., Soskin, D. P., Kerns, C., & Barlow, D. H. (2013). Positive emotion regulation in emotional disorders. *Clinical Psychology Review, 33*(3), 343-360.

Carter, D. J. (2018). Case study. *Clinical Case Studies, 17*(5), 296-310.

Carvalho, L., Reis, A. M., & Pianowski, G. (2019). Investigating correlations between defence mechanisms and pathological personality characteristics. *Revista Colombiana de Psiquiatria, 48*(4), 232-243.

Chambless, D. L., & Hollon, S. D. (1998). Defining empirically supported therapies. *Journal of Consulting and Clinical Psychology, 66*(1), 7.

Chambless, D. L., & Ollendick, T. H. (2001). Empirically supported psychological interventions. *Annual Review of Psychology, 52*(1), 685-716.

Chauhan, R., Awasthi, P., & Verma, S. (2014). Attachment and psychosocial functioning. *Social Science International, 30*(2), 331-344.

Chawla, N., & Ostafin, B. (2007). Experiential avoidance as a functional dimensional approach to psychopathology. *Journal of Clinical Psychology, 63*(9), 871-890.

Clarkson, P. (1990). A multiplicity of psychotherapeutic relationships. *British Journal of Psychotherapy, 7*(2), 148-163.

Clarkson, P. (1992). Physis in TA. *TAJ, 22*(4), 202-209.

Clarkson, P. (2013). *TA psychotherapy*. Routledge.

Cloitre, M., Cohen, L. R., Ortigo, K. M., Jackson, C., & Koenen, K. C. (2020). *Treating survivors of childhood abuse and interpersonal trauma: STAIR narrative therapy*. Guilford.

Cohen, A. N., Hammen, C., Henry, R. M., & Daley, S. E. (2004). Effects of stress and social support on recurrence in bipolar disorder. *Journal of Affective Disorders, 82*(1), 143-147.

Conkbayir, M. (2021). *Early childhood and neuroscience*. Bloomsbury.

Cornell, W. F. (2018). *At the interface of transactional analysis, psychoanalysis, and body psychotherapy: Clinical and theoretical perspectives*. Routledge.

Cornell, W. F., & Landaiche, N. M. (2006). Impasse and intimacy. *TAJ, 36*(3), 196-213.

Cornell, W. F. (1988). Life-script theory. *TAJ, 18*(4), 270-282.

Corrigan, P. W., Watson, A. C., & Barr, L. (2006). The self-stigma of mental illness. *Journal of Social and Clinical Psychology, 25*(8), 875-884.

Corsini, R. (2017). *Role playing in psychotherapy*. Routledge.

Côté, S., Vaillancourt, T., LeBlanc, J. C., Nagin, D. S., & Tremblay, R. E. (2006). The development of physical aggression from toddlerhood to pre-adolescence: A nation wide longitudinal study of Canadian children. *Journal of Abnormal Child Psychology, 34*, 68-82.

Cox, B. J., Fleet, C., & Stein, M. B. (2004). Self-criticism and social phobia in the US national comorbidity survey. *Journal Journal of Affective Disorders, 82*(2), 227-234.

Craig, C., Hiskey, S., & Spector, A. (2020). Compassion focused therapy. *Expert Review of Neurotherapeutics, 20*(4), 385-400.

Crișan, Ș., Stoia, M., Predescu, E., Miu, A. C., & Szentágotai-Tătar, A. (2023). The association between adverse childhood events and cluster C personality disorders. *Clinical Psychology & Psychotherapy, 30*(6), 1193-1214.

Crisanti, U. (2023). Can the phylogeny of compassion-focused therapy and the ontogeny of TA go beyond dual-process theories and propose multiple modes of thinking? In S. Crisan (Ed.), *Brain, decision-making and mental health* (pp. 395-415). Springer.

Cristea, I. A., Gentili, C., Cotet, C. D., Palomba, D., Barbui, C., & Cuijpers, P. (2017). Efficacy of psychotherapies for borderline personality disorder. *JAMA, 74*(4), 319-328.

Cross, W. E. (2012). The enactment of race and other social identities during everyday transactions. In C. L. Wijeyesinghe & B. W. Jackson (Eds.), *New perspectives on racial identity development* (pp. 192-215). Routledge.

Cuijpers, P., Van Straten, A., & Warmerdam, L. (2007). Behavioral activation treatments of depression. *Clinical Psychology Review, 27*(3), 318-326.

Cuijpers, P., Van Straten, A., Andersson, G., & Van Oppen, P. (2008). Psychotherapy for depression in adults: A meta-analysis of comparative outcome studies. *Journal of Consulting and Clinical Psychology, 76*(6), 909.

Cuijpers, P., Sijbrandij, M., Koole, S. L., Andersson, G., Beekman, A. T., & Reynolds, III, C. F. (2013). The efficacy of psychotherapy and pharmacotherapy in treating depressive and anxiety disorders: A meta-analysis of direct comparisons. *World psychiatry*, *12*(2), 137-148.

Cuijpers, P., Sijbrandij, M., Koole, S., Huibers, M., Berking, M., & Andersson, G. (2014). Psychological treatment of generalized anxiety disorder. *Clinical Psychology Review*, *34*(2), 130-140.

Cuijpers, P., Donker, T., Weissman, M. M., Ravitz, P., & Cristea, I. A. (2016). Interpersonal psychotherapy for mental health problems. *American Journal of Psychiatry*, *173*(7), 680-687.

Cuijpers, P., Karyotaki, E., Eckshtain, D., Ng, M. Y., Corteselli, K. A., Noma, H., Quero, S., & Weisz, J. R. (2020). Psychotherapy for depression across different age groups. *JAMA Psychiatry*, *77*(7). https://doi.org/10.1001/jamapsychiatry.2020.0164

Dalzell, H. J. (2000). Whispers: The role of family secrets in eating disorders. *Eating Disorders*, *8*(1), 43-61.

Dana, D. (2018). *The Polyvagal theory in therapy*. Norton.

Dang, K., Kirk, M. A., Monette, G., Katz, J., & Ritvo, P. (2021). Meaning in life and vagally-mediated heart rate variability. *International Journal of Psychophysiology*, *165*, 101-111.

Davidson, P. R., & Parker, K. C. (2001). Eye movement desensitization and reprocessing. *Journal of Consulting and Clinical Psychology*, *69*(2), 305.

David, D., Lynn, S. J., & Montgomery, G. H. (Eds.). (2018). *Evidence-based psychotherapy: The state of the science and practice*. Wiley Blackwell.

Davies, D. (1996). *Pink therapy*. McGraw-Hill.

Davies, J. (2013). *Cracked: Why psychiatry is doing more harm than good*. Icon.

Dawson, D., & Moghaddam, N. (2015). *Formulation in action*. Gruyter.

de Francisco Carvalho, L., Reis, A. M., & Pianowski, G. (2019). Investigating correlations between defence mechanisms and pathological personality characteristics. *Revista Colombiana de Psiquiatria (English ed.)*, *48*(4), 232-243.

Degruy-Leary, J. (1994). *Post-traumatic slave syndrome*. Caban.

Delorme, R., Ey, E., Toro, R., Leboyer, M., Gillberg, C., & Bourgeron, T. (2013). Progress toward treatments for synaptic defects in autism. *Nature Medicine*, *19*(6), 685-694.

DeRoten, Y., Darwish, J., Stern, D. J., Fivaz-Depeursinge, E., & Corboz-Warnery, A. (1999). Nonverbal communication and alliance in therapy. *Journal of Clinical Psychology*, *55*(4), 425-438.

DeYoung, P. A. (2003). *Relational psychotherapy*. Brunner-Routledge.

Dhananjaya, D. (2022). We are the oppressor and the oppressed. *TAJ*, *52*(3), 244-258.

Diener, M. J., Hilsenroth, M. J., & Weinberger, J. (2007). Therapist affect focus and patient outcomes in psychodynamic psychotherapy. *American Journal of Psychiatry*, *164*(6), 936-941.

Dishion, T. J., McCord, J., & Poulin, F. (1999). When interventions harm. *American Psychologist*, *54*(9), 755-764.

Divac-Jovanovic, M., & Radojkovic, S. (1987). Treating borderline phenomena across diagnostic categories. *TAJ*, *17*(2), 4-10.

Dodge, K. A., & Conduct Problems Prevention Research Group. (2007). Fast track randomized controlled trial to prevent externalizing psychiatric disorders: Findings from grades 3 to 9. *Journal of the American Academy of Child & Adolescent Psychiatry*, *46*(10), 1250-1262.

Donker, T., Griffiths, K. M., Cuijpers, P., & Christensen, H. (2009). Psychoeducation for depression, anxiety and psychological distress. *BMC Medicine*, *7*(1), 79-86.

Drego, P. (1983). The cultural parent. *Transactional Analysis Journal*, *13*(4), 224-227.

Drego, P. (2006). Freedom and responsibility. *TAJ*, *36*(2), 90-104.

Drye, R. C. (1974). Stroking the rebellious child: An aspect of managing resistance. *Transactional Analysis Journal, 4*(3), 23-26.

Duffy, K. E., Simmonds-Buckley, M., Haake, R., Delgadillo, J., & Barkham, M. (2024). The efficacy of individual humanistic-experiential therapies for the treatment of depression. *Psychotherapy Research, 34*(3), 323-338.

Ehring, T., Fischer, S., Schnulle, J., Bosterling, A., & Tuschen-Caffier, B. (2008). Characteristics of emotion regulation. *Personality and Individual Differences, 44*(7), 1574-1584. https://doi.org/10.1016/j.paid.2008.01.013

Ehring, T., Tuschen-Caffier, B., Schnülle, J., Fischer, S., & Gross, J. J. (2010). Emotion regulation and vulnerability to depression: Spontaneous versus instructed use of emotion suppression and reappraisal. *Emotion, 10*(4), 563.

Ekers, D., Richards, D., & Gilbody, S. (2008). A meta-analysis of randomized trials of behavioural treatment of depression. *Psychological Medicine, 38*(5), 611-623.

Eklund, J. H., & Meranius, M. S. (2021). Toward a consensus on the nature of empathy: A review of reviews. *Patient Education and Counseling, 104*(2), 300-307.

Elison, J., Lennon, R., & Pulos, S. (2006). Investigating the compass of shame. *Social Behavior and Personality: An International Journal, 34*(3), 161-168.

Elliott, R., Watson, J. C., Timulak, L., & Sharbanee, J. (2021). Research on humanistic-experiential psychotherapies. In A. E. Bergin & S. L. Garfield (Eds.), *Handbook of psychotherapy and behavior change* (pp. 421-467).

Elliott, R. (2002). The effectiveness of humanistic therapies. In D. J. Cain (Ed.), *Humanistic psychotherapies: Handbook of research and practice* (pp. 57-81). APA.

English, F. (2006). Unconscious constraints to freedom and responsibility. *TAJ, 36*(2), 172-175.

Enstad, F., & Kjeldsen, A. (2018). Alcohol use in adolescence. In K. S. Mathiesen, A. V. Sanson, & E. B. Karevold (Eds.), *Tracking opportunities and problems from infancy to adulthood* (pp. 119-126). Hogrefe.

Erikson, E. H. (1994). *Identity and the life cycle.* Norton.

Erskine, R. G., & Trautmann, R. L. (1996). Methods of an integrative psychotherapy. *TAJ, 26*(4), 316-328.

Erskine, R. G., & Zalcman, M. J. (1979). The racket system. *TAJ, 9*(1), 51-59.

Erskine, R., Moursund, J. P., & Trautmann, R. L. (1999). *Beyond empathy.* Brunner/Routledge.

Erskine, R. G. (1980). Script cure. *TAJ, 10*(2), 102-106.

Erskine, R. G. (1994). Shame and self-righteousness: Transactional analysis perspectives and clinical interventions. *Transactional Analysis Journal, 24*(2), 86-102.

Eslinger, P. J., Anders, S., Ballarini, T., Boutros, S., Krach, S., Mayer, A. V., Moll, J., Newton, T. L., Schroeter, M. L., de Oliveira-Souza, R., Raber, J., Sullivan, G. B., Swain, J. E., Lowe, L., & Zahn, R. (2021). The neuroscience of social feelings: Mechanisms of adaptive social functioning. *Neuroscience & Biobehavioral Reviews, 128*, 592-620.

Etemadi-Chardah, N., Matinpour, B., & Heshmati, R. (2017). Effectiveness of TA group therapy on addiction intensity of woman patients treated with methadone. *Addiction & health, 9*(3), 146.

Eve, P. M., Byrne, M. K., & Gagliardi, C. R. (2014). What is good parenting? *Family Court Review, 52*(1), 114-127.

Everaert, J., Koster, E. H., & Derakshan, N. (2012). The combined cognitive bias hypothesis in depression. *Clinical Psychology Review, 32*(5), 413-424.

Evinç, Ş. G., Gençöz, T., Foto-Özdemir, D., Akdemir, D., Karadağ, F., & Ünal, F. (2014). Child maltreatment and associated factors among children with ADHD: A comparative study. *The Turkish Journal of Pediatrics, 56*(1), 11-22.

Farber, B. A., Suzuki, J. Y., & Lynch, D. A. (2018). Positive regard and psychotherapy outcome: A meta-analytic review. *Psychotherapy, 55*(4), 411.

Farrington, D. P. (1995). The development of offending and antisocial behaviour from childhood. *Journal of Child Psychology and Psychiatry, 6*(36), 929-964.

Fehlinger, T., Stumpenhorst, M., Stenzel, N., & Rief, W. (2013). Emotion regulation is the essential skill for improving depressive symptoms. *Journal of Affective Disorders, 144*(1-2), 116-122.

Felici, C., Madeddu, F., Doering, S., Clarkin, J. F., & Preti, E. (2023). Knowing me, knowing you: A systematic review of object relations assessment. *Psychoanalytic Psychology.* https://doi.org/10.1037/pap0000460

Ferenchak, S. (2022). *De-pathologizing BDSM.* Widener.

Fiorentino, F., Buglio, G. L., Morelli, M., Chirumbolo, A., Di Giuseppe, M., Lingiardi, V., & Tanzilli, A. (2024). Defensive functioning in individuals with depressive disorders. *Journal of Affective Disorders.* https://doi.org/10.1016/j.jad.2024.04.091

Fischer, T. D., Smout, M. F., & Delfabbro, P. H. (2016). The relationship between psychological flexibility, early maladaptive schemas, perceived parenting and psychopathology. *Journal of Contextual Behavioral Science, 5*(3), 169-177.

Fonagy, P., Gergely, G., & Target, M. (2007). The parent-infant dyad and the construction of the subjective self. *Journal of Child Psychology and Psychiatry, 48*(3-4), 288-328.

Fonagy, P. (2003). The development of psychopathology from infancy to adulthood: The mysterious unfolding of disturbance in time. *Infant Mental Health Journal: Official Publication of the World Association for Infant Mental Health, 24*(3), 212-239.

Forghani, M., Rajaei, A., & Bayazi, M. H. (2021). Effect of TA approach group training on psychological capitals and the temptation of methadone-treated addicts. *Avicenna Journal of Neuro PsychoPhysiology, 8*(4), 167-171.

Fowlie, H. (2005). Confusion and introjection: A model for understanding the defensive structures of the parent and child ego states. *Transactional Analysis Journal, 35*(2), 192-204.

Fowlie, H., & Sills, C. (2011). *Relational TA. Principles in practice.* Karnac.

Fowlie, H., & Sills, C. (Eds.). (2018). *Relational transactional analysis: Principles in practice.* Routledge.

Fraley, C. R. (2002). Attachment stability from infancy to adulthood. *Personality and Social Psychology Review, 6*(2), 123-151.

Frankl, V. E. (1985). *Man's search for meaning.* Simon & Schuster.

Fredrickson, B. L. (2004). *The psychology of gratitude.* OUP.

Fruzzetti, A. E., Shenk, C., & Hoffman, P. D. (2005). Family interaction and the development of borderline personality disorder: A transactional model. *Development and Psychopathology, 17*(4), 1007-1030.

Fullen, T., Jones, S. L., Emerson, L. M., & Adamou, M. (2020). Psychological treatments in adult ADHD. *Journal of Psychopathology and Behavioral Assessment, 42*(3), 500-518.

Gable, S. L., Reis, H. T., Impett, E. A., & Asher, E. R. (2004). What do you do when things go right? *Journal of Personality and Social Psychology, 87*(2), 228-245.

Gable, S. L., Gonzaga, G. C., & Strachman, A. (2006). Will you be there for me when things go right? *Journal of Personality and Social Psychology, 91*(5), 904-917.

Gaddy, M. A., & Ingram, R. E. (2014). A meta-analytic review of mood-congruent implicit memory in depressed mood. *Clinical Psychology Review, 34*(5), 402-416.

Galatzer-Levy, I. R., Huang, S. H., & Bonanno, G. A. (2018). Trajectories of resilience and dysfunction following potential trauma. *Clinical Psychology Review, 63*, 41-55.

Gayol, G. N. (2004). Codependence. *TAJ*, *34*(4), 312-322.

Gendlin, E. T. (1996). *Focusing-oriented psychotherapy*. Guilford.

Gilbert, P. (2009). Introducing compassion-focused therapy. *Advances in Psychiatric Treatment*, *15*(3), 199-208.

Gilbert, P. (2010). *Compassion-focused therapy*. Routledge.

Gladfelter, J. (1992). Redecision therapy. *International Journal of group psychotherapy*, *42*(3), 319-334.

Goldberg, S. B., Tucker, R. P., Greene, P. A., Davidson, R. J., Wampold, B. E., Kearney, D. J., & Simpson, T. L. (2018). Mindfulness-based interventions for psychiatric disorders. *Clinical Psychology Review*, *59*, 52-60.

Goldberg, S. B., Anders, C., Stuart-Maver, S. L., & Kivlighan, III, D. M. (2023). Meditation, mindfulness, and acceptance methods in psychotherapy. *Psychotherapy Research*, *33*(7), 873-885.

Goldman, B. M., & Kernis, M. H. (2002). The role of authenticity in healthy psychological functioning and subjective well-being. *Annals of the American Psychotherapy Association*, *5*(6), 18-20.

Goldman, R. N., Greenberg, L. S., & Pos, A. E. (2005). Depth of emotional experience and outcome. *Psychotherapy research*, *15*(3), 248-260.

Goldstein, S., & Brooks, R. B. (Eds.). (2023). *Handbook of resilience in children*. Springer.

Goli, E., Abdekhodaie, M. S., Mashhadi, A., & Bigdeli, I. (2019). The role of parent-child interaction patterns in the development of obsessive-compulsive disorder: A literature review study. *Journal Fundamentals of Mental Health*, *22*, 5-20.

Goodheart, C. D. (2006). Evidence, endeavor, and expertise in psychology practice. In C. D. Goodheart, A. E. Kazdin, & R. J. Sternberg (Eds.), *Evidence-based psychotherapy: Where practice and research meet* (pp. 37-61). American Psychological Association.

Goodman, R., & West-Olatunji, C. (2008). Transgenerational trauma and resilience. *Journal of Mental Health Counseling*, *30*(2), 121-136.

Goodwyn, E. D. (2016). *Healing symbols in psychotherapy: A ritual approach*. Routledge.

Gopakumar, A., & Vaidik, A. (2024). Recognizing invisible oppression with the drama pyramid. *TAJ*, *54*(2), 150-163.

Gorrese, A., & Ruggieri, R. (2012). Peer attachment. *Journal of Youth and Adolescence*, *41*(5), 650-672.

Gotlib, I. H., & Joormann, J. (2010). Cognition and depression. *Annual Review of Clinical Psychology*, *6*, 285-312.

Goulding, R., & Goulding, M. (1976). Injunctions, decisions, and redecisions. *TAJ*, *6*(1), 41-48.

Goulding, M. M., & Goulding, R. L. (1979). *Changing lives through redecision therapy*. Grove.

Greenberg, L. S., & Paivio, S. C. (1997). *Working with Emotions in psychotherapy*. Guildford.

Greenberg, L. S., & Watson, J. C. (2006). *Emotion-focused therapy for depression*. APA.

Greenberg, L. S., Auszra, L., & Herrmann, I. R. (2007). The relationship among emotional productivity, emotional arousal and outcome in experiential therapy of depression. *Psychotherapy Research*, *17*(4), 482-493.

Greenberg, L. S., Rice, L. N., & Elliott, R. (2007). *Facilitating emotional change*. Guilford.

Greenspoon, P. J., & Saklofske, D. H. (2001). Toward an integration of subjective well-being and psychopathology. *Social Indicators Research*, *54*(1), 81-108.

Grégoire, J. (2024). *Conceptualizing ego states in transactional analysis: three systems in interaction*. Taylor & Francis.

Grolnick, W. S., & Ryan, R. M. (1989). Parent styles associated with children's self-regulation and competence in school. *Journal of Educational Psychology, 81*(2), 143-154.

Grossman, P., Niemann, L., Schmidt, S., & Walach, H. (2004). Mindfulness-based stress reduction and health benefits. *Journal of Psychosomatic Research, 57*, 35-43.

Guntrip, H. Y. (2018). *Personality structure and human interaction: The developing synthesis of psychodynamic theory.* Routledge.

Haimowitz, C. (2000). Maybe it's not 'kick me' after all. *TAJ, 30*(1), 84-90.

Haines, J. E., & Schutte, N. S. (2023). Parental conditional regard. *Journal of Adolescence, 95*(2), 195-223.

Hames, J. L., Hagan, C. R., & Joiner, T. E. (2013). Interpersonal processes in depression. *Annual Review of Clinical Psychology, 9*, 355-377.

Hammen, C. (1992). Cognitive, life stress, and interpersonal approaches to a developmental psychopathology model of depression. *Development and Psychopathology, 4*(1), 189-206.

Hanish, L. D., Martin, C. L., Fabes, R. A., Leonard, S., & Herzog, M. (2005). Exposure to externalizing peers in early childhood. *Journal of Abnormal Child Psychology, 33*, 267-281.

Harding, C. (2018). *Dissecting the superego.* Routledge.

Hargaden, H., & Cornell, W. F. (Eds.). (2019). *The evolution of a relational paradigm in transactional analysis: What's the relationship got to do with it?* Routledge.

Hargaden, H., & Sills, C. (2002). *Transactional analysis. A relational perspective.* Brunner-Routledge.

Hargaden, H., & Sills, C. (2003). Who am I for you. In C. Sills & H. Hargaden (Eds.), *Key concepts in TA.* Worth.

Hargaden, H., & Sills, C. (2014). *Transactional analysis: A relational perspective.* Routledge.

Harold, G. T., & Sellers, R. (2018). Interparental conflict and youth psychopathology. *Journal of Child Psychology, 59*(4), 374-402.

Harris, T. (2012). *I'm OK, you're OK.* Random House.

Hartman, D., O'Donnell-Killen, T., Doyle, J. K., Kavanagh, M., Day, A., & Azevedo, J. (2023). *The adult autism assessment handbook.* Kingsley.

Haugh, J. A., Miceli, M., & DeLorme, J. (2017). Maladaptive parenting, temperament, early maladaptive schemas, and depression. *Journal of Psychopathology and Behavioral Assessment, 39*(1), 103-116.

Hawkes, L. (2011). With you and me in mind. *TAJ, 41*(3), 230-240.

Hay, P. (2013). A systematic review of evidence for psychological treatments in eating disorders: 2005-2012. *International Journal of Eating Disorders, 46*(5), 462-469.

Hayes, S. C., Strosahl, K. D., & Wilson, K. G. (1999). *Acceptance and commitment therapy.* Guilford.

Hayes, S. C., Luoma, J. B., Bond, F. W., Masuda, A., & Lillis, J. (2006). Acceptance and commitment therapy. *Behaviour Research and Therapy, 44*(1), 1-25.

Hayes, J. A., Gelso, C. J., Goldberg, S., & Kivlighan, D. M. (2018). Countertransference management and effective psychotherapy. *Psychotherapy, 55*(4), 496-507.

Hendricks, M. N. (2002). Focusing-oriented/experiential psychotherapy. In D. J. Cain (Ed.), *Humanistic psychotherapies* (pp. 221-251). APA.

Henggeler, S. W., Letourneau, E. J., Chapman, J. E., Borduin, C. M., Schewe, P. A., & McCart, M. R. (2009). Mediators of change for multisystemic therapy with juvenile sexual offenders. *Journal of consulting and clinical psychology, 77*(3), 451.

Herman, J. L., & van der Kolk, B. A. (2020). *Treating complex traumatic stress disorders in adults.* Guilford.

Herman, J. (2023). *Truth and repair.* Hachette.

Heyrat, A., & Fesharaki, F. M. (2021). Effectiveness of TA on parental stress of mothers with autistic children. *Clinical Schizophrenia and Related Psychoses, 15*(3), 134-150.

Hill, D. (2015). *Affect regulation theory.* Norton.

Hine, J. (1997). Mind structure and ego states. *Transactional Analysis Journal, 27*(4), 278-289.

Hine, J. (2005). Brain structures and ego-states. *TAJ, 35*(1), 40-51.

Hinrichsen, H., Sheffield, A., & Waller, G. (2007). The role of parenting experiences in the development of social anxiety and agoraphobia in eating disorders. *Eating Behaviors, 8*(3), 285-290.

Høglend, P., Gabbard, G. O., & Gabbard, G. O. (2012). When is transference work useful in psychodynamic psychotherapy? A review of empirical research. *Psychodynamic Psychotherapy Research: Evidence-Based Practice and Practice-Based Evidence,* 449-467.

Hoff, E., & Laursen, B. (2019). *Handbook of parenting.* Routledge.

Hofmann, S. G., Asnaani, A., Vonk, I. J., Sawyer, A. T., & Fang, A. (2012). The efficacy of cognitive behavioral therapy. *Cognitive Therapy and Research, 36*(5), 427-440.

Holdsworth, E., Bowen, E., Brown, S., & Howat, D. (2014). Client engagement in psychotherapeutic treatment and associations with client characteristics, therapist characteristics, and treatment factors. *Clinical psychology review, 34*(5), 428-450.

Honarparvaran, N., Khatoni, Z., Bagheri, S., Namjoo, F., & Haronizadeh, Z. (2017). Effectiveness of mother-child TA group therapy. *Journal of Applied Psychology, 11*(1), 557-578.

Hoyt, M. F. (1989). Psychodiagnosis of personality disorders. *TAJ, 19*(2), 101-113.

Horn, E. K., Verheul, R., Thunnissen, M., Delimon, J., Soons, M., Meerman, A. M., Ziegler, U. M., Rossum, B. V., Andrea, H., Stijnen, T., & Emmelkamp, P. M. (2015). Effectiveness of short-term inpatient psychotherapy based on transactional analysis with patients with personality disorders: A matched control study using propensity score. *Journal of Personality Disorders, 29*(5), 663-683.

Horner, A. J. (2005). *Dealing with resistance in psychotherapy.* Jason Aronson.

Hyams, H. (1998). Dissociation. *TAJ, 28*(3), 234-243.

Irish, L. A., Kline, C. E., Gunn, H. E., Buysse, D. J., & Hall, M. H. (2015). The role of sleep hygiene in promoting public health: A review of empirical evidence. *Sleep Medicine Reviews, 22,* 23-36.

Jabbari, R., Hassan, M., & Sadegh Mahboob, S. (2019). Effectiveness of group training of TA on distress tolerance and communication skills. *Journal of Iranian Psychologists, 16*(61), 73-85.

Jacoby, M. (2016). *Individuation and narcissism.* Routledge.

Jalali, M. R., Zargar, M., Salavati, M., & Kakavand, A. R. (2011). Comparison of early maladaptive schemas and parenting origins in patients with opioid abuse and non-abusers. *Iranian Journal of Psychiatry, 6*(2), 54-62.

Janoff-Bulman, R. (2010). *Shattered assumptions.* Simon & Schuster.

Jeffrey, A. J., & Fish, L. S. (2011). Clinical intuition: A qualitative study of its use and experience among marriage and family therapists. *Contemporary Family Therapy, 33*(4), 348-363.

Jeness, C. F. (1975). Comparative effectiveness of behavior modification and TA programs for delinquents. *Journal of Consulting and Clinical Psychology, 43*(6), 758-770.

Jennissen, S., Huber, J., Ehrenthal, J. C., Schauenburg, H., & Dinger, U. (2018). Association between insight and outcome of psychotherapy: Systematic review and meta-analysis. *American Journal of Psychiatry, 175*(10), 961-969.

Jericho, B., Luo, A., & Berle, D. (2022). Trauma-focused psychotherapies for post-traumatic stress disorder: A systematic review and network meta-analysis. *Acta Psychiatrica Scandinavica, 145*(2), 132-155.

Johnsson, R. (2011). Client assessment in transactional analysis - A study of the reliability and validity of the Ohlsson, Björk and Johnsson script questionnaire. *International Journal of Transactional Analysis Research & Practice, 2*(2), 19-33.

Johnsson, R., & Stenlund, G. (2010). The affective dimension of alliance in transactional analysis psychotherapy. *International Journal of Transactional Analysis Research & Practice, 1*(1), 45-59.

Johnson, S. M., & Whiffen, V. E. (1999). Made to measure: Adapting emotionally focused couple therapy to partners' attachment styles. *Clinical Psychology: Science and Practice, 6*(4), 366-381.

Johnson, J., Panagioti, M., Bass, J., Ramsey, L., & Harrison, R. (2017). Resilience to emotional distress in response to failure, error or mistakes. *Clinical Psychology Review, 52*(1), 19-42.

Johnson, R., Smith, A., & Brown, T. (2018). Transactional Analysis in psychotherapy: A study of transaction Reupert and therapeutic outcomes. *Journal of Clinical Psychology, 74*(5), 612-628.

Johnstone, L., & Boyle, M. (2018). The power threat meaning framework: An alternative nondiagnostic conceptual system. *Journal of Humanistic Psychology, 1*(1), 1-18.

Joiner, T. E., Jr., Alfano, M. S., & Metalsky, G. I. (1993). Caught in the crossfire. *Journal of Social and Clinical Psychology, 12*(2), 113-134.

Joiner, T. E., Jr. (1997). Shyness and low social support as interactive diatheses, with loneliness as mediator. *Journal of Abnormal Psychology, 106*(3), 386-394.

Joiner, T. E., Jr. (2000). Depression's vicious scree. *Clinical Psychologist, 7*(2), 203-218.

Kabat-Zinn, J. (2003). Mindfulness-based interventions in context: Past, present, and future. *Clinical Psychology: Science and Practice, 10*(2), 144-156.

Kabat-Zinn, J. (2018). *The healing power of mindfulness.* Hachette.

Kahler, T. (1975). Drivers: The key to the process of scripts. *Transactional Analysis Bulletin, 5*(3), 280-284.

Kahler, T., & Capers, H. (1974). The miniscript. *TA Bulletin, 4*(1), 26-42.

Kahneman, D. (2011). *Thinking fast and slow.* MacMillan.

Kantor, M. (2003). *Distancing.* Bloomsbury.

Karatzias, T., Murphy, P., Cloitre, M., Bisson, J., Roberts, N., Shevlin, M., Hyland, P., Maercker, A., Ben-Ezra, M., Coventry, P., & Mason-Roberts, S. (2019). Psychological interventions for ICD-11 complex PTSD symptoms. *Psychological Medicine, 49*(11), 1761-1775.

Karpman, S. (1971). Options. *TA Bulletin, 1*(1), 79-87.

Katakis, P., Schlief, M., Barnett, P., Rains, L. S., Rowe, S., Pilling, S., & Johnson, S. (2023). Effectiveness of outpatient and community treatments for people with a diagnosis of 'personality disorder': systematic review and meta-analysis. *BMC psychiatry, 23*(1), 57.

Katakis, C. D. (1989). Stages of psychotherapy: Progressive reconceptualizations as a self-organizing process. *Psychotherapy: Theory, Research, Practice, Training, 26*(4), 484.

Kato, T. (2015). The impact of coping flexibility on the risk of depressive symptoms. *PloS One, 10*(5), e0128307.

Katz, L. F., & Gottman, J. M. (1993). Patterns of marital conflict predict children's internalizing and externalizing behaviors. *Developmental Psychology, 29*(6), 940-950.

Kazdin, A. E., Sherick, R. B., Esveldt-Dawson, K., & Rancurello, M. D. (1985). Nonverbal behavior and childhood depression. *Journal of the American Academy of Child Psychiatry, 24*(3), 303-309.

Kazdin, A. E. (2021). The Kazdin Method for Developing and Changing Behavior of Children and Adolescents. *International Journal of Mental Health Promotion, 23*(4).

Kazdin, A. E. (2022). Research design. In *Clinical psychology*. CUP.

Keefe, J. R., McMain, S. F., McCarthy, K. S., Zilcha-Mano, S., Dinger, U., Sahin, Z., Graham, K., & Barber, J. P. (2020). A meta-analysis of psychodynamic treatments for borderline and cluster C personality disorders. *Personality Disorders: Theory, Research, and Treatment, 11*(3), 157.

Keenan, N. (2024). Brain hemisphere specialization and neurodiversity. *TAJ, 54*(1), 15-30.

Kendjelic, E. M., & Eells, T. D. (2007). Generic psychotherapy case formulation training improves formulation quality. *Psychotherapy, 44*(1), 66-77.

Kernberg, O. F. (1993). *Severe personality disorders: Psychotherapeutic strategies.* Yale University Press.

Khoury, B., Lecomte, T., Fortin, G., Masse, M., Therien, P., Bouchard, V., ..., Hofmann, S. G. (2013). Mindfulness-based therapy. *Clinical Psychology Review, 33*(6), 763-771.

Kiesler, D. J. (1996). *Contemporary interpersonal theory and research.* Wiley.

King, P., & Temple, S. (2018). Transactional Analysis and the Ludic Third (TALT): A model of functionally fluent reflective play practice. *Transactional Analysis Journal, 48*(3), 258-271.

Kins, E., Beyers, W., & Soenens, B. (2013). When the separation-individuation process goes awry. *International Journal of Behavioral Development, 37*(1), 1-12.

Kipper, D. A., & Ritchie, T. D. (2003). The effectiveness of psychodramatic techniques. *Group Dynamics: Theory, Research, and Practice, 7*(1), 13.

Kjeldsen, A., Nes, R. B., Sanson, A., Ystrom, E., & Karevold, E. B. (2021). Understanding trajectories of externalizing problems. *Development and Psychopathology, 33*(1), 264-283.

Klein, J. P., Schaich, A., & Furukawa, T. A. (2023). How should narcissism be treated best? *The Lancet Psychiatry, 10*(12), 914-916.

Koehn, C. V., & Cutcliffe, J. R. (2007). Hope and interpersonal psychiatric/mental health nursing. *Journal of Psychiatric and Mental Health Nursing, 14*(2), 134-140.

Kohut, H. (2009). *The restoration of the self.* University of Chicago Press.

Kolden, G. G., Wang, C. C., Austin, S. B., Chang, Y., & Klein, M. H. (2018). Congruence/genuineness. *Psychotherapy, 55*(4), 424.

Koopmans, M. (2001). From double bind to n-bind. *Nonlinear Dynamics, Psychology, and Life Sciences, 5*(4), 289-323.

Kothgassner, O. D., Goreis, A., Robinson, K., Huscsava, M. M., Schmahl, C., & Plener, P. L. (2021). Efficacy of dialectical behavior therapy for adolescent self-harm and suicidal ideation. *Psychological Medicine, 51*(7), 1057-1067.

Kotilahti, E., West, M., Isomaa, R., Karhunen, L., Rocks, T., & Ruusunen, A. (2020). Treatment interventions for severe and enduring eating disorders: Systematic review. *International Journal of Eating Disorders, 53*(8), 1280-1302.

Krebs, P., Norcross, J. C., Nicholson, J. M., & Prochaska, J. O. (2018). Stages of change and psychotherapy outcomes. *Journal of Clinical Psychology, 74*(11), 1964-1979.

Kuhfuß, M., Maldei, T., Hetmanek, A., & Baumann, N. (2021). Somatic experiencing - Effectiveness and key factors of a body-oriented trauma therapy: A scoping literature review. *European Journal of Psychotraumatology, 12*(1), 1929023.

Kulashekara, B., & Kumar, G. V. (2014). Impact of TA on parent-adolescent conflict and aggression among adolescent students. *SKUAST Journal of Research, 16*(1), 46-56.

Lambert, M. J., Fidalgo, L. G., & Greaves, M. R. (2016). Effective humanistic psychotherapy processes and their outcomes. In D. J. Cain, K. Keenan, & S. Rubin (Eds.), *Humanistic psychotherapies* (pp. 49-79). APA.

Landheer, P. L. (1981). A developmental script questionnaire. *Transactional Analysis Journal, 11*(1), 77-80.

Langford, P. E. (2018). *Approaches to the development of moral reasoning.* Psychology Press.

Larsen, D., Edey, W., & Lemay, L. (2007). Understanding the role of hope in counselling: Exploring the intentional uses of hope. *Counselling Psychology Quarterly, 20*(4), 401-416.

Lefcourt, H. M. (2014). *Locus of control.* Psychology Press.

Leichsenring, F., & Leibing, E. (2003). The effectiveness of psychodynamic therapy and cognitive behavior therapy in the treatment of personality disorders: A meta-analysis. *American journal of psychiatry, 160*(7), 1223-1232.

Leichsenring, F., & Rabung, S. (2011). Long-term psychodynamic psychotherapy in complex mental disorders. *British Journal of Psychiatry, 199*(1), 15-22.

Leichsenring, F., Rabung, S., & Leibing, E. (2004). The efficacy of short-term psychodynamic psychotherapy in specific psychiatric disorders. *Archives of General Psychiatry, 61*(12), 1208-1216.

Leiper, R., & Kent, R. (2001). *Working through setbacks in psychotherapy: Crisis, impasse and relapse.* SAGE.

Leong, C., & Graichen, R. (2024). Decentering neuronormativity. *TAJ, 54*(1), 91-106.

Levant, R. F., & Sperry, H. A. (2016). Components of evidence-based practice in psychology. In N. Zane, G. Bernal, & F. T. L. Leong (Eds.), *Evidence-based psychological practice with ethnic minorities: Culturally informed research and clinical strategies* (pp. 15-29). American Psychological Association.

Levine, P. A. (1997). *Waking the tiger.* North Atlantic.

Levitt, H. M., Collins, K. M., Morrill, Z., Gorman, K. R., Ipekci, B., Grabowski, L., Karch, J., Kurtz, K., Orduña Picón, R., Reyes, A., & Vaswani-Bye, A. (2022). Learning clinical and cultural empathy: A call for a multidimensional approach to empathy-focused psychotherapy training. *Journal of Contemporary Psychotherapy, 52*(4), 267-279.

Levy, K. N., & Scala, J. (2012). Transference, transference interpretations, and transference-focused psychotherapies. *Psychotherapy, 49*(3), 391.

Leyro, T. M., Zvolensky, M. J., & Bernstein, A. (2010). Distress tolerance and psychopathological symptoms and disorders: A review of the empirical literature among adults. *Psychological Bulletin, 136*(4), 576.

Lewis, C., Roberts, N. P., Andrew, M., Starling, E., & Bisson, J. I. (2020). Psychological therapies for post-traumatic stress disorder in adults. *European Journal of psychotraumatology, 11*(1), 1729633-1729639.

Ligabue, S., & Tenconi, P. M. (2021). The experience of anxiety in body and mind. *TAJ, 51*(4), 335-350.

Lilliengren, P., Johansson, R., Lindqvist, K., Mechler, J., & Andersson, G. (2016). Efficacy of experiential dynamic therapy for psychiatric conditions. *Psychotherapy, 53*(1), 90.

Lim, C. R., & Barlas, J. (2019). The effects of toxic early childhood experiences on depression according to Young schema model. *Journal of Affective Disorders, 246*(1), 1-13.

Lincoln, T. M., Wilhelm, K., & Nestoriuc, Y. (2007). Effectiveness of psychoeducation for relapse, symptoms, knowledge, adherence and functioning in psychotic disorders. *Schizophrenia Research, 96*(1-3), 232-245.

Lindhiem, O., Bennett, C. B., Orimoto, T. E., & Kolko, D. J. (2016). A meta-analysis of personalized treatment goals in psychotherapy. *Clinical Psychologist, 23*(2), 165.

Little, R. (2001). Schizoid processes. *TAJ, 31*(1), 33-43.

Liu, R. T., Kleiman, E. M., Nestor, B. A., & Cheek, S. M. (2015). The hopelessness theory of depression. *Clinical Psychologist, 22*(4), 345-365.

Lloyd, C. E., Duncan, C., & Cooper, M. (2019). Goal measures for psychotherapy: A systematic review of self-report, idiographic instruments. *Clinical Psychology: Science and Practice, 26*(3), e12281.

Lobbestael, J., van Vreeswijk, M., & Arntz, A. (2007). Shedding light on schema modes. *Netherlands Journal of Psychology, 63*(3), 69-78. https://doi.org/10.1007/BF03061068

Lobbestael, J., Van Vreeswijk, M. F., & Arntz, A. (2008). An empirical test of schema mode conceptualizations in personality disorders. *Behaviour Research and Therapy, 46*(7), 854-860.

Lopez, F. G., & Gover, M. R. (1993). Self-report measures of parent-adolescent attachment and separation-individuation. *Journal of Counseling & Development, 71*(5), 560-569.

LoPiccolo, J., & LoPiccolo, L. (Eds.). (2012). *Handbook of sex therapy.* Springer.

Lovejoy, M. C. (1991). Maternal depression. *Journal of Abnormal Child Psychology, 19*(6), 693-706.

Luborsky, L., & Crits-Christoph, P. (1998). *Understanding transference: The core conflictual relationship theme method.* American Psychological Association.

Luborsky, L., McLellan, A. T., Woody, G. E., O'Brien, C. P., & Auerbach, A. (1985). Therapist success and its determinants. *Archives of General Psychiatry, 42*(6), 602-611.

Luborsky, J. L. (1976). Helping alliances in psychotherapy. In J. L. Cleghorn (Ed.), *Successful psychotherapy* (pp. 92-116). Bruner/Mazel.

Luborsky, L., Rosenthal, R., Diguer, L., Andrusyna, T. P., Berman, J. S., Levitt, J. T., Seligman, D. A., & Krause, E. D. (2002). The dodo bird verdict is alive and well - mostly. *Clinical Psychology: Science and Practice, 9*(1), 2-12.

Luyten, P., Mayes, L. C., Fonagy, P., Blatt, S. J., & Target, M. (Eds.). (2017). *Handbook of psychodynamic approaches to psychopathology.* Guilford.

MacBeth, A., & Gumley, A. (2012). Exploring compassion. *Clinical Psychology Review, 32*(6), 545-552.

Maddux, J. E., & Kleiman, E. M. (2016). Self-efficacy. In A. M. Wood & J. Johnson (Eds.), *Wiley handbook of positive clinical psychology* (pp. 89-101). Wiley-Blackwell.

Mahler, M. S. (2018). *The psychological birth of the human infant.* Routledge.

Mahler, M. S., Pine, F., & Bergman, A. (1975). *The psychological birth of the human infant: Symbiosis and individuation.* Basic Books.

Mahoney, A., Karatzias, T., & Hutton, P. (2019). A systematic review and meta-analysis of group treatments for adults with symptoms associated with complex post-traumatic stress disorder. *Journal of Affective Disorders, 243*, 305-321.

Mahrer, A. R. (1989a). *The integration of psychotherapies: A guide for practicing therapists.* Human Sciences.

Mahrer, A. R. (1989b). The case for fundamentally different existential-humanistic psychologies. *Journal of Humanistic Psychology, 29*(2), 249-262.

Maier, S. F., & Seligman, M. E. P. (2016). Learned helplessness at fifty. *Psychological Review*, *123*(4), 349-367.

Mallinckrodt, B., & Wei, M. (2005). Attachment, social competencies, social support, and psychological distress. *Journal of Counseling Psychology*, *52*(3), 358-367.

Malouff, J. M., Thorsteinsson, E. B., & Schutte, N. S. (2007). The efficacy of problem solving therapy in reducing mental and physical health problems: A meta-analysis. *Clinical Psychology Review*, *27*(1), 46-57.

Manor, O. (1992). TA, object relations, and the systems approach. *TAJ*, *22*(1), 4-15.

Manusov, V. L. (Ed.). (2014). *The sourcebook of nonverbal measures*. Psychology Press.

Marcia, J. E. (2010). Life transitions and stress in the context of psychosocial development. In *Handbook of Stressful Transitions Across the Lifespan* (pp. 19-34).

Marks, R., & Allegrante, J. P. (2005). A review and synthesis of research evidence for self-efficacy-enhancing interventions for reducing chronic disability. *Health Promotion Practice*, *6*(2), 148-156.

Marroquin, B. (2011). Interpersonal emotion regulation as a mechanism of social support in depression. *Clinical Psychology Review*, *31*(8), 1276-1290.

Martin, D. J., Garske, J. P., & Davis, M. K. (2000). Relation of the therapeutic alliance with outcome and other variables: A meta-analytic review. *Journal of Consulting and Clinical Psychology*, *68*(3), 438.

Massey, R. F. (2007). Reexamining social psychiatry as a foundational framework for transactional analysis. *TAJ*, *37*(1), 51-79.

Masuda, A., Hayes, S. C., Sackett, C. F., & Twohig, M. P. (2004). Cognitive defusion and self-relevant negative thoughts: Examining the impact of a ninety year old technique. *Behaviour Research and Therapy*, *42*(4), 477-485.

Mathews, A., & MacLeod, C. (2005). Cognitive vulnerability to emotional disorders. *Annual Review of Clinical Psychology*, *1*(1), 167-195.

Mausbach, B. T., Moore, R., Roesch, S., Cardenas, V., & Patterson, T. L. (2010). The relationship between homework compliance and therapy outcomes. *Cognitive Therapy and Research*, *34*(1), 429-438.

Mavranezouli, I., Megnin-Viggars, O., Daly, C., Dias, S., Welton, N. J., Stockton, S., Bhutani, G., Grey, N., Leach, J., Greenberg, N., & Katona, C. (2020). Psychological treatments for post-traumatic stress disorder in adults: A network meta-analysis. *Psychological Medicine*, *50*(4), 542-555.

Mazzetti, M. (2018). Cross-cultural TA. In H. Hargaden & C. Sills (Eds.), *Relational transactional analysis* (pp. 189-197). Routledge.

McCallie, M. S., Blum, C. M., & Hood, C. J. (2006). Progressive muscle relaxation. *Journal of Human Behavior in the Social Environment*, *13*(3), 51-66.

McCormick, P., & Pulleyblank, E. F. (1979). A more comprehensive life script interview. *Transactional Analysis Journal*, *9*(4), 234-236.

McNeel, J. R. (1976). The parent interview. *Transactional Analysis Journal*, *6*(1), 61-68.

McNeel, J. R. (1982). Redecisions in psychotherapy. *TAJ*, *12*(1), 10-26.

McNeel, J. R. (2010). Understanding the power of injunctive messages and how they are resolved in redecision therapy. *TAJ*, *40*(2), 159-169.

McNeel, J. R. (2016). The heart of redecision therapy. In R. G. Erskine (Ed.), *TA in contemporary psychotherapy* (pp. 55-78). Karnac.

Mellacqua, Z. (2014). Beyond symbiosis. *TAJ*, *44*(1), 8-30.

Mellacqua, Z. (2020). *Transactionala analysis of schizophrenia*. Routledge.

Mergenthaler, E. (1996). Emotion–abstraction patterns in verbatim protocols. *Journal of Consulting and Clinical Psychology, 64*(6), 1306-1315.

Messina, I., & Sambin, M. (2015). Berne's theory of cathexis and its links to modern neuroscience. *TAJ, 45*(1), 48-58.

Mikulincer, M., Shaver, P. R., & Pereg, D. (2003). Attachment theory and affect regulation. *Motivation and Emotion, 27*, 77-102.

Millard, L. A., Wan, M. W., Smith, D. M., & Wittkowski, A. (2023). The effectiveness of compassion focused therapy with clinical populations. *Journal of Affective Disorders, 326*, 168-192.

Minikin, K. S. (2023). *Radical-relational Perspectives in transactional analysis psychotherapy.* Routledge.

Mitchell, S. A., & Black, M. J. (2016). *Freud and beyond.* Hachette.

Mohr, D. C., Beutler, L. E., Engle, D., Shoham-Salomon, V., Bergan, J., Kaszniak, A. W., & Yost, E. B. (1990). Identification of patients at risk for nonresponse and negative outcome in psychotherapy. *Journal of Consulting and Clinical Psychology, 58*(5), 622-628.

Moiso, C., & Novellino, M. (2000). An overview of the psychodynamic school of TA and its epistemological foundations. *TAJ, 30*(3), 182-187.

Monajem, A., & Aghayousefi, A. (2015). Effectiveness of group psychotherapy of TA in craving beliefs, attachment styles and cognitive emotion regulation in addicts under treatment. *Scientific Quarterly Research on Addiction, 9*(34), 123-144.

Monajem, A. (2013). The comparison of schemas, parenting style, and life traps in married and divorced women. *International Journal of Behavioral Sciences, 7*(2), 133-142.

Moncrieff, J. (2008). *The myth of the chemical cure.* Palgrave Macmillan.

Monteleone, A. M., Pellegrino, F., Croatto, G., Carfagno, M., Hilbert, A., Treasure, J., Wade, T., Bulik, C. M., Zipfel, S., Hay, P., & Schmidt, U. (2022). Treatment of eating disorders: A systematic meta-review of meta-analyses and network meta-analyses. *Neuroscience & Biobehavioral Reviews, 142*, 104857.

Moores, J., & Oates, S. (2024). What is psychological and what is neurological? *TAJ, 54*(1), 63-77.

Morena, S. (2014). Children and their monsters. *TAJ, 44*(2), 118-127.

Moriyama, T. S., Polanczyk, G. V., Terzi, F. S., Faria, K. M., & Rohde, L. A. (2013). Psychopharmacology and psychotherapy for the treatment of adults with ADHD. *CNS Spectrums, 18*(6), 296-306.

Morley, T. E., & Moran, G. (2011). The origins of cognitive vulnerability in early childhood. *Clinical Psychology Review, 31*(7), 1071-1082.

Morris, G. L. (2006). *Altered states.* Capella University.

Moyers, T. B., & Rollnick, S. (2002). A motivational interviewing perspective on resistance in psychotherapy. *Journal of Clinical Psychology, 58*(2), 185-193.

Mruh, O. F. (2020). Assessment of the adaptive personal potential of the patients with paranoid schizophrenia. *Wiadomości Lekarskie, 73*(7), 1391-1396.

Nagin, D. S., & Tremblay, R. E. (2001). Analyzing developmental trajectories of distinct but related behaviors. *Psychological Methods, 6*(1), 18-34.

Neal, S. B. (2017). A therapist's review of process: Rupture and repair cycles in relational transactional analysis psychotherapy for a client with a dismissive attachment style: 'Martha'. *International Journal of Transactional Analysis Research & Practice, 8*(2), 24-34.

Neff, K. (2011). *Self-compassion.* Hachette.

Neimeyer, R. A., Harris, D. L., Winokuer, H. R., & Thornton, G. F. (2011). *Grief and bereavement in contemporary society*. Routledge.

Neimeyer, R. A. (Ed.). (2015). *Techniques of grief therapy*. Routledge.

Neimeyer, R. A. (Ed.). (2021). *New techniques of grief therapy*. Routledge.

Nia, M. K., Sovani, A., & Forooshani, G. R. S. (2014). Exploring correlation between perceived parenting styles, early maladaptive schemas, and depression. *Iranian Red Crescent Medical*, *16*(12), e17492–e17499.

Nienhuis, J. B., Owen, J., Valentine, J. C., Winkeljohn Black, S., Halford, T. C., Parazak, S. E., Budge, S., & Hilsenroth, M. (2018). Therapeutic alliance, empathy, and genuineness in individual adult psychotherapy: A meta-analytic review. *Psychotherapy Research, 28*(4), 593–605.

Nolen-Hoeksema, S., Wisco, B. E., & Lyubomirsky, S. (2008). Rethinking rumination. *Perspectives on Psychological Science, 3*(5), 400–424.

Norcross, J. C., & Karpiak, C. P. (2017). Our best selves: Defining and actualizing expertise in psychotherapy. *The Counseling Psychologist, 45*(1), 66–75.

Norcross, J. C., & Lambert, M. J. (Eds.). (2019). *Psychotherapy relationships that work: Volume 1: Evidence-based therapist contributions*. Oxford University Press.

Norcross, J. C., & Wampold, B. E. (2011). What works for whom: Tailoring psychotherapy to the person. *Journal of Clinical Psychology, 67*(2), 127–132.

Norcross, J. C. (2002). *Psychotherapy relationships that work*. OUP.

Noriega, G. (2010). The transgenerational script of transactional analysis. *Transactional Analysis Journal, 40*(3–4), 196–204.

Novak, E. T. (2008). Integrating neurological findings with TA in trauma work. *TAJ, 38*(4), 303–319.

Novak, E. T. (2013). Combining traditional ego-state theory and relational approaches to TA in working with trauma and dissociation. *TAJ, 43*(3), 186–196.

Novak, E. T. (2015). Are games, enactments, and reenactments similar? *TAJ, 45*(2), 117–127.

Novellino, M. (2003). Transactional psychoanalysis. *TAJ, 33*(3), 223–230.

Novellino, M. (2018). *The transactional analyst in action: Clinical seminars*. Routledge.

Nuttall, J. (2006). The existential phenomenology of transactional analysis. *Transactional Analysis Journal, 36*(3), 214–227.

O'Reilly-Knapp, M., & Erskine, R. G. (2010). The script system. *International Journal of Integrative Psychotherapy, 1*(2), 113–127.

Oates, S. (2021). What if my "I'm ok, you're ok" is different from yours? *TAJ, 51*(1), 63–76.

Obegi, J. H., & Berant, E. (Eds.). (2010). *Attachment theory and research in clinical work with adults*. Guilford.

Odgers, C. L., Moffitt, T. E., Broadbent, J. M., Dickson, N., Hancox, R. J., Harrington, H., Poulton, R., Sears, M. R., Thomson, M., & Caspi, A. (2008). Female and male antisocial trajectories. *Development and Psychopathology, 20*(2), 673–716.

O'Donohue, W., Buchanan, J. A., & Fisher, J. E.(2000).Characteristics of empirically supported treatments. *The Journal of Psychotherapy Practice and Research, 9*(2), 69.

Ogden, P. (2021). *The pocket guide to sensorimotor psychotherapy in context*. Norton.

Ohlsson, T. (2002). Effects of TA psychotherapy in therapeutic community treatment of drug addicts. *TAJ, 32*(3), 153–177.

Ohlsson, T. (2010). Scientific evidence base for TA in the year 2010. *International Journal of TA Research, 1*(1), 1–30.

Oller-Vallejo, J. (2005). Neurological subtrata of the basic ego-states. *Transactional Analysis Journal, 35*(1), 52–61.

Olson, S. L., & Lunkenheimer, E. S. (2009). Expanding concepts of self-regulation to social relationships: Transactional processes in the development of early behavioral adjustment. In A. Sameroff (Ed.), *The transactional model of development: How children and contexts shape each other* (pp. 55-76). American Psychological Association.

O'Reilly-Knapp, M., & Erskine, R. G. (2010). *Life-scripts*. Karnac.

Orlinsky, D. E., Ronnestad, M. H., & Willutzki, U. (2004). Fifty years of psychotherapy process-outcome research. In A. E. Bergin & S. L. Garfield (Eds.), *Handbook of psychotherapy and behavior change* (pp. 307-389). Wiley.

Orth, U., Erol, R. Y., & Luciano, E. C. (2018). Development of self-esteem from age 4 to 94 years. *Psychological Bulletin, 144*(10), 1045.

Page, A. C., Stritzke, W. G., & Mclean, N. J. (2008). Toward science-informed supervision of clinical case formulation. *Australian Psychologist, 43*(2), 88-95.

Pallini, S. (2018). The relation of attachment security status to effortful self-regulation. *Psychological Bulletin, 144*(5), 501.

Pally, R. (2001). A primary role for nonverbal communication in psychoanalysis. *Psychoanalytic Inquiry, 21*(1), 71-93.

Paniagua, F. A., & Yamada, A. M. (Eds.). (2013). *Handbook of multicultural mental health*. Academic Press.

Panos, P. T., Jackson, J. W., Hasan, O., & Panos, A. (2014). Meta-analysis and systematic review assessing the efficacy of DBT. *Research on Social Work Practice, 24*(2), 213-223.

Pargament, K. I., & Ano, G. (2004). Religious coping. In C. R. Snyder & S. J. Lopez (Eds.), *Handbook of positive psychology* (pp. 711-724). OUP.

Pargament, K. I., Exline, J. J., & Jones, J. W. (2013). APA handbook of psychology, religion, and spirituality. In *Context, theory, and research* (*Vol 1*, pp. xxvii-740). American Psychological Association.

Pargament, K. I., Koenig, H. G., Tarakeshwar, N., & Hahn, J. (2004). Religious coping methods as predictors. *Journal of Health Psychology, 9*(6), 713-730.

Pargament, K. I. (1997). *The psychology of religion and coping*. Guilford.

Parkin, F. (2002). Expanding permissions: New perspectives on working with transactional analysis and sexual difficulties. *Transactional Analysis Journal, 32*(1), 56-61.

Pascual-Leone, A., & Baher, T. (2023). Chairwork in individual psychotherapy. *Psychotherapy, 60*(3), 370.

Patel, N., & Smith, J. (2022). Neural correlates of complementary and crossed transactions: An fMRI study. *NeuroImage, 231*, 117865.

Pearrow, M., & Cosgrove, L. (2009). The aftermath of combat-related PTSD. *Communication Disorders Quarterly, 30*(2), 77-82.

Peek, J. H. (1975). *The effects of TA upon the self-concept of adjudicated delinquents*. Georgia State University.

Pennebaker, J. W., Kiecolt-Glaser, J. K., & Glaser, R. (1988). Disclosure of traumas and immune function. *Journal of Consulting and Clinical Psychology, 56*(2), 239-245.

Pennebaker, J. W. (2012). *Opening up*. Guilford.

Perry, N. B., Mackler, J. S., Calkins, S. D., & Keane, S. P. (2014). TA of the relation between maternal sensitivity and child vagal regulation. *Developmental Psychology, 50*(3), 784.

Pešić, M. H. (2009). Transactional analysis and attachment theory. *TAJ, 1*(1), 35-42.

Peterson, Z. D. (Ed.). (2017). *The Wiley handbook of sex therapy*. Wiley-Blackwell.

Pfammatter, M., Junghan, U. M., & Brenner, H. D. (2006). Efficacy of psychological therapy in schizophrenia. *Schizophrenia Bulletin, 32*(1), 64-S80.

Pinto, R. Z., Ferreira, M. L., Oliveira, V. C., Franco, M. R., Adams, R., Maher, C. G., & Ferreira, P. H. (2012). Patient-centred communication is associated with positive therapeutic alliance. *Journal of Physiotherapy, 58*(2), 77-87.

Popper, K. (1990). *The logic of scientific discovery*. Routledge.

Porges, S. W. (2011). *The polyvagal theory*. Norton.

Pos, A. E., Greenberg, L. S., & Elliott, R. (2008). *Experiential therapy. Twenty-First Century Psychotherapies: Contemporary Approaches to Theory and Practice* (pp. 80-122).

Power, N., Noble, L. A., Simmonds-Buckley, M., Kellett, S., Stockton, C., Firth, N., & Delgadillo, J. (2022). Associations between treatment adherence-competence-integrity (ACI) and adult psychotherapy outcomes. *Journal of Consulting and Clinical Psychology, 90*(5), 427-445.

Powers, M. B., Zum Vörde Sive Vörding, M. B., & Emmelkamp, P. M. (2009). Acceptance and commitment therapy: A meta-analytic review. *Psychotherapy and Psychosomatics, 78*(2), 73-80.

Prescott, D. S., Maeschalck, C. L., & Miller, S. D. (Eds.). (2017). *Feedback-informed treatment in clinical practice*. APA.

Prilleltensky, I. (2014). Meaning-making, mattering, and thriving in community psychology. *Psychosocial Intervention, 23*(2), 151-154.

Prochaska, J. O., & Norcross, J. C. (2001). Stages of change. *Psychotherapy, 38*(4), 443-448.

Prochaska, J. O., & Velicer, W. F. (1997). The transtheoretical model of health behavior change. *American journal of health promotion, 12*(1), 38-48.

Pulleyblank, E., & McCormick, P. (1985). The stages of redecision therapy. In L. Kadis (Ed.), *Redecision therapy* (pp. 51-59). Western Institute for Group and Family Therapy.

Rahmati, S., Hooshmani, R., Mousavi Anzehaei, A. S., & Dehaghin, V. (2020). Effectiveness of group training of TA (TA) on distress tolerance and social problem solving of delinquent adolescents. *Social Psychology Research, 10*(37), 45-64.

Ranson, K. E., & Urichuk, L. J. (2008). The effect of parent–child attachment relationships on child biopsychosocial outcomes. *Early Child Development and Care, 178*(2), 129-152.

Rasulova, V. V. (2022). Obsessive-compulsive dynamics of eating disorders. *TA in Russia, 2*(2), 24-31.

Ravitz, P., Maunder, R., & McBride, C. (2008). Attachment, contemporary interpersonal theory and IPT. *Journal of Contemporary Psychotherapy, 38*(1), 11-21.

Raya, A. F., Ruiz-Olivares, R., Pino, M. J., & Herruzo, J. (2013). A review about parenting style and parenting practices and their consequences. *International Journal of Higher Education, 2*(4), 205-213.

Rea, B. (2001). Finding our balance. *Psychotherapy, 38*(1), 97-106.

Reinhold, M., Bürkner, P. C., & Holling, H. (2018). Effects of expressive writing on depressive symptoms. *Clinical Psychologist, 25*(1), e12224.

Reupert, A. E., Maybery, D., & Nicholson, J. (2015). Gaining knowledge about parental mental illness. *Child & Family Social Work, 20*(2), 191-201.

Rice, K. G., FitzGerald, D. P., Whaley, T. J., & Gibbs, C. L. (1995). Cross-sectional and longitudinal examination of attachment, separation-individuation, and college student adjustment. *Journal of Counseling & Development, 73*(4), 463-474.

River, L. M., Borelli, J. L., Vazquez, L. C., & Smiley, P. A. (2018). Learning helplessness in the family. *Journal of Family Psychology, 32*(8), 1109-1119.

Robbins, A. (2004). *Conquering your quarterlife crisis*. Penguin.

Roberts, B. W., & DelVecchio, W. F. (2000). The rank-order consistency of personality traits from childhood to old age. *Psychological Bulletin, 126*(1), 3-25.

Robinson, S., Kissane, D. W., Brooker, J., & Burney, S. (2016). A review of the construct of demoralization. *American Journal of Hospice and Palliative Medicine, 33*(1), 93-101.

Rodenburg, R., Benjamin, A., Roos, C., Meijer, A. M., & Stams, G. J. (2009). Efficacy of EMDR in children. *Clinical Psychology Review, 29*(7), 599-606.

Rodrigues, P. M., Marques, D. R., & Gomes, A. A. (2019). Differences in early maladaptive schemas between young adults displaying poor versus good sleep quality. *Psychiatric Quarterly, 90*(4), 733-746.

Rogers-Sirin, L. (2017). Psychotherapy from the margins. *Journal for Social Action in Counseling & Psychology, 9*(1), 55-78.

Rosenau, K. A., Kim, J., Cho, A. C. B., Seltzer, M., Ugueto, A. M., Weisz, J. R., & Wood, J. J. (2024). Meta-Analysis of psychotherapy for autistic youth. *Child Psychiatry and Human Development, 1*(1), 1-12.

Rosenberg, R. A. (2013). *The human magnet syndrome.* PESI.

Rosendahl, S., Sattel, H., & Lahmann, C. (2021). Effectiveness of body psychotherapy. *Frontiers in Psychiatry, 12*, 709-798.

Roth, M., Neuner, F., & Elbert, T. (2014). Transgenerational consequences of PTSD. *International Journal of Mental Health Systems, 8*(1), 12-25.

Rothbart, M. K., & Bates, J. E. (2006). *Handbook of child psychology.* Wiley.

Rowland, H., & Cornell, W. F. (2021). Gender identity, queer theory, and working with the sociopolitical in counseling and psychotherapy. *TAJ, 51*(1), 19-34.

Rubinstein, D., & Lahad, M. (2023). Fantastic reality. *Traumatology, 29*(2), 102-111.

Ruini, C., & Mortara, C. C. (2022). Writing technique across psychotherapies. *Journal of Contemporary Psychotherapy, 1*(1), 1-12.

Ryan, S. M., Jorm, A. F., Toumbourou, J. W., & Lubman, D. I. (2015). Parent and family factors associated with service use by young people. *Early Intervention in Psychiatry, 9*(6), 433-446.

Saberinia, S., & Niknejadi, F. (2019). The effectiveness of TA on parent-child relationship in mothers of children with oppositional defiant disorder. *Avicenna Journal of Neuro Psycho Physiology, 6*(2), 83-90.

Sachse, R., & Elliott, R. (2002). Process–outcome research on humanistic therapy variables. In D. J. Cain (Ed.), *Humanistic psychotherapies* (pp. 83-115). APA.

Sachs-Ericsson, N., Verona, E., Joiner, T., & Preacher, K. J. (2006). Parental verbal abuse and the mediating role of self-criticism in adult internalizing disorders. *Journal of Affective Disorders, 93*(1-3), 71-78.

Scharff, J. S. (2005). *The Primer of object relations.* Aronson.

Schlegel, R. J., Hicks, J. A., Arndt, J., & King, L. A. (2009). Thine own self. *Journal of Personality and Social Psychology, 96*(2), 473-490.

Schlegel, R. J., Hicks, J. A., Davis, W. E., Hirsch, K. A., & Smith, C. M. (2013). The dynamic interplay between perceived true self-knowledge and decision satisfaction. *Journal of Personality and Social Psychology, 104*(3), 542.

Schlein, S. (2016). *The clinical Erik Erikson.* Routledge.

Schneider, K. (2015). Presence. *Existential Analysis, 26*(2), 304-313.

Schore, A. N. (1994). *Affect regulation and the origin of the self.* Lawrence Erlbaum.

Schore, A. N. (2001). The right brain as the neurobiological substratum of Freud's dynamic unconscious. In D. E. Scharff (Ed.), *The psychoanalytic century* (pp. 61-88). Other Press.

Schore, A. N. (2002). The neurobiology of attachment and early personality organization. *Journal of Prenatal and Perinatal Psychology and Health, 16*, 249-264.

Schore, A. N. (2003). *Affect dysregulation and disorders of the self*. Norton.

Schore, A. N. (2012). *The science of the art of psychotherapy*. Norton.

Schore, A. N. (2015). *Affect regulation and the origin of the self*. Norton.

Schrank, B., Bird, V., Rudnick, A., & Slade, M. (2012). Determinants, self-management strategies and interventions for hope in people with mental disorders: Systematic search and narrative review. *Social Science & Medicine, 74*(4), 554-564.

Schrank, B., Stanghellini, G., & Slade, M. (2008). Hope in psychiatry. *Acta Psychiatrica Scandinavica, 118*(6), 421-433.

Schwartz, A. (2021). *Complex PTSD treatment manual*. PESI.

Schwarzer, R. (2014). *Self-efficacy*. Taylor & Francis.

Sedgwick, J. M. (2020). *Contextual transactional analysis*. Routledge.

Segal, Z., Williams, M., & Teasdale, J. (2012). *Mindfulness-based cognitive therapy for depression*. Guilford press.

Segrin, C., & Passalacqua, S. A. (2010). Functions of loneliness. *Health Communication, 25*(4), 312-322.

Segrin, C. (2000). Social skills deficits associated with depression. *Clinical Psychology Review, 20*(3), 379-403.

Selavan, A. (1990). Berne's perspective on alcoholism: An addiction or a game? *TAJ, 20*(2), 135-136.

Setiya, K. (2014). *The midlife crisis*. Ann Arbor.

Shadbolt, C. (2004). Homophobia and gay affirmative TA. *TAJ, 34*(2), 113-125.

Shadbolt, C. (2022). The many faces of systemic oppression, power, and privilege. *TAJ, 52*(3), 259-273.

Shahbaz, C., & Chirinos, P. (2016). *Becoming a kink aware therapist*. Routledge.

Sharifi, M., Fatehizade, M. S., Bahrami, F., Jazayeri, R., & Etemadi, O. (2019). The effectiveness of mindfulness-integrated TA. *Quarterly Journal of Woman and Society, 9*(36), 177-196.

Shaw, D. S., Gilliom, M., Ingoldsby, E. M., & Nagin, D. S. (2003). Trajectories leading to school-age conduct problems. *Developmental Psychology, 39*(2), 189-200.

Shaw, D. S., Lacourse, E., & Nagin, D. S. (2005). Developmental trajectories of conduct problems and hyperactivity from ages 2 to 10. *Journal of Child Psychology and Psychiatry, 46*(9), 931-942.

Sheffield, A., Waller, G., Emanuelli, F., Murray, J., & Meyer, C. (2005). Links between parenting and core beliefs. *Cognitive Therapy and Research, 29*, 787-802.

Sheffield, A., Waller, G., Emanuelli, F., Murray, J., & Meyer, C. (2009). Do schema processes mediate links between parenting and eating pathology? *European Eating Disorders Review: The Professional Journal of the Eating Disorders Association, 17*(4), 290-300.

Sheldon, K. M., & Kasser, T. (1995). Coherence and congruence. *Journal of Personality and Social Psychology, 68*(3), 531-543. https://doi.org/10.1037/0022-3514.68.3.531

Shepherd, G. (2020). "Normally I'd get really agitated, but I just laughed!": What do participants reflect upon in a transactional analysis/mindfulness based anger management programme? *British Journal of Guidance & Counselling, 48*(4), 537-551.

Sherer, M., & Rogers, R. W. (1980). Effects of therapist's nonverbal communication. *Journal of Clinical Psychology, 36*(3), 696-700.

Shimamura, A. P. (2000). Toward a cognitive neuroscience of metacognition. *Consciousness and Cognition, 9*(2), 313-323.

Shor, E., Roelfs, D. J., & Yogev, T. (2013). The strength of family ties. *Social Networks, 35*(4), 626-638.

Shustov, D., Tuchina, O., Novikov, S., & Fedotov, I. (2016). Combinations of injunctions and personality types. *International Journal of TA Research, 7*(2), 1–20.

Siegel, D. J., Schore, A. N., & Cozolino, L. (2021). *Interpersonal Neurobiology and clinical practice.* Norton.

Sigmund, E. W. (1999). The pervasive victim self-image in clients with antisocial personality disorders. *TAJ, 29*(2), 109–114.

Sills, C. (Ed.). (2006). *Contracts in counselling & psychotherapy.* Sage.

Simerly, T. (2003). The risks and rewards of coming out in an uncertain world. *TAJ, 33*(1), 52–57.B.

Simon, W. (2009). Follow-up psychotherapy outcome of patients with dependent, avoidant and obsessive-compulsive personality disorders. *International Journal of Psychiatry in Clinical Practice, 13*(2), 153–165.

Singer, M. I., Anglin, T. M., Yu Song, L., & Lunghofer, L. (1995). Adolescents' exposure to violence and associated symptoms of psychological trauma. *Journal of the American Medical Association, 273*(6), 477–482. https://doi.org/10.1001/jama. 273.6.477

Singh, G. K. (2017). *Appreciation and well-being.* University of Pennsylvania.

Skipstein, A., Janson, H., Stoolmiller, M., & Mathiesen, K. S. (2010). Trajectories of maternal symptoms of anxiety and depression. *BMC Public Health, 10*(1), 589–602.

Smith, P. K., & Hart, C. H. (Eds.). (2022). *Wiley-Blackwell handbook of childhood social development.* Wiley.

Smits, J. A., Jacquart, J., Abramowitz, J., Arch, J., & Margraf, J. (Eds.), (2022). *Clinical guide to exposure therapy: Beyond phobias.* Springer.

Snyder, C. R., & Taylor, J. D. (2000). Hope as a common factor across psychotherapy approaches: A lesson from the dodo's verdict. In *Handbook of hope* (pp. 89–108). Academic Press.

Snyder, C. R., Lopez, S. J., Shorey, H. S., Rand, K. L., & Feldman, D. B. (2003). Hope theory, measurements, and applications. *School Psychology Quarterly, 18*(2), 122–139.

Sollarova, E., & Sollar, T. (2010). The psychologically integrated person. *Studia Psychologica, 52*(4), 177–192.

Spain, D., Harwood, L., & O'Neill, L. (2015). Psychological interventions for adults with autism spectrum disorders. *Advances in Autism, 1*(2), 79–86.

Spillius, E., & O'Shaughnessy, E. (2013). *Projective identification: The fate of a concept.* Routledge.

Sroufe, L. A., Egeland, B., Carlson, E. A., & Collins, W. A. (2005). *The development of the person.* Guilford.

Sroufe, L. A. (2005). Attachment and development: A prospective, longitudinal study from birth to adulthood. *Attachment & human development, 7*(4), 349–367.

Stahl, B., & Goldstein, E. (2019). *A mindfulness-based stress reduction workbook.* New Harbinger.

Stapleton, A. (2012). Coaching clients through the quarter-life crisis. *International Journal of Evidence Based Coaching & Mentoring, 3*(5), 39–50.

Stark, M. (1999). *Modes of therapeutic action.* Jason Aronson.

Steiner, C. (1974). *Scripts people live.* Grove.

Steinert, C., Munder, T., Rabung, S., Hoyer, J., & Leichsenring, F. (2017). Psychodynamic therapy. *American Journal of Psychiatry, 174*(10), 943–953.

Stern, D. (1985). *The interpersonal world of the infant.* Basic Books.

Stewart, I., & Joines, V. (1987). *TA today: A new introduction to TA.* Lifespace.

Stiles, W. B. (2001). Assimilation of problematic experiences. *Psychotherapy, 38*(4), 462.

Stoffers-Winterling, J. M., Storebø, O. J., Kongerslev, M. T., Faltinsen, E., Todorovac, A., Jørgensen, M. S., …, Simonsen, E. (2022). Psychotherapies for borderline personality disorder. *British Journal of Psychiatry, 221*(3), 538-552.

Stolorow, R. D., Brandchaft, B., & Atwood, G. E. (1987). *Psychoanalytic treatment: An intersubjective approach.* Analytic Press.

Strick, M., Dijksterhuis, A., Bos, M. W., Sjoerdsma, A., Van Baaren, R. B., & Nordgren, L. F. (2011). A meta-analysis on unconscious thought effects. *Social Cognition, 29*(6), 738-762.

Stuthridge, J. (2006). Inside out. *TAJ, 36*(4), 270-283.

Sue, D. W., & Spanierman, L. (2020). *Microaggressions in everyday life.* Wiley.

Sullivan, H. S. (2013). *The interpersonal theory of psychiatry.* Norton.

Summers, G., & Tudor, K. (2000). Cocreative TA. *TAJ, 30*(1), 24-40.

Summers, F. (2024). *Object relations theories and psychopathology.* Routledge.

Swift, J. K., Callahan, J. L., Cooper, M., & Parkin, S. R. (2018). The impact of accommodating client preference in psychotherapy. *Journal of Clinical Psychology, 74*(11), 1924-1937.

Symington, J., & Symington, N. (2002). *The clinical thinking of Wilfred Bion.* Routledge.

Tanaka, H., Johnson, L., & Garcia, M. (2021). Cross-cultural variations in the perception of transactional patterns. *International Journal of Intercultural Relations, 80*, 150-165.

Taşkale, N., & Soygüt, G. (2017). Risk factors for women's intimate partner violence victimization: An examination from the perspective of the schema therapy model. *Journal of Family Violence, 32*, 3-12.

Tao, K. W., Owen, J., Pace, B. T., & Imel, Z. E. (2015). A meta-analysis of multicultural competencies and psychotherapy process and outcome. *Journal of Counseling Psychology, 62*(3), 337-350.

Temple, S. F. (2002). *The Development of a TA psychometric Tool for enhancing functional fluency.* University of Plymouth.

Tepper, D. T., & Haase, R. F. (1978). Verbal and nonverbal communication of facilitative conditions. *Journal of Counseling Psychology, 25*(1), 35-44. https://doi.org/10.1037/0022-0167.25.1.35

Terlato, V. (2023). Bipolar dynamics of vitality. *TAJ, 53*(3), 222-236.

Thayer, S., & Schiff, W. (1975). Eye-contact, facial expression, and the experience of time. *The Journal of Social Psychology, 95*(1), 117-124.

Thompson, A., Hollis, C., & Dagger, D. R. (2003). Authoritarian parenting attitudes as a risk for conduct problems. *European Child & Adolescent Psychiatry, 12*(1), 84-91.

Thunnissen, M. (2010). Redecision therapy with personality disorders. *TAJ, 40*(2), 114-120.

Thunnissen, M. (2015). TA in a hospital setting with patients with personality disorders. In R. G. Erskine (Ed.), *Transactional analysis in contemporary psychotherapy.* Routledge.

Tomkins, S. S. (1978). Script theory. *Nebraska Symposium on Motivation, 26*, 201-236.

Torkaman, M., Farokhzadian, J., Miri, S., & Pouraboli, B. (2020). The effect of TA on the self-esteem of imprisoned women. *BMC Psychology, 8*, 1-7.

Tolin, D. F., McKay, D., Forman, E. M., Klonsky, E. D., & Thombs, B. D. (2015). Empirically supported treatment: Recommendations for a new model. *Clinical Psychology: Science and Practice, 22*(4), 317.

Torres-Giménez, A., Garcia-Gibert, C., Gelabert, E., Aïda Mallorquí, Segu, X., Roca-Lecumberri, A., Martínez, A., Giménez, Y., & Bàrbara, Sureda. (2024). Efficacy of EMDR for early intervention after a traumatic event: A systematic review and meta-analysis. *Journal of Psychiatric Research, 174*, 73-83. https://doi.org/10.1016/j.jpsychires.2024.04.019

Toth, S. L., Manly, J. T., & Cicchetti, D. (1992). Child maltreatment and vulnerability to depression. *Development and Psychopathology, 4*(1), 97-112.

Tozzi, C. (Ed.). (2023). *Active imagination in theory, practice and training.* Taylor & Francis.

Trett, R. (2004). From moral malevolence to autonomous performance. *TAJ, 34*(2), 156-169.

Tryon, G. S., & Winograd, G. (2011). Goal consensus and collaboration. *Psychotherapy, 48*(1), 50-57. https://doi.org/10.1037/a0022061

Tryon, G. S., Birch, S. E., & Verkuilen, J. (2018). Meta-analyses of the relation of goal consensus and collaboration to psychotherapy outcome. *Psychotherapy, 55*(4), 372.

Tudor, K. (2011). Understanding empathy. *TAJ, 41*(1), 39-57.

Tudor, K. (2020). Transactional analysis and politics. *Psychotherapy and Politics International, 18*(3), e1555-e1559.

Tudor, K., & Summers, G. (2014). *Co-creative transactional analysis: Papers, responses, dialogues, and developments.* Karnac Books.

Turner, R. J. (1988). The parent-adult-child projective drawing task: A therapeutic tool in TA. *Transactional Analysis Journal, 18*(1), 60-67.

Turner, D. T., van der Gaag, M., Karyotaki, E., & Cuijpers, P. (2014). Psychological interventions for psychosis. *American Journal of Psychiatry, 171*(5), 523-538.

Uchino, B. N. (2006). Social support and health. *Journal of Behavioral Medicine, 29*(4), 377-387.

Vaillant, G. E. (1992). *Ego mechanisms of defense.* American Psychiatric Pub.

Van den Bussche, E., Vandennoortgate, W., & Reynvoet, B. (2009). Mechanisms of masked priming. *Psychological Bulletin, 135*(3), 452.

Van der Kolk, B. A., Hostetler, A., Herron, N., & Fisler, R. E. (1994). Trauma and the development of borderline personality disorder. *Psychiatric Clinics of North America, 17*(4), 715-730.

Van der Kolk, B. A. (1994). *The body keeps the score.* Penguin.

van Rijn, B. (2014). *Assessment and case formulation in counselling and psychotherapy.* SAGE.

van Rijn, B., & Lukac-Greenwood, J. (Eds.). (2020). *Working with sexual attraction in psychotherapy practice and supervision: A humanistic-relational approach.* Routledge.

Van Tol, R. (2017). I love you, and you, and you too. *TAJ, 47*(4), 276-293.

Van Vlierberghe, L., Timbremont, B., Braet, C., & Basile, B. (2007). Parental schemas in youngsters referred for antisocial behaviour problems demonstrating depressive symptoms. *The Journal of Forensic Psychiatry & Psychology, 18*(4), 515-533.

Van Wijk-Herbrink, M. F., Bernstein, D. P., Broers, N. J., Roelofs, J., Rijkeboer, M. M., & Arntz, A. (2018). Internalizing and externalizing behaviors share a common predictor. *Journal of Abnormal Child Psychology, 46*(5), 907-920.

Vangelisti, A., Caughlin, J., & Timmerman, L. (2001). Criteria for revealing family secrets. *Communication Monographs, 68*(1), 1-27.

Vangelisti, A. L. (1994). Family secrets. *Journal of Social and Personal Relationships, 11*(1), 113-135.

Verhaeghe, P. (2017). *What about me?* Scribe.

Verheul, R., & Herbrink, M. (2007). The efficacy of various modalities of psychotherapy for personality disorders. *International Review of Psychiatry, 19*(1), 25-38.

Vohs, K. D., & Baumeister, R. F. (Eds.). (2016). *Handbook of self-regulation.* Guilford.

Vos, J. (2015). Meaning and existential givens in the lives of cancer patients: A philosophical perspective on psycho-oncology. *Palliative & Supportive care, 13*(4), 885-900.

Vos, J. (2016). Working with meaning in life in chronic or life-threatening disease. In P. Russo-Netzer, S. E. Schulenberg, & A. Batthyany (Eds.), *Clinical perspectives on meaning* (pp. 171–200). Springer.

Vos, J. (2017). *Meaning in life: An evidence-Based handbook for practitioners.* Bloomsbury.

Vos, J. (2018). Death in existential psychotherapies. In A. Menzies (Ed.), *Curing the dread of death* (pp. 145–170). Australian Academic Press.

Vos, J. (2020). *The Economics of Meaning in life.* University Professor's Press.

Vos, J. (2021a). Cardiovascular disease and meaning in life. *Palliative & Supportive Care, 19*(3), 367–376.

Vos, J. (2021b). *The psychology of COVID-19.* SAGE.

Vos, J. (2022). Meaning in life across cultures and times. In A. Chen (Ed.), *Meaning in life* (pp. 21–40). Atlantis.

Vos, J. (2023a). Phenomenology in the bedroom. life. In S. Simpson, M. Racho, B. D. Robiins, & L. Hoffman (Eds.), *Eros & psyche.* University Professors Press.

Vos, J. (2023b). *Doing research in psychological therapies: A step-by-step guide.* SAGE.

Vos, J. (2023c). The meaning sextet: A systematic literature review and further validation of a universal typology of meaning in Life. *Journal of Constructivist Psychology, 36*(2), 204–231.

Vos, J. (2024). The development and validation of the meaning approach scale: Traditional, functionalistic and critical-intuitive approaches to meaning in life. *Journal of Constructivist Psychology, 37*(4), 491–513.

Vos, J. (2025). Working as a therapist with victims of social injustice. In F. Gruba-McCallister & A. Cohen (Eds.), *Radical therapy.* Palgrave.

Vos, J. (2025b). Measuring meaning in life at macro and micro-level: Real-world implications and future directions (types, approaches, and number of envisioned and realized meanings in life). *Journal of Positive Psychology.* (In print).

Vos, J., & van Rijn, B. (2021a). A systematic review of psychometric TA instruments. *TAJ, 51*(2), 127–159.

Vos, J., & van Rijn, B. (2021b). The TA review survey: An investigation into self-reported practices and philosophies of psychotherapists. *TAJ, 51*(2), 111–126.

Vos, J., & van Rijn, B. (2021c). The evidence-based conceptual model of TA: A focused review of the research literature. *TAJ, 51*(2), 160–201.

Vos, J., & van Rijn, B. (2022). The effectiveness of TA treatments and their predictors: A systematic literature review and meta-analysis. *Journal of Humanistic Psychology.* https://doi.org/10.1177/00221678221117111

Vos, J., & van Rijn, B. (2023). Brief transactional analysis psychotherapy for depression: The systematic development of a treatment manual. *Journal of Psychotherapy Integration, 34*(1), 1–26.

Vos, J., & van Rijn, B. (2024a). Brief TA psychotherapy for depression: A randomized controlled trial. *The Journal of Humanistic Psychology.* [Accepted for publication].

Vos, J., & van Rijn, B. (2024b). *The experience of change in TA psychotherapy: Qualitative analysis of session evaluations and post-therapy interviews* [Internal Report].

Vos, J., & van Rijn, B. (2024c). *Using mixed methods in feasibility studies: The example of brief TA psychotherapy for depression* [Under review].

Vos, J., & Vitali, D. (2018). The effects of psychological meaning-centered therapies on quality of life and psychological stress: A meta-analysis. *Palliative & Supportive Care, 16*(5), 608–632.

Vos, J., Craig, M., & Cooper, M. (2015). Existential therapies: A meta-analysis of their effects on psychological outcomes. *Journal of Consulting and Clinical Psychology, 83*(1), 115.

Vos, J., Roberts, R., & Davies, J. (2019). *Mental health in crisis.* Sage.

Waldekranz-Piselli, K. C. (1999). What do we do before we say hello? The body as the stage setting for the script. *Transactional Analysis Journal, 29*(1), 31-48.

Waldhauser, G. T. (2023). *Neuropsychoanalysis.* Springer.

Wampold, B. E., & Imel, Z. E. (2015). *The great psychotherapy debate.* Routledge.

Wang, J., Lloyd-Evans, B., Giacco, D., Forsyth, R., Nebo, C., Mann, F., & Johnson, S. (2017). Social isolation in mental health. *Social Psychiatry and Psychiatric Epidemiology, 52*(12), 1451-1461.

Watts, B. V., Schnurr, P. P., Mayo, L., Young-Xu, Y., Weeks, W. B., & Friedman, M. J. (2013). Meta-analysis of the efficacy of treatments for posttraumatic stress disorder. *The Journal of Clinical Psychiatry, 74*(6), 11710.

Weeks, D. G., Michela, J. L., Peplau, L. A., & Bragg, M. E. (1980). Relation between loneliness and depression. *Journal of Personality and Social Psychology, 39*(6), 1238-2144.

Wei, M., Russell, D. W., & Zakalik, R. A. (2005). Adult attachment. *Journal of Counseling Psychology, 52*(4), 602-614.

White, T. (2017). A transactional analysis perspective on suicide risk assessment. *Transactional Analysis Journal, 47*(1), 32-41.

Widdowson, M. (2013). *The process and outcome of TA psychotherapy for the treatment of depression: An adjudicated case series* [Doctoral dissertation]. University of Leicester.

Widdowson, M. (2016). *Transactional Analysis for depression.* Routledge.

Wiggins, J. L., Mitchell, C., Hyde, L. W., & Monk, C. S. (2015). Identifying early pathways of risk and resilience. *Development and Psychopathology, 27*(4), 1295-1312.

Williams, I. C., & Glarino, G. G. (2023). The efficacy of TA as a community-based intervention for substance use disorder. *TAJ, 53*(3), 256-269.

Williams, S. R., Kertz, S. J., Schrock, M. D., & Woodruff-Borden, J. (2012). A sequential analysis of parent-child interactions. *Journal of Clinical Child & Adolescent Psychology, 41*(1), 64-74.

Wilson, H. A. (2014). Can antisocial personality disorder be treated?. *International Journal of Forensic Mental Health, 13*(1), 36-46.

Winell, M. (2008). *Leaving the fold.* Apocryphile.

Wisco, B. E. (2009). Depressive cognition. *Clinical Psychology Review, 29*(4), 382-392.

Wolfe, J. B., & Betz, N. E. (2004). The relationship of attachment variables to career decision-making self-efficacy and fear of commitment. *The Career Development Quarterly, 52*(4), 363-369.

Woods, M., & Woods, K. (1981). Ego splitting and the TA diagram. *TAJ, 11*(2), 130-133.

Woollams, S. J. (1979). Decision scale. *Transactional Analysis Bulletin, 9*(3), 209-212.

Woollams, S., & Brown, M. (1978). *Transactional analysis: A modern and comprehensive text of TA theory and practice.* Huron Valley Institute Press.

Woollams, S., & Brown, M. (1979). *Transactional analysis.* Prentice-Hall.

Wouters, A., & Smale, G. (1990). Diagnosis with Millon's personality system: Implications for TA therapy. *TAJ, 20*(2), 118-127.

Yılmaz, M., Türkarslan, K. K., Zanini, L., Hasdemir, D., Spitoni, G. F., & Lingiardi, V. (2024). Transference interpretation and psychotherapy outcome: A systematic review of a no-consensus relationship. *Research in Psychotherapy: Psychopathology, Process, and Outcome, 27*(1), 1-20.

Yontef, G. (2001). Psychotherapy of schizoid process. *TAJ, 31*(1), 7-23.

Young, J. E., Klosko, J. S., & Weishaar, M. E. (2006). *Schema therapy.* Guilford.

Zalcman, M. J. (1990). Game analysis and racket analysis. *TAJ, 20*(1), 4-19.

Zeigler-Hill, V. (2011). The connections between self-esteem and psychopathology. *Journal of Contemporary Psychotherapy, 41*(3), 157-164.

Zessin, U., Dickhauser, O., & Garbade, S. (2015). The relationship between self-compassion and well-being. *Applied Psychology, 7*(3), 340-364.

Zhao, X., & Epley, N. (2019). Why don't people give enough compliments? *Academy of Management Proceedings, 1*(1), 19535-19545.

Zilanawala, A., Sacker, A., & Kelly, Y. (2017). Longitudinal latent cognitive profiles and psychosocial well-being in early adolescence. *Journal of Adolescent Health, 61*(4), 493-500.

Zivkovic, A. (2023). Dependent personality and interpersonal dependency. *British Journal of Psychotherapy, 39*(1), 212-231.

Žvelc, G., Černetič, M., & Košak, M. (2011). Mindfulness-based TA. *TAJ, 41*(3), 241-254.

INDEX